Wesley and Whitefield?
Wesley versus Whitefield?

Wesley *and* Whitefield?
Wesley *versus* Whitefield?

EDITED BY
Ian J. Maddock

FOREWORD BY
David F. Wells

☙PICKWICK *Publications* · Eugene, Oregon

WESLEY AND WHITEFIELD? WESLEY VERSUS WHITEFIELD?

Copyright © 2018 Wipf and Stock Publishers. All rights reserved. Except for brief quotations in critical publications or reviews, no part of this book may be reproduced in any manner without prior written permission from the publisher. Write: Permissions, Wipf and Stock Publishers, 199 W. 8th Ave., Suite 3, Eugene, OR 97401.

Pickwick Publications
An Imprint of Wipf and Stock Publishers
199 W. 8th Ave., Suite 3
Eugene, OR 97401

www.wipfandstock.com

PAPERBACK ISBN: 978-1-4982-9067-8
HARDCOVER ISBN: 978-1-5326-1209-1
EBOOK ISBN: 978-1-5326-1210-7

Cataloguing-in-Publication data:

Names: Maddock, Ian J., editor. | Wells, David F., foreword

Title: Wesley and Whitefield? Wesley versus Whitefield? / edited by Ian J. Maddock, foreword by David F. Wells.

Description: Eugene, OR: Pickwick Publications, 2018 | Includes bibliographical references.

Identifiers: ISBN 978-1-4982-9067-8 (paperback) | ISBN 978-1-5326-1209-1 (hardcover) | ISBN 978-1-5326-1210-7(ebook)

Subjects: LCSH: Wesley, John, 1703–1791. | Whitefield, George, 1714–1770.

Classification: LCC BX8331.3 M32 2018 (print) | LCC BX8331.3 (ebook)

Extracts from The Book of Common Prayer, the rights in which are vested in the Crown, are reproduced by permission of the Crown's patentee, Cambridge University Press.

Scripture quotations from The Authorized (King James) Version. Rights in the Authorized Version in the United Kingdom are vested in the Crown. Reproduced by permission of the Crown's patentee, Cambridge University Press.

Manufactured in the U.S.A.   02/27/18

Contents

Contributors | vii
Foreword by David F. Wells | xi
Acknowledgments | xv

Introduction | 1
—Ian J. Maddock

1. "Beginning a Society of Their Own": John Wesley, George Whitefield, and the Bristol Division | 9
   —Joel Houston

2. The Vector of Salvation: The New Birth as (only) the Beginning of Conversion for Wesley and Whitefield | 27
   —Sean McGever

3. "The Whole World is Now My Parish": The Ecclesiological Conversions of Wesley and Whitefield | 42
   —Ian J. Maddock

4. Wesley, Whitefield, and the Church of England | 62
   —Edward Loane

5. "I Am Yet Persuaded, You Do Greatly Err": Whitefield, Wesley, and Christian Perfection | 87
   —David McEwan

6. Federalist Brothers: The Shared Covenantal Substructure of Whitefield and Wesley's Theology | 105
   —Jared Hood

CONTENTS

7. Whitefield and Wesley on Sin and Atonement | 124
   —Peter Adam

8. "Plain Truth for Plain People": Wesley, Whitefield, and Homiletics | 144
   —Martin Wellings

9. Freedom in the Atlantic World: John Wesley and George Whitefield on Slavery | 161
   —Glen O'Brien

10. Cultivating True Religion: The Nature and Dynamics of the Means of Grace | 183
    —Tom Schwanda

11. "Companions in the Way": Mentoring in the Ministry of Wesley and Whitefield | 204
    —Rhys S. Bezzant

12. The Hymnody of John Wesley and George Whitefield | 219
    —Robert S. Smith

Bibliography | 243

Contributors

Peter Adam (PhD, Durham University) was born and raised in Melbourne, Australia, and trained for the ministry at Ridley College, Melbourne. He has served as Lecturer at St. John's College, Durham, Vicar of St. Jude's in Carlton, Melbourne, and Principal of Ridley College. He also served as Canon of St. Paul's Cathedral, Melbourne. He is currently Vicar Emeritus of St. Jude's, Carlton. He has written and published on church history, preaching, and Bible commentaries.

Rhys S. Bezzant (ThD, Australian College of Theology) is Dean of Missional Leadership and Lecturer in Church History at Ridley College, Melbourne. He is the Director of the Jonathan Edwards Center Australia and is Visiting Fellow at the Yale Divinity School. He has published *Jonathan Edwards and the Church* (2014) and *Standing on Their Shoulders* (2015), and is presently writing a book on the mentoring ministry of Edwards. He also serves as Canon of St. Paul's Cathedral, Melbourne.

Jared Hood (PhD, University of Melbourne) is Senior Lecturer in Old Testament at Presbyterian Theological College, Melbourne, where he previously lectured in Church History, and is the Academic Dean. Jared has published several articles on the thought of George Whitefield and on the Pentateuch. He has spent thirteen years in pastoral ministry, and is editor of *Reformed Theological Review*.

Joel Houston (PhD, University of Manchester) is an Instructor in Biblical and Theological Studies at Nipawin Bible College, Saskatchewan, Canada, and Junior Fellow of the Manchester Wesley Research Centre. A contributor to *Wesleyan Theological Journal* and *Churchman*, Joel's continued research and writing explores the foundational elements of Wesley and Whitefield's doctrines of predestination as well as the social and theological developments of early Methodism.

Edward Loane (PhD, University of Cambridge) lectures in Doctrine and Church History at Moore Theological College, Sydney. He is an ordained Anglican clergyman and prior to pursuing doctoral studies was a minister in south-west Sydney. His research interests include Anglican and evangelical history as well as ecclesiology and eschatology. He has recently published *William Temple and Church Unity: The Politics and Practice of Ecumenical Theology* (2016), *From Cambridge to Colony: Charles Simeon's Enduring Influence on Australia* (2016), and *Celebrating the Reformation* (2017).

David McEwan (PhD, University of Queensland) is Associate Professor of Theology and Pastoral Theology at Nazarene Theological College, Brisbane, Honorary Associate Professor at the University of Queensland, and Fellow of the Manchester Wesley Research Centre, England. He also serves as the pastor of the Logan Community Church of the Nazarene in Logan, Queensland. He is the author of *Wesley as a Pastoral Theologian: Theological Methodology in John Wesley's Doctrine of Christian Perfection* (2011) and *The Life of God in the Soul: the Integration of Love, Holiness and Happiness in the Thought of John Wesley* (2015).

Sean McGever (MLitt, University of St. Andrews) is Area Director for Young Life in Phoenix, Arizona, and Adjunct Faculty in the College of Theology at Grand Canyon University. He is currently undertaking doctoral studies at the University of Aberdeen. Sean is a member of Young Life's training team that equips workers in over 100 countries. He has delivered papers on Wesley and Whitefield at the Society for the Study of Theology, the Wesleyan Theological Society, and the American Academy of Religion.

Ian J. Maddock (PhD, University of Aberdeen) is Senior Lecturer in Theology at Sydney Missionary and Bible College and a Research Fellow at the Jonathan Edwards Center, South Africa. Ian completed theological studies in Australia, the United States, and Scotland, and served as a pastor at Trinity Baptist Church in New Haven, Connecticut. He has published a number of journal articles on eighteenth-century transatlantic evangelicalism and is author of *Men of One Book: A Comparison of Two Methodist Preachers, John Wesley and George Whitefield* (Pickwick, 2011).

Glen O'Brien (PhD, La Trobe University) is Research Coordinator at Eva Burrows College within the University of Divinity and a member of the

University of Divinity's Centre for Research in Religion and Social Policy. He is a Research Fellow of the Australasian Centre for Wesleyan Research and an Honorary Fellow of the Manchester Wesley Research Centre. He has published widely on Wesleyan and Methodist themes. Along with Hilary M. Carey he co-edited and contributed chapters to *Methodism in Australia: A History* (2015) in the Routledge Methodist Studies Series.

Tom Schwanda (PhD, Durham University) is Associate Professor of Christian Formation and Ministry at Wheaton College, Illinois. Before teaching, he was a pastor for eighteen years. Among his recent books are *The Emergence of Evangelical Spirituality: The Age of Edwards, Newton, and Whitefield* (2016) and *Soul Recreation: The Contemplative–Mystical Piety of Puritanism* (Pickwick, 2012). He is currently working on two articles that explore different dimensions of Wesley and Whitefield.

Robert S. Smith (MTh, Australian College of Theology) teaches Theology, Ethics, and Music Ministry at Sydney Missionary and Bible College. He has written several articles on the importance of music and congregational song, and has recently co-authored *Songs of the Saints: Enriching our Singing by Learning from the Songs of Scripture* (2017). Rob is also a songwriter and producer for Emu Music. He is currently undertaking doctoral studies in the theology of sex and gender.

Martin Wellings (DPhil, University of Oxford) is Superintendent Minister of the Oxford Methodist Circuit and Minister of Wesley Memorial Church. His first book was *Evangelicals Embattled: Responses of Evangelicals in the Church of England to Ritualism, Darwinism and Theological Liberalism 1890–1930* (2003). His subsequent research has focused principally on Methodist history, and he co-edited the *Ashgate Research Companion to World Methodism* (2013). He is a Fellow of the Royal Historical Society and of the Society of Antiquaries of London.

Foreword

JOHN WESLEY AND GEORGE Whitefield are such pivotal figures, their ministries so remarkable, their personalities so large, their disputes with one another so jarring, it is no surprise that much has been written about them. Some of this literature does have a partisan flavor, because these good friends did diverge from one another on some key doctrines. And some, especially on the Wesleyan side, have looked at Wesley through the prism of the later development in this tradition when some Wesleyans departed from what he had thought.

I am therefore most appreciative for this very fine book, which does neither of these things. In fact, it has placed Wesley and Whitefield in their own historical context, side by side, in chapters that are developed with balance, accuracy, and insight.

These two towering figures catch our attention, of course, because they flourished in times that were far from easy. Travel, for example, was slow and sometimes difficult. The world might have become their parish, but they had to visit it on horseback and by ship. Whitefield sailed back and forth to the eastern coast of America more than did Wesley, but both rode countless miles by horseback—in Wesley's case, perhaps a quarter of a million miles. But that was the least of their difficulties.

In England in the eighteenth century, society had become deeply corrupted, more so, it would appear, than was the case in the American colonies. Indeed, English society had become so inhumane, so repressive of those lower down the class hierarchy, so wracked by crime, that it hardly seemed possible that it would be able to hold together. But then this evangelical revival swept through the land. So great is the difference between the England before the revival and the one that came after it that Lecky's well-known judgment may well be correct. Without this work of God, he said, England would have become engulfed in social revolution.

England at this time was no better off intellectually than it was socially. Deism had become the dominant framework for thinking about life. This had emerged at the beginning of the previous century but it gained fervor and momentum in the time of Wesley and Whitefield as it linked up with the Enlightenment. It then made its way across the ocean at the time of the American Revolution but it did not take hold in America until the beginning of the nineteenth century. But in England, Wesley and Whitefield found themselves up against a formidable intellectual opponent.

Deists made the argument that nature, including human nature, has within it all that people need to make their way through life. Nature does not need to be augmented by any supernatural revelation and, indeed, it is never disturbed by any divine interventions from outside. No miracles have ever occurred. Christ was, therefore, an earnest but deluded man. No gospel, no regeneration, no justification are needed for "salvation."

In addition to dismissing key biblical truths, this deism also undermined the idea that God is concerned for the world. That was its practical outcome. He had, in fact, withdrawn from it apparently in indifference. This meant that life was not framed by what is ultimate. Meaning is never more than provisional, temporary, and passing. Deists did speak of judgment but it was hard to know why God would take interest in a person's life after death when he had not taken much interest in that person's life before they died.

This alternative to Christian faith did provoke quite a vigorous counter-literature of an apologetic kind such as Bishop Butler's *Analogy of Religion* and William Law's *An Appeal to all that Doubt and Disbelieve the Truths of Revelation*. As needed as this counter-offensive was, though, what actually turned the tide in England was the recovery, through the ministries of Wesley and Whitefield, of "experiential religion" with its Christ-centered, Cross-focused message, its biblical doctrines of justification and regeneration, its vision of living life under the hand of God, and its hope of life everlasting. Theirs, in fact, was a sturdy, doctrinally shaped message that they advocated with energy and extraordinary tenacity. And, of course, this was also why their differences on election and sanctification were so deeply felt and were aired in ways that were sometimes sharp.

This book, of course, is a meticulous study of these two extraordinary people, Wesley and Whitefield. But one cannot read it without reflecting on the magnitude of what God did through them and on how urgently we need a comparable work of God in our own time.

Our world is like theirs in some ways and different in others. We are very aware, for example, that Christian faith is much in decline in the West today even as it was when Wesley and Whitefield lived. Today it lives on the margins of every Western society. It has been edged out of every public square. It now has to live in secularized contexts infused by a postmodern, relativistic mood where meaning is never more than individualistic and fragmentary and hope vanishes. Deism then and our postmodern world now achieve some of the same ends.

Our day, though, is also quite different from theirs in other ways. We travel and communicate with extraordinary ease. And we are far removed from the time of Wesley's quaint experiments in medical care such as placing sulfur and egg white on brown paper and then applying it to the side to cure tuberculosis!

But the most important difference is that in Wesley and Whitefield God had minds that were aflame with his truth. Their habits of thinking about Scripture were also deeply doctrinal. The same cannot always be said of those in the evangelical world today. In our churches, doctrinal thinking is quite rare. And in our pulpits, engagement with Scripture is not always deep. What Wesley and Whitefield had in their time, which God used mightily, we are often lacking in our time. May the essays in this book help us to see our world and ourselves with fresh eyes!

David F. Wells

Distinguished Research Professor
Gordon-Conwell Theological Seminary

Acknowledgments

APPRECIATION IS DUE TO the many who, in different ways, have contributed to this volume. I am grateful to the Board of Sydney Missionary and Bible College for granting me a sabbatical to pursue this project to its completion and for the hospitality extended by Richard Lints at Gordon-Conwell Theological Seminary during the Maddock family's six-month sojourn in South Hamilton, Massachusetts. I am especially thankful to the contributors to this volume who have collectively embraced the value of approaching Wesley and Whitefield with an irenic voice. Lastly, to my students, past and present, who might still be tempted to ask me whether Wesley or Whitefield is my favorite, the answer is still, and will always be, "Yes."

Ian J. Maddock

Croydon, July 2017

Introduction

Ian J. Maddock

You never really understand a person until you consider things from his point of view . . . until you climb into his skin and walk around in it.¹

An oft-repeated story—and one that has become enshrined in evangelical folklore—surrounds an encounter between John Wesley and one of his followers in the years immediately after George Whitefield's death. A contemporary of Wesley's, Edward Pease, was reported to have overheard "one of the godly band of Christian sisters who had been brought under [Wesley's] influences and who loved both Whitefield and himself" enquire of Wesley, "'Dear Mr. Wesley, do you expect to see dear Mr. Whitefield in heaven?'" After a lengthy pause that no doubt built dramatic tension, Wesley is said to have "replied with great seriousness, 'No, madam.' His inquirer at once exclaimed, 'Ah, I was afraid you would say so.'" John Wesley clarified, with intense earnestness, "'Do not misunderstand me, madam; George Whitefield was so bright a star in the firmament of God's glory, and will stand so near the throne, that one like me, who am less than the least, will never catch a glimpse of him.'"²

And yet if a different iteration of this story is anything to go by, Wesley did not have a monopoly on magnanimous gestures such as these. In this variant, the plotline is identical—but now it is *Whitefield* whose role it is to offer an assessment of his Arminian co-revivalist that takes his Calvinistic interlocutor by surprise. In the version described by Leslie Church,

---

1. Atticus Finch in Lee, *To Kill a Mockingbird*, 33.
2. A Methodist Preacher, *John Wesley the Methodist*, 168.

"One of [Wesley's] critics came to George Whitefield and said, 'Sir, do you think when we get to heaven we shall see John Wesley?' 'No, sir,' answered George Whitefield, 'I fear not, for he shall be so near the Eternal Throne and we shall be at such a distance, we shall hardly get a sight of him.'"[3] Whatever doubts might have surrounded the historical accuracy of these "possibly apocryphal"[4] events, they were overlooked as the anecdote began to quickly circulate and even make appearances in prominent pulpits. For example, Charles Spurgeon—though himself no endorser of Arminian soteriology—rehearsed Church's (not Pease's) version of the story and in the process affirmed its value as a rousing testimony to the value of maintaining evangelical unity in the midst of undoubted theological diversity: "In studying the life of Wesley, I believe Whitefield's opinion is abundantly confirmed—that Wesley is near the eternal throne, having served his Master, albeit with many mistakes and errors, yet from a pure heart, fervently desiring to glorify God upon earth."[5]

If the evocativeness of these stories lies at least in part in their presentation of Wesley *and* Whitefield as exemplars of evangelical ecumenicity, Spurgeon's comments nonetheless betray their undeniable theological differences. Without doubt their most visible doctrinal disagreement revolved around the nature of election during the so-called "Free Grace" episode. The dispute had a lasting ecclesiological legacy and resulted in the permanent separation of the Methodist Societies along Whitefieldian-Calvinist and Wesleyan-Arminian lines. Frank Baker went so far as to describe the "Free Grace" episode as "one of the most pregnant events in English church history," implicitly acknowledging that although they managed to achieve a measure of personal reconciliation in the years that followed, the Wesley-Whitefield relationship would forever be associated with conflict: Wesley *versus* Whitefield.[6]

In fact, Wesley and Whitefield's reputation for friction had become so ingrained in the British consciousness that even in the early twentieth century they were making appearances as combatants in the most unlikely places. In a memorable scene in Evelyn Waugh's 1930 satiric novel *Vile Bodies*, the novel's anti-hero, Adam Fenwick-Symes, receives a tour of the set of what is styled by its producer, a Mr. Isaacs of *The Wonderfilm Company of*

---

3. Church, *Knight of the Burning Heart*, 126.

4. Collins, *John Wesley: A Theological Journey*, 117.

5. Spurgeon, "John Wesley," 58. On another occasion he declared, "if there were wanted two apostles to be added to the number of the twelve, I do not believe there could be found two men more fit to be so added than George Whitefield and John Wesley." Spurgeon, *Autobiography*, 1:176.

6. Baker, "Whitefield's Break with the Wesleys," 103.

Great Britain, as the "most important All-Talkie super-religious film to be produced in this country by British artists and management and by British capital." Entitled *A Brand Plucked from the Burning*, the film focuses on the "life of that great social and religious reformer John Wesley"—but also features George Whitefield as his prime nemesis. Having been assured by Mr. Isaacs that the film "has been . . . supervised by a staff of expert historians and theologians," and that "Nothing has been omitted that would contribute to the meticulous accuracy of every detail," Fenwick-Symes arrives just in time for the shooting of the film's centerpiece: a sword duel between Whitefield and Wesley, who are cast as rivals for the affections of Selina, Countess of Huntingdon. "Of course, it's not really them," observes Isaac. "Two fencing instructors we got over from the gym at Aylesbury. That's what I mean when I say we spare no expense to get the details accurate. Ten bob we're paying them for the afternoon."[7] As Adam looked on, "He saw the two fencing instructors in long black coats and white neck bands lunging and parrying manfully until [Wesley] fell."[8] When he queries incredulously whether or not Wesley and Whitefield actually fought a duel, Isaacs responds confidently, "'Well, it's not actually recorded, but it's known that they quarrelled and there was only one way of settling quarrels in those days. They're both in love with Selina . . . you see. She comes to stop them, but arrives too late."[9]

Wesley and Whitefield: Two Peas in a Pod?

One of the convictions that motivates this present collection of essays is that John Wesley and George Whitefield are not paired and compared in print often enough. Although there have been myriad volumes focusing on the ministries of *either* Wesley *or* Whitefield, there are relatively few intentionally comparative studies of their full-orbed public ministries. As Timothy L. Smith observes,

> Aside from Luke Tyerman, a nineteenth-century Methodist, few historians have read and pondered the writings of both George Whitefield and John Wesley. Most have belonged, as Tyerman did, to one or the other partisan camp and allowed their knowledge of that tradition to guide their judgments. Preoccupation with supposed preeminence or priority has distorted their view of the two men's early cooperation.[10]

7. Waugh, *Vile Bodies*, 122.
8. Ibid., 124.
9. Ibid., 122.
10. Smith, *Whitefield and Wesley on the New Birth*, 7. There are, it must be

This lacuna is both surprising and regrettable given the manner in which their lives illuminated one another. Our understanding of Wesley and the legacy of his public ministry is impoverished apart from considering Whitefield (and vice versa).

When we compare Wesley and Whitefield, they can appear as "two peas in a pod": Wesley *and* Whitefield. After all, their biographies, career trajectories and doctrinal commitments reflect many and varied affinities. For example, although Wesley and Whitefield expressed retrospective ambivalence about their Oxford Holy Club experiences, the intensity of their time spent in this virtual holiness greenhouse was highly formative for both men: Wesley as the co-founder of the select group and Whitefield as his eager protégé. While Whitefield later followed Wesley as a missionary with the Society for the Propagation of the Gospel, succeeding him in Savannah, Georgia, it was Wesley who followed Whitefield into the fields in April 1739. Further, while both sought to be, in Wesley's language, *homo unius libri*, it was ultimately as extemporaneous *preachers* of one book that Wesley and Whitefield both found their homiletical and vocational homes. Both were ordained and remained clergy within the Church of England while at the same time exuding an evangelistic spirit that transcended national and denominational boundaries. Their parallel histories also included dramatic experiences of the new birth that became paradigmatic for their own respective proclamation of the necessity of regeneration and of being justified by faith, not works.

Wesley versus Whitefield: Apples and Oranges

But if "Wesley *and* Whitefield" have received surprisingly little attention given their many commonalities, then "Wesley *versus* Whitefield" as a dynamic has often been accentuated in a way that they can appear more like "apples and oranges." This historiographical trajectory often stresses their roles as theological champions of Arminianism and moderate Calvinism

---

acknowledged, some contemporary exceptions to the trends described above. And yet even these are limited in their scope and perspective. For example, while Smith's *Whitefield and Wesley on the New Birth* helpfully parses their shared commitment to proclaiming the necessity of regeneration, despite increasingly divergent views on the nature of grace and perfection, it is, by intention, narrowly doctrinal in its focus. James Schwenk's *Catholic Spirit* is more comprehensive in its treatment of Wesley and Whitefield's theological commitments, but in a bid to offer them as a "paradigm of evangelical ecumenicity, whereby evangelicals could work toward consensus-building, even though doctrinal and personal differences may not be completely rectified" (*Catholic Spirit*, 18), he accentuates their similarities in such a way as to run the risk of diminishing their theological differences as merely semantic.

respectively and is particularly evident in the partisan accounts of the "Free Grace" controversy. For example, Joseph Tracy evaluated this event from the vantage point of a self-professed Calvinist, contrasting Whitefield's unimpeachable character with what he styled the "cold-hearted selfishness of Wesley."[11] By contrast, the evaluations reached by some Wesleyan-Arminian authors are often diametrically opposed. McConnell presented Wesley as the victim of Whitefieldian theological partisanship and argued that throughout this dispute "Wesley shows at a considerable advantage over Whitefield."[12] That is, the theological differences between Arminians and Calvinists have led some Wesley and Whitefield biographers to assert not only the superiority of their respective champion's theology during the "Free Grace" controversy but also their moral acumen—especially at the expense of the other preacher.

In a similar vein, Arnold Dallimore's prodigious two-volume *George Whitefield: The Life and Times of the Great Evangelist of the 18th-Century Revival* was motivated not only by a desire to offer Whitefield as a model and spur to contemporary revival but also by a desire to correct what Dallimore perceives to be an egregious historiographical imbalance.[13] Dallimore considered Whitefield's "greatness" to have been illegitimately obscured and impoverished by a variety of mutually reinforcing factors, including "inadequate biography, poorly edited Works, lost documents, ineffective portraiture and the undue aggrandizement of his associate [that is, John Wesley]."[14] He wanted to address the deleterious impact on Whitefield's legacy caused by what he describes as the uncritical "admiration" and "unthinking veneration" shown towards Wesley by his early biographers.[15] These, he contends, collectively "proved incapable of viewing [Wesley's] career without bias," and have created a semi-legendary image of Wesley that has been tenaciously defended by the Methodist rank and file while simultaneously obscuring the contributions of fellow evangelists, most notably George Whitefield.[16]

---

11. Tracy, *Great Awakening*, 258.

12. McConnell, *Evangelicals, Revolutionists and Idealists*, 82–83.

13. Henry Rack describes Dallimore's work as being "detailed" though "uncritical." *Reasonable Enthusiast*, 565.

14. Dallimore, *George Whitefield*, 1:12.

15. Ibid.

16. Ibid., 1:12–13. Dallimore's tendency toward accentuating "Whitefield versus Wesley" has not gone unnoticed. Clifford observes, "The author's concern to compensate for the undue neglect of Whitefield's contribution makes him unnecessarily critical of Wesley." *Atonement and Justification*, 52.

The Scope and Purpose of This Volume

The historiographical trajectories we have briefly charted above threaten to pose something of a conundrum: which one most accurately describes the relationship that existed between these two foremost leaders of the eighteenth century transatlantic evangelical revival? Wesley *and* Whitefield? Or Wesley *versus* Whitefield? Depending on how selective a historical and/or theological aperture one chooses, it is possible to muster a wealth of substantiating evidence in support of either polarity. On the one hand, Wesley and Whitefield have served as enduring symbols of the possibility of an evangelical brotherly love that transcends intramural disagreements. After all, was it not Whitefield's desire that for all of their unresolved theological disagreements, Wesley should be given the honor of preaching at his memorial service in London? And yet, they have also functioned as exemplars of irreconcilable antagonism that veers towards theological fratricide. After all, it was also Whitefield who declared in 1742 that he and Wesley "preached two different gospels," and that not only would he "not join with [Wesley], or give [him] the right hand of fellowship," but that he was "resolved publicly to preach against [Wesley] . . . wheresoever he preached at all."[17]

Of course, this dilemma only persists for as long as we subscribe to the inviolability of the dichotomy and thus feel compelled to assert one narrative at the expense of the other. Perhaps then, rather than choosing to perpetuate this approach, there exists a more fruitful avenue of exploration—one in keeping with the complexity and longevity of their intertwined personal and theological biographies. This approach lies at the methodological heart of the present volume and consists in questioning and, as necessary, resisting the potential allure of either uncritically ecumenical "Wesley and" or parochial "Whitefield versus" narratives.

The ensuing twelve essays aim to test the validity of the dichotomies that have long characterized Wesley-Whitefield studies. Acknowledging the impossibility of attempting, let alone achieving, comprehensiveness—there is after all no end to the range of topics open to comparison across Wesley and Whitefield's respective overlapping ministries—this volume explores topics of recognized theological and historical significance from fresh perspectives while also forging innovative arenas of comparison. It possesses several distinctive features. First, as a multi-author volume, it is able to compare a variety of theological, historical, and pastoral facets of Wesley and Whitefield's full-orbed public ministry in a way that any single-author volume by nature cannot. Second, the authors bring a refreshing theological,

---

17. Ward and Heitzenrater, eds., *Journals and Diaries*, 19:188–89.

denominational, and regional diversity to their comparison of Wesley and Whitefield. And third, these essays introduce a multi-disciplinary approach towards its comparison of Wesley and Whitefield, encompassing theology, history, homiletics, and pastoral theology.

Chapters 1 and 2 approach some familiar terrain—Wesley and Whitefield's conception of conversion and their 1739–1742 dispute over predestination—from innovative perspectives. Sean McGever contends that, for all of their emphasis on the necessity of experiencing the new birth, the broader conception of both the new birth and progressive sanctification ought to be considered the fundamental structure of Wesley and Whitefield's unified theology of conversion. Joel Houston provides a fresh exploration of the so-called "Free Grace" episode, contending that while Wesley's stance on conditional election was a cherished theological commitment, the doctrine of election also functioned as a social demarcator and that by forcefully articulating a divergent doctrine of predestination from that of Whitefield, Wesley was thus able to lay the foundation of a Methodist movement of which he was the principal organizer.

Two chapters follow in which Ian Maddock and Ed Loane explore various facets of Wesley and Whitefield's evolving ecclesiology. Maddock contends that while Wesley and Whitefield shared a common ecclesiological motto, Whitefield's emphasis was on an evangelistic preaching ministry that placed a premium on maintaining mobility across spatial, social, and denominational boundaries. When Whitefield declared "The whole world is now my parish," his emphasis was more on "the world" and less on "the parish." By contrast, Wesley was equally committed to facilitating spiritual nurture for those converted under his preaching: I look upon all the world as *my parish*. Loane concludes that although Wesley was more tenaciously devoted to the Church of England, his legacy was ultimately more divisive. By contrast, Whitefield, whose adherence was less rigid, left a more enduring legacy in evangelical Anglicanism.

Chapters 5 to 7 compare elements of Wesley and Whitefield's theology. David McEwan takes up the contentious subject of Christian perfection, contrasting Whitefield's belief that God still required the same flawless life demanded of humanity prior to the fall with Wesley's belief that God moderated his requirements in the light of our fallen state. He concludes that while for Whitefield this meant Christian perfection was a goal to be pursued, for Wesley it was, by God's grace alone, an attainable goal in this present bodily life. Jared Hood explores the covenantal substructure of Wesley and Whitefield's theological systems, concluding that in surprising ways they might be considered "federalist brothers," while Peter Adam assesses their doctrines of original sin and the nature and extent of the atonement, concluding that despite some terminological misunderstanding, their genuine differences issued not only in pastoral consequences, but also shaped their ministries and messages.

Though thematically distinct, chapters 8 and 9 both focus on Wesley and Whitefield as products of their eighteenth-century times. Martin Wellings demonstrates how Wesley and Whitefield both brought to their preaching the shaping influences of a golden age of transatlantic sermon culture, transfigured by the evangelical revival. While Wesley and Whitefield shared a passionate conviction about the spiritual freedom provided in the new birth, in comparing their stances on slavery, Glen O'Brien concludes that they differed, tellingly, on the extent to which freedom should be considered a basic human right.

Finally, in chapters 10 to 12 our attention turns to pastoral and practical theology. Tom Schwanda explores how Wesley and Whitefield understood "true religion" and compares their utilization of specific spiritual disciplines and means of grace as a practical way of guiding believers into greater holiness. Rhys Bezzant creatively evaluates Wesley and Whitefield as "companions in the way," recipients and advocates of integrative and exhortative ministries, even if by personality and circumstances their own contribution as mentors was not fully developed. Lastly, while Wesley and Whitefield are not remembered as hymn writers, Rob Smith demonstrates the many ways each helped to establish the day of the evangelical English hymn: as passionate singers, promoters, collectors, compilers, editors, publishers, and (in Wesley's case) translators of hymns.

John Wesley and George Whitefield were in many ways larger-than-life figures during their own lifetimes—and indeed continue to be so today. And yet our ability to appreciate their abiding influence on contemporary evangelicalism is diminished if we consider them in isolation from one another. This volume serves as an invitation to grow in our awareness of their interdependence in a way that also acknowledges their undoubted differences. Whether one comes to these essays resonating more with Whitefield's Calvinistic parsing of the divine-human relationship in salvation, or with Wesley's commitment to spiritual nurture over and against a singularly evangelistic ministry, these chapters afford the opportunity to not only nuance our understanding of their respective theologies and ministry practices, but also better situate them in the wider eighteenth-century world. Echoing Atticus Finch's exhortation, they also offer a timely application of the inherent value of considering "things from [Wesley's] point of view," and of climbing "into [Whitefield's] skin and walk[ing] around in it." While the experience might well be awkward and uncomfortable, it is hoped that this volume will be a catalyst for irenic conversation both within evangelicalism and beyond.

1

"Beginning a Society of Their Own"

John Wesley, George Whitefield, and the Bristol Division

Joel Houston

HISTORICAL ANALYSES OF DOCTRINE often run the risk of flattening the concept into a simple ideological notion—doctrine becomes an abstract idea, a proposition to be assented to (or argued with) and little else.[1] Leif Dixon underscored this danger in his work on the rise of predestinarianism in Reformation England:

> When we study the "history of ideas" we always need to remember that these ideas do not exist except in the minds of individuals: it is too easy implicitly to reify concepts and ignore the importance of personality and intention when the question turns to the "big debates" about the theological character of the Church of England or the social functions of predestinarian ideas.[2]

The articulation of doctrine always occurs within a social nexus. Dixon's work uncovered much of the underlying psychological dynamics present

---

1. For the notion of doctrine as "informative proposition," see Lindbeck, *Nature of Doctrine*, 16.

2. Dixon, *Practical Predestinarians*, 253. Dixon's argument finds affinities with Alister McGrath's work on the historical and social contingencies of doctrine: "Without th[e] recognition of the social grounding of ecclesial reality, doctrine becomes an essentially idealist conception, divorced from its historical location and improperly separated from the matrix of social forces which shape it in manners that idealists prefer to overlook, yet are essential to a fully orbed account of the place of theory in the Christian life." McGrath, *Scientific Theology*, 3:66.

in predestinarian thinking up until the mid-seventeenth century.³ This investigation naturally leads to one of the most public predestinarian disputes since the Reformation, untouched by Dixon: the fracture in the evangelical revival between John Wesley and George Whitefield. This acrimonious dispute has come to be known as the "Free Grace" controversy (1739–1744).⁴ Dixon's argument, however, is not a new one and the understanding of the social elements of doctrine is not a novel concept.

A cursory understanding of the social elements of doctrine existed even in the immediate aftermath of the "Free Grace" controversy, exemplified in an anonymous anti-Methodist pamphlet entitled, "A Brief and Impartial Account of the Character and Doctrines of Mr. Whitefield and Mr. Wesley."⁵ The author painted Whitefield in unbecoming terms and argued that he was determined to establish a church "whereof he was to be the head."⁶ John and Charles Wesley were presented in equally unflattering language as men who "had hitherto gone hand in hand with [Whitefield] in everything, but they too perceive[d] that all the glory redounded to him, and that they were only considered as his private followers, began to set up for themselves."⁷ The author of the pamphlet asserted that the key to the establishment of a distinct brand of Wesleyan Methodism was Wesley's "Arminian" interpretation of the Reformed doctrine of predestination. The anonymous author is worth quoting at length:

> Mr. Whitefield's preaching up predestination, in the highest sense of the word, which he continued to do for a considerable time, afforded them a good opportunity of separating from him, which they immediately did, and beginning a society of their own, opposed Mr. Whitefield with great violence, by taking the other side, and preaching free grace in the greatest latitude. Though the insisting on either of these doctrines (however true any of them may be) tended very little to the edification of their hearers; they had their aim by it, making a distinct party, some following the one, and some the other.⁸

The anonymous author's assessment is instructive: the doctrine of predestination functioned as an instrument to differentiate and identify a distinct

---

3. Dixon, *Practical Predestinarians*, 26–32.

4. Sometimes referred to as the *First Calvinistic Controversy*, as per Brown-Lawson, *John Wesley and the Anglican Evangelicals*, 161–92.

5. Anonymous, *Impartial Account*, 5–6.

6. Ibid.

7. Ibid.

8. Ibid.

socio-religious entity, what would become the Wesleyan Methodist society. This new society existed within the broader ecclesiastical structure of the Church of England yet was "a distinct party" from Whitefield's Calvinistic Methodists through the preaching of "free grace" (by which the author means unlimited atonement and conditional election).

What follows is an examination of the events leading up to, and including, the "Free Grace" controversy itself. This essay will account for Wesley's rise to a position of leadership and authority in the early Methodist circles of Bristol and London from 1739 to 1740, superseding the position that Whitefield maintained before his second transatlantic voyage. Employing the insights of McGrath, Dixon, and the anonymous author of the *Impartial Account*, the present analysis seeks to uncover some of the less commented upon functions of doctrine, most notably, how doctrine functions as a "social demarcator."[9] This essay will argue that John Wesley used his interpretation of the doctrine of predestination as an instrument to uniquely identify his proto-Methodist societies over and above the supervision that Whitefield had over the early Bristol and London groups.[10] As such, predestinarian conflicts helped galvanize a particular brand of Methodism by imparting a sense of social identification while retaining the broadly orthodox features of a society within the Church of England.[11]

"A Fire Kindled in the Country": George Whitefield's Bristol Ministry[12]

Whitefield initiated his immediately successful, if ecclesiastically unorthodox, ministry in Bristol and surrounding areas in early 1739.[13] As Henry Rack notes, Whitefield was instrumental in promoting the revival from the early days of a loose coalition of "eccentric" close-knit colleagues and into

9. McGrath, *Genesis of Doctrine*, 37.

10. Dallimore has argued forcefully for this perspective as well. See *George Whitefield*, 2:19–41: "Wesley Enters into the Leadership of the Movement." It is important to note, however, that Dallimore saw Wesley's distinctive doctrine as being, primarily, Christian Perfection: ibid., 1:319. Dallimore was not without his detractors in this regard: see McGonigle, *Sufficient Saving Grace*, 151–52.

11. Because of the pendulum swing between Calvinism and Arminianism in the Church of England in the sixteenth and seventeenth centuries, either interpretation of predestination ("unconditional" or "conditional") could be considered within the bounds of orthodox church teaching. See Dixon's reading of Tyacke, *Practical Predestinarians*, 4–5; Tyacke, "Puritanism, Arminianism and Counter-Revolution," 120–21.

12. Whitefield, *Journals*, 217.

13. Dallimore, *George Whitefield*, 2:20.

"something more extensive and public."[14] Whitefield quickly realized he needed to enlist support and John Wesley was an obvious choice.[15] Admiring Wesley's expertise with "the great things of God," Whitefield wrote to his Oxford friend on 22 March 1739 and requested that he come and aid in the revival at Bristol.[16] Confident of Wesley's eventual agreement, Whitefield publically (and pre-emptively) advertised Wesley's impending visit and redoubled his exhortation: "I beseech you come next week. It is advertised in this day's journal. I pray for a blessing on your journey in our meetings. The people expect you much. Though you come after, I *heartily* wish that you may be preferred before me."[17] In his *Journal*, Wesley recounted receiving the letters;[18] after drawing lots, the Fetter Lane Society determined that Wesley should go to Bristol.[19] Wesley departed from London a week after Whitefield's request, on 29 March, and arrived in Bristol on 31 March 1739.[20]

As much as George Whitefield implored Wesley to come to Bristol, it did not come with unchecked endorsement. Aware of Wesley's theological leanings, Whitefield advised his friend that disputing over contentious topics, especially that of predestination, was unwise.[21] Wesley admitted this in his letter to James Hutton and the Fetter Lane Society on 30 April 1739:

> I was now in some doubt how to proceed. Our dear brethren, before I left London, and our brother Whitefield here, and our brother Chapman since, had conjured me to enter into no

---

14. Rack, *Reasonable Enthusiast*, 192.
15. Dallimore, *George Whitefield*, 2:20.
16. Baker, ed., *Letters*, 25:612.
17. Ibid.
18. "During my stay here I was fully employed between our own society in Fetter Lane and many others, where I was continually desired to expound. So that I had no thought of leaving London when I received . . . a letter from Mr. Whitefield . . . entreating me in the most pressing manner to come to Bristol without delay." Ward and Heitzenrater, eds., *Letters and Diaries*, 19:37.
19. It is of interest to note that the process of deliberation among the Fetter Lane brethren was likely something that Wesley chafed under, and may well have contributed to the fracture with Fetter Lane in June of 1740. Henry Rack notes that the Fetter Lane model of decision making "conflicted with Wesley's sense of authorized ecclesiastical authority (and perhaps his own sense of authority by virtue of the personal call of God)." Rack, *Reasonable Enthusiast*, 188. For a particularly penetrating analysis of John Wesley's use of lots in this instance, see Hammond, "Whitefield, Wesley, and Revival Leadership" in Hammond and Jones, eds., *George Whitefield: Life, Context, and Legacy*, 106–8.
20. Baker, ed., *Letters*, 25:619n1.
21. Dallimore, *George Whitefield*, 2:20, 26.

disputes, least of all concerning Predestination, because this people was so deeply prejudiced for it.[22]

Before proceeding to Wesley's subsequent proclamation of conditional election, the question must be asked: why did Whitefield ask Wesley to abstain from theological squabbles? Whitefield could simply have been counseling Wesley as to the best possible course of evangelism among a people group that was not well known to Wesley. While the health of the revival was important to both men, in this case it was especially important for Whitefield who had a personal attachment to Bristol, a city just 40 miles southwest of his hometown, Gloucester. Whitefield's advice seems to contain a note of foreboding caution as well, indicating that were Wesley to preach against predestination, the theological inclinations of Whitefield's following could result in strident opposition. What is clear in Whitefield's exhortation, however, is that his early following was built upon a foundation that was thoroughly Calvinistic.[23] To be "deeply prejudiced" for the doctrine of predestination would suggest that it was constitutive of the very identity of Whitefield's leadership over the societies in Bristol.

Furthermore, lurking behind Whitefield's exhortation is the appearance of wishing to remain foremost in the proto-Methodist movement in Bristol. By asking Wesley to simply conform, or at the very least not contradict, the doctrinal standards adhered to by Whitefield, Harris, and others, Whitefield attempted to limit Wesley's ability to exert a distinctive theological identity. As such, Wesley would simply be serving the work that Whitefield initiated.[24] Wesley was to be a partner in the revival, yes, but the role was arguably that of stewarding Whitefield's ministry, while Whitefield carried on the exciting (and exhausting) work of itinerant preaching. It is not unreasonable to suggest that Whitefield desired to retain the best of both worlds: charismatic speaker in the American colonies and chief of the evangelical Revival in England. In his absence, Whitefield desired that no personality supersede his own, evidenced by Whitefield's caution that Wesley not preach the very doctrine that would identify Wesley as a distinct leader in his own right.[25] In this way, predestination functioned both as a

22. Baker, ed., *Letters*, 25:639.

23. Dallimore argued that Whitefield's Calvinism was present from the earliest days of his ministry. See Dallimore, *George Whitefield*, 1:395–410.

24. At this juncture, Dallimore referred to Wesley as "something of a lieutenant to Whitefield," ibid., 2:20.

25. Geordan Hammond has argued that Whitefield's concluding signatures in his epistolary correspondence between the years of 1735 to 1739 support the conclusion that Whitefield saw himself less as Wesley's spiritual "son" and more as a peer in the evangelistic endeavors in the early years of the revival. See Hammond, "Revival

doctrine that delineated the shape of God's soteriological design, and also as an instrument to distinguish between the unique theological constitutions of Wesley and Whitefield. Thus, Whitefield could simultaneously say to Wesley, "I *heartily* wish that you may be preferred before me" yet not desire that Wesley break up the theological foundation that Whitefield had established upon Calvinistic principles, particularly those relating to predestination. Whitefield's sentiments to Samuel Mason near the beginning of the revival reflect his personal sense of ownership in the Bristol ministry: "The fire is not only kindled but blown up into a blaze. I hope brother [? Wesley] will under God keep it until I return from Georgia."[26] After all, Whitefield also wished to remind Wesley that "you come *after*."[27]

"Free Grace" and Subsequent Charismata

Whitefield's request that Wesley avoid preaching against predestination went unheeded. In Wesley's same letter to Hutton and Fetter Lane wherein he acknowledged Whitefield's caution, Wesley revealed that he was the recipient of a letter that "charg[ed] me roundly with 'resisting and perverting the truth as it is in Jesus' by preaching against God's decree of predestination."[28] The letter of which Wesley spoke is not extant, but given Wesley's dating, seems to indicate that the letter was in circulation some time before Wesley's arrival in Bristol.[29] Unwilling to have the anonymous letter tarnish his reputation, Wesley defended his theological integrity by mounting an offensive against the prevailing Calvinism in Bristol: Wesley preached on predestination on 26 April 1739 at Newgate.[30] Of note is Wesley's belief that he "was led, I know not how" to preach on predestination.[31] It is as though Wesley wished to dissolve his own agency in preaching against predestination, even though Wesley had good cause to speak against it: to absolve his good name from the slanderous circulating letter in Bristol. Herbert McGonigle ob-

---

Leadership," 114.

26. Roberts, "George Whitefield and Friends," 2:182.

27. Baker, ed., *Letters*, 25:612; emphasis mine. This sentiment is shared by Heitzenrater: "George realized his own limitations at organization but could lay his own subtle claim to some priority." Heitzenrater, *Wesley and the People Called Methodists*, 108. Coppedge disagreed: Coppedge, *John Wesley in Theological Debate*, 43–44. Coppedge, however, demonstrated an unwillingness to concede that Wesley was aggressive in the least in his early Bristol ministry.

28. Baker, ed., *Letters*, 25:639.

29. McGonigle, *Sufficient Saving Grace*, 114.

30. Baker, ed., *Letters*, 25:639–40.

31. Ibid., 25:639–40.

served that Wesley's sermon catapulted him to a position of equal standing with Whitefield, and effectively divided the proto-Methodist societies "into pro and anti-Calvinistic groups."[32]

Wesley's preaching at Newgate was but one outcome of his personal study and increasingly forceful articulation of an Arminian doctrine of predestination. Wesley's *Diary* on 25 April 1739 noted that he "writ upon Predestination" at 06:00,[33] and the following day at 12:00 "appealed to God concerning predestination."[34] The fruit of this focused meditation appeared on Saturday, 28 April, 06:30: "sermon upon predestination."[35] The next morning, Sunday, 29 April, Wesley preached the sermon "Free Grace" at 07:00 on the Bowling Green; in his *Diary* he recorded "four thousand there."[36]

A question must here be asked concerning Wesley's design in preaching on predestination. As stated, a letter had been circulating in Bristol, declaring that Wesley was "'resisting and perverting the truth as it is in Jesus' by preaching against God's decree of predestination."[37] If Whitefield was correct in evaluating the theological climate of Bristol, the prevailing sentiment would be *for* a Calvinistic understanding of God's predestining love towards his elect. Thus, a differing interpretation of this doctrine would be to suggest a corruption of the Calvinist understanding. Therefore, if Wesley was trying to dispel false accusations about his views on predestination and vindicate the unjust charges of being a false teacher, why did he preach in such a way as to openly contradict Whitefield and the prevailing understanding of predestination? Surely, to ameliorate the supposed misunderstanding of the anonymous letter, Wesley would have been far better off affirming or assuming a Calvinistic interpretation of Article Seventeen for the purposes of public discourse, or simply remaining silent on the issue and letting the letter pass into history. As it was, Wesley intentionally verified the "truth" of the anonymous letter by preaching *against* the popular support for Calvinistic predestination in Bristol. Consequently, it is reasonable to suggest that Wesley viewed the letter as an appropriate entry point into Bristol's religious culture, both to instruct erring believers in the true nature of God's electing love and to establish for himself a

---

32. McGonigle, *Sufficient Saving Grace*, 115.
33. Ward and Heitzenrater, eds., *Journals and Diaries*, 19:386.
34. Ibid.
35. Ibid., 19:387.
36. Ibid. See also McGonigle's summary of Wesley's preparation to speak against Calvinistic predestination, *Sufficient Saving Grace*, 114.
37. Baker, ed., *Letters*, 25:639.

distinct theological identity beside, and perhaps above, that of Whitefield. A predominantly Arminian doctrine of predestination was the key to an orthodox, yet markedly distinct, theological identity for Wesley.

Wesley's anti-predestinarian (in the Calvinist sense) preaching was instantaneously marked with charismatic responses from the crowds in Bristol, which Wesley interpreted as confirmation of the veracity of his message of conditional election and unlimited atonement.[38] Wesley's entry into open-air preaching "on Whitefield's coat-tails"[39] and subsequent campaign in Bristol has been interpreted as one prominent example of Wesley's "unusually forceful leadership style" and, indeed, the "uncompromising and at times ruthless imposition of personal authority."[40]

"A Division Between You and Me": Whitefield's Response[41]

A natural question arising from Wesley's actions is, what was Whitefield's response?[42] Given Wesley's "divine" guidance to preach and print against predestination and the apparent disregard of Whitefield's appeal, addressing the matter with Whitefield would be, arguably, prudent. Six weeks after Wesley preached against predestination, he found himself preaching in London alongside Whitefield.[43] Wesley recorded the surprising affair in his *Journal* for Thursday 14 June 1739.[44] Whitefield also noted the events of the same day in his *Journal*, seemingly unaware of Wesley's actions in Bristol.[45] No mention was made of Wesley's preaching against predestination.

Whitefield's ignorance did not last long; a few short days after their encounter at Blackheath, Whitefield learned of Wesley's actions and wrote two impassioned letters to Wesley, dated 25 June 1739 and 2 July 1739

---

38. Ward and Heitzenrater, eds., *Journals and Diaries*, 19:48–57. See also Ayling, *John Wesley*, 106.

39. Lloyd, *Charles Wesley*, 52. Lloyd commented further that "it is indicative of Wesley's insensitivity that he saw nothing wrong in joining Whitefield in open-air preaching in London, six weeks after he had described his friend's views as blasphemy." Ibid., 53–54.

40. Lloyd, *Charles Wesley*, 44.

41. Baker, ed., *Letters*, 25:662.

42. Dallimore, *George Whitefield*, 1:314–15.

43. Ibid., 1:314.

44. Ward and Heitzenrater, eds., *Journals and Diaries*, 19:69.

45. Whitefield, *Journals*, 284.

respectively.[46] In his first letter, Whitefield confessed his dismay concerning Wesley's intentions:

> I hear, honoured sir, you are about to print a sermon against predestination. It shocks me to think of it. What will be the consequence but controversy? If people ask my opinion, what shall I do? I have a critical part to act. God enable me to behave aright. Silence on both sides will be best . . . Oh! My heart within me is grieved![47]

Wesley's response to Whitefield's letters above has not survived; however, Whitefield's subsequent reply indicated that Whitefield viewed an open break as something to be avoided.[48] While it may be reasonably inferred that preserving the friendship was high on the list of priorities for both men, Wesley zealously pursued his efforts against Calvinist error, fearing antinomianism to be the natural outworking of Calvin's system.[49] Wesley's doctrinal concerns were sincere, yet his conspicuous silence towards Whitefield immediately after casting lots to preach *and* print against predestination presents a conflict that may be understood fruitfully as not simply a doctrinal disagreement but also a struggle for control. What emerges in the early disputes over predestination was the way in which doctrine, particularly the doctrines of election and predestination, functioned as an instrument to consolidate early Methodist identity.

Reports of the dispute between Wesley and Whitefield were likely exacerbated on the grounds of linguistic confusion, compounding the already tense theological disagreement. As James Schwenk and others have argued (Ian Maddock and Irwin Reist among them), Whitefield and Wesley's fracas was, in part, semantic.[50] "Free grace" was a favored phrase of both men, but Wesley and Whitefield interpreted it in different ways. Irwin Reist observed that "Wesley and Whitefield agreed in the matter of grace being the source of man's salvation and, as such, being free, but that they differed in the mode of its operation upon mankind."[51] Therefore, for Whitefield, "free grace" was God's sovereign saving initiative, from election of believers to glorification.[52] Whitefield argued that this grace was

---

46. Dallimore, *George Whitefield*, 1:315.
47. Baker, ed., *Letters*, 25:662.
48. Ibid., 25:668.
49. Heitzenrater, *Wesley and the People Called Methodists*, 133.
50. Schwenk, *Catholic Spirit*, 29–30; Maddock, *Men of One Book*, 193–94; Reist, "Wesley and Whitefield," 28–29.
51. Ibid.
52. Gilles, ed., *Works*, 6:77.

not open to everyone in equal measure as though it depended upon human agency: "Free, because not free to all; but free, because God may withhold or give it to whom and when he pleases."[53]

In Wesley's estimation, the grace that was freely dispensed cast a wider net: "salvation was gracious, but God moved upon all men, drawing them to Himself."[54] Wesley concurred with Whitefield that grace is free "in all," in the sense that "It does not depend on any power or merit in man; no, not in any degree, neither in whole, nor in part."[55] Yet, for Wesley, grace was plainly "for all" in the sense that in no way is the doctrine of election constructed so as to preclude any person from the offer of God's saving love.[56] Wesley's distinction underscored his commitment to the doctrine of "unlimited atonement" and shifted the meaning of the term "free" from the prerogative of God to the availability of saving grace. Both Wesley and Whitefield continued to use the phrase "free grace" in their own way, which sharpened the theological polemics. The terminological dispute over the phrase "free grace" is evidence of how both evangelists were "talking past one another" and may also be understood as Wesley's challenge to the theological assertions of a Calvinist interpretation of predestination.

Wesley continued to actively preach and print against predestination in Whitefield's absence between August 1739 and March 1741.[57] Fiery missives were exchanged across the Atlantic, with Whitefield becoming more and more agitated with Wesley's actions, and passing theological disagreement breaking out into a protracted personal and public argument.[58] Wesley saw an opportunity in Whitefield's absence to simultaneously correct the prevailing and erroneous doctrinal beliefs about predestination (among others), and also, consolidate power within the Methodist movement with himself at the helm. One of the instruments that Wesley employed to establish authority over the Methodist societies was the expulsion of members who were not in doctrinal accord.

53. Gilles, ed., *Works*, 4:72. See also Maddock, *Men of One Book*, 194.
54. Reist, "Wesley and Whitefield," 29.
55. Outler, ed., *Sermons*, 3:545.
56. Ibid.
57. It is important to note that Wesley's concentrated attacks against Calvinistic predestination were not always squarely aimed at Whitefield. Wesley's 1740 republication of the sermon "Free Grace" was in response to an anonymous pamphlet entitled "'Free Grace' Indeed!" that had called into question Wesley's sincerity and character. While Wesley's actions may have exacerbated the situation between he and Whitefield, the complexity of the pamphlet war cannot be overlooked. For further reading, see Maddock, "Solving a Transatlantic Puzzle?," 1–14.
58. For helpful, though slightly divergent, summaries, see Harrington, "Friendship Under Fire, "167–81; Maddock, "Solving a Transatlantic Puzzle?," 1–14.

"Purging the Societies"

Wesley's actions in Bristol were not simply an engagement with errant theology. Whitefield's letter to Wesley on 2 July 1739 revealed Wesley's tendency to remove those from the societies who held different opinions and disputed over controverted matters.[59] Wesley's decision to "purge the societies" warrants further attention to assess the way in which Wesley shaped the societies to function nearly exclusively under his control, effectively challenging the monopoly Whitefield held on early Methodism. Three events will be examined to demonstrate Wesley's drive for influence over the Methodist societies: The creation of the "United Societies," the expulsion of John Acourt, and the removal of John Cennick.[60]

The Creation of the "United Societies"

The early Bristol societies (not yet referred to as explicitly "Methodist")[61] had quickly grown too large for their meager accommodations.[62] Heitzenrater attested to Wesley's organizational capabilities: Wesley oversaw the construction of "The New Room" (previously, "our Room") in May of 1739.[63] Furthermore, Wesley provided stalwart leadership in this case, enabling the societies' own managerial independence and monetarily aiding them when necessary.[64] Heitzenrater continued: "[Wesley] also took a crucial step by assuming managing control (as well as financial responsibility) from the feoffees of the societies"[65]—this ensured that the societies could not be ejected from their facility by the feoffees in the event they disagreed with the style or content of Wesley's preaching.[66] Wesley's leadership at this juncture was truly necessary, yet there is little doubt that Wesley's much-

---

59. Baker, ed., *Sermons*, 25:667.

60. Space here constricts an investigation of the equally provocative break with the Moravians at Fetter Lane. See Heitzenrater, *Wesley and the People Called Methodists*, 121; Dallimore, *George Whitefield*, 2:30; Ward and Heitzenrater, eds., *Journals and Diaries*, 19:162; Baker, ed., *Letters*, 26:53.

61. Heitzenrater, *Wesley and the People Called Methodists*, 114.

62. Ibid., 113.

63. Ibid.

64. Ibid.

65. Ibid.; See Ward and Heitzenrater's explanation that Feoffees were "trustees of a freehold (rather than a leasehold) estate in land, displaced in general usage . . . by the term 'trustee.'" Ward and Heitzenrater, eds., *Works*, 19:56n70. See also ibid., 19:56–57.

66. Heitzenrater, *Wesley and the People Called Methodists*, 113; Ward and Heitzenrater, eds., *Journals and Diaries*, 19:56–57.

needed intervention also won him substantial influence over the fate and fortunes of the Bristol societies. A merger of Wesley's own followers and the remnant of those who broke with the Moravians at the Fetter Lane Society, the new organization was simply referred to as "The United Societies."[67] As Rack notes, while this term largely indicated that it was the combination of the two societies under one roof, it was also "becoming a description of the whole chain under Wesley's supervision."[68] Later on in 1739, Wesley would use this same "supervision" to shift the locus of the Methodist work from Bristol to the Foundery in London.[69] This action, as Dallimore argued, contributed to an "increased prominence and consolidation as a separate body."[70] Throughout Whitefield's absence, Wesley's identification as proto-Methodism's chief leader grew. Indeed, "early in 1741 there were clear signs that Wesley was taking a grip on his societies."[71]

The Expulsion of Mr. Acourt

One of the more inflammatory incidents of the "Free Grace" controversy was the expulsion of the pugnacious predestinarian, Mr. Acourt, from the United Societies. This incident is a useful case study of the way in which predestinarian theology was being used as an instrument to identify the emerging Methodist Societies and an indicator of Wesley's leadership of the early Methodist movement. Of interest in the Acourt occurrence is the conflict Wesley had with Whitefield's "people," that is, the Moorfields congregations that was left in Wesley's care during Whitefield's absence.[72] Mr. John Acourt was one such fellow. Wesley's *Journal* recorded the incident:

> In the evening Mr. Acourt complained that Mr. Nowers had hindered his going into our society. Mr. Nowers answered, "It was by Mr. C. Wesley's order." "What," said Mr. Acourt, "do you refuse admitting a person into your society only because he differs from you in opinion?" I answered, "No; but what opinion do you mean?" He said, "That of election. I hold a certain number is elected from eternity. And these must and shall be saved. And the rest of mankind must and shall be damned. And many of your society hold the same." I replied, "I never asked whether

---

67. Heitzenrater, *Wesley and the People Called Methodists*, 116.
68. Rack, *Reasonable Enthusiast*, 213.
69. Dallimore, *George Whitefield*, 2:29.
70. Ibid.
71. Rack, *Reasonable Enthusiast*, 212.
72. Dallimore, *George Whitefield*, 2:33.

they hold it or no. Only let them not trouble others by disputing about it." He said, "Nay, but I will dispute about it." "What, wherever you come?" "Yes, wherever I come." "Why, then, would you come among us, who you know are of another mind?" "Because you are all wrong, and I am resolved to set you all right." "I fear your coming with this view would neither profit you nor us." He concluded, "Then I will go and tell all the world that you and your brother are false prophets. And I tell you, in one fortnight you will all be in confusion."[73]

By Wesley's account, Mr. Acourt was far too divisive to be beneficial to a harmonious society meeting, and as such, his expulsion was warranted. Imperative to Wesley's argument was that "he did not expel for 'opinions' but only when they were forced on people and divided them."[74] Wesley's perspective was not without precedent: "several of the new forms of renewal within the church recognized that disputation was counterproductive."[75] John Wesley, therefore, was consistent with his principles in dismissing Acourt insomuch as it related to overt disputing.

It cannot be disregarded, however, that in each case of dismissal (Acourt, Stock, and Cennick) it was a dispute over predestination that occasioned a fracture. This disputing could rightly be called contentious, yet it is somewhat understandable.[76] The Foundery was chiefly composed of Whitefield's followers, particularly those of the Moorfields gathering. As such, Whitefield would have been viewed as the organizing force and founding leader of the movement.[77] On this view, Acourt was simply protesting what he believed to be a violation of the doctrinal vision proclaimed by the "original" leader, George Whitefield. Wesley's actions even have a Laudian ring to them.[78] Were any members ever expelled for disputing vocally about Arminianism? Was it really the case that the Calvinists were the only contributors to disputations? Was peace and harmony truly the desired aim, or, was uniting a society under Wesley's distinct theological vision of greater importance? Indeed, Wesley reportedly paid close attention those who leaned, or were suspected of leaning, in a Calvinistic direction. As John

---

73. Ward and Heitzenrater, eds., *Journals and Diaries*, 19:152–53.

74. Rack, *Reasonable Enthusiast*, 198.

75. Heitzenrater, *Wesley and the People Called Methodists*, 131.

76. "It was apparently right for Wesley to preach against Calvinism in Bristol, but wrong for Acourt to champion it in London." Williams, "English and Welsh Methodism," 10.

77. Dallimore, *George Whitefield*, 2:33; Rack, *Reasonable Enthusiast*, 191.

78. For Archbishop Laud's propensity to discipline vocal Calvinists, but not Arminians, see Como, "Predestination and Political Conflict in Laud's London," 289, 291.

Murray, a Methodist class leader, recounted in his memoir, "I was more than suspected of retaining my father's Calvinistic doctrines. Mr. Wesley received information against me. He set a watch over me; thus fixing upon me the evil eye of suspicion."[79] Predestination was, clearly, the watershed doctrine identifying two distinct proto-Methodist identities.[80]

John Cennick and the Kingswood School

Challenges multiplied for John and Charles Wesley in December of 1740, when the men were again disputing about the legitimacy of holding to unconditional election, this time with the schoolmaster of George Whitefield's Kingswood School, John Cennick.[81] Even though Kingswood was placed largely under Wesley's leadership in Whitefield's absence, Cennick believed Whitefield to be the rightful administrator of the Kingswood school, and that Wesley was subordinate to Whitefield in adjudicating matters of doctrine and practice.[82] Initially sympathetic to the Wesleys' doctrine of election, Cennick began to turn to a Calvinistic understanding in the fall of 1740,[83] gathering like-minded Calvinists for his cause, including Thomas Bissicks and Ann Allin.[84] Naturally, the arguments with Wesley began.

John Cennick wrote to Whitefield on 17 January 1741 and notified him of the Wesleys' interruptions at Kingswood, particularly over the doctrine of predestination, and begged Whitefield to come and set matters aright.[85] The letter was intercepted by Wesley and summarily presented to the Society on 22 February 1741.[86] Cennick, Bissicks, and Allin were, like

---

79. John Murray, *Life of Rev. John Murray*, 23, 52. Murray does not date the incident of Wesley's misgivings, however, given Murray's life (1741–1815), it would be considerably *after* the "Free Grace" controversy. Thanks are due to Kelly Yates for directing my attention to this particular incident.

80. Rack, *Reasonable Enthusiast*, 198.

81. Gunter, *Limits of "Love Divine,"* 229. Kingswood was a school funded and established by Whitefield for the Colliers of the area. "The Kingswood school . . . was more fully a Whitefield project. He had conceived the idea and had laid the first stone." See also Dallimore, *George Whitefield*, 2:36.

82. Ibid., 2:38.

83. Gunter, *Limits of "Love Divine,"* 229.

84. Ward and Heitzenrater, eds., *Journals and Diaries*, 19:182.

85. "With universal redemption bro. Charles pleases the world . . . Bro. John follows him in everything. I believe no atheist can more preach against predestination than they. And all who believe election are counted enemies to God, and called so. Fly, dear brother. I am as alone . . . I am in the midst of the plague . . . If God give thee leave, make haste." Ward and Heitzenrater, eds., *Journals and Diaries*, 19:183.

86. Dallimore, *George Whitefield*, 2:39.

Acourt and Stock before them, expelled from the Society. Wesley's writ of dismissal contained the predictable elements, namely, expulsion not over opinion, but division.[87] Further expulsions followed the Cennick incident. On 24 February 1741 at the Bands meeting in Bristol, John Wesley reviewed the membership list of the United Society and "pruned 'disorderly walkers' from the membership list."[88] Wesley wrote, "I took an account of every person (1) to whom any reasonable objection was made; (2) who was not known to and recommended by some on whose veracity I could depend."[89] Membership "tickets" were then issued, the first time Wesley's *Journal* records the practice.[90] To be a ticket-holder, therefore, was to be recognized as one who did not simply hold to the appropriate doctrinal content but also visibly conformed to the peculiar identity of the United Societies. A tangible link had been established, a corporeal correspondence to a theological system—and while doctrinal dissent was theoretically possible, it was practically nonexistent. Those who did not possess a ticket were "put upon trial again, unless they voluntarily expelled themselves."[91]

With over forty members removed from the Society, John Wesley reinforced his ban on Saturday, 28 February, "this time reading a 'paper' that censured the principal leaders of the predestinarian party."[92] The expulsion of Cennick, Acourt, and the others could reasonably be interpreted as John Wesley consolidating his leadership of the Revival by eliminating those of a divergent doctrinal opinion.[93] Wesley "shut up this melancholy subject" in his journal by including an extract from a letter that Charles Wesley wrote to John Cennick.[94] Charles chastised Cennick,

> You came to Kingswood upon my brother's sending for you. You served him in the gospel as a son. I need not say how well he loved you. You used the authority he gave you to overthrow his doctrine. You everywhere contradicted it. (Whether true or false is not the question.) But you ought first to have fairly told him, "I preach contrary to you. Are you willing, notwithstanding,

---

87. Ward and Heitzenrater, eds., *Journals and Diaries*, 19:184.

88. Tyson, *Charles Wesley*, 290; Ward and Heitzenrater, eds., *Journals and Diaries*, 19:183.

89. Ibid., 19:183–84.

90. Ibid., 19:184n29.

91. Ibid., 19:184.

92. Tyson, *Charles Wesley*, 290.

93. Dallimore, *George Whitefield*, 2:32, 40.

94. Ward and Heitzenrater, eds., *Journals and Diaries*, 19:186.

that I should continue *in your house*, gainsaying you? If you are not, I have no more place in these regions."[95]

Two observations are drawn from Charles's rebuke. The first is that John Wesley could be indicted for his actions in opposition to George Whitefield using Charles Wesley's exact words. John Cennick's behavior, while inappropriate in some measure, found precedent in John Wesley's usurpation of Whitefield's leadership of the early Methodist movement in Bristol in 1739. The second observation is that Charles was quite content to leave the veracity of the doctrine of Calvinist predestination out of the question. Herein is a demonstration of the potent, identity-giving characteristics of doctrine—an additional facet from its propositional content. If a given doctrine were true, would not Charles (or John for that matter) desire it to be proclaimed, regardless of the consequences? Indeed, the answer is in the negative if the balance of power swayed away from the control of the Wesleys.

In the Spring of 1741, the transformed leadership of the Revival had taken place; as Henry Rack notes,

> There were major societies in London, Bristol and Kingswood, with some others under Wesley's influence. There was a hard core of bands within the societies on the old Fetter Lane model. Members were subject to discipline over their conduct, and although there was ostensibly no doctrinal test, they were pursuing faith and good works were expected, while the notion of a later perfection experience was being explored.[96]

There may have been no "doctrinal test," yet members were encouraged along in a clearly delineated Arminian understanding of predestination that provided little deviation from the Wesleys' sanctioned interpretation of election. Predestinarian doctrine did divide the two men, yet this contentious tenet of theology functioned *both* as a marker of orthodox and proper Christian teaching *and* as an instrument to manage and maintain distinct Methodist societies in the bourgeoning cities of London and Bristol. Combative actions persisted and, at times, the *Journal* of John Wesley can read like the battle plans of a general, mobilizing his troops for conflict.[97] When Whitefield landed at Deal in March of 1741, Charles wrote to John exhorting him to come quickly, as Whitefield's "fair" language was not enough to mollify fears that he would attack the Wesley brothers in print over the doctrine

---

95. Ibid.
96. Rack, *Reasonable Enthusiast*, 212–13.
97. Baker, ed., *Letters*, 26:65.

of predestination.⁹⁸ Aware that Whitefield would be printing his riposte to John's sermon "Free Grace," Charles urged a counter-offensive: "Behold, the hope of him is in vain . . .Warn all among you not to make mention of his name within their lips, except in prayer. Bring up Barclay if ready—(to be published the day *after* his reply), with the Hymns."⁹⁹ The Barclay tract to which Charles referred was William Barclay's *Serious Considerations on Absolute Predestination*, which John had abridged.¹⁰⁰ Charles's strategy was patently militaristic, seeking to discharge a response only after the opposing contestant had offered his "reply." John Wesley replied to his brother:

> I must go round and glean after G. W[hitefield]. I will take care of the books you mention. My Journal is not written yet. The bands and society are my first care. The bands are purged; the society is purging; and we continually feel whose hand is in the work. Send the new-printed *Hymns* immediately. We presented a thousand of Barclay [*Serious Considerations on Absolute Predestination*] to G. W.'s congregation on Sunday. On Sunday next I propose to distribute a thousand more at the Foundery.¹⁰¹

Wesley sought to displace Whitefield's societies and establish himself as the leader. Indeed, it was Wesley's distinctive doctrines, among them conditional election and Christian perfection, that enhanced Wesley's distinct brand of Methodism—one that remained orthodox according to the canons and formularies of the Church of England, yet was a stark departure from Whitefield's Calvinism.¹⁰² Such a strategy was useful for Wesley to develop and maintain a distinct Methodist identity in light of Whitefield's Calvinistic societies that saw Whitefield as their founder and leader.¹⁰³ It is manifestly clear from John Wesley's words, "the bands are purged; the society is purging," that the purge intended was a cleansing of those who held, not just to any incorrect doctrine, but to a Calvinistic stance on predestination.

98. Ibid., 26:54–55.

99. Ibid., 26:54–55.

100. Ibid., 26:55n17. See McGonigle, *Sufficient Saving Grace*, 131–35, for an incisive analysis of Barclay's work.

101. Baker, ed., *Letters*, 26:55.

102. Dallimore, *George Whitefield*, 1:319; 2:31–32.

103. Ibid., 2:32.

Conclusion

The identity-giving characteristics of doctrine are often underdeveloped in analyses of theological disagreement; the "Free Grace" controversy in in 1739 is no exception. Perhaps more disappointing than a one-dimensional understanding of doctrine is the uncritical approach that seeks to understand the *resolution* of doctrinal dispute. Luke Tyerman is an example of the characteristic gloss:

> Whitefield and Wesley were separated; but within eighteen months after the publication of Whitefield's letter, their old friendship was entirely re-established; and ever afterwards, to the end of life, Wesley and Whitefield loved each other with a love like that of David and Jonathan.[104]

Tyerman's comments were mirrored with minor adjustment in G. R. Balleine's sentiment (highlighted by Gatiss[105]) that, "the ["Free Grace" controversy] blew itself out; better feelings began to prevail; and although the two sections never quite came together again, they continued to work side by side in perfect harmony."[106] An analysis of the aftermath of the "Free Grace" controversy that takes into account the social dimensions of doctrine is outside the purview of this essay. What remains is simply the fact that the doctrine of predestination in the "Free Grace" controversy was constitutive of much more than the theological predisposition of either Wesley or Whitefield. The doctrine of predestination was the means through which Wesley could identify himself as a leader, in his own right, of the Methodist movement. By forcefully articulating a divergent doctrine of predestination from that of Whitefield, Wesley could lay the foundation of a Methodist movement wherein he was the principal organizer. While Wesley's stance on conditional election was a cherished theological commitment, and by no means a mere political device, it nonetheless served a social function. Echoing over the lawns of Bowling Green on 29 April 1739 was the proclamation of not only a divergent doctrine of predestination but also a new and different Methodism, whereof *Wesley* was to be the head.

---

104. Tyerman, *Life of the Rev. George Whitefield*, 1:475. Tyerman also made little effort to conceal his own prejudices regarding Wesley's opinion of Calvinism: "['Free Grace'] presents [predestination] in all its naked, hideous deformity; but it is fair, and no Calvinian dexterity can make it otherwise." Ibid., 1:319.

105. Gatiss, *True Profession of the Gospel*, 31.

106. Balleine, *A History of the Evangelical Party*, 42.

2

The Vector of Salvation

The New Birth as (Only) the Beginning of Conversion for Wesley and Whitefield

Sean McGever

In his 1760 sermon "The New Birth," John Wesley's declared: "If any doctrines within the whole compass of Christianity may be properly termed fundamental they are doubtlessly these two—the doctrine of justification, and that of the new birth."[1] George Whitefield wrote in his 1737 sermon "On Regeneration": "The doctrine of our regeneration, or new birth in Christ Jesus . . . is the very hinge on which the salvation of each of us turns."[2] While the doctrine of the new birth was undoubtedly an important facet of the theology and teaching of Wesley and Whitefield, some have recently suggested that revivalist soteriology might instead be better understood to revolve around the experience of conversion; scholars such as David Bebbington, W. R. Ward, Mark Noll, and Timothy Larson elevate conversion, not the new birth, in their readings of the evangelical revival.[3]

The contention of this chapter is that, while Wesley and Whitefield both preached the necessity of regeneration, they nonetheless recognized it constituted only the beginning of God's work in Christians. Wesley may have strained his point in isolating justification and the new birth as the entire compass of Christianity. Perhaps Wesley was being intentionally

---

1. Outler, ed., *Sermons*, 2:187.
2. Gillies, ed., *Works*, 6:257.
3. These scholars do not minimize the new birth, but instead elevate conversion as their focus. See: Bebbington, *Evangelicalism in Modern Britain*, 5–10; Ward, *Early Evangelicalism*, 4; Noll, *Rise of Evangelicalism*, 19–21; Larsen, "Defining and Locating Evangelicalism," 1.

reductionist. Wesley's theology required at least one more primary doctrine: holiness.[4] The broader conception of both the new birth and continued growth is the fundamental structure of Wesley and Whitefield's unified theology of conversion.

This chapter will demonstrate that conversion is not synonymous with the new birth. Conversion is inclusive of the new birth as a beginning and pushes further to describe Christian growth as a journey away from sin and self and toward holiness. A proper appraisal of conversion is important and relevant since focusing on the single moment of the new birth can avert people from Christian growth. A robust view of conversion is a better approach for practical discipleship and captures the soteriology of Wesley and Whitefield more fully than the limited metaphor and theological concept of the new birth. The new birth and conversion are not the same thing and do not attempt to describe the same thing. Thus, the new birth and conversion should distinguished. Conversion is initiated by the new birth, but like a vector has both a magnitude and a direction. The *magnitude* is set by the initial moment of instantaneous conversion whereby justification is appropriated and one is regenerated, while the *direction* of continued holiness is established through the introduction of sanctification.

The New Birth Is Not the Same with Sanctification

Wesley on the New Birth

John Wesley taught that the new birth is the inward moment when justification is applied, an individual is regenerated, and sanctification and the renewal of the image of God begin in the life of the believer through the prevenient grace of God.[5] While some place their salvation in outward works, the new birth, the beginning of a right relationship with God, is an

---

4. In the introduction of Wesley's "Explanatory Notes on the Old Testament," Wesley gave several recommendations for daily Bible reading. He exhorted: "Have a constant eye to the analogy of faith; the connexion and harmony there is between those grand, fundamental doctrines, Original Sin, Justification by Faith, the New Birth, Inward and Outward Holiness." Wesley repeatedly lists holiness as being integrally connected to the new birth and justification. See also Wesley's sermons "On the Fall of Man" and "Causes of the Inefficacy of Christianity." Wesley, *Explanatory Notes upon the Old Testament*, ix; Outler, ed., *Sermons*, 2:411; 4:89.

5. Wesley's three most important sermons regarding the new birth are, "The Marks of the New Birth," "The Great Privilege of Those that are Born of God," and "The New Birth." Outler, ed., *Sermons*, 1:415–43; 2:186–201; Also see: Maddox, *Responsible Grace*, 157–91; Collins, *Theology of John Wesley*, 195–236; Oden, *Christ and Salvation*, 2:217–36; and Rack, *Reasonable Enthusiast*, 394–95.

inner work. Wesley states in his *Journal* on 13 September 1739: "I believe [the new birth] to be an inward thing; a change from inward wickedness to inward goodness; an entire change of our inmost nature from the image of the devil (wherein we are born) to the image of God."[6] For Wesley, the new birth itself does not provide an immediate and externally distinguishable mark; the new birth is an inner work which changes and rebirths one's divine nature.

The new birth occurs, in Wesley's estimation, instantaneously. It is not an ongoing event: we are not born again, and again, and again. Wesley states: "at the very moment of justification, we are born again: In that instant, we experience that inward change."[7] The new birth has a first moment. Wesley taught: "the spiritual life, which commences when we are born again, must, in the nature of the thing, have a first moment, as well as the natural."[8] While the exact moment of the new birth may be difficult to identify experientially, theologically the new birth is a singular and inward occasion.

The new birth for Wesley is synonymous with regeneration and happens in the same moment as justification. Biblically, the new birth is exemplified in John 3 with the discussion of what it means to be "born again." To be born again is literally to be generated again, that is, re-generation.[9] Wesley makes the definition of regeneration very clear in the dictionary he first authored in 1753. Wesley wrote: "Regenerate: born again, thoroughly changed in all his tempers."[10] Similarly, in a letter to Mr. Downes, Wesley declared that the "plain English" meaning of regeneration was the new birth.[11] Justification, while inseparable chronologically from regeneration, is defined by Wesley in the first question of Methodist doctrine in the

---

6. Ward and Heitzenrater, eds., *Journals and Diaries*, 19:32, 97; See also: Outler, ed., *Sermons*, 1:350–51; 3:506–7; Ward and Heitzenrater, eds., *Journals and Diaries*, 19:32.

7. Outler, ed., *Sermons*, 1:350–51; Wesley states in his sermon "The Great Privilege of Those That Are Born of God": "In one point of time his sins are blotted out, and he is born again of God." Ibid., 1:431. In "The Principles of a Methodist" Wesley writes: "The moment a man comes to Christ (by faith) he is justified, and born again." Davies, ed., *Methodist Societies*, 9:360.

8. Davies, ed., *Methodist Societies*, 9:360.

9. While Wesley separated the new birth from sanctification, at times the distinction was subtle. For instance, in Wesley's *Notes* on Titus 3:5, Wesley wrote: "Sanctification: expressed by the laver of regeneration, (that is, baptism, the thing signified, as well as the outward sign) and the renewal of the Holy Ghost; which purifies the soul as water cleanses the body, and renews it in the whole image of God." Wesley did not divorce the new birth from sanctification; he saw the new birth as the required catalyst for sanctification. Wesley, *Explanatory Notes upon the New Testament*, Titus 3:5.

10. Wesley, *Complete English Dictionary*.

11. Davies, ed., *Methodist Societies*, 9:360.

Minutes of 1744: "To be pardoned and received into God's favour, and into such a state that, if we continue therein, we shall finally be saved."[12] The pardon of justification is of a different nature than being born again. A full discussion of Wesley's justification is beyond the scope of this chapter, but within the framework of this chapter it is important to note that Wesley understands the new birth and justification to occur in the same moment, but logically justification precedes the new birth.[13]

The new birth marks when sanctification and the renewal of the image of God *begin* in the life of the believer. Wesley calls the new birth the threshold, the first entrance, the first point, the beginning, and the gate of sanctification.[14] In other words, the new birth coincides with the beginning of sanctification, but the new birth does not bring the entirety of sanctification into the life of the believer instantaneously. Similarly, the new birth marks the renewal of the image of God in the life of the believer. At times Wesley describes an entire change from the image of the devil to the image of God through the new birth.[15] At other times, Wesley does not speak of an *entire* change but the *renewal* of the image of God.[16] In his sermon "The Repentance of Believers," Wesley clarifies the extent of change in the image of God in the new birth:

> We allow, that at the very moment of justification, we are born again: In that instant we experience that inward change from "darkness into marvellous light"; from the image of the brute and the devil, into the image of God; from the earthly, sensual, devilish mind, to the mind which was in Christ Jesus. But are we then entirely changed? Are we wholly transformed into the image of him that created us? Far from it: We still retain a depth of sin; and it is the consciousness of this which constrains us to groan, for a full deliverance, to Him that is mighty to save.[17]

12. Rack, ed., *Methodist Societies*, 10:126.

13. This is because, as Wesley states: "We first conceive his wrath to be turned away, and then his Spirit to work in our hearts." Outler, ed., *Sermons*, 2:187. The subtle priority Wesley gives justification before regeneration is critical to properly understand Wesley's view of original sin and the need for the prevenient grace of God whereby justification is in no way synergistic with works. While Wesley and Whitefield agreed substantively on justification, Maddock shows how they differed in regard to the "tense" of justification, in other words whether one is justified past, present, or future in regard to perseverance. Maddock, *Men of One Book*, 205–11.

14. Outler, ed., *Sermons*, 3:506–7; Maddox, ed., *Doctrinal and Controversial Treatises*, 12:300.

15. Outler, ed., *Sermons*, 3:507. Also see: ibid., 1:351.

16. Ibid., 2:194.

17. Ibid., 1:351.

In other words, both sanctification and the image of God begin but are not brought to completion upon the coming of the new birth.[18] With the basic features of Wesley's theology of the new birth in place, several observations can be made regarding the new birth, and more specifically the new birth as a metaphor. First, just as in physical birth, so too in spiritual rebirth there is an inherent passivity on the part of the one being reborn. While not antithetical to an Arminian soteriology, the new birth is nonetheless more sympathetic with monergistic and Reformed conception of the divine-human relationship in salvation.[19]

Second, a "birth" metaphor naturally forces the concept of a "birthday." Debate continues regarding Wesley's understanding of his date of salvation, but there is enough evidence directly from Wesley to agree that he was not always clear about his "spiritual birthday."[20] In his letter to Mr. Downes, Wesley wrote: "But we say again and again, we are concerned for the substance of the work, not the circumstance. Let it be wrought at all, and we will not contend whether it be wrought gradually or instantaneously."[21] Wesley was more concerned with the change, the substance, or the work of the new birth than pinpointing the exact date. Following Jesus' comments on the mysterious nature of the new birth, Wesley warns that we cannot know every detail.

---

18. There exists a broad scholarly consensus regarding Wesley's conception of the new birth. Maddox distinguishes between the moment of the new birth and the subsequent gradual therapeutic transformation through sanctification. Campbell says the new birth marked the beginning of new life in Christ and the start of the process of sanctification. Collins says that the new birth "refers not to the entirety of the process of sanctification (as in other uses of Wesley), but to the integrity, the thoroughness, of its beginning." Despite this unanimity among Wesleyan scholars who say that Wesley understood the new birth as a momentary beginning, Rack writes, "as used by Wesley [the new birth] often means not simply the moment of justification but the whole process by which the believer becomes transformed from sin to holiness." However, Rack concludes in the same paragraph: "[Wesley] came to see new birth as only the beginning of the sanctifying process." Therefore, despite Rack's momentary conceptualization of the new birth as a "whole process," he concludes along with the other leading Wesleyan scholars that the new birth is a theological concept focusing on the appropriation of the beginning of Christian salvation and not the entirety of it. Maddox, *Responsible Grace*, 170; Campbell, *Wesleyan Beliefs*, 101; Collins, *Theology of John Wesley*, 207; See also: Runyon, *New Creation*, 80–82; Rack, *Reasonable Enthusiast*, 394.

19. This point has been acknowledged by those within the Wesleyan-Arminian tradition. For example, Methodist biblical scholar Ben Witherington comments on John 1:12–13: "The unborn does not make a decision to be born . . . the emphasis in John is placed squarely on the divine side of the equation, not on the voluntarist side of the ledger, as is so often the case in Wesleyan and Arminian discussions of conversion." Witherington III, "New Creation or New Birth?," 123.

20. See Maddox, *Aldersgate Reconsidered*; Tyson, "John Wesley's Conversion at Aldersgate"; Olson, "Exegeting Aldersgate."

21. Davies, ed., *Methodist Societies*, 9:360.

In Wesley's sermon "The New Birth" he writes: "Not that we are to expect any minute, philosophical account of the manner how this is done . . . The precise manner how it begins and ends, rises, and falls, no man can tell . . . how the Holy Spirit works this in the soul, neither thou nor the wisest of children of men is able to explain."[22] Pressing for clockwork scientific theological precision of the timing of the new birth in a believer demands too much out of the doctrines of justification and regeneration.

Whitefield on the New Birth

The new birth was a key term within Whitefield's soteriological vocabulary and had a significant role in his theology of conversion.[23] Right from the beginning of his epiphany at Oxford, Whitefield understood the importance of the new birth.[24] He immediately wrote to his family upon learning about the new birth as Henry Scougal taught it. Whitefield stated: "I wrote letters to my relations, telling them there was such a thing as the new birth."[25] Later, in his sermon "All Mens Place," Whitefield warmly recalled: "whenever I go to Oxford, I cannot help running to that place where Jesus Christ first revealed himself to me, and gave me the new birth."[26] Right from the outset of Whitefield's ministry, the new birth was a distinctive feature of his preaching and often a reason why he was banned from pulpits and the target of endless controversies with ministers.[27]

22. Outler, ed., *Sermons*, 2:191.

23. Lambert comments, "Although Whitefield did not invent the concept of the new birth, he constructed his own meaning of the conversion process. Proclaiming that salvation transcended traditional church boundaries, the revivalist delivered his message to a mass audience" (Lambert, "The Great Awakening as Artifact," 226). Hindmarsh declares the new birth as Whitefield's "great theme" (Hindmarsh, *Evangelical Conversion Narrative*, 104). Perhaps most significantly, in his funeral sermon for Whitefield, John Wesley declared the new birth and justification by faith the "fundamental doctrines which [Whitefield] everywhere insisted on" (Outler, ed., *Sermons*, 2:343). Kidd observes, "Preaching the new birth would become the center of Whitefield's gospel ministry and the defining cause of his life" (Kidd, *George Whitefield*, 9).

24. Not only did the new birth inaugurate Whitefield's evangelical understanding of salvation, his view of the new birth really did not change throughout his career. Smith writes: "neither Wesley nor the increasingly Calvinist Whitefield ever altered his basic stance on the primacy of the experience of the new birth." Smith, *Whitefield and Wesley on the New Birth*, 7.

25. Whitefield, *A Short Account*, 15.

26. Whitefield, *Eighteen Sermons*, 360.

27. In his *Further Account*, Whitefield recalls, "[T]wo clergymen sent for me, and told me they would not let me preach in their pulpits any more, unless I renounced that part of my sermon on regeneration, wherein I wished, 'that my brethren would

Whenever Whitefield had the opportunity he would preach on the new birth; the new birth was what he called the "one thing needful." Whitefield described the "one thing" in a letter on 2 October 1738: "But what shall I write to you about? Why, of our common salvation, of that one thing needful, of that new birth in Christ Jesus, that ineffable change which must pass upon our hearts, before we can see God, and of which you have heard me discourse so often. Let this, this, my dear friends, be the end of all your actions."[28] The new birth was the focus of Whitefield's preaching and ministry; the new birth was the singular cause Whitefield relentlessly expressed anytime the opportunity arose.

While the new birth was an undeniably important term for Whitefield, what exactly did he understand it to mean and entail? Throughout Whitefield's preaching and writing the new birth was understood in its most basic sense. This metaphor was applied to the new spiritual life in Christ one received when one converted and became a true Christian. Whitefield wrote in a letter from 15 December 1749: "There must be a closing with Christ, a vital union of the soul with God, or, in other words, 'Christ formed within us.' This was the expression that first convinced me of the new birth."[29] Whitefield at times spoke of the new birth in similar terms such as the "new creation," "new man," "new heart," "new mind," "new nature"; each highlights a different angle of the same reality.[30]

Another important aspect of the *delivery* of the new birth was Whitefield's frequent reference to the "pangs" of the new birth. This description was reminiscent of the challenge and pain that mothers face leading up to their delivery. These pangs not only occurred before conversion but also could continue after conversion.[31]

Whitefield linked the new birth with regeneration so frequently that the new birth and regeneration can be thought of as synonyms in his teaching. Whitefield's sermon "On Regeneration" opened by stating: "The doctrine of our regeneration, or new birth in Christ Jesus . . . is the very

---

entertain their auditories oftener with discourses upon the new birth.' This I had no freedom to do, and so they continued my opposers." Whitefield, *Journals*, 90.

28. Gillies, ed., *Works*, 3:428–29.

29. Ibid., 2:305. Note the probable influence of Scougal's *Life of God in the Soul of Man* on Whitefield's theology.

30. Ibid., 5:258, 260, 262, 267.

31. Whitefield speaks of these pangs in a letter from 11 March 1749: "Various are the trials inward and outward that you will meet with. It is in the spiritual as in the natural birth. The after-pangs are sometimes sharper than those that precede the new-birth itself." Ibid., 2:245.

hinge on which the salvation of each of us turns."[32] One need only turn to Whitefield's letter *An Answer to the Bishop of London's Last Pastoral Letter* to see the synonymous link between regeneration and the new birth.[33]

While regeneration and the new birth were virtual synonyms for Whitefield, justification was not a synonym with either. Justification did happen in the "instant" or moment of instantaneous conversion, just as regeneration did.[34] Yet justification for Whitefield should be thought of in relation to sin and merit, regarding righteousness, while regeneration and the new birth should be thought of as the change of a new nature. Justification and regeneration/new birth happened in the same moment in Whitefield's understanding, yet they described two different effects that were brought about by instantaneous conversion. Whitefield stated in his *Further Account*: "The doctrine of the New Birth and Justification by Faith in Jesus Christ (though I was not so clear in it as afterwards) made its way like lightning into the hearers' consciences."[35] The new birth and justification stood apart but happened in the same moment in Whitefield's theology of conversion. However, as we will see, Whitefield understood conversion as an overarching concept that included, but went beyond, the new birth.

We have thus far observed that while Wesley and Whitefield emphasized the new birth, regeneration did not capture the fullness of their message. Wesley and Whitefield shared a unified theology of the new birth, which is highlighted in three basic features. First, they both believed that the new birth happened in the same moment as justification. Second, they believed that the new birth was distinguished from justification, and justification was logically, but not chronologically, prior to the new birth. Third, both taught that the new birth and regeneration were synonymous. The unanimity of their beliefs is not surprising since Article Twenty-Seven and the infant baptism rite of the Church of England declared the new birth and regeneration as synonymous.[36] Further, the Church of England distinguished justification and regeneration.[37]

---

32. Ibid., 6:257.

33. See especially ibid., 4:10.

34. Justification spoken of here is applied or appropriated justification in the life of an individual. Whitefield teaches that justification was accomplished upon Christ's resurrection. Ibid., 4:478; 6:128, 319.

35. Whitefield, *Journals*, 81.

36. *Book of Common Prayer, 1662 Edition*, 263–64.

37. The Thirty-Nine Articles, Book of Common Prayer, and the Edwardian Homilies never discuss justification and regeneration (or the new birth) in the same sections. However, these sources show the features of justification are different than the features of regeneration, thereby maintaining the distinction Wesley and Whitefield gave to the

As an isolated doctrine, the new birth as taught by Wesley and Whitefield may not have spurred on the evangelical revival. The very nature of the "birth" metaphor is a passive act on behalf of the one being "birthed." Furthermore, the new birth and regeneration (and justification) were part and parcel of the rite of baptism, which, by and large, was performed in infancy, another passive moment for the one being "birthed." At the heart of Wesley and Whitefield's message in the evangelical revival was not the new birth as an end in itself, but rather regeneration as the beginning of the renewal of the image of God in the soul of man through progressive sanctification, encapsulated in their dual commitment to conversion.

Conversion: a Thorough Change of Heart and Life From Sin to Holiness; A Turning

We have thus far suggested that the Wesley and Whitefield's doctrine of the new birth cannot be isolated as the hallmark doctrine of their preaching in the evangelical revival. We now proceed to suggest that conversion captures the robust nature of Wesley and Whitefield's soteriological vision.

What did Wesley and Whitefield teach regarding conversion?

Wesley on Conversion

A thoroughgoing and theological description of Wesley's theology of conversion is difficult to find. When conversion is discussed the focus often becomes sociological or psychological in nature.[38] When forced back to more theological discussions, conversion is misunderstood as being synonymous with the new birth or kept within the realm of biblical studies apart from the discussion of Christian doctrine.[39] The new birth and

---

new birth and justification.

38. For examples, see Rambo, *Understanding Religious Conversion*; Rambo, "Conversion Studies, Pastoral Counseling, and Cultural Studies"; James, *Varieties of Religious Experience*; Nock, *Conversion*, and McKnight and Ondrey, *Finding Faith, Losing Faith*.

39. Most theologians and historians of the eighteenth century use the terms "conversion" and "new birth" / "regeneration" interchangeably. Runyon, *New Creation*, 57; Collins, *Theology of John Wesley*, 215; Henry, *George Whitefield*, 26; Kidd, *George Whitefield*, 17, 26; Lambert, *Pedlar in Divinity*, 15–24; Hindmarsh, *Evangelical Conversion Narrative*, 110; Noll, *Rise of Evangelicalism*, 15; Bebbington, *Evangelicalism in Modern Britain*, 15. This interchangeability is reflected in the common understanding of the terms. For instance, the *New Dictionary of Theology* contends that conversion is "commonly referred to as 'new birth' or regeneration" (Davie et al., *New Dictionary of Theology*, 218). Two Methodist scholars who are more careful to use the term

conversion share many of the same features in the initial *moment* of true faith, but the concept of conversion distinguishes itself from the new birth via the direction, growth, and continuance one must possess, by the grace of God, to be considered a true convert.

While the new birth is inward, conversion is both inward and outward. While the new birth is limited to an instant, conversion has a beginning that continues. Conversion includes justification, regeneration, and not only the beginning of sanctification and the renewed image, but also continued growth of sanctification and the ongoing renewal of the image of God in the believer. In short, conversion encompasses both the beginning and ongoing essence of salvation in the life of a believer.

Wesleyan scholars have overlooked the word "conversion," and perhaps understandably, since Wesley discouraged the inquiry of this word himself. In his 1750 response to George Lavington in *A Letter to the Author of The Enthusiasm of the Methodists and the Papists Compared*, Wesley wrote: "you say, I 'represent conversion as sudden and instantaneous.' Soft and fair! Do you know what conversion is? (A term, indeed, which I very rarely use, because it rarely occurs in the New Testament.)"[40] Wesley is very clear to say that he does not use the term "conversion" because it occurs rarely in the New Testament.

The basic essence of conversion is captured in Wesley's dictionary entry: "Conversion: 'a thorough change of heart and life from sin to holiness; a turning.'"[41] Wesley's definition is not surprising since the English word "conversion" has direct roots in French, *convertir* (to convert), and Latin, *converto* (to turn around) and *conversio* (a turning around). In the King James Version, variants of convert/conversion terms occur fifteen times with Acts 15:3 as a prime example of the word's proper use.[42] This passage describes Paul and Barnabas telling other churches about the "conversion" of the gentiles. Wesley's dictionary definition of conversion is consistent with the French, Latin, and Greek understanding, which is to turn "from" and "to" something or someone.

"conversion" in its nuanced sense are Maddox and Knight: Maddox, *Responsible Grace*, 152; Knight III, "The Transformation of the Human Heart: The Place of Conversion in Wesley's Theology," 44. Biblical studies on conversion have centered on Paul's so-called conversion and then tend to turn to the analysis of the meaning of conversion in Second Temple Judaism.

40. Cragg, ed., *Appeals to men of Reason and Religion*, 11:368.
41. Wesley, *Complete English Dictionary*.
42. Ps 19:7; 51:13; Isa 1:27; 6:10; 60:5; Matt 13:15; 18:3; Mark 4:12; Luke 22:32; John 12:40; Acts 3:19; 15:3; 28:27; Jas 5:19, 20.

Wesley's definition of conversion has an aim: turning toward holiness. Wesley understood a convert to be someone who could show continued evidence and continued holiness in his or her life. One example is found in a letter to John Smith on 22 March 1748 where Wesley speaks of the expectation of outward works for true converts. Wesley writes: "[those who are converted] are converted from all manner of wickedness 'to a sober, righteous, and godly life.' Such an uniform practice is true outward holiness. And where this is undeniably found, we ought to believe, there is holiness of heart, seeing the tree is known by its fruits."[43] So the true convert is expected to show true outward holiness in their actions and works. Conversion built upon and extended Wesley's understanding of the new birth to encompass the radical change embedded in his soteriology and evidenced in the evangelical revival.

Whitefield on Conversion

While Wesley was well known to differ from Whitefield on several important topics, they had much overlap regarding the theology of conversion. Whitefield understood conversion as the experience of turning "from" self-righteousness and "to" the righteousness of Christ through the power of the Holy Spirit. While instantaneous conversion was a focal point of his theology of conversion, Whitefield understood that there was a "holy variety" in the way God works; conversion must be thought of in several different ways.[44]

First, Whitefield believed that some individuals might not have a recollection or a specific date of any instantaneous moment when they converted; for Whitefield, the recollection of a conversion date or a conversion moment was normative but not required. For instance, in 1747 Whitefield published his sermon "Christ the Believer's Husband," in which he observed: "it is not so very material, though no doubt it is very satisfactory, if we cannot relate all the minute and particular circumstances, that attended our conversion; if so be we are truly converted now, and can say, the work is done, and that, 'our Maker is our husband.'"[45] When the "moment" of conversion was unknown, or not even required, conversion was understood more as a process or "ongoing" since the beginning was unknown.

---

43. Baker, ed., *Letters*, 26:290.

44. For an excellent analysis of Whitefield's early theological formation of his view of the new birth, justification, and conversion, see Olson, "Whitefield's Early Theological Formation."

45. Gillies, ed., *Works*, 5:180.

Second, Whitefield understood conversion as an ongoing and repeated "turning" to God throughout the Christian life; at times calling the repeated turning to God a "second" conversion. An ongoing conversion for one who was already firmly converted is a good way to understand some otherwise perplexing self-reflections found in Whitefield's correspondence. On 20 December 1752 Whitefield wrote: "And O that I may be converted myself more and more every day and hour! I am ashamed of my being such a dwarf in religion, and of my having so little of the mind of CHRIST."[46] On 26 March 1754, Whitefield recorded: "O that I may begin to begin to be converted myself.—I am a dwarf.—Less than the least of all, shall be my motto still."[47] Again, on 1 December 1763 Whitefield wrote: "LORD JESUS, spare root and branch, for thy own glory, and thy people's good! LORD JESUS, convert us all more and more, and make us all like little children!"[48] In each of these instances, Whitefield desired more and more "turning" for himself and his recipients. He was leading, humbly and pastorally, the call to rededicate oneself to Jesus repeatedly. There is no indication that Whitefield thought that he had lost his initial conversion to Christ.

Third, conversion for Whitefield could never be reduced to only one moment in time; conversion was always part of a bigger picture in the life of the believer. The picture of conversion in the life of the believer included "marks" of a sound conversion such as ongoing repentance, obedience, and love. These ongoing marks did not *merit* a Christian's conversion, but they did *mark* a true Christian's conversion.

The marks of a sound conversion for Whitefield were the general trend of growth in the Christian life. These marks were indicated by the forsaking of sin through repentance, bringing forth fruit in godly living, and generally going beyond general civility toward actual godliness. Instances abound in Whitefield's writing regarding the marks of a sound conversion.[49] These examples show that Whitefield frequently drew explicit correlations between an individual's claims to Christian conversion and their outward behavior. These behaviors are understood as the "marks" of a sound conversion.

Last, the ongoing nature of conversion for Whitefield was an appropriate manifestation of Whitefield's doctrine of election. Whitefield claimed that his view of election did not lead to antinomianism, as it could for some hyper-Calvinists.[50] Instead, the ongoing nature of conversion showed the

---

46. Ibid., 2:463.
47. Ibid., 3:69.
48. Ibid., 3:303.
49. Whitefield, *Journals*, 145–47; Gillies, ed., *Works*, 4:90, 363.
50. See Toon, *Emergence of Hyper-Calvinism*, 49–69, 143–52. Whitefield distanced

proper fruits of a rightly understood doctrine of election in Whitefield's moderate Calvinism.

Soon after Whitefield began to emphasize election in his teaching, he responded to those who thought election would negate the seeking of these "marks." The sermon "The Conversion of Zaccheus," published in 1739 as Whitefield's theological progression towards more explicitly Calvinistic doctrines was well underway, spoke directly to these accusations. In this sermon, Whitefield explained that justification by faith and not by works could happen in a moment since God is a sovereign agent who "works upon his children in their effectual calling, according to the counsel of his eternal will." Whitefield continued: "Say not within yourselves, this is a licentious Antinomian doctrine; for this faith, if true, will work by love, and be productive of the fruits of holiness. See an instance in this convert Zaccheus: no sooner had he received JESUS CHRIST by faith into his heart, but he evidences it by his works."[51] True faith and true conversion resulted, for Whitefield, in true fruits of holiness in the life of the elect. A genuine mark of conversion was simply that a true convert would bring forth fruit.

Wesley and Whitefield both understood conversion in its most basic sense, to turn "from" and "to" something or someone. The turn was from self-righteousness and to the righteousness of Christ. Salvation entailed not merely a one-time conversion, but the life of salvation was the ongoing conversion of an individual into the image of God. The evangelical revival was shaped significantly, and foundationally, on the unified theology of conversion which Wesley and Whitefield shared. Conversion is distinguished at its outset by the new birth and in its *telos* by the ongoing restoration of the image of God in individuals, or in other words, holiness. While Wesley and Whitefield differed significantly in their precise articulation of election, perseverance, and perfection, they nonetheless shared a common conception of the importance of conversion. This shared conviction helped to sustain their influential ministries and the transatlantic evangelical revival itself.

---

and defended himself from the threat of being labeled an antinomian (Gillies, ed., *Works*, 1:367; 4:48, 155–56, 217; 5:26, 187; 6:56; Whitefield, *Journals*, 323–24). In Wesley's "Free Grace" sermon, he implies that Whitefield taught a doctrine which led to antinomianism. However, in a letter to Samuel Furly on 14 October 1757, Wesley explicitly stated that he did not believe Whitefield was an antinomian (Outler, ed., *Sermons*, 3:548–49; Baker, ed., *Letters*, 27:102).

51. Gillies, ed., *Works*, 6:56.

Redemption Applied: The Vector of Conversion

In the opening of Wesley's sermon "The New Birth" he states: "How great importance, then, must it be of to every child of man thoroughly to understand these fundamental doctrines!"[52] For Wesley and Whitefield the new birth was the gateway to salvation and full life in Christ. While the new birth is a helpful and biblical metaphor, it stalls, as it largely describes only the beginning of salvation and full life in Christ, both in its theological content and as a metaphor.

While the revivals of the eighteenth century saw many who experienced the pangs of the new birth and a salvation testimony, much more energy was needed to form true converts who continued in their faith. The need for ongoing Christian growth birthed the Methodist Societies, initially the Whitefieldian, and later, and more lasting, the Wesleyan. As the decades and centuries progressed, revivalism became known more for its sawdust trail than for the ongoing marks of the new birth of which Wesley and Whitefield preached. We might go so far as to suggest that an overemphasis on the new birth produced many short-lived Christians.

Wesley and Whitefield teach us that, as a metaphor, conversion is relatable because it is a subjective term in which one participates relationally, unlike the new birth. The Christian turns in response to the prevenient grace of God.[53] As a metaphor, conversion does not necessarily imply a conversion "date" since it concerns itself with the continued direction of the Christian life rather than focusing on a one-time occurrence. Less emphasis on the "date" deflects an overemphasis on a single moment, since conversion is more focused on the current state of the Christian disciple. Wesley and Whitefield showed that conversion works well as a metaphor because one can have an initial conversion and then keep converting and turning to God over and over throughout the Christian life in a way that seems inapplicable when speaking of birth. Parallel to a metaphor from physics, while the new

---

52. Outler, ed., *Sermons*, 2:187.

53. Without a proper understanding of the prevenient grace of God, the "turning" of conversion could be seen as a Pelagian or semi-Pelagian doctrine. Prevenient, or preventing, grace was not only an Arminian concept, it is one Calvinists also utilized. For instance, in his sermon *Conversion of Zaccheus* Whitefield wrote: "Praise, magnify, and adore sovereign, electing, free, preventing love." Similarly, in a letter on 10 November 1739, Whitefield wrote: "Man is nothing: he hath a free will to go to hell, but none to go heaven, till GOD worketh in him to will and to do after his good pleasure. It is GOD must prevent, GOD must accompany, GOD must follow with his grace, or JESUS CHRIST will bleed in vain." For the Calvinist, preventing grace allows one to "accompany" the work God initiated. Unlike Wesley, Whitefield would have added that grace was effectual, irresistible, and persevering. Gillies, ed., *Works*, 1:90; 6:53.

birth might be thought of as the initial moment when an object overcomes static friction, or static deadness brought upon by original sin, thereby giving an initial velocity via an external force of God's grace, conversion can be thought of as a vector, having a continued velocity and direction toward Christian holiness and the restoration of the image of God in the life of the believer. Rather than a sole focus on the initial beginning provided by the new birth, it was the continued direction of the vector of conversion that was at the heart of the message of Wesley and Whitefield.

3

"The Whole World is Now My Parish"

The Ecclesiological Conversions of Wesley and Whitefield

IAN J. MADDOCK

THE YEAR 1739 WAS a highly significant one for John Wesley and George Whitefield, one that found them staking out their respective theological and territorial space as two of the foremost leaders of the transatlantic evangelical revival. Not only did they tussle over the definition of key pieces of contested theological nomenclature like "free grace"[1] and "perfection,"[2] they also began the highly contentious and vocation defining practice of itinerant field preaching. Wesley and Whitefield both described what amounted to momentous homiletical, if not ecclesiological, conversions using remarkably similar language. Just a matter of weeks after his first foray into field preaching at Kingswood, Whitefield wrote to Daniel Abbot on 3 March 1739, "The whole world is now my parish," while a week before Wesley "became more vile" and followed Whitefield's lead in Bristol, on 28 March he likewise declared, "I look upon *all the world as my parish*."[3]

This chapter will first situate their conversion to extemporaneous, itinerant field preaching in the context of a series of preceding experiential and theological turning points that also reflect considerable similarities. These include their shared zeal for holiness (nurtured, if not quite originating, during their experiences as members of the Holy Club at Oxford), a "conversion" that eventually paved the way for their experience of regeneration and a shared recognition that justification precedes sanctification (what

---

1. See Maddock, *Men of One Book*, 193–95; and Maddock, "Solving a Transatlantic Puzzle," 1–15.

2. See Maddock, "George Whitefield: Christian Perfectionist?," 147–61.

3. Whitefield, *Letters*, 105; Baker, ed., *Letters*, 25:616.

is commonly described as their "evangelical" conversions). We shall then turn to explore how. despite Whitefield and Wesley coming to the point of articulating their ecclesiological/vocational mottos using virtually identical language, their conceptions of what it meant to live out this expansive ministry charter were far from identical. We shall observe that, on the one hand, Whitefield's emphasis was on an evangelistic preaching ministry that placed a premium on maintaining mobility across spatial, social, and denominational boundaries: the *whole world* is my parish. But if Whitefield's ministry was, in his own assessment, primarily focused on "planting" the seed of the gospel, then Wesley's ministry entailed a significant emphasis on "watering," or the ongoing spiritual nurture of those awakened under his preaching: I look upon all the world as *my parish*. In this way, their divergent applications of this memorable phrase function as accurate reflections of their differing aspirations for their respective public ministries.

Mothers and Their Exceptional Sons: Susanna and John, Elizabeth and George

"Few great people," suggests Stout, "achieve fame without aspiring to it, and Whitefield was no exception."[4] While the same could equally be said of Wesley, it is also true that few acquire the level of widespread recognition that Wesley and Whitefield managed during their lifetimes and beyond without first possessing a strong conviction that they had been destined for importance. This sense of providential exceptionalism—of having been set apart by God to pursue and achieve remarkable accomplishments in God's service—was nurtured in the homes of Whitefield and Wesley, and especially by their respective mothers, Elizabeth and Susanna.

If Whitefield's decision to begin publish his *Journal* at the tender age of twenty-four was not considered precocious enough, his mode of describing his birth cemented this suspicion in the eyes of his critics. In the earliest edition of his *Journals* (in equal measure religious autobiography, revival narrative, and gripping travelogue, intentionally delivered for public consumption as an apologia for his conviction that he had been called to fulfill a "public work"[5]), Whitefield famously, or perhaps infamously, began by closely identifying his own birth with that of Jesus. Although the ensuing criticism would prompt him to omit this passage from subsequent editions, Whitefield's audacious sense of destiny is clearly evident. He declared:

---

4. Stout, *Divine Dramatist*, xxi.
5. Whitefield, *Journals*, 35.

> As God has been pleased of late to call me to a public work, I thought His children would be glad to know how I was trained up for it . . . the circumstance of my being born in an inn, has often been of service to me in exciting my endeavours to make good my mother's expectations, and so follow the example of my dear Saviour, who was born in a manger belonging to an inn.[6]

After describing how "even as an infant, [his mother, Elizabeth] expected more comfort from me than any other of her children,"[7] Whitefield recounts Elizabeth's instrumental role in facilitating an unlikely route to Pembroke College, Oxford, as a servitor, thus saving him from the life of a Gloucester innkeeper. Subsuming any of his own ambitions for upward mobility beneath hers, he wrote:

> Having thus lived with my mother for some considerable time, a young student, who was once my schoolfellow, and then a servitor of Pembroke College, Oxford, came to pay my mother a visit. Amongst other conversation, he told her how he had discharged all college expenses that quarter, and received a penny. Upon that my mother cried out, "This will do for my son." Then turning to me, she said, "Will you go to Oxford, George?" I replied, "With all my heart."[8]

If Whitefield's mother was crucial in instilling in her son a conviction that he had been set apart for some great work, then the same can most certainly be said of Wesley's mother Susanna. It was she who, after John's dramatic escape from the inferno that consumed the Epworth Rectory on 9 February 1709, likened him to, "a brand plucked from the burning," echoing the words of Zechariah 3:2. Soon after she resolved "to be more particularly careful of the soul of this child, that Thou hast so mercifully provided for, than ever I have been, that I may do my endeavour to instill into his mind the principles of Thy *true* religion and virtue."[9]

Wesley's flirtation with a fiery death, along with his mother's assessment of the near-miraculous providential favor that had been bestowed upon the then five-year-old, resonated with him for many years to come. Indeed, on 26 November 1753, as he lay seriously ill and "not knowing how it might please God to dispose of me," Wesley took the preventative (and, as it turned out, premature) step of writing the inscription for his own tombstone, ostensibly to stop the "vile panegyric" that might ensue following

---

6. Ibid., 35, 37.
7. Ibid., 35.
8. Ibid., 42.
9. Wallace, *Susanna Wesley: The Complete Writings*, 235.

his death. His choice of words echoed Susanna's over four decades earlier, evidence of the strong influence she continued to exert over her son's psyche long after her own death:

> Here lieth the Body of JOHN WESLEY, A brand plucked out of the burning, Who died of consumption in the fifty first year of his age, Not leaving, after his debts are paid, Ten pounds behind him, Praying, God be merciful to me, an unprofitable servant.[10]

In their own ways, Elizabeth Whitefield and Susanna Wesley both instilled in their sons awareness of having been saved—not simply *from* unbecoming vocations or untimely deaths, but *for* the purpose of achieving great things in God's service. That being said, it took Wesley and Whitefield some time to discover their vocational homes that would see them variously collude and collide as key leaders of the burgeoning Methodist movement.

A Tale of Two (Initial) Conversions

Whitefield: "If this Not Be True Religion, What Is?"

Whitefield arrived in Oxford in 1732 with a passionate concern for deepening his personal holiness. Throughout the preceding twelve months he "began to be more and more watchful over [his] thoughts, words, and actions," distanced himself from an expanding list of activities that he identified as ungodly, and struggled repeatedly to wrestle himself free from "an abominable secret sin, the dismal effects of which I have felt and groaned under ever since."[11] While Kidd contends that "Whitefield had not yet experienced conversion"[12]—at least not in the sense of having yet experienced *regeneration*—he was nonetheless thoroughly converted to the pursuit of holiness, devoting himself to various religious "duties," including "receiving the Sacrament monthly, fasting frequently, attending constantly on public worship, and praying often more than twice a day in private."[13] Whitefield's reading habits were especially formative, Thomas á Kempis's *The Imitation of Christ* and William Law's *Serious Call to a Devout and Holy Life* and *Christian Perfection* not only providing fuel for his quest for spiritual purity but also sowing seeds of the necessity of inward renewal. Having now been embraced by "both the Mr. Wesleys" and the Holy Club, Whitefield reflected how,

---

10. Ward and Heitzenrater, eds., *Journals and Diaries*, 20:482.
11. Whitefield, *Journals*, 41–42.
12. Kidd, *George Whitefield*, 17.
13. Whitefield, *Journals*, 44.

> I now began, like them, to live by rule, and to pick up the very fragments of my time, that not a moment of it might be lost. Whether I ate or drank, or whatsoever I did, I endeavoured to do all to the glory of God. Like them, having no weekly sacrament, although the Rubric required it, at our own college, I received every Sunday at Christ Church. I joined with them in keeping the stations by fasting Wednesdays and Fridays and left no means unused, which I thought would lead me nearer to Jesus Christ.[14]

Evident in the above quotation is a sense of Whitefield's retrospective ambivalence regarding the efficacy of these efforts. Nonetheless, throughout his *Journal* account of this period he was prepared to describe those who joined the Holy Club in terms of having "converted." Of his own decisive, even evangelistic, role he wrote, "God enabled me to do much good to many, as well as to receive much from the despised Methodists, and made me instrumental in converting one who is lately come into the Church, and, I trust, will prove a bright and shining light."[15]

But it was not until 1735, after reading, at Charles Wesley's recommendation, Henry Scougal's *The Life of God in the Soul of Man*, that Whitefield first came to embrace the necessity of spiritual regeneration. It was only then that he acknowledged that "true religion" did not consist in fulfilling religious duties, but rather in a thoroughgoing inward change:

> At my first reading it, I wondered what the Author meant by saying, "That some falsely place Religion in going to Church, doing hurt to no one, being constant in the Duties of the Closet, and now and then reaching out their hands to give Alms to their poor Neighbours."—Alas! Thought I, "If this be not true religion, what is?" God soon showed me . . . "true religion was a Union of the soul with God, and Christ formed within us," . . . and from that moment, but not till then, did I know that I must be a new creature.[16]

It was one thing for Whitefield to become convinced of the necessity of spiritual regeneration; it was another for him to experience it personally. His *Journals* describe the process towards what Olson categorizes as his "evangelical"[17] conversion in highly visceral terms. Whitefield recounts

---

14. Ibid., 47.
15. Ibid., 48.
16. Ibid., 47.
17. Olson, "Whitefield's Conversion," 29. Olson suggests that Whitefield's theological formation during the period 1734–1740 saw him journey from Oxford Methodist to

"groaning under an unspeakable Pressure both of Body and Mind"[18] as his spiritual anguish expressed itself physically and mentally. It was not until May 1735 that he experienced what he would later describe as "the pangs of the new birth."[19] Whitefield was especially fond of alluding to parallels between Jesus' words and example when it came to describing crucial turning points in his own preparation for public ministry. Not only his birth as we have previously observed, but also his ordination and first foray into field preaching were recounted in such terms. Similarly, Whitefield described the moment of his conversion as an experience of release preceded by intense anguish, contemporaneous with Jesus' sufferings prior to his death as described in John 19:28. Whitefield wrote,

> One day, perceiving an uncommon drought and a disagreeable clamminess in my mouth and using things to allay my thirst, but in vain, it was suggested to me, that when Jesus Christ cried out, "I thirst," His sufferings were near at an end. Upon which I cast myself down on the bed, crying out, "I thirst! I thirst!" Soon after this, I found and felt in myself that I was delivered from the burden that had so heavily oppressed me.[20]

Having undergone what he later styled "the pangs of the new birth,"[21] regeneration became a staple focal point of Whitefield's spoken and printed sermons. In early 1737, Whitefield first preached his influential sermon, "On Regeneration," in which he described the "doctrine of our regeneration" as "the very hinge on which the salvation of each of us turns."[22] Not only was this sermon Whitefield's earliest published work, he credited it with being the instrument by which God "began the awakening at London, Bristol, Gloucester, and Gloucestershire."[23] Whitefield might have been committed to the normative authority of Scripture, but that did not preclude him from appealing to his own experience of regeneration as paradigmatic. Near the time of his death, he described the way he had known the reality of the new birth "for about thirty-five years as clear

---

evangelical Methodist (precipitated by his 1735 conversion) to Calvinistic Methodist.

18. Whitefield, *Journals*, 58.
19. Ibid., 108.
20. Ibid., 58.
21. Ibid., 108.
22. Gillies, ed., *Works*, 6:257. Timothy Smith describes it as "one of the most influential sermons ever published in Christendom." *Wesley and Whitefield on the New Birth*, 63.
23. Whitefield, *Journals*, 86.

as the sun is in the meridian."[24] Whitefield's own conversion experience thus provided a template for the experience he encouraged his readers and hearers to undergo. As Lambert observes,

> Whitefield based his qualifications for proclaiming the necessity of the new birth on his acquaintance with "experimental religion" not his mastery of prescribed theology. He linked his message to the personal experience of the messenger, filtering the message of the new birth through his own intense conversion."[25]

Wesley: "They Saw Likewise That Men Are Justified before They Are Sanctified; But Still Holiness Was Their Point"

Wesley acquired a taste for holiness during his formative years at Epworth, an appreciation that was further developed as an undergraduate student at Oxford. By 1725 he had established in his own mind "that the call to righteousness pervading the Old and the New Testaments was the central theme of Scripture."[26] A voracious and eclectic reader, Wesley's appetite for holiness was nurtured as he immersed himself in the writings of Lorenzo Scupoli, Thomas á Kempis, Jeremy Taylor, William Law, and the devotional tradition of Eastern Orthodoxy, including Clement of Alexandria, Gregory of Nyssa, and Macarius of Egypt, all of whom in varying ways emphasized the pursuit of *inward* holiness as the core of the Christian life. On 10 December 1734, he wrote to his father,

> By holiness I mean, not fasting, or bodily austerity, or any other external means of improvement, but that inward temper to which all these are subservient, a renewal of soul in the image of God. I mean a complex habit of lowliness, meekness, purity, faith, hope and love of God and man.[27]

---

24. Whitefield, *Eighteen Sermons*, 306. Although the subjective experience of regeneration was vital, Whitefield's firm sense of assurance was equally predicated upon the objective work of Christ. For instance, on 10 November 1739, he wrote to Mr. S [Seward?], "Blessed be God, the Lord Jesus is my whole righteousness. By virtue of that I know I am justified, I believe I shall be sanctified, and am assured I shall be everlastingly redeemed: for God loved me with an everlasting love." Gillies, ed., *Works*, 1:114.

25. See Lambert, "The Great Awakening as Artifact," 223–46. See also Lambert, *Pedlar in Divinity*, 13, 15–25.

26. Smith, *Wesley and Whitefield on the New Birth*, 11.

27. Baker, ed., *Letters*, 25:399.

Like Whitefield after him, Wesley's Herculean pursuit of inward and outward holiness through all manner of religious commission and austerity was no match for his sensitive conscience. Thoroughly disillusioned with his own lack of holiness, on 3 October 1731, Wesley resignedly concluded that as Christians "our hope is sincerity, not perfection, not to do well, but to do our best. If God were to mark all that is done amiss, who could abide it?"[28] In other words, at this point in his theological formation, Wesley argued that the imperfect zeal with which a person pursues holiness, augmented by God's leniency, provided the grounds of assurance of salvation. Collins suggests that Wesley's "resolve was actually a prescription for a deep and long-lasting malaise . . . for it, in effect, made obedience to the moral law the basis of acceptance . . . put another way, this approach [to holiness] made sanctification the ground of justification."[29] In a retrospective evaluation of the period prior to his Aldersgate Street experience, Wesley concluded that, "by my continued *endeavour to keep his whole law*, inward and outward, *to the utmost of my power*, I was persuaded that I should be accepted of him, and that I was even then in a state of salvation."[30] Wesley came to recognize that from his "youth up" he had depended and grounded his hope of salvation, "in whole or in part, upon my own works or righteousness"; "being ignorant of the righteousness of Christ," even his time as a missionary in Georgia was spent "beating the air."[31] He was thus able to reflect, "I was ordained Deacon in 1725, and Priest in the year following. But it was many years after this before I was convinced of the great truths above recited. During all that time I was utterly ignorant of the nature and condition of justification. Sometimes I confounded it with sanctification; (particularly when I was in Georgia)."[32]

Wesley's Aldersgate Street experience, on 24 May 1738, was undoubtedly a seminal turning point in his life, quickly enshrined in Methodist folklore as the date of Wesley's evangelical conversion.[33] Just as Whitefield's personal experience of the new birth buttressed and emboldened his appeals to undergo regeneration, Aldersgate Street became paradigmatic for Wesley "as a defining moment in his life in which belief and experience were joined

28. Baker, ed., *Letters*, 25:318.
29. Collins, *John Wesley: A Theological Journey*, 41.
30. Ward and Heitzenrater, eds., *Journals and Diaries*, 18:244–45.
31. Ibid., 18:246, 248.
32. Jackson, ed., *Works*, 8:111.
33. The precise nature and significance of Wesley's Aldersgate Street experience has been the subject of recent re-evaluation. See Maddox, ed., *Aldersgate Reconsidered*, and Collins's response to revisionist accounts in "Other Thoughts on Aldersgate," 10–25.

together."[34] Wesley famously wrote in his *Journal* that as he heard the preface to Luther's Epistle to the Romans being read, and particularly the description of the "change which God works in the heart through faith in Christ, I felt my heart strangely warmed. I felt I did trust in Christ, Christ alone for salvation; and an assurance was given me that He had taken away *my* sins, even *mine*, and saved *me* from the law of sin and death."[35]

It was during this period that Wesley's understanding of the relationship between justification and sanctification also began to change. From 1738 forward, Wesley came to understand that whereas justification entails a *"relative* change" and "implies what God *does for us* through his Son," sanctification entails a *"real"* change.[36] Sanctification is "the immediate *fruit* of justification," the change that God *"works in us* by his Spirit."[37] And yet even after his pivotal realization that justification must precede sanctification, Wesley never entirely gave up on his first love, the pursuit of holiness still retaining a privileged place in his theology and practice. In the "Large Minutes," Wesley wrote:

> In 1729, two young men, reading the Bible, saw they could not be saved without holiness, followed after it, and incited others so to do. In 1737 they saw holiness comes by faith. They saw likewise that men are justified before they are sanctified; but still holiness was their point. God then thrust them out, utterly against their will, to raise a holy people. When Satan could no otherwise hinder this, he threw Calvinism in the way; and then Antinomianism, which strikes directly at the root of all holiness.[38]

Beneath the pithiness of this summary lies profound insight into the impulses that drove Wesley's life-long theological activity. Wesley might have converted to the position that "justification always stands first, without any antecedent 'holiness' or merit of any kind as a *necessary* precondition to human salvation," but the practical locus of his attention never shifted from the pursuit of "holiness of heart and life" as the core of the Christian life.[39] Outler observes that "it is important, therefore, always to start with Wesley's first conversion (1725), a conversion to the ideal of holy living, and to remember

---

34. Schwenk, *Catholic Spirit*, 38.

35. Ward and Heitzenrater, eds., *Journals and Diaries*, 18:250.

36. See Wesley's sermons "The Scripture Way of Salvation," in Outler, ed., *Sermons*, 2:158; "Justification by Faith," in ibid., 1:187; and "On Working Out Our Own Salvation," in ibid., 3:204.

37. Outler, ed., *Sermons*, 1:187.

38. Jackson, ed., *Works*, 10:300.

39. Outler, *Theology in the Wesleyan Spirit*, 71.

that he never thereafter abandoned this ideal even when further conversions . . . complicated his interpretation of it by a good deal."[40]

A Third Conversion: 1739 and Itinerant Field Preaching

And yet as formative as these first and second conversions undoubtedly were in the personal lives of Wesley and Whitefield, a third conversion was needed to set them both on a trajectory towards becoming the public figures they were known for during their lifetimes and are remembered for today. Since Whitefield was the first to "break the ice" and experiment with extemporaneous and itinerant field preaching, and since it was at Whitefield's "invitation" that Wesley followed suit shortly after, we begin with Whitefield's ecclesiological or homiletical conversion.

Whitefield: "Field Preaching Is My Plan: In This I Am Carried as on Eagles Wings"

It is "doubtful if there would have been any Evangelical Revival," suggests Belden, "if Whitefield had been other than he was—the master evangelist of all time, and if he had not discovered the grace and the audacity to initiate out-of-church preaching."[41] Whitefield's conversion to itinerant field preaching was in various ways both gradual and inexorable. As early as December 1737, on the eve of his departure for Savannah, Georgia, he had begun to experiment with extempore preaching and had found the experience to be both exhilarating and liberating. Whereas there is no indication that Wesley's first experience of extempore preaching at All Hallows Church in 1735 was in any way premeditated, Whitefield considered his initial foray to have been "granted in answer to prayer."[42] He reflected,

> It happened providentially that a lecture was to be preached that evening at Deptford, and several importuned me to preach it; at first I was fearful (O me of little faith), having no notes. But afterwards (having got the consent of the minister), I went up, depending on the promise, "Lo! I am with you always even unto

---

40. Ibid., 70.
41. Belden, "Whitefield," 2.
42. Whitefield, *Journals*, 98.

the end of the world," and was enabled to preach to a large congregation without the least hesitation.[43]

From the irregularity of extempore preaching, it was only a short homiletical step to the vocation-defining irregularity of extempore field preaching. Whitefield would soon become the most visible exponent of the genre across the transatlantic world, but as he set out he had examples to emulate. The evangelical revivalist Howell Harris had been field preaching throughout Wales since 1735 and provided a ready paradigm for Whitefield's innovative preaching postures. Aspiring "to catch some of his fire," Whitefield commented approvingly: "He discourses generally in a field, but at other times in a house, from a wall, a table, or anything else."[44] Once again identifying himself closely with Jesus at a momentous turning point in his public ministry, Whitefield described his first field preaching venture in his *Journal* entry for Saturday, 17 February 1739:

> About one in the afternoon, I went with my brother Seward, and another friend, to Kingswood . . . My bowels have long since yearned toward the poor colliers, who are very numerous, and as sheep having no shepherd. After dinner, therefore, I went upon a mount, and spake to as many people as came unto me. There were upwards of two hundred. Blessed be God that I have now broken the ice! I believe I was never more acceptable to my Master than when I was standing to teach those hearers in the open fields. Some may censure me; but if I thus pleased men, I should not be the servant of Christ.[45]

Whitefield initially justified his radical homiletical redirection in terms of an uncomplicated either-or: reminiscent of the Apostle Paul's language in Galatians 1:10, either he could preach in the fields to the socially-economically and spiritually impoverished and thus please God, or he could cease and desist in order to "please men," in this instance, his ecclesiastical authorities. When the chancellor of Bristol challenged the legitimacy of his actions on the grounds that the collections he had taken up for the Orphan House he had recently established in Savannah, Georgia, had stifled their generosity towards the Bristol clergy, Whitefield was again confrontational. In a private meeting with the chancellor on 24 February 1739 Whitefield "resolved to go on preaching, and that if collections were not made here for the poor Georgians, [he] would lay it entirely upon him; adding, withal, [he] would

---

43. Ibid., 98.
44. Ibid., 229.
45. Ibid.,, 215–16.

not be the one who should hinder such a design for the universe."[46] If ever challenged in this way, Whitefield's Bethesda Orphanage would frequently function as a justification for the itinerant nature of his ministry.

On other occasions he went on the offensive and provocatively deployed scriptural justifications for his irregular ministry. He insinuated that not only was his own ministry in direct alignment with Jesus' public ministry, but that his detractors were spiritually akin to the Pharisees of Mark 8:11–12 whose demand "to know by what authority we preach" confirmed their calloused hearts. Responding to the rhetorical question "has not God set His seal to our ministry in an extraordinary manner?", Whitefield asked:

> Have not many that were spiritually blind received their sight? Many that have been lame strengthened to run the way of God's commandments? Have not the deaf heard? The lepers been cleansed? The dead raised? And the poor had the Gospel preached unto them? That these notable miracles have been wrought, not in our own names, or by our own power, but in the Name and by the power of Jesus of Nazareth cannot be denied. And yet they require a sign.[47]

Whitefield at times offered glimpses of a more conciliatory tone in his defense of field preaching. For instance, he made efforts to demonstrate that itinerant field preaching did not contravene Church of England canon law,[48] made sure that when he preached on the Sabbath it did not coincide with the stated times of regular worship, and claimed that "we went not into the fields till we were excluded from the churches."[49] But his most constructive and strident defenses of the practice came from the Scriptures. Reflecting in 1745 on six years of itinerant field preaching, he wrote:

> What do you think of *Jesus Christ* and his Apostles? Were they not field-preachers? Was not the best sermon that was ever delivered, delivered from a *Mount*? Was not another very excellent one preached from a place called *Mars-Hill*? And did not *Peter* and *John* preach above seventeen hundred years ago in *Solomon's Porch*, and elsewhere, though the clergy of that generation commanded them to speak no more in the name of Jesus? These were the persons I had in view, when I began my *adventures* of field-preaching. Animated by their example,

---

46. Ibid., 218.
47. Ibid., 293–94.
48. Ibid., 249ff., 259.
49. Ibid., 293.

when causelessly thrust out, I took the field; and if this be my shame, I glory in it.[50]

By the time he embarked on his journey to the American colonies in 1739, fresh from a phenomenally successful series of field preaching events throughout England during the previous year, Whitefield's ecclesiological conversion was complete and his vocational die was cast. He pronounced, "Everyone hath his proper gift. Field preaching is my plan. In this I am carried as on eagles' wings."[51]

Wesley: "I Became More Vile"

If Whitefield's temperament and inclinations rendered him well suited to his "adventures" in field preaching, Wesley found himself embracing what he styled "*this strange way* of preaching in the fields"[52] almost in spite of his natural gifts, inclinations, and inherited ecclesiological convictions. By March 1739, Whitefield's affecting, itinerant, and, by this point, *field* preaching saw him in increasingly high demand both in London and in Bristol. Not able to be in two places at once, Whitefield turned to Wesley for help, not so much inviting his Oxford mentor to join him as much as virtually conscripting Wesley as a fellow field preacher.

In Wesley's estimation, the whole matter was scandalous: not so much *how* Whitefield had drafted him into action (Whitefield put out an advertisement that Wesley was soon to preach in his place in Bristol, and then informed Wesley *after* the fact[53]), but *what* acts he had been conscripted to perform. After observing Whitefield preach outdoors on 29 March, Wesley reflected, "I had been all my life (till very lately) so tenacious of every point relating to decency and order that I should have thought the saving of souls *almost a sin* if it had not been done *in a church*."[54]

It is difficult to overstate the hurdles Wesley must have overcome even to consider field preaching. "Occasional preaching in the open air was one thing," observes Baker: "the deliberate acceptance of preaching outside parish churches as a normal method of evangelism quite another, especially for this staid little clergyman so prejudiced in favour of doing everything decently

---

50. Gillies, ed., *Works*, 4:232.
51. Quoted in Philip, *Life and Times*, 385.
52. Ward and Heitzenrater, eds., *Journals and Diaries*, 19:46.
53. Baker, ed., *Letters*, 25:612.
54. Ward and Heitzenrater, eds., *Journals and Diaries*, 19:46.

and in order according to the rules and customs of his beloved church."[55] Wesley's *Journal* entry for Monday, 2 April 1739 bears witness to his awareness of having reached a momentous, vocation-defining turning point in his public ministry. Setting aside the palpable sense of shame he associated with field preaching, he proceeded to preach on Jesus' words in Luke 4:18–19: "At four in the afternoon I submitted to be more vile, and proclaimed in the highways the glad tidings of salvation, speaking from a little eminence in a ground adjoining to the city [Bristol], to about three thousand people."[56] Just as Wesley appropriated 2 Samuel 6:22, so too did Whitefield—but with significantly more bravado.[57] Hammond suggests that "the contrast at this stage between Whitefield's revelling in innovative evangelistic methods and Wesley the High Churchman turned reluctant open-air preacher is striking."[58] Similarly, Doughty observes that in Wesley,

> There is a note of pathos in the words as though he had stooped to something of which part of him was ashamed. The Oxford scholar and don, with his inherited aristocratic instincts and ingrained respect for what was regular and constitutional, had become a "field preacher," a man beyond the pale of the regular ministry, knowing that the hand of authority would be increasingly against him; that he would forfeit the regard and friendship of many of his own order: that he was making himself a "fool for Christ's sake."[59]

Compared to Whitefield, Wesley was much more anxious to establish a plausible ecclesiastical defense of his actions, appealing variously to the "extraordinary"[60] nature of his calling along with the indeterminate scope of his ministry as a Fellow of Lincoln College. By his own reckoning, Wesley did not actively pursue field preaching; instead, it was forced upon him. He

---

55. Baker, *John Wesley and the Church of England*, 67.

56. Ward and Heitzenrater, eds., *Journals and Diaries*, 19:42.

57. For instance, after preaching at Moorfields on Sunday, 13 May 1739, Whitefield recorded in his *Journal*: "But if this is to be vile, Lord grant that I may be more vile. I know this foolishness of preaching is made instrumental to the conversion and edification of numbers. Ye Pharisees mock on, I rejoice, yea, and will rejoice." *Journals*, 265.

58. Hammond, "Whitefield, Wesley and Revival Leadership," 106.

59. Doughty, *John Wesley: Preacher*, 37.

60. Wesley appealed to Book VII of Richard Hooker's *Laws of Ecclesiastical Polity* in support of his field-preaching ministry, arguing that in addition to the "ordinary call" to "preach the Word of God" he received through ordination "by the bishop," the empirical results of his field preaching proved that he had also received an "extraordinary call" to fulfill this ministry. Wesley wrote to his brother Charles, "God bears witness in an *extraordinary manner* that my *thus exercising* my *ordinary call* is well-pleasing in his sight." Baker, ed., *Letters*, 25:660.

wrote, "Being thus excluded from the churches, and not daring to be silent, it remained only to preach in the open air; which I did at first, not out of choice, but necessity."[61] He used all of these modes of justification, prefaced with an appeal to the Bible's normative authority, in his pre-emptive defense of field preaching on 20 March:

> I allow no other rule, whether of faith or practice, than the Holy Scriptures. But on Scriptural principles I do not think it hard to justify whatever I do. God in Scripture commands me, according to my power, to instruct the ignorant, reform the wicked, confirm the virtuous. Man forbids me to do this in another's parish; that is, in effect, to do it at all; seeing as I have now no parish of my own, nor probably ever shall. Whom then shall I hear? God or man? "If it be just to obey man rather than God, judge you." A dispensation of the gospel is committed to me, and woe is me if I preach not the gospel. . . . Suffer me now to tell you my principles in this matter. I look upon *all the world as my parish*; thus far I mean, that in whatever part of it I am, I judge it meet, right, and my bounden duty to declare unto all that are willing to hear the glad tidings of salvation. This is the work which I know God has called me to. And I am sure his blessing attends it. Great encouragement have I therefore to be faithful in fulfilling the work he hath given me to do.[62]

But if Wesley had become a fully persuaded field preacher, he was nonetheless a reluctant field preacher, making little effort either to romanticize his experiences. His natural habitats were libraries and lecture halls, not preaching to coal miners in the open fields. By his own admission, his preference was "To be a saunterer *inter sylvas academicas*, a philosophical *sluggard*, than an itinerant *preacher*."[63] Even after twenty years' experience field preaching, the struggle to abandon the practice for a more sedentary, comfortable ministry was still strong. He wrote, "What a marvel the devil does not love field-preaching! Neither do I." [64]

Although he would continue to protest his devotion to the Church of England, as late as 1775 declaring "I am a High Churchman and the son of a High Churchman,"[65] by now Wesley's churchmanship had undergone decisive changes. He had come to embrace a form of ecclesiological pragmatism

---

61. Jackson, ed., *Works*, 8:273.
62. Baker, ed., *Letters*, 25:615–16.
63. Ibid., 26:197.
64. Ward and Heitzenrater, eds., *Journals and Diaries*, 21:203.
65. Telford, ed., *Letters*, 6:156.

where the ends determined the usefulness of the means, no matter how cherished those inherited ecclesiastical structures might have been. Wesley asked,

> What is the end of all ecclesiastical order? Is it not to bring souls from the power of Satan unto God? And to build them up in his love? Order, then is so far valuable as it answers these ends; and if it answers them not it is worth nothing. Now I would fain know, Where has *order* answered these ends? Not in any place where I have been: not among the tinners in Cornwall, the keelmen at Newcastle, the colliers in Kingswood and Staffordshire; not among the drunkards, swearers, Sabbath-breakers of Moorfields, or the harlots of Drury Lane.[66]

These drastic times called for drastic ecclesiological measures. And yet it was not simply the eternal destiny of those to whom Wesley preached that was at stake. In Wesley's estimation, if he failed to "play the part of an itinerant evangelist" he would not only betray God, but also run the risk of forfeiting his own salvation. In response to critics who queried the propriety of his ecclesiological conversion, he wrote,

> But you know no call I have to preach up and down, to play the part of an itinerant evangelist. Perhaps *you* do not. But I do; I know God hath required this at my hands. To me his blessing my work is an abundant proof, although such a proof often makes me tremble. But "is there not pride or vanity in my heart?" There is, yet this is not my motive to preaching. I know and feel that the spring of this is a deep conviction that it is the will of God; and that were I to refrain I should never hear that word, "Well done, good and faithful servant," but "Cast ye the unprofitable servant into outer darkness, where there is weeping and gnashing of teeth."[67]

The Whole World Is Now My Parish?

By 1739 Wesley and Whitefield had undergone a series of profound conversions. The third of these saw them independently articulating their ecclesiological mottos using virtually identical language, declaring "the whole world" to be their "parish." Yet, given that Wesley and Whitefield's shared usage of key theological terminology like "free grace" and "perfection"

66. Baker, ed., *Letters*, 26:206.
67. Ibid., 26:237.

masked divergent theological conceptions, this phrase begs the question: they might well have shared a ecclesiological motto, but did Wesley and Whitefield also share a common understanding of that motto? Since it appears Whitefield was the first to appropriate the term, we begin with how his application of this memorable phrase functioned as a window into his aspirations for his public ministry.

Whitefield conceived of his own ministry more or less exclusively in terms of evangelism. When he declared on 3 March 1739, "The whole world is now my parish," his emphasis was more on "the world" and less on "the parish", more on evangelism and less, unlike Wesley, on also facilitating spiritual nurture for those converted under his preaching.

Whitefield envisaged his ministry in expansive terms: "My business seems to be, to evangelize, to be a Presbyter at large."[68] He placed a premium on establishing, maintaining, and maximizing this evangelistic mobility across spatial, denominational, and social boundaries. For instance, while Whitefield retained his status as a presbyter in the Church of England, he wore the affiliation lightly. When Dr. Cutler queried the nature of his allegiance to Church of England doctrine and ecclesiology in September 1740 in Boston, Whitefield asserted that "a catholic spirit was best" and that he

> saw regenerate souls among the Baptists, among the Presbyterians, among the Independents, and among the Church folks,— all children of God, and yet all born again in a different way of worship: and who can tell which is the most evangelical?[69]

The following year, and on the other side of the Atlantic, the Erskine brothers in Scotland attempted to persuade Whitefield to renounce his Church of England ordination and join their breakaway Presbyterian movement. Whitefield resisted their overtures, perhaps conscious that any hint of sectarianism or provincialism would dilute the trans-denominational appeal of his transatlantic ministry. Even Whitefield's critics attested to the intentionality of his intramural evangelical catholicity, despite it being interpreted as being motivated by a cynical desire to maximize financial gain. For instance, the 18 June 1741 edition of the *South Carolina Gazette* provocatively and pejoratively described Whitefield as

> a staunch Churchman in Old England! A thorough Independent in new England! An Anabaptist among Anabaptists! A true-blue Kirkman in Scotland! And a Quaker among Quakers!

---

68. Whitefield, *Letters*, 262.
69. Whitefield, *Journals*, 458.

Becoming all things to all men, not that he might gain some, but make some gain of all![70]

Despite opportunities to do so, Whitefield never deviated from his singular evangelistic focus and recognized that in this respect his aspirations differed from those held by Wesley who was also committed to the task of spiritual nurture. In a letter to Wesley on 25 August 1740, he wrote: "My business seems to be chiefly in planting; if God send you to water, I praise his name—I wish you a thousandfold increase."[71] Similarly, he wrote to James Hutton on 13 July 1741, "God lets me see more and more, that I must evangelize . . . I have no freedom, but in going about to all denominations. I cannot join with any one, so as to be fixed in any particular place."[72] He consistently resisted overtures to diversify his ministry and assume the mantle of leadership over the Calvinistic wing of the Methodist movement. Come 1748, having just returned to England from his third (and lengthiest) venture in the American colonies, he met with Howell Harris and the Countess of Huntingdon at Chelsea, where Harris sought not only to convince Whitefield of the importance of gathering converts together but also to encourage him to assume a leadership role over the Calvinist Methodist Societies. But when the Countess of Huntingdon installed Whitefield as one of her personal chaplains for the purpose of evangelizing, in Whitefield's words, "some of the *Mighty* and *Noble*," his mind was definitively settled. Whitefield wrote to Wesley soon afterwards,

> My attachment to America will not permit me to abide very long in England; consequently I should but weave a *Penelope's* web if I formed societies; and if I should form them I have not proper assistants to take care of them. I intend therefore to go about preaching the gospel to every creature. You, I suppose, are for settling societies everywhere; but more of this when we meet.[73]

Whereas Whitefield focused his energies narrowly on the task of widespread evangelism, Wesley considered the long-term spiritual nurture and oversight of Methodist societies to be inextricably linked to his vocation as a field preacher. He saw himself as a shepherd of "the people called Methodists": I look upon all the world as *my parish*. Doughty observes, "Wesley insisted on following up his initial work and, as a rule, declined to preach

---

70. Quoted in Lambert, *"Pedlar in Divinity,"* 21.
71. Whitefield, *Letters*, 205.
72. Ibid., 277.
73. Gillies, ed., *Works*, 2:169–70.

where continuity and consolidation seemed to be impossible."[74] For instance, after meeting with the members of the Methodist society at Tanfield on 13 March 1743, Wesley was grieved at the "terrible instances" of people who had been "half-awakened and then left to themselves to fall asleep again." He therefore resolved, "by the grace of God, not to strike one stroke in any place where I cannot follow the blow."[75] By 1763 Wesley's sentiments had strengthened:

> I was more convinced than ever that the preaching like an apostle, without joining together those that are awakened and training them up in the ways of God, is only begetting children for the murderer. How much preaching there has been for these twenty years all over Pembrokeshire![76] But no *regular societies*, no discipline, no order or connection. And the consequence is that nine in ten of the once awakened are now faster asleep than ever.[77]

The above quotation hints at Wesley's occasionally explicit criticism of Whitefield's failure to consolidate the fruits of his field-preaching ministry into societies to facilitate continuing spiritual nurture. As early as 1741, Wesley commented in a letter written to his brother Charles, "I must go round and glean after G. Whitefield."[78] In fact, it appears Whitefield would later come to regret his decision not to diversify the scope of his public ministry and apply himself to the spiritual nurture of those who had experienced regeneration. He acknowledged, "My brother Wesley acted wisely. The souls that were awakened under his ministry he joined in class, and thus preserved the fruit of his labour. This I neglected, and my people are a rope of sand."[79] Cragg's memorable encapsulation of these different emphases, while verging on the hyperbolic (and perhaps also a little uncharitable), nonetheless confirms Whitefield's retrospective introspection: "Wher-

---

74. Doughty, *John Wesley: Preacher*, 57. Turner agrees, suggesting that Wesley was well aware "that his own movement owed more to careful institutionalization than to violent bursts of collective religious excitement" that often followed in the wake of Whitefield's preaching events (*John Wesley: The Evangelical Revival*, 13).

75. Ward and Heitzenrater, eds., *Journals and Diaries*, 19:318.

76. Ward and Heitzenrater observe that while South Pembrokeshire was the domain of "the Moravians and Welsh Calvinistic Methodists," there "is no evidence that John Wesley's preachers had been there for so long." Ibid., 21:424n26.

77. Ibid., 21:424.

78. Baker, ed., *Letters*, 26:55.

79. Quoted in Doughty, *John Wesley: Preacher*, 57. Turner concludes, "Whitefield's unconcern with organization guaranteed that English Methodism would become almost entirely Arminian in its theology." *John Wesley: The Evangelical Revival*, 13.

ever Whitefield went he left an overwhelming impression of impassioned eloquence. Wherever Wesley went, he left a company of men and women closely knit together in a common life."[80]

Conclusion

As significant as their embrace of the pursuit of holiness and subsequent experience of regeneration undoubtedly were in the biographies and theological formation of Wesley and Whitefield, we have observed that another, third, conversion—to itinerant field preaching—was needed to propel them both on a trajectory towards their eventual status as two of the foremost leaders of the eighteenth-century evangelical revival. And yet as vocationally momentous as this ecclesiological turning point proved to be, the role field preaching occupied in their respective public ministries differed. For while Wesley and Whitefield might both have declared "the whole world" to be their "parish," this shared terminology did not manifest itself in identical ecclesiological visions. Reflecting on the different ways each understood the scope and purpose of their public ministry, Belden suggests that while Whitefield's legacy lies in being "the pioneer evangelist of the great revival," by contrast Wesley is best understood as "the constructive evangelist,"[81] an acknowledgement of Whitefield's evangelistic and Wesley's organizational entrepreneurialism.

Wesley and Whitefield held varying aspirations for their respective public ministries and these led them to emphasize different facets of a shared ecclesiological motto that was simultaneously controversial and conceptually elastic. On the one hand, Whitefield's emphasis was on an evangelistic preaching ministry that placed a premium on maintaining mobility across spatial, social, and denominational boundaries: the *whole world* is my parish. But if Whitefield's ministry was, in his own assessment, primarily focused on "planting" the seed of the gospel, then Wesley's ministry also entailed a significant emphasis on "watering," or the ongoing spiritual nurture of those awakened under his preaching: I look upon all the world as *my parish*.

---

80. Cragg, *Church and the Age of Reason*, 145.
81. Belden, "George Whitefield: His Influence on His Time," 2.

4

Wesley, Whitefield, and the Church of England

Edward Loane

There is no doubt that the relationship of John Wesley and George Whitefield to the Church of England was both formative and of ongoing significance for the shape of their ministries. Yet the myriad aspects from which these relationships can be studied, along with their dynamic nature, open a labyrinth of potential explorations. Moreover, the multidimensional structure of the Church of England is itself problematic to the study. After all, the Church of England is more than merely its articulated doctrine or its officers (the bishops and clergy) or its congregations or its practices. Rather, it is a conglomeration of all of these factors together. Thus, in order to provide an adequate account of the similarities and differences between Wesley and Whitefield in these relationships, we must, on the one hand, consider their adherence to the church's beliefs and their conformity, or lack thereof, to her practices. On the other hand, we must also consider *the Church of England's* view of Wesley and Whitefield. Furthermore, the changes in these attitudes and relationships over time must be accounted for.

Frank Baker begins his major study on Wesley's relation to the Church of England by affirming the impossibility of understanding John Wesley apart from his relationship with the established Church. He argues, "In thought and affection, in habit and atmosphere, his whole being was inextricably interwoven with that of the church."[1] To highlight this point, he uses Whitefield as a strong contrastive, contending that Whitefield's churchmanship was merely an incidental feature of his religious background to which he sat lightly. This chapter, however, demonstrates that Wesley and White-

---

1. Baker, *Wesley and Church of England*, 1.

field shared more in common in their relation to the Church of England than Baker's juxtaposition acknowledges. Nevertheless, while the paths they trod were often parallel, there were also significant differences, and various realizations took place at different times. All of these factors contribute to the interesting kaleidoscope of connections between these men and the church in which they were members. Paradoxically, although Wesley was more tenaciously devoted to the Church of England, his legacy was ultimately more divisive, whereas Whitefield, whose adherence was less rigid, left a more enduring legacy in evangelical Anglicanism.

Wesley's and Whitefield's Attitude to the Church of England

Anglican Doctrine and Liturgy

Wesley and Whitefield were both born and bred as loyal adherents of the Church of England. Each had numerous clerical ancestors and their early experiences were bound to the established church. These foundations led to intimate familiarity with the formularies of the church as well as earnest convictions that they were correct articulations of Christianity. Both men offered themselves for ordination and willingly made the requisite oaths and declarations. Throughout their lives, they repeatedly declared themselves to be loyal to the church's doctrine and claimed that their emphases and practices were more in line with its confessions than the beliefs and practices that were common in their day.

Rather than undermine the Church of England, Harry Stout has noted that the Methodist movement as a whole "originated as a purifying element within a compromised Church of England."[2] Again, this motivation is attributed to both Wesley and Whitefield. For example, Richard Heitzenrater shows Wesley believed he was simply preaching the "old religion" of the Church of England, which had virtually vanished since the Restoration.[3] In Wesley's final University Sermon at Oxford, he closed with a challenge for the Church of England to promote, once again, the doctrine which had brought about the Reformation: salvation by faith.[4] Likewise, J. I. Packer has pointed out that "Whitefield insisted that the religion he modeled and

---

2. Stout, *Divine Dramatist*, 20.
3. Heitzenrater, *Wesley and the People Called Methodists*, 141.
4. Outler, ed., *Sermons*, 1:117–30.

taught was a straightforward application of Anglican doctrine as defined in the Articles, the Homilies and the Prayer Book."[5]

At face value, Wesley and Whitefield were not seeking to supplant the Church of England, but rejuvenate it. In 1763, Wesley would write that there were only a few true Christians in England and he questioned, "as for a Christian visible Church, or a body of Christians visibly united together, where is this to be seen?"[6] Likewise, Whitefield boldly declared that it was moribund clergy who were "schismatics" and "the bane of the church of England" because they "subscribe to our Articles . . . and then preach contrary to those very Articles . . . "[7] In other words, Wesley and Whitefield believed that while the doctrine and structures of the church were not corrupt, many of the officers of the church subverted its principles and purpose.

Although both of John Wesley's grandfathers had been dissenters, his parents had both conformed at an early age and, as a high church clerical family, they zealously raised their children to revere the Church of England as sacrosanct.[8] Indeed, Wesley was not aware of his heritage of dissent until 1765, and by that point the trajectory of his own convictions had been determined.[9] Baker contended that in childhood the *Book of Common Prayer* "became almost as familiar to [the Wesley children] as the Bible itself."[10] This would have been further reinforced for John when he attended the Charterhouse School where students attended chapel every day. Having gone up to Oxford, Wesley desired the life of a don, which necessitated him to be in Orders. From this point it is clear that his personal commitment to the Church of England had become "more conscious and concerned."[11] He was ordained deacon on 19 September, 1725, and the significance of his ordination for Wesley should not be underestimated. Many years later, when he was field preaching near Bath, he was challenged as to what authority he had to behave in such a manner. Wesley replied "By the authority of Jesus Christ, conveyed to me by the Archbishop of Canterbury, when he

---

5. Packer, *Shorter Writings*, 51.

6. "The Principles of a Methodist Farther Explained: Occasioned by The Rev. Mr. Church's Second Letter to Mr. Wesley: In a Second Letter to that Gentleman," in Davies, ed., *Methodist Societies*, 9:160–237.

7. Gatiss, ed., *Sermons*, 2.121.

8. Cf. Pollock, *Wesley the Preacher*, 16–18. John's paternal grandfather (and namesake) was one of the clergy ejected in 1662 and his maternal grandfather was a leading London dissenter.

9. Baker, *Wesley and Church of England*, 7, 237.

10. Ibid., 9.

11. Ibid., 15.

laid hands upon me, and said, 'Take thou authority to preach the gospel.'"[12] Wesley took his ordination promises very seriously and used them to his advantage in the proclamation of the gospel for the rest of his life.

While George Whitefield's immediate family was not clerical, his grandfather was the son, grandson, nephew and brother of clergymen.[13] As such, from a young age Whitefield had contemplated being a clergyman, and one of his favorite childhood games was pretending to be a minister reading prayers.[14] He was encouraged along this course as a viable way to raise his—and his family's—station in life.[15] Even before his encounter with the Wesleys at Oxford, Whitefield was very earnest and while still in Gloucester he personally adopted many of the Methodist practices such as fasting, visiting the poor, regularly receiving the sacrament, and daily attendance at church.[16] However, Whitefield's journey toward ordination was complicated by internal reservations surrounding personal ambition. At various points he felt he could not pursue ordination because his desire for ministry was tainted with ambition to become a bishop.[17] When his local bishop in Gloucester, Martin Benson, declared he would not ordain candidates under the canonical age of twenty-three, Whitefield felt relieved that the decision could be postponed. However, the combination of a vivid dream and personal encouragement of Bishop Benson that he would ordain Whitefield whenever he offered himself convinced him that ordination was God's call.[18] The ordination of the twenty-one-year-old Whitefield took place on 27 June 1736.

At their ordinations, both Wesley and Whitefield promised that they would always diligently "minister the doctrine and sacraments, and the

---

12. "An Extract of The Rev Mr. John Wesley's Journal," 5 June 1739. Ward and Heitzenrater, eds., *Journals and Diaries*, 19:64. Bishop Potter had been translated to Canterbury in 1737.

13. For the family tree, see Dallimore, *George Whitefield*, 1:39.

14. Gledstone, *George Whitefield*, 4.

15. Pollock, *Whitefield the Evangelist*, 13.

16. Ibid., 15.

17. Ibid., 14. As an interesting turn of events, after Whitefield had reached the height of his fame, the problem of how to deal with him was of great concern to the leading figures of the land including Walpole. According to Gledstone, when Walpole and his companions complained to the king that Whitefield needed to be stopped, the king replied, "I believe the best way will be to make a bishop of him." Gledstone, *George Whitefield: M.A. Field Preacher*, 253. When discussions took place about the establishment of an Anglican bishop in the New World Whitefield's name was constantly put forward as a candidate from the mid-1740s to the mid-1760s. Kidd, *George Whitefield*, 237.

18. Parr, *Inventing George Whitefield*, 17; Dallimore, *George Whitefield*, 1:94–95.

discipline of Christ, as the Lord hath commanded, and as this Church and Realm hath received the same . . . " As we shall see, both men declared themselves to be loyal servants of the established church throughout their lives. Nevertheless, there were few officers of the church who would have advocated Wesley and Whitefield's version of loyalty, and both men would have had difficulty maintaining that they had kept their promise to "reverently obey your Ordinary, and other chief Ministers, unto whom is committed the charge and government over you." In fact, Wesley was explicit about his stance. For example, at the Methodist Convention in 1746 he declared "We will obey the rules and the governors of the Church, whenever we can consistently with our duty to God. Whenever we cannot, we will quietly obey God rather than men."[19]

As has been noted, Wesley was schooled from the cradle in high churchmanship. Even as late as 1775 Wesley claimed: "I am an High Churchman, the son of an High Churchman, bred up from my childhood in the highest notions of passive obedience and non-resistance."[20] Howard Snyder captured some of the tensions within Wesley, stating: "He was at once a High Churchman and a Pietist; a traditionalist and an innovator; a Biblicist and an experientialist."[21] Iain Murray argues that Wesley's high churchmanship was one of the most influential factors shaping his theology.[22] As evidence for this claim, he points to Wesley's asceticism and high sacramentalism, demonstrated by his willingness to appoint lay preachers but strictly forbidding them to administer the sacraments.[23] This theology manifested itself in Wesley's insistence that Methodists, although meeting in their own meeting houses at other times, should always attend their local parish on Sunday and receive Holy Communion from there as regularly as it was offered. Despite his irregularities, Wesley was persistent in his advocacy of participation in Church of England rites.

Whitefield believed his ministry was essentially a revival of authentic doctrine in the Church of England. He claimed it was not field preaching that was the chief cause of offence, but "the doctrine that I preach there," which he believed was nothing other than a revival of "the essential articles

---

19. "Minutes of the 1747 Conference, Wednesday June 17," in Rack, ed., *Methodist Societies*, 10:201.
20. Telford, ed., *Letters*, 6:56.
21. Snyder, *Radical Wesley*, 71.
22. Murray, *Wesley*, 44.
23. Ibid., 44–45.

of the Church of England."[24] When he was defending himself against accusations from the bishop of London he protested his loyalty, declaring,

> My constant way of preaching is, first to prove my propositions by Scripture, and then to illustrate them by the Articles and collects of the Church of England. Those who have heard me can witness how often I have exhorted them to be constant at the public service of the church. I attend on it myself, and would read the public liturgy every day if your Lordship's clergy would give me leave.[25]

William Gibson suggested that Whitefield's reluctance to adhere to the liturgy indicated some hostility to it.[26] On the contrary, Whitefield articulated his devotion to the Church of England's doctrinal formularies declaring: "I should rejoice to see all the world adhere to her Articles . . . I am a friend of her Articles, I am a friend to her Homilies, I am a friend to her liturgy."[27] Indeed, Whitefield claimed that "our English liturgy is, without doubt, one of the most excellent established forms of public prayer in the world."[28] Such statements stand in contrast to the common perception that Whitefield was "indifferent to denominational allegiance."[29] Nevertheless, he qualified his statement by saying that no form can suit every particular case, and lamented that many never prayed for the things they most need because they were tied to the established forms. As such, Gibson is on firmer ground in his position that Whitefield's irregularity implied "the inadequacy and insufficiency of the Church's form of worship."[30] Whitefield sat more loosely to the laws of the church than Wesley. Whitefield experienced nothing like the crisis of conscience that Wesley suffered as they took the innovative step into field preaching. As Church of England pulpits were closed to him, Whitefield brashly commented, "little do my enemies think what service they do to me. If they did one would think, out of spite they would even desist from opposing me."[31]

Wesley also regularly commended the Church of England formularies. Not long after his conversion, Wesley read the Homilies and, delighted

24. Gillies, ed., *Works*, 4:115.

25. Ibid., 4:5–16, esp. 10; see also Baker, *Wesley and Church of England*, 67.

26. Gibson, "Whitefield and the Church of England," 61.

27. Gatiss, ed., *Sermons*, 1:177.

28. George Whitefield to Dr. Durell, 12 April 1768, in Gillies, ed., *Works*, 4:316.

29. Rivers, "Whitefield's Reception in England," 261; Baker, *Wesley and Church of England*, 1.

30. Gibson, "Whitefield and the Church of England," 61.

31. Cited in Stout, *Divine Dramatist*, 103.

at the doctrine he found there, he published an abridged version.[32] Baker described this as "a deliberate attempt to discover and publish the authorized views of the Church of England on this central theme of the Methodist Revival."[33] As the years progressed, Wesley became more comfortable publicly declaring his reticence at subscribing to everything contained in the *Book of Common Prayer* and the Thirty-Nine Articles.[34] Indeed, in 1746 he published his own *Sermons on Several Occasions*, which effectively functioned as Methodist homilies. Such criticisms and deviations would probably have resulted in ejection a century earlier, but laxity of eighteenth-century ecclesiastical discipline proffered no official sanction. Nevertheless, even in the 1780s he still claimed, "I believe there is no liturgy in the world, either in ancient or modern language, which breathes more of a solid, scriptural, rational piety, than the Common Prayer of the Church of England."[35] Although in his last decade Wesley published a revision of the Prayer Book, in general both Wesley and Whitefield found the formularies of the church to be in concurrence with their newfound evangelical faith.

One of the factors that contributed to the Wesley's firm belief that he was acting in good faith within the established parameters of the Church of England was his thorough knowledge of her rubrics and canons. Wesley, at times, found himself in trouble for his excessive zeal in adhering to Anglican rubrics.[36] In 1743 Wesley published *An Earnest Appeal to Men of Reason and Religion* in which he defended Methodism against the charge that they were undermining the Church of England.[37] He defended himself against the charge that he did not observe the laws of the church, claiming, "I have observed the rubrics with a scrupulous exactness, not for wrath, but for conscience's sake." He pointed to rubrics he kept that he knew were commonly neglected by most clergy. He also made similar points in relation to the church's canons.[38] His point was that he was more loyal to the Church of England than those who charged him with disloyalty.

Wesley's attitude to the polity of the Church of England was modified significantly from his early high-church understanding. Snyder argued that by 1747 Wesley had come to the position that the succession of

32. "The Doctrine of Salvation, Faith, and Good Works, Extracted from the Homilies of the Church of England" in Outler, *John Wesley*, 123–33.

33. Baker, *Wesley and Church of England*, 56.

34. Ibid., 238.

35. "Preface to the *Sunday Service*, 1784." Cited in ibid., 234.

36. Ibid., 47.

37. Cragg, ed., *Appeals to Men of Reason and Religion*, 11:37–94.

38. Ibid., 11:79. He followed up this work with the publication of the *Further Appeal*, which restated his case. Ibid., 11:95–325.

Anglican bishops was not unbroken from the Apostles.[39] He described his position in 1779:

> I still believe "the episcopal form of church government to be both Scriptural and Apostolical": I mean, well agreeing with the practice and writings of the apostles. But that it is *prescribed* in Scripture I do not believe. This opinion, which I once heartily espoused, I have been heartily ashamed of ever since I read Bishop Stillingfleet's *Irenicon*. I think he has unanswerably proved that "neither Christ nor his apostles *proscribed* any form of church government, and that the plea of divine right for diocesan episcopacy was never heard of in the primitive church."[40]

This changed understanding of the nature of the episcopal office led to a denouncing of practices that as a young man he upheld. For example, in 1788 he declared that he did not want a bishop to consecrate one of this chapels or graveyards; in fact, he would not suffer it because he was "clearly persuaded the thing is wrong."[41] This radical alteration in his understanding of episcopacy eased his conscience about appointing lay preachers, and towards the end of his life even ordaining his own ministers.

Both Wesley and Whitefield took a common path towards deviations in protocol, albeit far more reluctantly for Wesley. In 1738 it was Whitefield who led the way in open-air preaching, with Wesley reluctantly following this novelty.[42] Field preaching, by necessity, involved preaching in a local incumbent's parish; there was no way around this. Wesley pointed to the general license to preach associated with his Oxford fellowship, but the practice, while not illegal per se, was nevertheless irregular and an infringement on parochial jurisdiction.

Likewise, Whitefield was the first to break with Church of England conventions relating to extempore prayer. He began to find the collects and the written prayers of Bishop Andrewes too confined and formal. On Christmas morning in 1738, for the first time, Whitefield prayed extempore before a congregation of several hundred people.[43] Wesley again followed suit.

---

39. Snyder, *Radical Wesley*, 81.

40. *Arminian Magazine*, 1779, 598–601, cited in ibid., 70.

41. *Arminian Magazine*, 1788, 541–43, cited in Baker, *Wesley and Church of England*, 214.

42. This was a pivotal moment for each man and their relation to the Church of England, but as it is the sole focus of another chapter in this volume we will not dwell on it.

43. Whitefield, *Journals*, 103.

Wesley was always more reluctant than Whitefield in pursuing these innovations. His high church conscience inclined him to shun novelty. He described the tension he felt stating his two principles: "The one, that I dare not separate from the Church, that I believe it would be a sin so to do; the other, that I believe it would be a sin not to vary from it in the points mentioned."[44]

At the same time, despite the major divergences in accepted practice, neither man was ever defrocked or officially sanctioned throughout their ministry. Wesley believed this fact should be evidence enough of his allegiance to the Church of England, regardless of how far his movement drifted from her conventions or was ostracized by her officers. He explained to Thomas Church, "Nothing can prove I am no member of the church till I either am excommunicated or renounce her communion, and no longer join in her doctrine, and in the breaking of bread, and in prayer."[45] However, it was in the development of Methodist Societies that provided Wesley and Whitefield, particularly Wesley, a structural avenue for deviation from the Church of England.

Church of England Society, or Sect?

Religious societies aiming at renewal of the Church of England were certainly not an invention of the Methodist movement. Since the 1670s religious societies had established local and national programs for Christian education, publication, and missions.[46] At least forty such societies were meeting around London by the turn of the century. These organizations were by no means considered distinct from the Church of England; on the contrary, these parachurch groups were encouraged by authorities and enfranchised as an aspect of the church's work. John Wesley would have been very familiar with these structures as his father was an avid supporter of religious societies.[47] Likewise, Whitefield was familiar with these religious societies and he had preached to some of them before he first went to America.[48]

As the revival began to take hold and Methodist societies flourished, both Wesley and Whitefield were adamant that they did not want to establish an organization that could be considered a sect. In 1744, the year before the uprising of Bonnie Prince Charlie, Wesley had drafted a letter

---

44. "Prophets and Priests" in Outler, ed., *Sermons*, 4:81.
45. Davies, ed., *Methodist Societies*, 9:195.
46. Heitzenrater, *Wesley and the People Called Methodists*, 107.
47. Snyder, *Radical Wesley*, 15.
48. Gledstone, *George Whitefield: M.A. Field Preacher*, 69.

to George II declaring the loyalty of the Methodist societies.[49] However, he was convinced by his brother Charles not to send it because doing so would constitute the societies as a distinct sect. Charles wrote, "At least it would *seem to allow* that we are a body distinct from the National Church, whereas we are only a sound part of that Church."[50] John certainly did not want to concede that his societies should be considered a dissenting body. Likewise, Whitefield was adamant he did not want to establish a separate body. He claimed in a letter the Hervey, "You judge right when you say, it is your opinion that I do not want to make a sect, or set myself at the head of a party. No; let the name of Whitefield die, so that the cause of Jesus Christ may live . . ."[51] Both Wesley and Whitefield may have intended for the Methodist societies to remain wedded to the Church of England and renew the Church from within, but this became increasingly difficult as the officers of the church railed against them with growing hostility.

Understandably, as parish pulpits were closed to Wesley and Whitefield and Methodists were finding themselves refused Holy Communion by antagonistic clergy, the question of formal separation from the Church of England was felt with growing urgency. Wesley prepared a paper, "Ought We to Separate from the Church of England?" which he read to his conference of preachers in May 1755.[52] Wesley was firm in his resolve that they most certainly should not separate. In 1760, when three of lay preachers administered the Sacrament in a Methodist chapel in Norwich, Charles Wesley wrote that it was a crisis and the movement "must now resolve either to separate from the Church, or to continue in it for the rest of our days."[53] John Wesley rebuked the preachers and made clear at the next conference that the "people called Methodists" would remain within the Church of England.[54] Nevertheless, as the years went by there was less and less conformity to Church of England protocols and practices. Furthermore, as Baker is right to point out, without a clearly defined and universally accepted formula for separation, the situation became entrenched allowing

---

49. "The Humble Address of the Societies in England and Wales, In Derision called Methodists," 5 March 1744 in Baker, ed., *Letters*, 26:104–6.

50. Charles Wesley to John Wesley, 6 March 1744 in Newport and Lloyd, *Letters of Charles Wesley*, 1:112.

51. George Whitefield to James Hervey, 5 April 1749 in Gillies, ed., *Works*, 2:248. Cf. Gledstone, *George Whitefield: M.A. Field Preacher*, 257.

52. Heitzenrater, *Wesley and the People Called Methodists*, 216.

53. Charles Wesley to William Grimshaw, 27 March 1760 in Jackson, *Life*, 2:187–88.

54. Pollock, *Wesley the Preacher*, 222.

the ambiguous situation of Wesley maintaining his loyalty to the Church of England while others proclaimed his treason.[55]

John Wesley's structure of independent societies added further ambiguity. The orders of the Fetter Lane Society lacked reference to the Church of England, a fact that could be construed as Wesley implicitly distancing himself from the established church. However, Baker shows that such a notion is unsustainable when it is put alongside the fact that "they went in a body to communion at St Paul's Cathedral, expelled two members 'because they disowned themselves from the Church of England', and 'readmitted' another lapsed member after he had 'gladly returned to the church.'"[56] Wesley's structures provide evidence of both independence and adherence.

In August 1739, Wesley was invited to give a defense of his position by the scholarly Joseph Butler, Bishop of Bristol. Wesley argued that his teaching was in accordance with the *Homilies*, and when charged with having administered communion in his societies he denied it: "My lord, I never did yet; and believe I never shall."[57] Ultimately, Wesley's firm stance on this conformity to Anglican convention weakened in the years ahead. The opposition of clergy denying Methodists the sacrament left Wesley in a difficult situation. Part of his solution was the 1743 procuring of the West Street Chapel in London for his societies. This was an episcopally consecrated building and, as such, Wesley felt at liberty to administer communion in it. Elsewhere, he began the practice of administering private communion for the sick, which was allowable, but he would extend this to a large company of the sick person's friends.[58] Heitzenrater is correct that Wesley "at times stretched the rubrics in order to provide the Sacrament."[59] Wesley's misgivings about using non-episcopally consecrated buildings for communion dissipated and he began to regularly offer the Lord's Supper at his meetinghouses.[60]

Both Wesley's and Whitefield's activities became more irregular in relation to Church of England practice. While Wesley had established his societies as an adjunct to the parish church, Whitefield's patron, the Countess of Huntingdon, began establishing private chapels.[61] A privilege of peerage was the legal right to build chapels and appoint chaplains. These

---

55. Baker, *Wesley and Church of England*, 161.
56. Ibid., 75.
57. Ward and Heitzenrater, eds., *Journals and Diaries*, 19:472.
58. Baker, *Wesley and Church of England*, 84.
59. Heitzenrater, *Wesley and the People Called Methodists*, 154.
60. Baker, *Wesley and Church of England*, 213.
61. Pollock, *Whitefield the Evangelist*, 247–48.

foundations remained within the Church of England but were independent of episcopal interference. As such, while Wesley's societies eventually became an independent denomination after his death, Whitefield's legacy was more profound in the established church itself.[62] This outcome is somewhat paradoxical considering the general perception that Wesley was far more devoted the Church of England than Whitefield.

The reality was that Whitefield was less concerned than Wesley about the establishment and organization of societies. Such endeavors were not his priority; Thomas Kidd has pointed out that "instead of building an Anglican renewal movement (or worse, in his mind, a Dissenting denomination), he simply wished to 'go about preaching the gospel to every creature.'"[63] This lack of emphasis on the organization of societies meant he was not nearly as concerned as Wesley with the perception his societies were sectarian. Indeed, the London meetinghouses where Whitefield's followers congregated were registered by him as "meeting-places of certain congregations of Protestant Dissenters from the Church of England calling themselves Independents."[64] Whitefield's ministry did not result in a strong sense of belonging to "Whitefield." Rather, Whitefield encouraged his converts to join any church to which they felt drawn.[65]

Wesley, on the other hand, organized his followers into distinct societies. He defended his organization against the charge of schism by declaring that most of the members were heathens who did not belong to any other church.[66] The legacy of these different emphases was that Whitefield's ministry did not lead to a separate denomination while Wesley's did.

It was in relation to 1780s America that Wesley took his most divisive action. Baker has argued that Wesley's views on valid church government had altered substantially by 1745; indeed, this led to his appointment of lay preachers.[67] Wesley was always adamant that these preachers were not pastors and his appointment of them was not ordination and therefore was not a breach of Anglican order.[68] It was, however, following the War of Independence and at the request of American Methodists that Wesley viewed the ecclesiastical situation in the New World with fresh eyes.[69] He made

62. Ibid., 249.
63. Kidd, *George Whitefield*, 207.
64. Gledstone, *George Whitefield: M.A. Field Preacher*, 305.
65. Ibid., 349.
66. Baker, *Wesley and Church of England*, 77.
67. Ibid., 140.
68. Snyder, *Radical Wesley*, 92.
69. Baker, *Wesley and Church of England*, 239.

plans for an independent Methodist Church in America that would be liturgical and episcopal. Wesley prepared and published a "drastic revision of the *Book of Common Prayer* and Thirty-Nine Articles."[70] In 1784, "Wesley committed the outrageous breach of Anglican order" by ordaining presbyters and appointing Thomas Coke as General Superintendent of Methodists in America.[71] Coke was a bishop of American Methodists in all but name. Charles Wesley was devastated, saying, "Lord Mansfield told me last year, that 'ordination is separation.' But my Brother does not and will not see; or that he has renounced the Principles and Practice of his whole life."[72] Charles expressed his concern in verse:

> So easily are Bishops made
>
> By man's, or woman's whim?
>
> W[esley] his hands on C[oke] hath laid,
>
> But who laid hands on Him?[73]

John Wesley refused to accept that it created a breach in his standing with the Church of England. By the time he died, he had ordained twenty-seven presbyters and two superintendents. Yet, even after 1784, he still publicly proclaimed, "I am now, and have been from my youth, a member and a minister of the church of England. And I have no desire nor design to separate from it, till my soul separates from my body."[74] Regardless of how legitimate Wesley's claim to not have broken with the Church of England in these actions was, the nature of what he established was itself evidence of his relation to the Church of England. His new church was clearly modeled on Anglican polity, liturgy, and doctrine.

Was there ever a breach between Wesley and the Church of England? Baker contends impartial observers would agree that Wesley had practically separated from the Church of England well before his 1784 ordinations. He had founded his distinctive "connexion" of preachers operating without reference to ecclesiastical order. His societies possessed numerous properties founded on trust deeds independent of the Church of England.[75] All of this was under the authority of a single priest who had no parochial charge

---

70. Ibid., 218.
71. Ibid., 162; Pollock, *Wesley the Preacher*, 250.
72. Tyson, *Charles Wesley: A Reader*, 60.
73. Ibid., 429.
74. Outler, ed., *Sermons*, 3:67.
75. Baker, *Wesley and Church of England*, 109.

and operated unsupervised by episcopal authority.[76] As early as the 1739 Wesley's older brother, Samuel, had warned that by his behavior "though the church would not excommunicate *you*, you would *excommunicate the church*."[77] And yet, Wesley encouraged his followers to attend their local parish churches. He stipulated that his preaching houses must proclaim nothing contrary to the *Homilies* or the Thirty-Nine Articles. Baker makes the point that while Wesley maintained he would never separate from the Church of England, he had effectively separated *within* the church.[78] In this sense, he felt at ease to declare his movement a reform movement of the church.[79] In Wesley's mind, separation from the Church of England involved renunciation of the Church's doctrines or refusal to participate in its services. On these grounds he felt on sure ground in declaring his loyalty. He did say, however, that he would sooner separate from the church than give up his support of lay preaching, field preaching, extempore preaching or forming societies.[80] Murray argues that Wesley's priorities in these matters were not ecclesiological, but rather, evangelistic.[81] Thus, while Wesley's own tenacious claim of loyalty never led to formal separation in his lifetime, his divergent structures, principles and practices ensured separation was an obvious and easy path for his followers after his death.

Church of England and Other Denominations

In 1789 Wesley described himself in his youth as "not only a member of the Church of England, but a bigot to it, believing none but the members of it to be in a state of salvation."[82] Even well after his heart was strangely warmed, Wesley continued to rebaptize converts from dissent.[83] Considering his own tenacious loyalty to the Church of England despite major persecution, he found it very difficult to support dissenters who left the church by choice rather than necessity.[84] Nevertheless, as the years progressed Wesley came to be more favorably disposed to dissenters. This change in sentiment was the result of correspondence with the Presbyterian, Ralph Erskine. Erskine had

---

76. Ibid., 283.
77. Samuel Wesley to John Wesley, 3 September 1739, in Clarke, ed., *Memoirs*, 341.
78. Baker, *Wesley and Church of England*, 116–17.
79. Ibid., 118.
80. Heitzenrater, *Wesley and the People Called Methodists*, 218.
81. Murray, *Wesley*, 41.
82. Telford, ed., *Letters*, 8:140.
83. Baker, *Wesley and Church of England*, 71.
84. Ibid., 133.

deliberately sought to reshape Wesley's thinking and began sending him Presbyterian literature.[85] In 1775, Wesley claimed to "have an opportunity of conversing freely with more persons of every denomination than anyone else in the three kingdoms."[86]

The change in Wesley's stance is exemplified in his sermon *Catholic Spirit*, which he published in 1755.[87] In this sermon Wesley warned against a sectarian spirit that divides the people of God and he sought to show that God was working through other denominations. At the same time, he was firm that the catholic spirit did not mean doctrinal indifference. Herbert McGonigle has claimed that John Wesley's sermon "has something to say to all of us in the twenty-first century" as it is a model of Christian ecumenical spirit.[88] In fact, in 1790 Wesley would still claim: "I advise all our brethren that have been brought up in the Church to continue there." But he then conceded, "The Methodists are to spread life in all denominations; which they will do till they form a separate sect."[89] Yet, even in his newfound ecumenical stance, Wesley maintained his belief that the established church was the best place from which to proclaim Christ.[90] As such, he was not prepared to advance in unity with other groups, regardless of how evangelical they were, if he perceived it would result in a worsening relationship between Methodists and the Church of England.[91]

Frank Baker contrasts Wesley to Whitefield, who, he declared, was "the true focal point for evangelical dissenters."[92] According to James Schwenk, however, Whitefield would have been content to preach exclusively in Church of England pulpits; it was only the fact that they were closed to him that he ventured onto the platforms of other denominations.[93] Indeed, Whitefield once preached that if the Church of England would preach its stated "doctrine of Christ and the Articles" then the number of dissenters would decrease and his denomination would "become the joy of the whole earth."[94]

---

85. Ibid., 143–44.
86. John Wesley to Lord Dartmouth, 15 June 1775 in Telford, ed., *Letters*, 6:163.
87. Outler, ed., *Sermons*, 2:79–96.
88. McGonigle, "Catholic Spirit," 50.
89. Telford, ed., *Letters*, 8:211.
90. Baker, *Wesley and Church of England*, 121.
91. Ibid., 129.
92. Ibid., 135.
93. Schwenk, *George Whitefield*, 44.
94. Gatiss, ed., *Sermons*, 2:121.

There is little doubt, though, that Whitefield became open to dissenters long before Wesley. As early as 1735 Whitefield had modified his view that those outside the established church must be damned. He met a faithful dissenter named Cole and concluded that dissenters like Cole knew more about grace and justification by faith than many of the clergy.[95] Whitefield was encouraged in these years by reading famous Protestant dissenters like Matthew Henry.[96] In Whitefield's early travels in America he became more impressed with forms of Christianity other than Anglicanism and he envisaged a Christian cooperation that transcended denominational affiliation. One sermon he preached in Philadelphia included the provocative anti-sectarian dialogue with Abraham,

> Father Abraham, whom have you in heaven? Any Episcopalians? *No!* Any Presbyterians? *No!* Any Independents or Seceders, New Sides or Old Sides, any "Methodists? *No! No! No!* Whom have you there, then Father Abraham? *We don't know those names here! All who are here are Christians—believers in Christ, men who have overcome by the blood of the Lamb and the word of his testimony.* Oh is that the case? Then God help me, God help us all, to forget having names and to become *Christians* in deed and in truth.[97]

In America, Whitefield began to preach to the congregations of different denominations. Pollock remarked that he "thus became ecclesiastically all things to all men."[98] As the years went on he received many invitations from dissenters, far more than from the clergy of his own church.[99] He claimed, "There is nothing that grieves me more than the differences amongst God's people."[100] He even went so far as to say that if the Pope lent him his pulpit he "would gladly proclaim the righteousness of Jesus Christ therein!"[101] This attitude was somewhat programmatic for evangelical ecumenism in the centuries since Whitefield as gospel fidelity and proclamation became cherished more dearly than denominational loyalty.

This ecumenical ideal not only clashed against the prevailing paradigm within the Church of England, but also among Whitefield's gospel partners in other denominations. An excellent example of this was his interaction with

95. Pollock, *Whitefield the Evangelist*, 32.
96. Ibid., 41.
97. Gillies, "Memoirs of Rev. George Whitefield," 116.
98. Pollock, *Whitefield the Evangelist*, 128.
99. Ibid., 186.
100. Whitefield, *Sermons on Important Subjects*, 279.
101. Gillies, ed., *Works*, 1:308.

Ebenezer and Ralph Erskine in 1741. The two Scotsmen attempted to persuade Whitefield to break away from the "wicked, bishop-bound Church of England" and join their newly established Presbyterian church.[102] The invitation to come and help them came at first by letter, to which Whitefield responded, "I come only as an occasional preacher, to preach the simple gospel to all who are willing to hear me, of whatever denomination. It will be wrong in me to join a reformation in Church government and further than I have light given me from above."[103] On the sixth day after Whitefield arrived in Scotland. The men, along with a number of their associates, again attempted to induce him to secede from his ecclesiastical allegiances. Whitefield confounded them by declaring that he would not separate from his communion till he was "either cast out or excommunicated."[104]

One aspect of this meeting that is puzzling was Whitefield's solemn declaration that he would not be episcopally ordained again for a thousand worlds.[105] Robert Philip has argued that this declaration is quite unique from Whitefield and is not repeated in any of his letters or any popular anecdotes of his preaching or conversation.[106] Philip concludes that Whitefield "had neither fixed nor definite opinions upon the subject of episcopacy."[107] As such he supported episcopacy when it supported faithful gospel proclamation but did not when bishops hindered it. Certainly, Whitefield's encounter with the Erskines demonstrated his belief that, in contrast to his opponents, no ecclesiastical polity was of divine origin. Nevertheless, in something of an irony considering his firm resolve against the Erskines, Whitefield was buried inside the Presbyterian Church at Newbury Port. He was not anti-Presbyterian in outlook, but wanted to maintain and expand his trans-denominational ministry.

Gledstone describes Whitefield as "practically an independent minister, while remaining a clergyman of the Church of England."[108] This paradox was a manifestation of Whitefield's truly ecumenical spirit, which was quite contrary to the prevailing paradigm of his age. He was willing to preach and

---

102. The Erskines, particularly Ebenezer, were leaders in secession from the Church of Scotland in the 1730s and were deposed by that church in 1740. They believed strongly in the Reformed and Covenantal tradition of the church and were opposed to Erastianism.

103. George Whitefield to Ralph and Ebenezer Erskine, 16 May, 1741, in Gillies, ed., *Works*, 1:262.

104. Gledstone, *George Whitefield: M.A. Field Preacher*, 174.

105. Philip, *Life and Times of the Reverend George Whitefield, M.A.*, 448.

106. Ibid., 273.

107. Ibid., 274.

108. Gledstone, *George Whitefield: M.A. Field Preacher*, 305.

minister in partnership with Christians despite differing denominational affiliations. J. I. Packer has critiqued the itinerant and independent nature of Whitefield's ministry, noting that he "saw himself as serving all the churches all the time," which led to "an individualistic piety of what we would call the a parachurch type, a piety that gave its prime loyalty to transdenominational endeavours . . . and that conceived of evangelism as typically an extra-ecclesial activity."[109] In other words, this ministry fostered a concept now commonplace in evangelicalism: that successful evangelism takes place at "evangelistic events" that are quite separate from regular corporate worship. Mark Noll observed this shift stating, "Up to the early 1700s, British Protestants preached on God's plans *for the Church*. From the mid-1700s, however, evangelicals emphasized God's plans *for the individual*."[110] Such observations are helpful in demonstrating the continuing influence of Whitefield's legacy in contemporary evangelicalism, Anglican or otherwise.

The Church of England's Attitude towards Wesley and Whitefield

Thus far we have compared something of Wesley's and Whitefield's understanding and attitudes towards the Church of England. Of course, every relationship has two sides, so now we turn to explore the Church of England's relationship to Wesley and Whitefield. The dynamic and pluriform nature of these attitudes make generalization necessary, but the common trend was to move from friendly encouragement and welcome by bishops and clergy to outright opposition and hostility.[111]

Episcopacy

Both Wesley and Whitefield received a measure of support in their early ministry from the episcopacy. We have already noted the support Bishop Benson gave Whitefield towards ordination, but this support continued well into Whitefield's ministry. The week after his ordination, the bishop received a complaint following Whitefield's first sermon: that fifteen people had been driven mad. The bishop's brief response was that he hoped the

---

109. Packer, *Shorter Writings*, 59.

110. Cited in ibid., 59.

111. Gibson has argued that, in the case of Whitefield, this antagonism was motivated by "four specific and reasonable concerns: ecclesiastical authority, popery, Jacobitism, and antinomianism" (Gibson, "Whitefield and the Church of England," 46). It is not too difficult to trace these fears as the root of opposition to Wesley also.

madness might not be forgotten by the next Sunday.[112] After Whitefield's meteoric rise to fame in both England and America, he returned to Benson in order to be ordained to the Priesthood in January 1739. On this occasion Benson was affectionate towards him. Not long after, Benson wrote to the Earl of Huntingdon who was concerned about his wife's Methodist associations, and said of Whitefield,

> Though mistaken on some points, I think him a very pious, well-meaning young man, with good abilities and great zeal. I find his grace of Canterbury thinks highly of him. I pray God grant him great success in all his undertakings for the good of mankind, and the revival of true religion and holiness among us in these degenerate days.[113]

Even though this was written before the advent of field preaching, Benson's attitude remained benevolent in his admonition for this innovation and he assured Whitefield of his prayers.[114]

Likewise, Wesley's early interactions with bishops were generally positive. He had been advised early on to seek the support of those in authority over him, which he was anxious to do.[115] When Wesley first proposed to visit prisoners he sought the bishop's approval. John Potter, Bishop of Oxford, replied that he "was greatly pleased with the undertaking."[116] Potter was also a high churchman and, according to Charles Wesley, Potter's early support was because he believed the Methodists might "leaven the whole lump" of the Church of England.[117] After Potter's translation to Canterbury, the Wesleys went to see him in February 1739. Charles Wesley recorded that they were received with "great affection" by the Archbishop.[118] They also went to meet with the Bishop of London, Edmund Gibson. Wesley was quite familiar with Gibson. He had enjoyed an extended meeting with him in October 1738 and, according to his brother Charles, the bishop found nothing objectionable in their teaching and assured them: "you may have free access to me at all times."[119] This was quite an invitation

---

112. Gledstone, *George Whitefield: M.A. Field Preacher*, 31.

113. Bishop Benson to Lord Huntingdon in Seymour, *Life and Times of Selina Countess of Huntingdon*, 1:196.

114. See Gibson, "Whitefield and the Church of England," 47–48.

115. Baker, *Wesley and Church of England*, 24, 58.

116. Ward and Heitzenrater, eds., *Journals and Diaries*, 18:126.

117. Charles Wesley to Benjamin La Trobe, 20 July 1786 in Baker, *Wesley and the Church of England*, 59.

118. Wesley, *Charles Wesley Journal*, 1:162–63.

119. Ibid., 1:151.

from one of the most dignified prelates in the country. The day after he had returned from Georgia, Whitefield also visited Potter and Gibson and was favorably received.[120] Charles Wesley recorded Gibson's belief that, "G. Whitefield's *Journal* was tainted with enthusiasm, though he was himself a pious, well-meaning youth."[121] However, just a few months later, Whitefield was the subject of Gibson's attack in his published pastoral letter against lukewarmness and enthusiasm.[122]

What had changed the attitude of the bishops in such a short period of time? The answer, in short, was the advent of field preaching. Whitefield wrote to Wesley in the middle of 1739 saying, "I hear we shall be excommunicated soon."[123] Although excommunication was never really likely, certainly episcopal hostility attempted to inhibit the Methodist's work.[124] In August 1739, Wesley's interview with Bishop Butler descended to an argument in which Butler told Wesley "You have no business here. You are not commissioned to preach in this diocese. Therefore I advise you to go hence." Wesley doggedly informed the bishop that he was going to stay and that as a Fellow of an Oxford College he had a license to preach anywhere in England.[125] In 1742, Wesley and Whitefield were summoned twice to frosty meetings with the Archbishop of Canterbury and Bishop of London, who implored them to desist from their activities. However, the Methodists were firm in their resolve to continue. Such defiance did not endear Wesley or Whitefield to those in episcopal authority. Indeed, Gibson is accurate in his assessment of Whitefield that "A more restrained leader might have established Calvinistic Methodism without needlessly shaking the hornets' nests that so agitated many bishops and clergy."[126] Furthermore, as both men began to make their private interviews with bishops public through the publications of their journals, the hostility increased. Both Wesley and Whitefield wrote open letters and pamphlets aimed directly at the attitudes of episcopal authorities. Whitefield had been the first to do this, and he virtually chal-

---

120. Dallimore, *George Whitefield*, 1:218.

121. Jackson, ed., *Charles Wesley Journal*, 1:162–63.

122. *Bishop of London's Pastoral Letter against LukeWarmness and Enthusiasm*; Gledstone, *George Whitefield: M.A. Field Preacher*, 108.

123. Whitefield, *Letters*, 498.

124. "Anglican discipline was very lax, that Convocations no longer met, and that the bishops were unlikely to move unless pushed very hard. All this, indeed, was part of the malady which the Methodists were seeking to remedy. Nevertheless the danger of an unexpected episcopal reaction which might destroy their effectiveness was always present." Baker, *Wesley and Church of England*, 58.

125. Ward and Heitzenrater, eds., *Journals and Diaries*, 19:472.

126. Gibson, "Whitefield and the Church of England," 63.

lenged the bishops to take a stand against the Methodist movement. In his published *Journal* he recorded his feeling that "If we have done anything worthy of the censures of the church why do not the Right Reverend the Bishops call us to a public account? If not, why do not they confess and own us?"[127] This brash attitude was something he later regretted, saying "Alas, alas, in how many things I have judged and acted wrong . . . I have hurt the cause I would defend, and also stirred up needless opposition."[128]

Following Gibson's *Pastoral Letter*, Whitefield promptly published his response. His defense was acerbic in tone and was as much an attack on the bishop as a defense of his ministry. Far from retreating, Whitefield criticized Gibson's preaching for failing to elicit the ecstatic responses in question: "Has your lordship been a preacher in the Church of England for so many years, and have you never seen any sudden or surprising effects consequent upon your lordship's preaching?"[129] There was another clash between Whitefield and Gibson early in 1744. Anonymous papers had been circulated denouncing the Methodists and Whitefield in particular. What is more, it was widely believed that none other than Gibson was the anonymous author.[130] Whitefield wrote directly to Gibson to clarify if the rumors were true.[131] There was no response from the bishop, but his printer sent a suggestive note to Whitefield two days later, which indicated the bishop was responsible. Despite the weight of episcopal pressure, Whitefield was adamant that the Methodists continued to have a rightful place in the established church. He declared: "As yet we see no sufficient reason to leave the Church of England and turn Dissenters; neither will we do it till we are thrust out." [132]

Sometimes the ire of bishops was misdirected at Wesley and Whitefield through no fault of their own. For example, George Lavington, Bishops of Exeter, probably would have continued to tolerate the Methodists, except in 1748 a forged document was circulated which was supposedly from his primary charge to his clergy. The document portrayed the bishop as promoting Methodism, which enraged him, and he accused Wesley and Whitefield of sponsoring or even authoring the document. Lavington maintained the rage for almost the rest of his life, himself attacking the Methodists through virulent pamphleteering. However, in 1762, the year of Lavington's death,

127. Whitefield, *Journals*, 153.
128. 24 June 1748, Gillies, ed.,*Works*, 2:144.
129. Gledstone, *George Whitefield: M.A. Field Preacher*, 110.
130. Ibid., 217.
131. Ibid., 218.
132. Ibid.

both Wesley and Whitefield independently met with the bishop and some form of reconciliation was achieved.[133] Benson's successor in Gloucester, William Warburton, provides another example of antagonism; Warburton was vehemently opposed to the Methodists and actively sort to pervert their activities.[134] Despite these attacks, at a meeting in 1749 Wesley and Whitefield resolved "to abide in the communion of the Established Church and to look upon bishops as fathers till thrown out."[135]

Although the general tenor of episcopal opinion was antagonistic towards Wesley and Whitefield, there were exceptions, even later in life. For example, the Bishop of Derry ordained Tom Maxfield "to assist that good man [Wesley] that he may not work himself to death."[136] Furthermore, Lavington's successor in Exeter, John Ross, was also sympathetic and invited Wesley to dinner. At the end of the evening the kind bishop said "Mr. Wesley, I hope I may sit at your feet in the kingdom of heaven."[137] These examples demonstrate the pluriform responses to Wesley and Whitefield and the dynamic nature of episcopal support.

Clergy

There may not have been any official sanctions ever imposed against Wesley and Whitefield by the Church of England, yet in practice they were "thrust out." It was not long after the revival began that pulpits in previously supportive parishes began to be closed to them. Early in 1739 Wesley and Whitefield together met their critics and attempted to explain their understanding of the gospel, but it was to no avail.[138] Whitefield's immense popularity was soon despised by parish clergy who denied him access to their pulpits. He exclaimed: "I hope I shall learn more and more and more every day that no place is amiss for preaching the gospel. God forbid that the word of God should be bound because some out of misguided zeal deny the use of their churches."[139] Pamphlets were published by clergy declaring Whitefield was a "peddler of strange doctrines, a menace to the good order of the church."[140] Kidd has shown that there were also those who came to his defense and, as

---

133. Gibson, "Whitefield and the Church of England," 54–56.
134. Gledstone, *George Whitefield: M.A. Field Preacher*, 314–15.
135. Cited in Baker, *Wesley and Church of England*, 127.
136. Ward and Heitzenrater, eds., *Journals and Diaries*, 21:409.
137. Pollock, *Wesley the Preacher*, 255.
138. Kidd, *George Whitefield*, 64.
139. Whitefield, *Journals*, 108.
140. Pollock, *Whitefield the Evangelist*, 82.

such, "by mid-1739, the literature for and against Whitefield had reached a flood tide."[141] Gibson argues that, at least initially, there was a distinction between Wesley and Whitefield in the openness of clergy: Wesley being invited to preach in parish churches and Whitefield not.[142] Perhaps there is evidence of this and it would further highlight the dynamic nature of their relationships with the Church of England. However, there is also early evidence of Wesley complaining that pulpits were closed. In 1738 he wrote to the church in Herrnhut, "my brother and I are not permitted to preach in most of the churches of London."[143] In 1743 Wesley was even denied the sacrament and opportunity to preach in the parish church he grew up at and where his father had been the rector.[144] He continued to seek the cooperation of local clergyman before engaging in extra-parochial ministry, but these gestures of partnership and courtesy were usually met with hostility.[145] Both Whitefield and Wesley began to claim that the whole world was their parish.[146] It was the rejection from Church of England pulpits that was a major factor in Wesley and Whitefield expanding their field-preaching ministry.

Although most of the clergy did not welcome the Methodists, there were a few evangelical clerics who supported their ministry. Whitefield tended to have more clerical followers than Wesley. Nevertheless, following a friendly meeting in March 1761 with Henry Venn, Wesley took positive steps towards bringing about a fraternal union among sympathetic clergy.[147] He was convinced that working together was the best hope of reviving the church from within.[148] He stated, "I think it a great pity that the few clergymen in England who preach the three grand scriptural doctrines—Original sin, Justification by Faith, and Holiness consequent thereon—should have any jealousies or misunderstandings between them."[149] It was particularly painful for him, however, that cooperation became more difficult as evangelicals such as John Newton, John Berridge, Henry Venn, and Augustus

---

141. Kidd, *George Whitefield*, 78.
142. Gibson, "Whitefield and the Church of England," 62.
143. Baker, ed., *Letters*, 25:572.
144. Ward and Heitzenrater, eds., *Journals and Diaries*, 19:309.
145. Baker, *Wesley and Church of England*, 62.
146. This quote is most famously attributed to Wesley; however, Gatiss has shown that Whitefield declared "The world is now my parish" a month before Wesley was recorded as saying it. Gatiss, "Anglican Evangelist," 33.
147. This topic has been given fresh exploration in a recent monograph, Danker, *Wesley and the Anglicans*.
148. Baker, *Wesley and Church of England*, 185, 191–94.
149. Campbell, ed., *Letters*, 27:250.

Toplady, "turned to Calvinism."[150] Wesley's efforts through the 1760s proved futile. Even though Whitefield was supportive, other Calvinistic ministers were reluctant. By 1770, Wesley had given up hope. He stated to the Methodist Conference of 1769,

> It has long been my desire that all those ministers of our Church who believe and preach salvation by faith might cordially agree between themselves, and not hinder but help one another. After occasionally pressing this in private conversation whenever I had opportunity, I wrote down my thoughts upon the head and sent them to each in a letter. Out of fifty or sixty to whom I wrote only three vouchsafed me an answer. So I give this up. I can do no more. They are a rope of sand: and such they will continue.[151]

This lament was published the following year, the year of Whitefield's death. These two events marked the end of Wesley's chances to unite the evangelical clergy. Baker concludes that from this point Wesley focused on the future of the Methodist societies, "preferably as a movement within the Anglican Church, but if not as a denomination distinct from it."[152]

Laity

As we have reflected on the attitude of the bishops and clergy, we should note that the Church of England is more than those holding official rank. The vast majority of the church is laity and, although we cannot develop this point expansively, it is essential to see that Wesley's and Whitefield's popularity with the laity was unique among church leaders. For example, the Sunday after it became known that the chancellor of Bristol had forbidden Whitefield from preaching in every pulpit in the city, ten thousand residents of the city gathered to hear him at Kingswood.[153] Likewise, in 1753 when Whitefield assisted William Grimshaw in administrating Communion, the crowd filled the church four times over and "sipped away thirty-five bottles of wine."[154] The reason this period has become known as the great awakening is because of the popular impact these preachers had among ordinary people. Thousands responded positively to their message. In this sense, it is possible to argue that Wesley and Whitefield, while enduring hostility

150. Murray, *Wesley*, 69–70.
151. Rack, ed., *Works*, 10:377.
152. Baker, *Wesley and Church of England*, 197.
153. Pollock, *Whitefield the Evangelist*, 95.
154. Heitzenrater, *Wesley and the People Called Methodists*, 214.

from bishops and rejection from clergy, did enjoy a large measure of support from members of the Church of England.

Conclusion

The relationship with the Church of England was an integral aspect of the ministries of both Wesley and Whitefield. In many ways, the treatment by officials in the church was formative for the innovations they took. On the other side, they declared their loyalty while pioneering novel and provocative practices. In 1834, a Methodist described Wesley as like an oarsman who faced the Church of England while he rowed steadily away.[155] This image is accurate in portraying Wesley's tenacious adherence to the established church while at the same time taking steps towards separation. In 1739 Wesley broke with established conventions by field preaching. In 1749 he united his societies across England. In 1763 the societies sought a measure of legal protection. In 1769 Wesley gave up his efforts to work with evangelical clergy and in the 1780s he began to ordain and consecrate his own ministers. Whitefield, on the other hand, treated the Church of England more like a good ship that he had been commissioned to sail on. He was happy to modify the rigging and tackle. He readily criticized other crew. He was more than willing to use his skills to help other vessels. But he was never willing to give up his commission.

Ultimately, Wesley's legacy was a separate denomination heavily indebted to the structures and theology of the Church of England. Whitefield's legacy, however, was felt more within Anglican evangelicalism and the higher allegiance to the noun rather than the adjective. Dallimore stated, "Much of the harvest resulting from Whitefield's lifetime of labours was garnered within the Church of England."[156] Nevertheless, both Wesley and Whitefield have been profoundly influential on the Church of England and they stand out as two of the denomination's most impressive leaders. This is a fact that Anglicans should readily cherish, and for which they should give thanks to God.

---

155. Cited in Chadwick, *Victorian Church*, 1:370.

156. Dallimore, *Whitefield*, 1:321. For two excellent recent contributions to the legacy of George Whitefield, see Rivers, "Whitefield's Reception in England"; and Atherstone, "Commemorating Whitefield."

5

"I Am Yet Persuaded, You Do Greatly Err"[1]

Whitefield, Wesley, and Christian Perfection

DAVID McEWAN

Introduction

JOHN WESLEY AND GEORGE Whitefield were effective evangelists and key leaders in the eighteenth-century revival that impacted both sides of the Atlantic. They had a deep personal friendship but as the revival progressed this was often strained due to their differing theological perspectives on the nature of the divine-human interaction in salvation; Whitefield's Reformed Calvinism and Wesley's evangelical Arminianism setting them apart.

Reading their sermons leaves a clear impression of how close they are in terminology and emphasis on such matters as the nature of humanity as created, the consequences of human sin, God's initiative in providing salvation in Christ as a free gift of grace arising from love alone, genuine religion as a personal and transformative relationship with God, the call to live a holy life, the work and witness of the Spirit and the spiritual habits and practices that form us into Christlikeness and deepen our fellowship with God and neighbor.[2]

Despite these shared emphases, Wesley's Arminian and Whitefield's Reformed theological frameworks do influence their views at a number of critical points, and this is evident in their debates over Christian perfection. In a recent article, Ian Maddock briefly explored their differences of

---

1. Whitefield to Wesley, quoted in Baker, ed., *Letters*, 26:43.

2. In researching the material for this chapter I was struck by how alike they were in so many ways. Their agreement is also noted by Maddock, *Men of One Book*, 176–231; Smith, "Whitefield and Wesleyan Perfectionism," 64–68.

opinion on Christian perfection. Maddock points out that the key points of theological debate over perfection could be attributed to their differing frameworks.³

This chapter does not trace the history of their dispute over perfection,⁴ but seeks to explore the critical theological elements at the heart of their debate. We begin with a brief look at their understanding of the character of the Christian life and the call to perfection. This is followed by an examination of their views on the nature of perfection and its implications for our present bodily life. The chapter concludes by contrasting George Whitefield's belief that God still required the same flawless life demanded of humanity prior to the fall with John Wesley's belief that God moderated his requirements in the light of our fallen state. This meant that for Whitefield Christian perfection was a goal to be pursued, while for Wesley it was, by God's grace alone, an attainable goal in this present bodily life.

Whitefield and the Christian Life: "salvation is all of God"

For Whitefield, salvation was a gift of grace, rising solely from the love of God for sinful humanity, with the righteousness of Christ imputed to us while we are still sinners.⁵ The goal of salvation is a total renovation of our sinful nature through Christ: "by sanctification I mean a *total renovation of the whole man*: by the righteousness of Christ, believers come legally, by sanctification they are made spiritually, alive; . . . They are sanctified, therefore, throughout, in spirit, soul, and body."⁶ Whitefield completely rejected the notion of the new life in Christ as one of endless sinning and forgiveness. He urged every Christian "to leave all thy sinful lusts and pleasures; renounce, forsake, and abhor thy old sinful course of life, and serve God in holiness and righteousness all the remaining part of life. If you lament and bewail past sins, and do not forsake them, your repentance is in vain, you are mocking of God, and deceiving your own soul."⁷ Commenting on Romans 6:1, he wrote, "'Shall we continue in sin then, that grace may abound?' But as he [Paul] rejected such an inference with a 'God forbid!' so do I."⁸ In his sermon, "Marks of Having Received the Holy Ghost," Whitefield wrote:

3. Maddock, "George Whitefield," 147–61.
4. See Smith, "Whitefield and Wesleyan Perfectionism," 63–85.
5. Gatiss, ed., *Sermons*, 1:93–94. See also ibid., 1:57, 409–12; 2:276.
6. Ibid., 2:218–19 (emphasis mine). See also ibid., 2:28, 331–32.
7. Ibid., 2:31. See also ibid., 1:416 –179; 2:81–82, 275–76, 282.
8. Ibid., 1:411–12. See also ibid., 1:386; 2:33.

> "Whosoever is born of God, (says St. John) sinneth not, neither can he sin, because his seed remaineth in him." Neither can he sin. This expression does not imply the impossibility of a Christian's sinning: for we are told, that "in many things we offend all": It only means thus much: that a man who is really born again of God, doth not *willfully commit sin, much less live in the habitual practice of it*. For how shall he that is dead to sin, as every converted person is, live any longer therein?[9]

This language reflects very closely that of Wesley, as he made the same point from I John: "He that is by faith born of God sinneth not, (1), by any habitual sin, for all habitual sin is sin reigning; but sin cannot reign in any that believeth. Nor, (2), by any wilful sin; for his will, while he abideth in the faith, is utterly set against all sin."[10] Both men believed that the Christian life is one in which, by the power of the Holy Spirit, the believer need not commit "willful sin."

Whitefield had a very strong emphasis on love and relationships as the clear evidence of the new life in Christ. It is love that is the essence of our relationship with Christ: "God is well pleased, when all our actions proceed from love, love to himself, and love to immortal souls."[11] It is love that is to be the mark of a genuine Christian life: "O love one another; 'he that dwells in love dwells in God, and God in him.' . . . O walk in love. If I could preach no more, if I was not able to hold out to the end of my sermon, I would say as John did, when he was grown old and could not preach, 'Little children, love one another:' if ye are God's children, then love one another."[12] This love of God in the heart is not an end in itself, but is to lead to obedience.[13] However, as we shall see later, this obedience flowing from love would always be imperfect. Whitefield affirmed that a deep, loving relationship with Christ took time to develop:

> I confess, indeed, that the heart of a natural man is not thus enlarged all at once; and a person may really have received the Holy Ghost, (as Peter, no doubt, had when he was unwilling to go to Cornelius) though he be not arrived to this: but then, where a person is truly in Christ, all narrowness of spirit decreases in

---

9. Ibid., 2:191–92 (emphasis mine).

10. Outler, ed., *Sermons*, 1:124. The balance of this quotation in its original setting was too strong and Wesley would nuance it later. See ibid., 1:235–38, 240; Jackson, ed., *Works*, 14:276.

11. Gatiss, ed., *Sermons*, 2:258. See also ibid., 1:227.

12. Ibid., 1:399–400.

13. Ibid., 1:144.

> him daily; the partition wall of bigotry and party zeal is broken down more and more; and the nearer he comes to heaven, the more his heart is enlarged with that love, which there will make no difference between any people, nation, or language.[14]

Though Whitefield rejected the notion of salvation as mere forgiveness and emphasized the centrality of the love of God, his language on perfection is much more guarded. In a large measure, this is a reflection of his Reformed soteriology.

Wesley and the Christian Life: "Are You a Witness of the Religion of Love?"

As much as Whitefield, Wesley upheld the central tenet of the Protestant evangelical faith that salvation is a free gift of God's grace, received by faith, and that the righteousness of Christ is imputed to those who trust in Christ at the moment they believe.[15] While imputed righteousness is the "*ground* of our acceptance with God," implanted righteousness is "the *fruit* of it."[16] Wesley's theological understanding of the power of God's imparted righteousness to deal with the whole sin issue is critical for his doctrine of perfection.[17] It is important to note that Wesley defined righteousness primarily in terms of love: "Righteousness is the fruit of God's reigning in the heart. And what is righteousness but love? The love of God and of all mankind, flowing from faith in Jesus Christ, and producing . . . every right disposition of heart toward God and toward man."[18]

This implies that righteousness is primarily a right relationship rather than meeting some standard of law or rule. Wesley had a much more explicit relational focus to his soteriology, and this relationship is essentially defined by love.[19]

> For to this end was man created, to love God; and to this end alone, even to love the Lord his God with all his heart and soul, and mind, and strength. But love is the very image of God: it is

---

14. Ibid., 2:194–95. See also ibid., 1:179–80; 2:291, 310, 342.

15. Outler, ed., *Sermons,* 1:453–62. See also Telford, ed., *Letters,* 3:371–88. A thorough examination of this topic can be found in McGonigle, *Sufficient Saving Grace,* 217–39.

16. Outler, ed., *Sermons,* 1:458.

17. See McGonigle, *Sufficient Saving Grace,* 217–39.

18. Outler, ed., *Sermons,* 1:642. See also ibid., 2:188.

19. Ibid., 1:225–35, 348–50; 4:356

the brightness of his glory. By love, man is not only made like God, but in some sense one with him.[20]

Wesley was convinced that authentic love required freedom—the ability to say yes or no to the relationship. A love that is compelled through original design, or by simple coercion from a greater power, would not be love at all: "Love is perfect freedom. As there is no fear, or pain, so there is no constraint in love."[21] Without freedom "both the will and the understanding would have been utterly useless. Indeed without liberty man had been so far from being a *free agent* that he could have been no *agent* at all. For every *unfree being* is purely passive, not active in any degree."[22]

This was at the heart of Wesley's rejection of the Reformed understanding of predestination and election.[23] At every moment of the God-human relationship there had to be a genuinely free choice because "'liberty necessitated', or overruled, is really no liberty at all. It is a contradiction in terms. It is the same as 'unfree freedom', that is, downright nonsense."[24] Wesley declared that God's wisdom, power, and goodness were seen in governing us as humans made in his image, so he would not overrule our understanding, will, or liberty and therefore could not save us by compulsion or denying our freedom to choose.[25] He strongly believed that we must be "free in believing, or not believing . . . Indeed if man were not free he could not be accountable either for his thoughts, words, or actions. If he were not free he would not be capable either of reward or punishment . . . Virtue or vice, of being either morally good or bad."[26] This means that however salvation in Christ is effected, it must enable the restoration of choice that had been forfeited in the garden: "least of all did he take away your liberty, your power of choosing good or evil; he did not *force* you; but being *assisted* by his grace you . . . *chose* the better part."[27] This assistance Wesley called preventing (prevenient) grace, and it restored to humanity the ability to choose for or

---

20. Ibid., 4:355. See also ibid., 1:184, 581.

21. Ibid., 4:355. See also ibid., 4:295.

22. Ibid., 2: 475. See also ibid., 2:376, 401, 417; 4:225–35, 356.

23. This can be explored further in Collins, *Scripture Way of Salvation*, 19–45; McGonigle, *Sufficient Saving Grace*, 265–331.

24. Outler, ed., *Sermons*, 2:475. See also ibid., 4:295–96.

25. Ibid., 2:541. See also ibid., 2:531.

26. Ibid., 2: 417. See also: ibid., 2:376, 488–89. For a full treatment of predestination by Wesley, see Chilcote and Collins, eds., *Doctrinal and Controversial Treatises II*, 13:227–38, 258–320.

27. Outler, ed., *Sermons*, 2:489.

against a relationship with God again "without depriving any of them of that liberty which is essential to a moral Agent."[28]

Here is a critical point of difference between the two men. It impacts their understanding of the possibilities of grace in this life and it lies at the heart of their disagreement over perfection.

Our ability to exercise a free choice is connected to our understanding and our motives. Reflecting on the creation account and the test that God gave to humanity regarding the fruit of the tree of the knowledge of good and evil (Gen. 2:16), Wesley doubted that Adam would choose evil knowing it to be such. "But it cannot be doubted he might mistake evil for good. He was not infallible; therefore not impeccable."[29] Wesley believed that we were not created knowing all things (that would make us divine), so ignorance is not in itself evil. It may lead to evil if intentional wrong choices, based on what we do know, are made. In his opinion, the choice made in the garden was not due to limited knowledge, but to doubting God's love and an unwillingness to continue to trust him; it is this that lies at the core of his understanding of the nature of sin. Wesley believed that humanity now needed to be aware of the consequences of their choice in Genesis 3 and their inability to remedy it. It is for this reason that God gave us the law, as it "pointed out all those thoughts, and words, and works, by so many express injunctions, which the love of God, when that was the spring of his soul, produced without any injunction."[30] In other words, what would once have sprung naturally from a heart of love is now codified to demonstrate the problem, not to be its solution.[31] Wesley, like Whitefield, affirmed that the only answer is Jesus Christ, who as the great Physician came to heal our diseased souls: "Know your disease! Know your cure! . . . By nature ye are *wholly corrupted*; by grace ye shall be *wholly renewed*."[32]

Wesley agreed with Whitefield that it is the love of God in the heart that enables the Christian to obey God, but Wesley was more optimistic about its power to transform the heart in this present bodily existence: "It was by a sense of the love of God shed abroad in his heart that every one of them was enabled to love God. Loving God, he loved his neighbour as himself, and had power to walk in all his commandments blameless."[33] In

---

28. Ibid., 2:489. See also Outler, ed., *Sermons* 3:203 and particularly n24 on prevenient grace. On prevenient grace, see Crofford, *Streams of Mercy*..

29. Outler, ed., *Sermons*, 2:476.

30. Ibid., 4:331.

31. Ibid., 4:332, emphasis mine.

32. Ibid., 2:185.

33. Ibid., 2:419. See also ibid., 2:188.

harmony with this, Wesley defined the goal of salvation in Christ in terms of love: "'thou shalt love the Lord thy God with all thy soul, and thy neighbor as thyself.' The Bible declares, 'Love is the fulfilling of the Law,' 'the end of the commandment,' of all the commandments which are contained in the oracles of God."[34] In his landmark sermon, "The Circumcision of the Heart," it is love that is the evidence of a perfect life: "add love, and thou hast the 'circumcision of the heart' . . . it is the essence, the spirit, the lie of all virtue. It is not only the first and great command [Matt. 22:38], but it is all the commandments in one. Whatsoever things are just, whatsoever things are pure, whatsoever things are amiable or honourable; if there be any virtue, if there be any praise, they are all comprised in this one word—love. In this is perfection and glory and happiness"[35] The evidence we are not self-deceived comes from keeping his commandments: "Love rejoices to obey, to do in every point whatever is acceptable to the Beloved. A true lover of God hastens to do his will on earth as it is done in heaven."[36] Though Wesley, like Whitefield, linked love and obedience, he did not believe that obedience had to be flawless.

The Call to Perfection in Whitefield and Wesley

The call to perfection is commonly associated with Wesley and the developing Methodist movement; Whitefield was equally passionate about this:

> The injunction given by God to Abraham is very strong: "Walk before me, and be thou perfect." The same he again lays upon all Israel, in the eighteenth of Deuteronomy: "Thou shalt be perfect, and without blemish, with the Lord thy God." And lest any should think to excuse themselves from this obligation, by saying, it ceased when the old law was abolished, our blessed Savior ratified and explained it: "Be ye, therefore, perfect, even as your Father who is in heaven is perfect."[37]

Though this is stated in very bold terms here, he nuances his message in other sermons. In particular, the focus is on the pursuit of perfection and not its attainment: "Fulfill you then my joy, by continuing thus minded, and

---

34. Ibid., 3:585. See also ibid., 5:448, 453.
35. Ibid., 1:407.
36. Ibid., 1:80.
37. Gatiss, ed., *Sermons*, 1:187–88. Wesley also quotes a similar range of texts and for the same purpose—the call to perfection directed to all who would follow Christ. See, for example, Outler, ed., *Sermons*, 1:402–3, 428.

labor to go on to perfection."[38] Christians who do this are "my beloved lovers of Christian perfection."[39] For Whitefield, perfection is to be longed for and pursued wholeheartedly, but it is clearly not to be experienced in this life: "lead us on perpetually *towards that perfection to which thou hast taught us to aspire*; that keeping us here in a constant imitation of thee, and peaceful union which each other, thou mayest at length bring us to that everlasting glory, which thou hast promised to all such as shall *endeavor to be perfect, even as the Father who is in heaven is perfect, . . .*"[40]

Wesley's letters and sermons are filled with the same urgings to pursue perfection and at every Conference Methodist preachers were asked: "are you *going on to perfection*? Do you expect to be *perfected in love* in this life? Are you groaning after it?"[41] Note that, unlike Whitefield, they were to expect to be made perfect. This call is found throughout Wesley's writings and is applied to all Christians, not just the preachers.[42] There is an evident optimism of grace in Wesley that is not found in the soteriological framework of Whitefield, and this arises from their theological understanding of the nature and extent of salvation provided by Christ in this present existence.[43]

The Nature of Perfection in Whitefield

Both Wesley and Whitefield agreed that humans could perfectly love and obey God prior to the fall.[44] Neither of them saw salvation as mere forgiveness and both emphasized the transforming power of the Holy Spirit in the believer's life. Yet their similarities masked a deep division between them on the actual nature of perfection and its achievability prior to death. Whitefield, in a sermon to correct the false views of perfection held by Dr. Trapp, wrote:

38. Gatiss, ed., *Sermons*, 1:145–46 (emphasis mine).

39. Ibid., 1:201.

40. Ibid., 1:187–88 (emphasis mine).

41. Rack, ed., *Methodist Societies*, 10:315. These question have been asked of every preacher (now ordination candidate) in the Methodist church since first recorded in Wesley's own conference minutes.

42. There is a very large body of evidence for this. See McEwan, *Wesley as a Pastoral Theologian*.

43. Once again, this is a topic that is beyond the scope of this chapter and here I want to focus more narrowly on those elements that directly inform their understanding of perfection. A good overview of the Reformed and Arminian positions on salvation can be found in Peterson and Williams, *Why I Am Not an Arminian*; and Walls and Dongell, *Why I Am Not a Calvinist*.

44. See Gatiss, ed., *Sermons*, 1:139–40; and Outler, ed., *Sermons*, 2:439; 1:204–5, 208–9.

"Raise up, I beseech thee, O Lord, some true pastors, who may acquaint them with the nature and *necessity of perfect righteousness*, and lead them to that love of Christian perfection which the angry-minded, pleasure-taking Doctor Trapp, labors to divert them from . . ."[45] The link between righteousness and perfection is borne out in another sermon: "To you I speak, all ye lovers and strugglers after the *perfect righteousness* of your divine Master Christ; what wonder is it, that you should be charged with enthusiasm, with folly, with fanaticism and madness?"[46] Unlike Wesley, righteousness is not seen primarily in relational terms but in character qualities and these are tied to the perfect character of God as revealed to us in Christ. As a consequence, Whitefield firmly believed that the only standard acceptable to God is perfect obedience to the moral law, because "the least deviation from the moral law, according to the covenant of works, whether in thought, word, or deed, deserves eternal death at the hand of God."[47] He made it plain that even after the disobedience recorded in Genesis 3, "they were as much under a *covenant of works* as ever. And though, after their disobedience, they were without strength; yet they were obliged not only to do, but continue to do all things, and that too in *the most perfect manner*, which the Lord had required of them."[48] Clearly, to be perfect we must offer complete obedience to the whole moral law of God, with absolutely no deviation or imperfection allowed. Such an understanding led him to state that we can never attain such a "perfect" righteousness in this life.[49]

In Whitefield's view, while a genuine transformation occurred at the moment of accepting Christ, it remained an incomplete transformation as long as we live in this present body. He did not believe that the in-being of sin was removed by the new birth, though its power was taken away: "Observe me, I say, the prevailing power of this enmity must be taken away; for the in-being of it will never be totally removed, till we bow down our heads, and give up the ghost. . . . But as for its prevailing power, it is destroyed in every soul that is truly born of God, and gradually more and more weakened as the believer grows in grace, and the Spirit of God gains a greater and greater ascendancy in the heart.[50] This impacts the daily experience of every Christian:

---

45. Gatiss, ed., *Sermons*, 1:191–92. See also ibid., 2:276, 282–83. For Trapp's position, see Maddock, "George Whitefield."

46. Gatiss, ed., *Sermons*, 1:199–200 (emphasis mine).

47. Ibid., 2:425–27.

48. Ibid., 1:265 (emphasis mine). See also ibid., 2:242–43.

49. Ibid., 1:199–200.

50. Ibid., 1:67–68. Whitefield says that Paul's testimony in Romans 7 is that of a Christian. Wesley rejected the idea that Paul was describing the normal Christian state

> After we are renewed, yet we are renewed but in part, indwelling sin continues in us, there is a mixture of corruption in every one of our duties; so that after we are converted, were Jesus Christ only to accept us according to our works, our works would damn us, for we cannot p[u]t up a prayer but it is far from that perfection which the moral law requireth. I do not know what you may think, but I can say that I cannot pray but I sin—I cannot preach to you or any others but I sin—I can do nothing without sin.[51]

This indwelling sin is a presence, a power or influence that impacts every area of life, though the deeply committed Christian can find a measure of victory over it by the power of God's grace: "Let indwelling sin be your daily burden; and not only bewail and lament, but see that you subdue it daily by the power of divine grace."[52] Whitefield's own testimony was: "no sin has *dominion* over me, yet I feel the strugglings of indwelling sin day by day."[53]

For Whitefield, perfection in this life was very much a limited reality due to the damage that has been wrought on our body and all its functions since that first sin:

> these depraved natures of ours, must necessarily undergo an *universal moral change; our understandings must be enlightened; our wills, reason, and consciences, must be renewed;* our affections must be drawn toward, and fixed upon things above; and because flesh and blood cannot inherit the kingdom of heaven, this corruptible must put on incorruption, this mortal must put on immortality. And thus old things must literally pass away, and behold all things, *even the body* as well as the faculties of the soul, must become new.[54]

It is only at the resurrection that we shall finally be delivered from indwelling sin:

> The most perfect Christian, I am persuaded, must agree, according to one of our Articles, "That the corruption of nature remains even in the regenerate; that the flesh lusteth always

---

in Romans 7:7ff; see his very strong comments in *Explanatory Notes on the New Testament* and Outler, ed., *Sermons*, 1:322, 332–33. See also Gatiss, ed., *Sermons*, 2:218–19; Baker, ed., *Letters*, 26:66.

51. Gatiss, ed., *Sermons*, 2:429.

52. Ibid., 2:228–29. See also ibid., 1:199–200; 2:428.

53. Quoted in Baker, ed., *Letters*, 26:11. This is an early testimony by Whitefield (24 March 1740), but there is no evidence he changed his position later.

54. Gatiss, ed., *Sermons*, 1:256 (emphasis mine).

> against the spirit, and the spirit against the flesh." So that believers cannot do things for God with that perfection they desire; this grieves their righteous souls [sic] day by day, and, with the holy apostle, makes them cry out, "Who shall deliver us from the body of this death!" I thank God, our Lord Jesus Christ will, but not completely before the day of our dissolution; they will the very being of sin be destroyed, and an eternal stop put to inbred, indwelling corruption.[55]

This effectively means that no human being can be perfectly righteous in this life: "Till we come up to the perfection of our heavenly father, we can never be righteous enough, much less perfectly righteous: wherefore, as in this life, men cannot attain to the perfection of their heavenly father, it follows in course that the persons here spoken to, cannot be men perfectly righteous, there being no such men existing."[56] As a result, he confirmed that he was "no friend to sinless perfection. I believe the being (though not the dominion) of sin remains in the hearts of the greatest believers."[57] It is not surprising that he would write to Wesley expressing his deepest sorrow that his friend seemed "to own a sinless perfection in this life attainable."[58] Accordingly, he told him: "I am yet persuaded, you greatly err. You have set a mark you will never arrive at, till you come to glory."[59]

The Nature of Perfection in Wesley

Not surprisingly, like Whitefield, Wesley rejected any notion of "sinless perfection," and in his Preface to his *Hymns and Sacred Poems* he listed some twenty-six Scripture passages to refute the charge.[60] He affirmed that he upheld the doctrines of the Church of England: "the *perfection* I hold is so far from being contrary to the doctrine of our Church that it is exactly the same which every clergyman prays every Sunday: 'Cleanse the thoughts of our hearts by the inspiration of thy Holy Spirit, that we may *perfectly love thee*, and *worthily magnify* thy holy name.' I mean neither more nor less than

---

55. Ibid., 2:224–25. See also ibid., 1:139–40.
56. Ibid., 1:199–200.
57. Gillies, ed., *Works*, 1:58.
58. Quoted in Baker, ed., *Letters*, 26:32. The letter from Whitefield strongly affirms his belief that sin remains in the believer till death and impacts their life. See also Higgins, "Achieving Human Perfection," 61.
59. Quoted in Baker, ed., *Letters*, 26:43. See also ibid., 26:261.
60. Cragg, ed., *Appeals to Men of Reason and Religion*, 11:339–40.

this."[61] By perfection "I mean 'perfect love', or the loving God with all our heart, so as to rejoice evermore, to pray without ceasing, and in everything to give thanks. I am convinced every believer may attain this."[62]

The phrase "perfect love" does not appear in Whitefield's writings, but it is found in Wesley's and it was a critical element in his understanding of the Christian life.[63] It is "the humble, gentle, patient love of God and man ruling all the tempers, words, and actions, the whole heart and the whole life."[64] Wesley believed that the only perfection possible in this life was to love God and neighbor with our whole being: "This is the sum of Christian perfection: *it is all comprised in that one word, love.*"[65] Such a transformative experience of love was not something that was given to the believer as a possession, but arises solely from our moment by moment relationship with Christ. This was affirmed in a letter to Joseph Benson: "Christ does not give light to the soul separate from, but in and with, Himself. . . . our perfection is not like that of a tree, which flourishes by the sap derived from its own root; but like that of a branch, which, united to the vine, bears fruit, but severed from it is 'dried up and withered.'"[66] It is the linking of love and relationship that lies at the heart of the difference between the men on the possibilities of grace in this life, and whether perfection can be experienced before death.

Wesley, like Whitefield, confessed that the being of sin remained even in those who are regenerate and they were utterly helpless to change this by themselves.[67] Only Christ can change the heart; only then is "the leprosy cleansed . . . the evil root, the carnal mind, is destroyed and inbred sin subsists no more. But if there be no such *second change*, if there be *no instantaneous deliverance after justification*, if there be none but a gradual

---

61. Davies, ed., *Methodist Societies*, 9:409. See also ibid., 9:49–53; Cragg, ed., *Appeals to Men of Reason and Religion*, 11:108–17.

62. Telford, ed., *Letters*, 4:10. See also ibid., 4:157–58.

63. See Outler, ed., *Sermons*, 2:134–35; Baker, ed., *Letters*, 25:151; Telford, ed., *Letters*, 4:71; 5:78; 6:45; 7:369; 8:14, 184, 188. Wesley also refers to "holy love," and "pure love" in connection with our relationship with God. The references to love in connection with the Christian life are substantial; see McEwan, *Life of God in the Soul*.

64. Outler, ed., *Sermons*, 2:187. See also Telford, ed., *Letters*, 5:299, 341–42.

65. Outler, ed., *Sermons*, 3:74 (emphasis mine). Outler mentions in n. 19 that there are more than fifty summaries of "perfection" as love in Wesley's writings. Some of the key Scripture passages are Rom 12:1; Gal 5:22–23; Eph 4:24; Phil 2:5; Col 3:10; 1 Thess 5:23; 1 Pet 1:15, 2:5. See ibid., 3:74–76. See also Telford, ed., *Letters*, 6:335; ibid., 7:206–7.

66. Telford, ed., *Letters*, 5:204.

67. Outler, ed., *Sermons*, 1:339–45.

work of God (that there is a gradual work none denies) then we must be content, as well as we can, to remain full of sin till death."[68]

This is another critical point. Wesley believed that God would deal with in-being sin (the root) just as thoroughly as he did the sinful acts (the fruit) through a subsequent work of grace.[69] Wesley's confidence rested in his belief that what God had promised in his word, he would surely fulfil: "For [God] cannot mock his helpless creatures, calling us to receive what he never intends to give."[70] He emphasized that "Through him [Christ] I cannot only overcome, but expel all the enemies of my soul. Through him I can 'love the Lord my God with all my heart, mind, soul, and strength'; yea, and walk in holiness and righteousness before him all the days of my life."[71] In response to faith "the heart is cleansed from all sin, and filled with pure love to God and man. But even that love increases more and more, till we 'grow up in all things unto him that is our head', 'till we attain the measure of the stature of the fullness of Christ.'"[72] This fullness of love Wesley called "Christian Perfection" and it is defined in terms of our present human condition, not our condition before the fall or after the resurrection.[73]

Given the damage that sin has done to the human race, he agreed with Whitefield that we can no longer keep the original covenant of works, requiring absolute obedience and perfect performance. Unlike Whitefield, he believed that God of love has now offered us a covenant of grace that suits the realities of the present human condition.

> Adam in Paradise was able to apprehend *all* things distinctly, and to *judge truly* concerning them; therefore it was his duty so to do. But no man living *is* now *able* to do this; therefore neither is it the duty of any man now living. Neither is there any man now in the body who does or can walk in this instance by that rule which was bound upon Adam. Can anything be more plain than this—that Adam *could*, that I *cannot* avoid mistaking? Can anything be plainer than this—if he *could* avoid it, he *ought*? or

---

68. Ibid., 1:346 (emphasis mine).

69. See Smith, "Wesley and Whitefield," 67–69, for the early historical background.

70. Outler, ed., *Sermons*, 3:76–77. Wesley listed such texts as Deut 30:6; Matt 19:19; 22:37; Heb 10:16; Eph 4:21, 23–24; 1 Thess 5:23; Ps 130:8; Matt 1:21; Heb 7:25; Ezek 36:25–27. See also Outler, ed., *Sermons*, 2:483, 410–12, 23–32; 3:78.

71. Ibid., 1:350.

72. Ibid., 3:204.

73. This is dealt with in some detail in "Thoughts on Christian Perfection," "Further Thoughts upon Christian Perfection," and especially "A Plain Account of Christian Perfection." Chilcote and Collins, eds., *Doctrinal and Controversial Treatises II*, 13:57–80, 95–131, and 132–91. See also Noble, *Holy Trinity*.

> than this—If I *cannot*, I *ought not*? I mean it is not my duty: for the clear reason that no one can do the impossible. Nothing in the Sermon [on the Mount] or the Law contradicts this.[74]

This is confirmed in Wesley's understanding of Paul's teaching in 1 Thessalonians 5:23: "As if he [Paul] had said, 'Ye shall enjoy as high a degree of holiness as is *consistent with your present state of pilgrimage* . . . loving him with all your heart (which is the sum of all perfection.'"[75] For God to hold us to a standard of performance we can no longer achieve would be a violation of love: "Faith working or animated by love is all that God now requires of man. He *has* substituted (not sincerity, but) love, in the room of angelic perfection."[76] Both covenants are suited to the capacities and abilities of their subjects, with a corresponding responsibility and accountability. That is why we always need the merits of Christ's death

> for innumerable violations of the Adamic as well as the angelic law. It is well therefore for us that we are not now under these, but under the law of love. 'Love is now the fulfilling of the law', which is given to fallen man. This is now, with respect to us, the perfect law. But even against this, through the present weakness of our understanding, we are continually liable to transgress. Therefore every man living needs the blood of atonement, or he could not stand before God.[77]

Wesley acknowledged that our minds, emotions, and bodies were impacted by sin and therefore could not possibly function as they did in the original creation. He agreed that we cannot be free from mistakes, wrong judgments, wrong practice, wrong tempers, or passions while in the body.

> We willingly allow, and continually declare, there is no such perfection in this life as implies either a dispensation from doing good and attending all the ordinances of God; or a freedom from ignorance, mistake, temptation, and a thousand infirmities necessarily connected with flesh and blood.[78]

---

74. Telford, ed., *Letters*, 4:98. See also ibid., 4:155.

75. Outler, ed., *Sermons*, 3:179 (emphasis mine). Wesley was careful to clarify that he did not preach either angelic or adamic perfection; see ibid., 2:405–6, 74, 81–82; 3:73, 159–62; Telford, ed., *Letters*, 5:255.

76. Jackson, ed., *Works*, 11:416. See also Telford, ed., *Letters*, 4:155.

77. Outler, ed., *Sermons*, 3:73–74. See also Outler, ed., *Sermons*, 2:100–102; Ward and Heitzenrater, ed., *Journals and Diaries*, 21:337–338; Jackson, ed., *Works*, 14:328–29.

78. Davies, ed., *Methodist Societies*, 9:53. See also Jackson, ed., *Works*, 14:329.

He warned that "some have vehemently maintained; yea, have affirmed that none are perfected in love unless they are so far perfected in understanding that all wandering thoughts are done away; unless not only every affection and temper be holy, and just, and good, but every individual thought which arises in the mind be wise and regular."[79] Wesley said this was an unscriptural notion.[80] He agreed that these were all violations of the Adamic law and thus sin under those conditions; however, we are not now under Adamic law, but the law of love (Rom 13:10) and here sin was defined as "a voluntary transgression of a known law" of God.[81]

> Nothing is sin, strictly speaking, but a voluntary transgression of a known law of God. Therefore every voluntary breach of the law of love is sin; and nothing else, if we speak properly. To strain the matter farther is only to make way for Calvinism. There may be ten thousand wandering thoughts and forgetful intervals without any breach of love, though not without transgressing the Adamic law. But Calvinists would fain confound these together. Let love fill your heart, and it is enough![82]

This required Wesley to distinguish between "sin properly so called" and "involuntary transgressions" or infirmities.[83] The former were willfully chosen, and therefore culpable and brought condemnation; the latter were not willfully chosen and consequently not culpable and did not bring condemnation.[84] He agreed that both sins and infirmities were deviations from the perfect will of God and so needed Christ's gracious atonement, but he was insistent that the latter brought no condemnation: "There is no guilt, because there is no choice."[85] He felt the Scriptures gave no grounds for believing God condemned us for things beyond our power to change.[86] This is based

---

79. Outler, ed., *Sermons*, 2:126. See Outler's introduction in ibid., 2:125–26. He mentions the role of two later sermons in qualifying Wesley's views of perfection: "On Sin in Believers"; and "The Repentance of Believers." See also Goodwin, "Setting Perfection Too High."

80. Ibid., 2:134–35.

81. Ibid., 3:79.

82. Telford, ed., *Letters*, 5:322. See also ibid., 5:255, 313, 315,

83. For further insight on Wesley's understanding of sin and infirmities, see Peckham, *Wesley and Human Infirmities*. For material on Wesley's understanding in the light of current developments in neuroscience and psychology, see Armistead, *Wesleyan Theology*, 129–42, 177–92; Noble, *Holy Trinity*, 97–127.

84. In particular, see Outler, ed., *Sermons*, 1:317–52. See also ibid., 2:103; Jackson, ed., *Works*, 9:281.

85. Outler, ed., *Sermons*, 1:241. See also Jackson, ed., *Works*, 11:394–97.

86. Outler, ed., *Sermons*, 1:242–43.

on his conviction that there must be personal culpability before we can be held accountable. A critical development that hinges, at least in part, on his developing understanding of the centrality of love, is the distinction he made between intention and performance. The person may have a perfect intention, but the performance might be marred due to the realities of present bodily existence. If God sees the intention, then is the person condemned simply because of faulty execution? Wesley, given his understanding of God's love, did not think that was the case. Wesley sought to demonstrate from Scripture that there was no condemnation for "sins of infirmity" due to the present limitations of our human condition:

> Christian perfection therefore does not imply ... an exemption either from ignorance or mistake, or infirmities or temptations. Indeed, it is only another term for holiness.... Thus everyone that is perfect is holy, and everyone that is holy is, in the Scripture sense, perfect. Yet we may ... observe that neither in this respect is there any *absolute perfection* on earth.... So that how much soever any man hath attained, or in how high a degree soever he is perfect, he hath still need to "grow in grace," and daily to advance in the knowledge and love of God his Saviour.[87]

As long as we are in the body, mistakes will arise from defects of knowledge, understanding and judgment, but they need no longer arise from a defect of love. He was careful to maintain that we never achieve a state of grace in which we no longer needed the priestly work of Christ: "we should still need His Spirit, and consequently His intercession for the continuance of that love from moment to moment. Beside, we should still be encompassed with infirmities and liable to mistakes, from which words or actions might follow, even though the heart was all love, which were not exactly right. Therefore in all these respects we should still have need of Christ's priestly office."[88]

Wesley believed that 1 John 1:5-6, 9; 3:7-10; 4:17 all confirmed that Christians can experience "perfect love" in this life, not just at the moment of death.[89] To set perfection to high (flawless perfection) was to effectively destroy it as a valid hope for all who were in Christ now. While Whitefield is not specifically in view, this observation fits perfectly with the heart of the disagreement between the two friends:

---

87. Ibid., 2:104-5.
88. Telford, ed., *Letters*, 3:380.
89. Outler, ed., *Sermons*, 2:119-20 (emphasis mine). See also ibid., 2:117-18. His case is supported by extensive Scripture quotation. See Jackson, ed., *Works*, 8:279.

> I have frequently observed, . . . that the opposers of perfection are more vehement against it when it is placed in this view than in any other whatsoever. They will allow all you say of the love of God and man, of the mind which was in Christ, of the fruit of the spirit, of the image of God, of universal holiness, of entire self-dedication, of sanctification in spirit, soul, and body; . . . All this they will allow, so we will allow sin, a little sin, to remain in us till death.[90]

Conclusion

John Wesley and George Whitefield have much in common in their theological understanding, ministry practice, and Christian lifestyle. There is little doubt that a casual listener to their preaching would not discern a great deal of difference in either their topics or their language. Both men essentially agree on the nature of human life as created by God and as it will be post-resurrection; it is the possibilities of life in this present age that are disputed.

Whitefield's soteriological framework rested on God's love for humanity and our response to that love. The evidence of having received God's love is primarily obedience to God's law as revealed in Christ and in Scripture. Because he is convinced that God offers no accommodation for our present bodily existence, this obedience must be as perfect now as it was before sin entered the world. He believed that God's standard for us has not changed and it requires absolute perfection in word, deed, and thought. Any deviation from that flawless standard is sin and will bring condemnation unless the person repents. No matter the degree of grace experienced, the presence of indwelling sin remains and impacts every area of life so that even the most victorious Christian sins in some form or other every day. They should seek to reduce these failures as much as possible through grace and the power of the Spirit—so the call to perfection is genuine and must not be neglected. However, it is a call to pursue perfection; it will not be experienced this side of death due to the present corruption of our understanding, will, reason, and conscience.

Wesley's soteriological framework also rested on God's love for humanity and our response to that love. Unlike Whitefield, he believed that a loving God makes an accommodation for our present bodily existence and what is now possible for us due to the consequences of sin. The interdependent relationship of love and freedom leads Wesley to conclude that

---

90. Outler, ed., *Sermons*, 3:85.

culpability is intimately linked with our intentions and willful choices. Consequently, God makes a gracious allowance for the present limitations of our understanding, will, reason and conscience and the impact these have on our performance. God still has an absolute requirement for us, but it is for love and relationships, not flawless obedience to the law. The evidence of having received God's love lies primarily in the heart, in terms of personal trust, rather than outward obedience; Christian perfection is to love God with our whole being and our neighbor as ourselves. In this framework sin is, strictly speaking, a voluntary (willful) breach of the law of love. Breaches of the relationship may occur without the concurrence of the will, and they are strictly speaking an infirmity, and do not bring condemnation. All such imperfections need the atoning work of Christ, and a grace-enabled, whole-hearted endeavor to do better in the future. For Wesley, such a perfection is possible by divine grace and human openness, receptivity and ever-deeper trust.

For Whitefield, the only perfection acceptable before God is a perfected perfection—a flawless performance of every last requirement of the law. For Wesley, the perfection acceptable before God is a perfecting perfection—a dynamic relationship of love that shows itself in character transformation and service to God and neighbor. In the end, it comes down to a decision about the essential nature of our life with God—performance (Whitefield) or passion (Wesley)? Does God require the same level of performance now as he did in the original creation, or does he make an allowance for the reality of present bodily existence? This is the crucial point on which his whole claim to Christian perfection as a reality in this life stands or falls. Depending on how you evaluate their theological perspectives, you will find either Wesley's or Whitefield case the more convincing. Whatever our judgment on their respective theologies, both men sought with all their hearts to lead a holy life, be faithful in God's service and minister the gospel to all who would hear them.

6

Federalist Brothers

The Shared Covenantal Substructure of Whitefield and Wesley's Theology

JARED HOOD

Introduction

THAT JOHN WESLEY ADHERED to federal, covenant theology, or something akin to it, is beginning to be appreciated by scholars, whereas the federalism of George Whitefield is assumed, not often explored, and sometimes taken to contradict his evangelistic fervor. This study compares and contrasts the covenantal theologies of these two superlative eighteenth-century evangelists. To state the case at the outset, Wesley and Whitefield were brothers in arms, federalist friends, despite their infamous Reformed-Arminian rivalry. It was not only evangelism that bound them together, nor a basic Protestant orthodoxy, but an even deeper intellectual or hermeneutical synergy.

Focus

Since Whitefield's theology is more easily quantifiable,[1] whereas Wesley was the more deliberately-creative theologian, this study places an inevitable emphasis on Wesley over Whitefield. Furthermore, there is the incongruity of an Arminian theologian adhering to what appears to be Reformed federalism. Recent scholarship has Wesley incorporating federalism (either Reformed, or an Arminianized iteration) seamlessly and consciously into an

---

1. Hood, "The Methodical George Whitefield," 311–22; Hood, "I Never Read Calvin," 7–20; Hood, "Whitefield: The Heart of an Evangelist," 164–79.

Arminian system, but this needs further exploration. The suggestion of this studyrather is that Wesley adopted a covenantal structure comparable with that of Whitefield, yet was unaware of the implications, and was unaware of the extent to which it was Reformed covenantalism. Comparisons between Wesley and Arminius will indicate that Wesley's covenantal thought was less connected with Arminian covenantalism.[2]

Wesley had a Reformed-Arminian rivalry with Whitefield, but the proposal is that the rivalry also existed in himself. This produced points of tension that surface in his well-known distinctives on justification, universal atonement, the servant-son metaphor,[3] perfection, and assurance, although these points cannot be explored in detail here. The question will be whether the substructure or superstructure of his theology won out. The impact of the substructure is seen as he gradually moved to moderate some of his more controversial teachings. His covenant theology[4] does not appear to have modified his core doctrine of the universal atonement, even though the two are often regarded as incompatible, but it can explain his movement on justification and some of the complexity in his notion of servanthood, and it could also alleviate a typical Reformed criticism that Wesley placed too much emphasis on the individual over against divine sovereignty.

The Difficulty of the Wesleyan Question

Determining the nature of Wesley's covenantalism is complex. Firstly, Wesley's comments on the topic were brief. Brevity is not a telling observation. Whitefield's comments were also sparse, but federalism was pervasive for him. Secondly, federalist and Arminian covenantal theology can be misunderstood.

---

2. On whether Wesley had read Arminius, see Stanglin and McCall, *Jacob Arminius*, 193–94; Gunter, "John Wesley," 65–82. On his covenant theology in particular, Outler has Wesley drawing on Ames, Perkins, and especially the Westminster Confession. Outler, ed., *Sermons*, 1:203n2. Rodes, *From Faith to Faith*, 37–58, takes up the matter of ancestry at length. Cf. Monk, *John Wesley*, 99, "Wesley follows . . . Ames . . . and . . . Isaac Ambrose"; ibid., 106, prioritizes the role of Susanna.

3. Rodes, *From Faith to Faith*, 12, takes the servant-son metaphor as the chief evidence of the influence of covenant theology upon Wesley. The difficulty is that Wesley's servant idea crosses the Old and New Testament divide, and so is not a reflection of Wesley's view of the nature of the old covenant.

4. On the terms "covenant theology" and "federalism," the former is embracive of Reformed theological perspectives on covenant, including inceptive beliefs in the sixteenth century. "Federalism" is used as a sub-set of covenant theology, with its clearer view of the headship of Adam and Christ. Of the eighteenth century, the distinction is somewhat trivial. Arminius's perspective is termed covenantal rather than covenant theology.

Federalism has a deep commitment to pact and conditionality (over against the stereotype of covenantal unconditionality), so at the level of covenantal theology alone, Arminian and Reformed coventantalism look similar.[5] The mere presence of conditionality is not determinative.

Thirdly, there are more options than are sometimes considered. Vickers sees in Wesley an Arminian covenantal theology.[6] Rodes sees a Reformed system consciously adapted to Arminian ends.[7] Could he have held to a variant Reformed scheme such as Amyraldianism?[8] These initially appear to be markedly different conclusions, although on closer inspection, each posits substantial Reformed covenantal influence in Wesley's thought. They also portray Wesley as consistent and self-aware.[9] But to what degree was he conscious of the real nature of his position?

Procedure

Whitefield's more straightforward covenant theology will be used to elucidate Wesley's position, and Wesley will also be read in the light of Arminius. The following understanding of federalism's distinctions will be used for evaluation, particularly points iii–v:

---

5. The broad similarities between Arminian and Reformed theology leads Reist, "Theologies of Grace," 26–40, to argue that Wesley and Whitefield were not as divided as they thought they were. All he really shows is that one was Arminian and one was Reformed.

6. Vickers, "Wesley's Theological Emphases," 192, on the English Arminian adaptation of the classical Reformed covenant of grace, says, "Wesley brought to full expression the two-fold Arminian emphasis on free grace and holiness."

7. Rodes, *From Faith to Faith*, 8, points out that Outler and Noble both acknowledge a connection between Wesley and covenant theology, but leave it unexplored. Rodes provides several reasons why so many have failed to see the relationship.

8. Adamthwaite, *Through the Christian Year*, 236, has briefly suggested it of Charles Wesley, on the basis of the inclusion of a treatise by Daniel Brevint in the 1746 collection of Communion hymns. "[I]t is quite possible that Wesley had read more widely in the Saumur theology . . . I cannot prove this." The brothers betray no concern with the order of decrees—see below.

9. Ironically, while some claim Wesley to the federalist camp, others believe that Whitefield was compromised by Arminianism in his free offer of the gospel. Of the free offer, Packer says, "Well, Calvinists do that too!" (Packer, *Honouring the People of God*, 215). Packer called Wesley a "confused Calvinist," whereas Jerry Walls sees Wesley as coherent and the Reformed as confused: Walls and Dongell, *Why I Am Not a Calvinist*, 154; Walls, "John Wesley on Predestination and Election," 619.

i. Theology proper: belief in the hiddenness or incomprehensibility of God, who can only be known if he condescends to reveal or impart himself.

ii. Emphasis: the insistence upon the centrality of the covenant, particularly with regard to hermeneutics and soteriology.

iii. Hermeneutics: the Old and New Testaments are held to be a unity.

iv. Federal headship: Adam and Christ are seen as the heads of fallen and redeemed humanity respectively, one disobedient for all, and the other obedient for all.

v. Bilateralism, or law-grace interplay: divine sovereignty and human responsibility are held in tension, with an emphasis on the absolute necessity of grace for salvation, to the exclusion of all human merit, yet without denying the necessity of works and the presence of "conditions" in the covenant.

vi. Terminology: the language of the covenants of works and grace, and/or their equivalents, is employed.

vii. Reformed: all of the above exist within the Reformed system of theology.[10]

The procedure is not to work through the list, but to correlate Whitefield and Wesley to the federalist covenants each in turn, in this way: the covenant of redemption (which is not mentioned in the above list, since it was not integral to federalism from its inception), the covenant of works, and the covenant of grace in the Old Testament and New Testament.

The Covenant of Redemption

Whitefield reveled in the covenant of redemption.[11] Whitefield held union with Christ—or more specifically, relationship with Christ—to be both foundational and the apex of Christianity, so there was congruity with the eternal, intra-Trinitarian relationship. The Christian enters into

---

10. The list is the author's own, but each point can be discerned from the chapter on covenant (chapter 7) in the Westminster Confession of Faith. See Karlberg, *Covenant Theology in the Reformed Perspective*, 111–22. Van Til rather saw the covenant of redemption as foundational to covenant theology, though this is historically problematic. Van Til, "Covenant Theology," 240–41.

11. "God . . . hath let me see more into the covenant of redemption between the Father and the Son," Gillies, ed., *Works*, 1:287; 6:199.

a relationship that had existed through all eternity at a level beyond the Christian's comprehension (so there is no tinge of theosis).

Leaving aside the debate as to how he moved into his Reformed views, this "everlasting covenant," as he usually spoke of it, also accorded well with his doctrine of predestination, putting a personal face (faces) on the doctrine. It also connected with one of his evangelistic emphases, on immediate and entire assurance following conversion. Those who are converted have the Spirit, for faith comes only from the Spirit, but undergirding this is the eternal, divine commitment. The covenant of redemption says to the convert that God is on his or her side. Although the covenant of redemption is arguably a lesser-known doctrine among evangelicals today, it was vital to one of the fathers of evangelicalism.

> Dear Sir, get acquainted more and more with electing love; study the covenant of redemption, and see how GOD loved you with an everlasting love. This will cause you to glory only in the LORD, and to pass through the valley of the shadow of death, with a full assurance of faith; knowing that CHRIST hath engaged to lodge you safe in eternal glory.[12]

This doctrine brought the only complete, covenantal divergence between Wesley and Whitefield. Wesley prioritized supernaturally enabled free will. On account of prevenient grace, people are free to choose the salvation that God offers. Therefore, reprobation, the corollary of predestination, is anathema, for it says that some cannot choose.[13] Wesley is so adamant, that he says that the Bible would be in error if it taught reprobation—a surprising comment from a biblicist.[14] Rejecting reprobation, Wesley necessarily rejected predestination and the eternal covenant. Wesley rejected predestination "calmly" and at length. The covenant of redemption, however, is summarily dismissed. No time is allocated to sifting through the proof-texts.

The irony is that Arminius embraced the doctrine, and was positive about predestination, too. On these points, Arminius was more Reformed than Wesley, as it were. Both men had the same fundamental argument: predestination is based on prescience. For Arminius, this meant he could speak about predestination at length, without feeling theologically threatened.

12. Ibid., 1:269.

13. For the nature of Wesley's Arminianism, see McGonigle, *Sufficient Saving Grace*, and for his view on the five points of Calvinism, see Poole-Connor, *Evangelicalism*, 153–59, 172–75.

14. Chilcote and Collins, eds., *Doctrinal and Controversial Treatises II*, 13:317. Monk, *John Wesley*, 102, suggests that Wesley only succeeded in moving the problem of a discriminating God back from election to prevenient grace. Why do some resist? "[H]as God endowed men equally with prevenient grace?"

Arminius saw correlation between a free pact in eternity, based on prescience of human belief, and the conditional covenant of grace. Wesley still spoke about predestination, but his predominant language was of rejection. He evidenced little direct contact with Arminius. As an English Arminian, Wesley's predestinarianism was a reaction against classical Reformed theology rather than an adoption of continental Arminianism.

The Covenant of Works

Whitefield's mind was never far from Genesis 2–3. His preaching constantly touched on the historical fall and its theological and covenantal counterparts, total depravity and the covenant of works. The full title, "covenant of works," is a term that Whitefield only used in his sermons, but it is used repeatedly.

Whitefield held to an uncomplicated form of the covenant of works, devoid of speculation or even of defensive argumentation. Adam could have obeyed and attained eternal life—a perennially controversial point, but never questioned or debated by Whitefield—but instead disobeyed. Adam's actions were on behalf of humankind, and so by obedience, all would have been rewarded, and by his disobedience, the whole world has been plunged into judgment. Thus, for example, he wrote:

> And so infinite was the condescension of the high and lofty One who inhabiteth eternity, that although he might have insisted on the everlasting obedience of him and his posterity; yet he was pleased to oblige himself, by a covenant, or agreement, made with his own creatures, upon condition of an unsinning obedience, to give them immortality and eternal life.[15]

The correlation with the *Westminster Confession of Faith* 7.1–2 is striking, even in the use of vocabulary: "condescension," "posterity," "pleased," "creature/s," "upon condition of ... obedience."

Whitefield seldom deals with complexities, but on the nature of merit in the covenant, the above quote gives an indication of his thought. The merit of works was a covenantal merit, and apart from God's covenanting "condescension" would have attained nothing.

The covenant of works gives the federalist structure of the two heads of humanity. Adam was the "head, the representative of all his seed."[16]

---

15. Gillies, ed., *Works*, 5:233, 255, 375–76. See also ibid., 5:23.

16. Whitefield, *Additional Sermons*, 261. In an early sermon on justification, he speaks of Adam as a "Publick Person, as the common Representative of all Mankind," in

Christ was the second Adam, who not only undoes Adam's sin but does what Adam failed to do. Christ obeyed and attained eternal life for the elect. "In this body he formed a complete obedience to the law of GOD; whereby he in our stead fulfilled the covenant of works . . . "[17] The covenant of works thus explained humankind's problem, and the covenant of grace gave the solution.

For Whitefield, every person in a sense repeats Adam's failure. It is not that each person is a second Adam, given the promise of life upon obedience. Still, each person seeks to gain life for him or herself, and fails. The "old" covenant thus now only curses.[18] Whitefield had no misgiving with this one-for-many corporate concept. Not only did it provide for salvation in Christ, but it simply was a reality from the beginning of history. It was thus to be preached, and, indeed, Whitefield expected converts not only to confess themselves sinners in their own right, but sinners in Adam.[19]

Wesley also affirmed the covenant of works.[20] He rarely used the full term, but the concept was widespread,[21] being part of a construct that shaped his thinking—a defining hermeneutics. Leviticus 18:5, "he shall live by them," could not have signified salvation by works, since the only legal principle leading to life was in the Garden.

> They should follow God's commands . . . because their life and happiness depend upon it. And though in strictness, and according to the covenant of works they could not challenge life for so doing, except their obedience was universal, perfect, constant and perpetual, and therefore no man since the fall could be justified by the law, yet by the covenant of grace this life is promised to all that obey God's commands sincerely.[22]

---

the "first covenant." Whitefield, *Sermons on Several Practical Subjects*, 12, 15.

17. Gillies, ed., *Works*, 5:24.

18. Ibid., 5:230; Whitefield, *Additional Sermons*, 275; Gillies, ed., *Works*, 6:34, 230.

19. Whitefield, *Additional Sermons*, 277.

20. Wesley did not deny original sin. See McCall, "But a Heathen Still," 148–51; Oden, *John Wesley's Scriptural Christianity*, 159. McCall, "But a Heathen Still," 149, highlights that "Wesley defends the federalism of the Westminster Catechism," speaking of the Larger Catechism as "a very excellent composition." See Maddox, *Works*, 12:240.

21. The substance of the covenants of works and grace is present in Sermon 5, *Justification by Faith*. Six uses of the full title—the majority—are in Sermon 6, *Righteousness of Faith*. See Outler, ed., *Sermons*, 1:181–99, 200–216.

22. Wesley, *Explanatory Notes on the Old Testament*, Leviticus 18:5, 1288. The same argument is made in Sermon 6. See also Sermon 12 (1746): the Christian has joy in obedience, "and yet not in keeping them as if we were thereby to fulfil the terms of the *covenant of works* . . . But we rejoice in walking according to the *covenant of grace*,"

This is in contradistinction to Arminius's covenantalism.[23] Arminius drew a distinction between the value of the tree of life itself, and the symbolism of the tree. In itself, the tree had some power. As long as Adam ate it (with an obedience "far inferior" to obedience to natural law), he had continuing physical life (not eternal life) in the garden. Symbolically, it indicated that, upon fuller obedience to the moral law, Adam would have eternal life.[24] There is thus a distinction between outward/legal and inward/real obedience. The distinction is useful when approaching the rest of the Old Testament. The bulk of the Old Testament focuses upon legal obedience.

The ideas of outward and inward obedience and two levels of life in the Garden were not replicated in Wesley. He did seem to hold to the view that the tree gives continuing life rather than a higher state of life. However, he refused to make a substantial distinction between the obedience leading to "eternal continuance" of physical life in the garden and to "life everlasting." Obedience leading to the former is the same obedience that results in the latter, thus cleverly holding together two views that are sometimes seen as dichotomous.[25]

Holding to the doctrine in this way created a conflict within Wesley on original sin and Christ's imputation. He affirmed original sin (with ameliorating prevenient grace, the "first" moral salve applied to the will[26]), yet he wanted to avoid a person's fate being dependent upon another, for this infringes personal responsibility and free will.

> "But with regard to parents and their posterity, God assures us children 'shall not die for the iniquity of their fathers.'" No,

---

Outler, ed., *Sermons*, 1:312; "And who ever was under the covenant of works? None but Adam before the fall," Outler, ed., *Sermons*, 2:27; Jackson, ed., *Works*, 8:289.

23. As a small point that demonstrates the historical separation between Wesley and Arminius, the covenant for Arminius was designed to secure worshippers for God—not an emphasis found in Wesley. Arminius, *Works*, Oration I, The Object of Theology, 1:8, 10–11; ibid., Disputation XXXIX, On the Will, 1:73.

24. Arminius, *Works*, Disputation XXIX, On the Covenant, 2:54. The same views are stated in Disputation LXI, On the Sacraments, 2:118.

25. Wesley, *Explanatory Notes on the Old Testament*, Genesis 2, 811: "[A]ssuring him of the continuance of life and happiness upon condition of his perseverance in innocency and obedience." Sermon 6: "This law or covenant (usually called the covenant of *works*) given by God to man in paradise, required an obedience perfect in all its parts, entire and wanting nothing, as the condition of his eternal continuance in the holiness and happiness wherein he was created." Outler, ed., *Sermons*, 1:204. Entire obedience needed to continue "until the days of his trial should be ended, and he should be confirmed in life everlasting." Ibid., 1:205.

26. "The first wish to please God," Outler, ed., *Sermons*, 3:203.

not eternally. I believe none ever did or ever will die eternally, merely for the sin of our first father.[27]

Free will was not his most fundamental principle, but revulsion at unconditional reprobation.[28] He feared a sovereign God who divided people into eternal categories, not even upon prescience of individual human action.

The reservation about the corporate nature of the covenant of works is found in what Arminius said about its promise of life. For Arminius, if Adam had obeyed, each individual still would themselves have come into the covenant of works and have to obey individually to eternal life. In a comment that also begins to elucidate how Arminius saw the Old Testament and its ceremonial requirements, he wrote:

> We are of opinion that, if our first parents had remained in their integrity by obedience performed to both these laws, God would have acted with their posterity by the same compact, that is, by their yielding obedience to the moral law inscribed on their hearts, and to some symbolical or ceremonial law; though we dare not specially make a similar affirmation, respecting the tree of the knowledge of good and evil.[29]

Thus, both wanted to retain the place of the individual, notwithstanding federal headship.[30] Both also had a dialectic, though, so that both affirmed at least an aspect of that which they seemed to deny. Arminius went on to say that "the gifts Adam would have received would be for his posterity too . . . the gifts conferred on them should be transmitted to their posterity."[31] There are thus gifts passed on, but individual responsibility was still affirmed.

Wesley, on the negative side of the equation, knew that the Canaanites suffered because of Ham.[32] The one disobeyed for the many. Wesley wanted to maintain individual responsibility, but in his treatise, *On Original Sin*, he

27. Maddox, ed., *Doctrinal and Controversial Treatises*, 12:307.

28. Adapting Walls, "John Wesley on Predestination and Election," 620. Chilcote and Collins, eds., *Doctrinal and Controversial Treatises II*, 13:290: "You may drive me . . . unless I will contradict myself . . . to own a measure of free will in every man . . . And . . . I can drive you . . . to own unconditional reprobation."

29. Arminius, *Works*, Disputation XXIX, On the Covenant, 2:54.

30. Stanglin and McCall, *Jacob Arminius*, 194, rather believes that Arminius affirmed the corruption of original sin but denied guilt, for guilt attaches to what individuals actually do, whereas Wesley affirmed the Westminster Confession on the role of Adam *in toto*. McGonigle, *Sufficient Saving Grace*, 159, has it as above, though, that Wesley did not have "a doctrine of imputed guilt as in classic Calvinism," despite his "Augustinian understanding of original sin."

31. Arminius, *Works*, Disputation XXIX, On the Covenant, 2:58.

32. Maddox, ed., *Doctrinal and Controversial Treatises*, 12:308.

struggled to resolve the problem.³³ Against the charge that it is unfair that all die in Adam, he did say that "all may recover through the *Second Adam* whatever they lost through the *first*."³⁴ No one loses "but by his own choice" (in the context of prevenient grace, not just a free offer).³⁵ In this sense, no one dies eternally "merely" because of Adam. Still, those that do die eternally die partly because of Adam, and all still die temporally and spiritually because of Adam. That there is subsequent culpability from resisting grace does not solve the first problem. All people still suffer for a fault not their own. Whether made in a Reformed or Arminian context, this is not a strong defense of free will or of God's justice.

Wesley settled on discrediting the federalist language while accepting something akin to the substance.

> But as neither "representative" nor federal head are Scripture words, it is not worth while to contend for them. The thing I mean is this: the state of all mankind did so far depend on Adam that by his fall they all fell into sorrow and pain and death, spiritual and temporal.³⁶

Wesley made this comment in response to what he saw as the Pelagianism of John Taylor. Whilst the first sentence might seem to be an insubstantial concession, it is not without effect.³⁷ It left Wesley with a less precise expression of the relationship of Adam to humankind. He still used "representative," but what does "depend" signify?³⁸ He appears as a man struggling with the

---

33. Bryant, "Original Sin," 535, points out that in *True Origin of the Soul* in the *Arminian Magazine*, 1783, "Wesley used traducianism as a way of explaining how humanity shares in the corruption of Adam without focusing on the guilt . . . we participated in body and soul, in both the guilt and consequences of Adam's sin." The imputation of guilt was still by Adam as federal head, though, as is imputation in relationship to Christ. Thus, the problem was not resolved by traducianism, and Wesley still hesitated to say that any dies for the sin of Adam.

34. Maddox, ed., *Doctrinal and Controversial Treatises*, 12:327. See also ibid., 12:215.

35. Outler, ed., *Semons*, 1:434.

36. Maddox, *Doctrinal and Controversial Treatises*, 12:327.

37. Arguably he evidenced that he still struggled against original sin as late as 1784, when he omitted the article on original sin from his abridgement of the Thirty-Nine Articles. Contrary to Maddox, *Responsible Grace*, 75, it is not that he rejected an earlier error of adopting original sin, but, per McCall ("But a Heathen Still," 150), he does not want original sin to be affirmed apart from affirming individual judgment for resisting grace (in the context of the doctrine of prevenient grace).

38. A similar imprecision is seen in the 1757 *Doctrine of Original Sin*. "Adam *alone or single* was, in some sense, on trial for all mankind." What is meant by "in some sense"? However, he is clear about the legal and existential outcome. "Adam fell, and hereby the sentence of death came on him and all his posterity . . . death, the penalty of

train of his own logic, unable to address it at its point of origin, but resisting the destination. He certainly knew how close he was to Calvinism, being even within a hair's breadth, as he put it, but he had to struggle to keep the gap from being closed.[39]

Despite reservations, Wesley was committed to original sin, because he knew that Adam was a type of Christ, and Christ brings salvation to others. Swimming in this Reformed stream (he cited Hervey, Watts, and Boston's *Fourfold State* throughout his interaction with Taylor), he inevitably ended up affirming a version of the imputed righteousness of Christ,[40] but it needed qualifying. Christ was the "representative for all mankind,"[41] just as Adam was head for all. The very heart of the federalist scheme is the efficacy of the representatives' actions, so that Christ is the head only of the elect, but the universalism of Arminianism and Wesleyanism detract from this parallel. Christ is really only the potential representative (prevenient grace excepted)—federalism in prevaricated terms but not in power.

Wesley struggled with imputed righteousness, for much the same reasons that he struggled with original sin and unconditional predestination: it functioned as a disincentive to pursue holiness. Still, his covenant theology meant he was unable to resist a form of it. He eventually showed his qualified acceptance of the doctrine in the well-known sermon of 1765, *The Lord our Righteousness*.[42] The sermon holds no discussion of covenantal issues, which might seem to counter the argument that federalism was driving Wesley's theological development. Still, federalism was a key issue in the righteousness debate, as evidenced in the significant discussion of the covenants of works and grace in the apparent rejection of the doctrine in Wesley's preface to his abridgement of Goodwin's *A Treatise on Justification*.[43] Wesley was so locked in confrontation that he even was willing to say that there was no covenant in Genesis 3. In other words, he saw clearly that he could not adopt the covenant of works and disallow imputed righteousness. The sermon shows that it was federalism that prevailed.

In historical order in the sixteenth century, imputed righteousness existed prior to the covenant of works. The former can exist without the latter. The opposite is improbable, though. Wesley did not accept a version

---

the old covenant, came (more or less) on all mankind." Maddox, *Doctrinal and Controversial Treatises*, 12:350.

39. Telford, ed., *Letters*, 4:298.
40. Maddox, ed., *Doctrinal and Controversial Treatises*, 12:397–401.
41. Ibid., 12:328, 378.
42. Outler, ed., *Sermons*, 1:447–65.
43. Chilcote and Collins, eds., *Doctrinal and Controversial Treatises II*, 13:374–90 (1765, as part of a debate with James Hervey dating to 1756).

of imputed righteousness because Arminius did, but he journeyed to it through a federalist pathway.

The Covenant of Grace

The covenant of grace, holding the Old and New Testaments together in their salvational focus, was a core distinctive of the Swiss Reformers, and was modified so as to be all but rejected by Arminius. Whitefield and Wesley together agree with the Reformed stance as expressed in documents such as the Thirty-Nine Articles. Article Seven says, "The old Testament is not contrary to the new, for both in the old and new Testament everlasting life is offered to mankind by Christ." The Old Testament is not only about "transitory promises." Its moral law is therefore binding, but the ceremonial and civil are not.[44]

Both Whitefield and Wesley employed the language of the covenant of grace. Both spoke frequently of the eternal covenant (although for Whitefield, that expression prioritized the covenant of redemption). Whitefield favored speaking of Christ as the "angel" of the covenant,[45] and Wesley spoke of Christ as the mediator of the new covenant,[46] and of the blood of the (everlasting) covenant.[47]

Both affirmed the canonical unity of the Scriptures, then. The covenant of grace was inaugurated in Genesis 3, the Abrahamic covenant is an expression of that covenant, and both broadly spoke positively of the Mosaic covenant, too. Whitefield had only two covenants, the first that was only in the Garden, and the "second covenant" made after the Fall.[48] Similarly, in Sermon 6, *The Righteousness of Faith*, Wesley contrasted not the Mosaic and new covenants, but the covenant of grace in old and new with the covenant

---

44. For Wesley on the temporary ceremonial law and the abiding moral law, see Wesley, *Explanatory Notes on the New Testament*, Galatians 3:19, 465. For Wesley's formative reading on the Thirty-Nine Articles, see McGonigle, *Sufficient Saving Grace*, 91–92. He points to the influence of John Ellis's *A Defence of the Thirty-Nine Articles of the Church of England* in particular. Ellis gives an entirely standard, Reformed explanation of Article Seven.

45. Gillies, ed., *Works*, 4:492; 5:57, 223.

46. Outler, ed., *Sermons*, 3:187; Cragg, ed., *Appeals to Men of Reason and Religion*, 11:51; Wesley, *Explanatory Notes on the New Testament*, Hebrews 9:15, 596; Chilcote and Collins, eds., *Doctrinal and Controversial Treatises II*, 13:380.

47. Ward and Heitzenrater, eds., *Journals and Diaries*, 19:176; Outler, ed., *Sermons*, 1:199, 261, 351, 407, and 527.

48. *A Letter to Some Church-Members of the Presbyterian Persuasion*, Gillies, ed., *Works*, 4:58.

made with Adam.[49] Wesley readily appropriated the Ten Commandments, and explicitly defended its continued applicability for those living under the new covenant. When he seemed to attack the Mosaic economy, it was the ceremonial law that was in view. "Stand fast therefore in the liberty—From the ceremonial law."[50] Both men were in accord with Article Seven.

In contrast, for Arminius, the Mosaic administration was neither a covenant of works nor a covenant of grace. It was not a covenant of works, for "There was only a single sacrament of the covenant of works, and that the tree of life."[51] In places, it had "covenants of promise" that were of one "substance" with the new,[52] but otherwise it was about legalism, designed to expose sin. The Mosaic was law, and contrasted with the grace of the covenants of promise and the New Testament.[53] Even though it exposed sin, driving people to the sacrifices, it must not be called the covenant of grace.[54] Arminius spoke of the covenant of works as having a legal obedience that led to long life rather than eternal life.[55]

---

49. He finds the gospel in Genesis 3:15, and with increasing clarity in Genesis 12:15, 18, with Moses, and then with David to all the prophets. In this Old Testament context, he says that this "covenant of *grace* doth not require us to *do* anything at all, as absolutely and indispensably necessary in order to our justification, but only to *believe* in him . . . " Outler, ed., *Sermons*, 1:207.

50. Wesley, *Explanatory Notes on the New Testament*, Galatians 5:1, 470; see also ibid., Hebrews 3:8, 593: "It is new in many respects, though not as to the substance of it: . . . 2. Freed from those burdensome rites and ceremonies."

51. Arminius, *Works*, Disputation LI, On the Church of the Old Testament, 2:117.

52. Ibid., Disputation XLIV, On Faith in God and Christ, 2:84. Also, he readily appropriated the Ten Commandments. Ibid., Disputation LXXIII, On Particular Acts of Obedience, 2:135.

53. "The old law was 'weak and beggarly,' and incapable of giving life." Ibid., Disputation 13, On the Comparison of the Law and the Gospel, 395. Wesley uses the Mosaic-sounding language, "Do this and live" of the covenant of works in the Garden (Maddox, ed., *Doctrinal and Controversial Treatises*, 12:350), while remaining positive about the Mosaic economy. The expression is an adaptation of Lev 18:5; Deut 4:1; Rom 10:5. Sermon 6, on Romans 10:5–8, puts it that the covenant of works says, "Do this and live," while the covenant of grace says "Believe, and live." Outler, ed., *Sermons*, 1:204.

54. "'II. The Old Testament' is never used in the Scriptures for the covenant of grace. III. The confounding of the promise and of the Old Testament is productive of much obscurity in Christian theology, and is the cause of more than a single error." Arminius, *Works*, Disputation LI, On the Church of the Old Testament, 2:96. Contra Wesley, *Explanatory Notes on the Old Testament*, Introduction to Genesis, 795: "Tis called the Old Testament with relation to the New, which doth not cancel, but crown and perfect it."

55. Grotius was clear that this was the Mosaic function as well. "God promised them, in the covenant made with Moses, a quiet possession of the land of Palestine, so long as they conformed their lives to the precepts of the law: and, on the contrary, if they sinned grievously against it, he threatened to drive them out." Grotius, *Truth of the Christian Religion*, Book V, Section XVI, 208. As an aside, Kline and Horton maintain

Thus, Wesley did not follow Arminius's view of the Mosaic covenant. He did muse that the covenant of works has a parallel with the symbolic nature of the Mosaic, but did not pursue this.[56] He adopted a Reformed hermeneutical position. Before exploring the problematic nature of this for one who consciously sought to be Arminian, there is a further twist. Wesley understood that the covenant of grace was a Reformed position, but believed that he had recast it in an Arminian way.

Wesley seldom discussed covenantal matters reflectively. One place in which he does so, though, is *Predestination Calmly Considered*. He debated whether the covenant of grace is unconditional or conditional.[57] In accordance with the typical English Arminian perspective, he perceived Reformed covenant theology to teach that the covenant of grace is unconditional.[58] This Wesley could not accept, and he set out to prove from Scripture that the covenant of grace is conditional. Lest he go too far towards works, though, he added an important qualification, that God gives the grace to fulfill the conditions. Wesley thought by this that he had arrived at a unique system, distinguishable from both the Reformed, which overplayed God's grace and devalued works, and the Arminian, which underplayed the degree to which grace enabled works.

The problem is that covenantal conditionality was original and prevalent within Reformed covenantal thought. The earliest Swiss exponents, Zwingli and Bullinger, saw the covenant in bilateral terms, and recurrent in federalism was the use of the very term, "conditions"—conditions met in the believer by grace. The idea of testament, the bestowal of grace, was also emphasized,[59] at the back of which were unconditional election and irresistible grace, but the idea of contracting parties was inherent. Wesley's

---

that by obedience to the Mosaic covenant, long life in the land is attained, and that as a symbol of the eternal life that the second Adam would bring by his obedience.

56. "The Mosaic history, as well as the Mosaic law, has rather the patterns of heavenly things, than the heavenly things themselves." Wesley, *Explanatory Notes on the Old Testament*, Genesis 2, 810. A reference to the covenant of grace being a "state of personal trial" is unusual, but it is not a comment on the Mosaic economy in particular, but the entire covenant of grace. Maddox, ed., *Doctrinal and Controversial Treatises*, 12:350. This means that the covenant of grace parallels to some extent the covenant of works, in which Adam was "on trial." Wesley was perhaps thinking of his doctrines of perseverance and perfection here. The comment seems to exclude the real parallel between the covenants of works and grace, that "Adam . . . was . . . on trial for all mankind," and Christ was on trial. That is, it seems to deny the very essence of federalism—yet Wesley's other comments indicate that this was not what was intended.

57. Chilcote and Collins, eds., *Doctrinal and Controversial Treatises II*, 13:298–300.

58. Olsen has the same perspective. Olson, *Arminian Theology*, 53.

59. Cf. Arminius, *Works*, Disputation XXXIX, On the Will, 2:73.

comment could have been written by any number of Reformed theologians, particularly with the words, "enables us to perform": "God now vouchsafes, on one only condition, (which himself also enables us to perform) both to remit the punishment due to our sins, to reinstate us in his favour, and to restore our dead souls to spiritual life, as the earnest of life eternal."[60]

Wesley denied that any other than Adam was under the covenant of works, but rather Christ's sons "are under the covenant of grace."[61] He held the one condition of the covenant to be faith.[62] He might have thought that it was not Reformed to add that faith works itself out with love, but this, of course, was precisely a Reformed distinctive.[63] "The manner of their acceptance is this: the free grace of God, through the merits of Christ, gives pardon to them that believe, that believe with such a faith as, working by love, produces all obedience and holiness."[64]

Formally speaking, without wider consideration of the nature of predestination, prevenient grace and universal atonement,[65] Wesley's covenant of grace was the Reformed covenant of grace. Wesley was not only unaware of the extent to which his covenantalism aligned with Reformed theology

---

60. Outler, ed., *Sermons*, 1:186. McGonigle (*Sufficient Saving Grace*, 160–61) describes the acceptance of the 1745 Conference of repentance and works as "conditions" of justification, in the context of discussing Baxter's neonomianism. This was not Wesley's settled position on justification, and the instinct to give works a significant place, and even to speak of works as conditions, was not contrary to Reformed thought. Bullinger held that the Decalogue is "almost a paraphrase of the conditions [not of justification, but] of the covenant" (*De Testamento seu Foedere Dei Unico et Aeterno* in McCoy and Baker, *Fountainhead of Federalism*, 113). Wesley tied works so closely to faith that he could speak of works as part of the "ordinary condition of final salvation," but faith remains the only condition of present salvation. Wesley has in this connected faith alone to present justification, whilst giving works an evidentiary place thereafter, although this present/final salvation was not always consistently clear. Cragg, ed., *Appeals to Men of Reason and Religion*, 11:130. See also Chilcote and Collins, eds., *Doctrinal and Controversial Treatises II*, 13:332, "The conditions of the new covenant are, 'Repent and believe.'"; McGonigle, *Sufficient Saving Grace*, 266–69.

61. Outler, ed., *Sermons*, 2:27.

62. The covenant "requires only *faith*." Outler, ed., *Sermons*, 1:209.

63. While being clear that it is not lively faith that is instrumental of justification. Wesley also signified this when he wrote in Sermon 35, "Whereas now all good works, though as necessary as ever, are not antecedent to our acceptance, but consequent upon it. Therefore the nature of the covenant of grace gives you no ground, no encouragement at all, to set aside any insistence or degree of obedience, any part or measure of holiness." Outler, ed., *Sermons*, 2:27.

64. Ibid., 2:27.

65. See Vickers, "Wesley's Theological Emphases," 196–97, on the universal scope of the covenant of grace in Wesley.

but he also consciously and mistakenly believed that his stance was discrete from Reformed thought.

This adherence to the covenant of grace created a tension with Wesley's emphasis on conditional election and free will. It did not have to be a destabilizing force, remembering that covenant theology is rooted in Augustinianism, yet Augustine had placed an emphasis on works, fusing justification and sanctification. However, for Wesley, while he wanted to say "free will" (assisted by prevenient grace), the covenant of grace gave him a whole Bible that always emphasized God's gift of salvation. Therefore, Wesley found himself oscillating back to God's grace, and God's sovereignty. To restate it, adherence to the covenant of grace produced for Wesley an instability between the objective and subjective elements of salvation.

There is no proof-text that directly demonstrates the connection, but given his view of the covenant, it is no surprise to see that Wesley struggled with one of his signature doctrines, the doctrine of assurance, as he tried to balance the objective with the subjective.[66] This was not theoretical, but part of his personal struggle. At his Aldersgate conversion (or assurance of conversion) experience, he emphasized his own faith (see below). There is evidence of ensuing lack of assurance that seems to fit the narrative. In a 1766 letter to Charles, he exclaimed, 'Therefore [I never] believed in the Christian sense of the word.'[67] In the face of this, he describes his frenetic evangelistic efforts. This could be explained as an Arminian overemphasis on works, although lack of assurance was also a seventeenth-century Puritan phenomenon. Alternatively, he may have been contrasting his own sinfulness with God's power ("hedged in", φερόμενος—borne along, probably connecting his experience to Pentecost or the prophets, Acts 2:2; 2 Peter 1:21). This could well be Wesley oscillating back to an emphasis on grace.[68] Wesley arguably concluded his life not with an Arminian-Reformed tension on assurance, but simply with a Reformed tension.

Whitefield believed that he understood Wesley's predicament. Pinpointing the underlying problem, he advised John to "study the covenant of grace that you may be consistent with yourself."[69]

---

66. Monk's conclusion is that "Wesley does not stress the covenant idea as a means of assurance," but he accepts that his covenantal thinking still impacted the doctrine, since covenant deals with "man's dependence upon God's grace and the relationship thereto of works." Monk, *John Wesley*, 96–97.

67. Telford, ed., *Letters*, 5:16.

68. His journal entry of 4 January 1739 can be interpreted similarly. Ward and Heitzenrater, eds., *Journals and Diaries*, 19:29–30.

69. Gillies, ed., *Works*, 1:248.

A Personal Covenant

The above analysis suggests that covenant theology formed the substructure of both Whitefield and Wesley's theology, although for Wesley, Arminianism was unstably balanced atop the foundation. The significance of the notion of covenant emerged for both men when turning from the *historia salutis* to the *ordo salutis*, that is, when considering the individual's relationship to God. Both construed relationship with God as covenantal. The covenant of grace had to be actualized in the individual's life.

Whitefield favored the imagery of a marriage covenant, which was the theme of one of his popular sermons.[70] For him, this placed the emphasis not so much on the new birth and commitment[71] but on the nature and experience of the mystical relationship. The emphasis arose from Whitefield's own conversion and religious experience, and from his reading of Puritan figures such as Scougal. Whitefield's insistence on entering personally into covenant thus ameliorates criticisms (or commendations) that Whitefield the emphatic evangelist had Wesleyan-Arminian leanings with regard to faith and conversion. Insisting that individuals covenant with God is the natural outworking of a federalist position.[72] Whitefield held that unconditional election and the free offer of the gospel are not mutually exclusive, a stance consistent with Reformed creedal statements.

Wesley also sought to bring people to faith (as part of obedience and holiness), but arguably placed more emphasis on this than on union with Christ. This correlates with the Arminian view that election itself is contingent upon human response. Dallimore notes the strong emphasis placed on faith.[73] It is as though faith replaced the legalistic endeavors of the Holy Club.[74]

---

70. The sermon preached to the Fetter Lane Society of Young Women. Gillies, ed., *Works*, 5:77.

71. Contra Lambert, "The Great Awakening as Artifact," 230–31, who says that for Whitefield, "Only the condition of one's soul mattered." See also Dallimore, *George Whitefield*, 1:345.

72. Clarkson, *Welsh Calvinistic Methodism*, 33–50, is puzzled by the combination, and sees the emphasis on the place of the will as Arminianism. See, rather, Dallimore, *George Whitefield*, 2:61. Whitefield's comment is: "No more does God's absolute purpose of saving his chosen preclude the necessity of the Gospel revelation, or the use of any of the means through which he has determined the decree shall take effect." Gillies, ed., *Works*, 4:79.

73. Dallimore, *George Whitefield*, 1:181.

74. Murray, *Wesley and Men Who Followed*, 9, 55, sees Wesley's Aldersgate Street experience as conversion-consciousness. Whether it was conversion or the awareness of conversion, the key is that it was a faith-feeling moment. He found he had the faith for which he was looking.

The idea of a personal covenant thus was highly prominent in Wesley's teaching, well beyond Whitefield's employment of the theme. He drew up "Directions for Renewing Our Covenant with God."[75] His journals are replete with details of services of joining in covenant, particularly on Good Fridays and on New Year's Days (1773, 1776, 1777, 1783, 1785), and with notes of exhortations to renew covenant with God.[76] The "Directions" have only limited contact with the objective covenants, although it is clear enough that it is the covenant of grace into which a person enters.[77] Moreover, even the blessings of the Mosaic covenant will belong to the one covenanting.[78] Faith is the central element, for prayer, Scripture, and the sacraments do not save.[79] The conditions of the covenant also include obedience, and the result is that the triune God becomes "my Covenant-Friend, and I through thine infinite grace, am become thy Covenant-Servant."[80]

Framing this as a covenant demonstrates how dominant the covenant notion was in Wesley's thinking and practice, reminiscent of the seventeenth-century covenanting Scots, and Dickson's appeal to "close a bargain, and a formal covenant with God."[81] In fact, Wesley's covenant was based on the covenant of "that blessed man," the Puritan, Richard Alleine (1611–1681).[82] His later movement on his doctrine of assurance can be pointed to

---

75. First published in 1780. See the discussion in Finley, *Nature's Covenant*, 71–73, including on the importance of the Spirit to those entering the pact. Finley ties the Wesleyan emphasis on covenant back to a softer rather than the high-Calvinist Reformed theology of the sixteenth century (citing Ursinus). This fails to understand that pact has an integral role in covenant theology, and adopts a predestinarian stereotype, a stereotype to which Wesley adhered, as discussed above.

76. The first such note is on Friday 25 December 1747, and then Saturday 9 July 1748. Monk, *John Wesley*, 105, has the first date as January 1748 (but there is no note in Ward and Heitzenrater, eds., *Journals and Diaries*, 20:204), and says the next reference is not until 1755. On the Service, much has been published. See Davies, *From Watts and Wesley to Maurice*, 197–201; Rupwate, "The Covenant Theology of John Wesley," 79–90.

77. Interestingly, one of the warrants for coming to Christ is God's ordination. The Father has chosen the Son for this, referencing Isaiah 42:1. Wesley, *Covenant*, 9. This is a standard proof-text for the covenant of redemption, but it is not clear if Wesley was not rather referring to the sending of the Son into the world.

78. Ibid., 15, citing Deut 26:17–18 in particular.

79. Ibid., 7.

80. Ibid., 18, 23.

81. Dickson, "The Sum of Saving Knowledge," 332.

82. Also author of *Heaven Opened, or A Brief and Plain Discovery of the Riches of God's Covenant of Grace*. Alleine's *Vindiciae Pietatis* had been included in *A Christian Library* in 1753 (vol. 29 is often cited. Green, *Works of John and Charles Wesley*, 84–85, has it in volumes 24 and 30, of the same year). The first service using the covenant is recorded in the journal entry for Monday 11 August 1755. "After I had recited the tenor of the covenant proposed, in the words of that blessed man, Richard Alleine." Jackson,

as the evidence that there was decreasing emphasis on human commitment, and so his notion of personal covenanting fitted into what was increasingly a Reformed view of works and grace.[83]

Conclusion

Whitefield's covenant theology was straightforward and pervasive in his thinking and ministry. Perceiving no clash with his evangelistic fervor, he even held to the covenant of redemption, and reveled in Christ as the "angel" of that covenant. For Whitefield, the covenant of works explained what humankind's problem was, and the covenant of grace proclaimed the solution. He had no qualms with the federal headship of Adam or Christ, and forcefully proclaimed both.

Wesley's relationship to federalism was more complicated. In his wider theology, he knew he was within a hair's breadth of Calvinism, but was less aware of why that was the case. As Wesley strove to bring consistency to his Arminian system, Whitefield pinpointed the underlying problem: the covenant of grace. Wesley's theological superstructure was balanced not on Arminius's covenantalism, to which Wesley had only passing affinity, but unstably on a federalism shared with Whitefield. Wesley rejected the covenant of redemption out of hand, but only partly qualified the corporate nature of the covenant of works, and more significantly, mistakenly believed that he had tamed federalism by affirming conditionality in the covenant of grace. The key components of federalism remained. In this surprising way, Whitefield and Wesley were federalist brothers.

---

ed., *Works*, 2:339. Tripp (*Renewal of the Covenant*, 2), oddly has the first use between 1658 and 1660. See also Jackson, "Directions for Renewing Our Covenant with God," 176–84.

83. Note that in his well-known letter to John Wesley dated 24 December 1740, Whitefield complained that Wesley pleaded "so vehemently for a sinless perfection," but by 11 September 1747, he rejoiced that "you and your brother are more moderate with respect to *sinless perfection*." Gillies, ed., *Works*, 4:74, 643. See also ibid., 2:130. On the debate between Wesley and Whitefield over perfection, see Maddock, "George Whitefield: Christian Perfectionist?," 147–61.

7

Whitefield and Wesley on Sin and Atonement

Peter Adam

Gospel Unity, Gospel Conflict

WHAT AN EXTRAORDINARY IRONY. It was a movement focused so clearly and strongly on the gospel of Christ's atoning death. It held this as God's remedy for human sin as the center of its theology and the heart of its activity. And yet, within the evangelical movement, there was severe disagreement on the theology and practice of this gospel. What's more, this disagreement occurred between the close friends who were the significant leaders of this movement: George Whitefield, and John and Charles Wesley. Their disagreement profoundly influenced the evangelical movement at that time, and continues to be felt around the world.

Whitefield had joined John and Charles Wesley's Holy Club in Oxford University in the 1730s, and together they were committed to the search for holiness in heart and life. They studied, prayed, fasted, engaged in self-mortification, received the Holy Communion, and did good works. Whitefield was converted and received assurance of salvation in 1735, and was influenced by such Calvinist writings as Bishop Joseph Hall's *Meditations* and Matthew Henry's *Commentary on the Whole Bible*. He wrote of the effect of this reading on his Holy Club friends:

> About this time God was pleased to enlighten my soul, and bring me into the knowledge of His free grace, and the necessity of being justified in His sight by *faith only*. This was more extraordinary, because my friends at Oxford rather inclined to

the mystic divinity; and one of them . . . lately confessed he did not like me . . . because I held justification by faith *only*.[1]

The Wesleys came from a different theological background to Whitefield. Their parents were firmly Arminian.[2] As early as 1725, John Wesley doubted predestination. "How is this consistent with either divine justice or mercy?"[3]

It is commonly believed that John and Charles Wesley came to full evangelical faith in London in 1738. John then published *The Doctrine of Salvation, Faith and Good Works*, in which he made it clear that justification by faith must precede sanctification. "Justification" referred to the beginning of the Christian life, and "sanctification" to its subsequent progress. The two Wesleys now joined Whitefield in vigorous evangelistic and pastoral ministry, preaching in churches and then in the open air.

Agreements

The central themes of Whitefield's preaching were original sin, justification by faith alone, and regeneration. The central themes of John Wesley's preaching were original sin, justification by faith, and holiness of heart in the lives of those who had been born again.[4] They agreed on original sin and total depravity, the centrality of Christ's atoning death, and the need for regeneration or new birth.

Original Sin and Total Depravity[5]

Whitefield and Wesley were of the same mind on these. Whitefield taught: "We all stand in need of being justified, on account of the sin in our natures: for we are all chargeable with original sin, or the first sin of our parents . . . [for] 'in Adam all died'; that is, Adam's sin was imputed to all . . . this point seems to be excellently summed up in the article of our Church, where she declares, 'Original sin . . . is the fault and corruption of every man.'"[6]

---

1. Whitefield, *Journals*, 62.
2. McGonigle, *Sufficient Saving Grace*, 73–105, 127–28.
3. Baker, ed., *Letters*, 25:175.
4. Maddock, *Men of One Book*, 177–78.
5. "Original sin" means sin originating in Adam, and Adam's sin damaged all his descendants. "Total depravity" means that the corruption and sickness of sin is found in every part of humans: minds, hearts, wills, affections, and actions.
6. Gillies, ed., *Works*, 6:217–18. "Article" here means one of the Thirty-Nine Articles

Wesley preached similarly on Genesis 6:5, "And God saw that the wickedness of man was great in the earth, and that every imagination of the thoughts of his heart was only evil continually." He said:

> He saw "all the imaginations." It is not possible to find a word of more extensive signification. It includes whatever is formed, made, fabricated within; all this or passes in the soul; every inclination, affection, passion, appetite; every temper design, thought. It must of consequence include every word and action, as naturally flowing from these fountains . . . Allow this, and you are so far a Christian. Deny it, and you are but a heathen still.[7]

And again,

> Indeed we are already bound hand and foot by the chains of our own sins . . . They are wounds, wherewith the world, the flesh, and the devil have gashed and mangled us all over. They are diseases that drink up our blood and spirits, that bring us down to the chambers of the grace. But considered as they are here, with regard to God, they are debts immense and numberless.[8]

So while many thought of Wesley as Pelagian or semi-Pelagian, this was not true. Wesley's optimism about Christian sanctification was based on God's gratuitous grace. Their disagreements were about the reception and human response to this grace, and the possibility of transformation in this life.

The Centrality of Christ's Atoning Death

The Wesleys and Whitefield also agreed on the centrality of Christ's death as the atonement for sin. Whitefield preached:

> Whilst we were his enemies, God sent forth his Son, made of a woman, made under the law, that he might become a curse for us. Oh, the freeness, as well as the infinity, of the love of God our Father! . . . Think, O believers, think of the love of God, in giving Jesus Christ to be the propitiation for our sins . . . think how your heavenly Father bound Jesus Christ, his only Son, and offered him upon the altar of his justice, and laid upon him the iniquities of us all.[9]

---

of Religion. See Article Nine, "Of Original or Birth-sin."

7. Wesley, *Standards*, 1:439, 444.
8. Ibid., 1:267.
9. Whitefield, *Sermons*, 1:290.

He contrasts Isaac, whose substitute was a ram, with Jesus, who died as the substitute for others. "Isaac is saved, but Jesus, the God of Isaac dies: a ram is offered up in Isaac's room, but Jesus has no substitute; Jesus must bleed, Jesus must die: God the Father provided this Lamb for himself from all eternity."[10]

John Wesley wrote,

> Christian faith is then, not only an assent to the whole Gospel of Christ, but also a full reliance on the blood of Christ; a trust in the merits of his life, death, and resurrection; a recumbency upon him as our atonement and our life, as *given for us*, and *living in us*. It is a sure confidence which a man hath in God, that through the merits of Christ, *his* sins are forgiven, and *he* reconciled to the favour of God; and, in consequence thereof, a closing with him, and cleaving to him, as . . . our salvation.[11]

Charles Wesley continued the same theme:

> Alas! What evil hath He done,
>
> The spotless Lamb of God?
>
> Cut off, not for himself, but me,
>
> He bears my sins on yonder tree,
>
> And pays my debt in blood.[12]

This common focus was based on a common acceptance of the doctrine of the Trinity, and of the incarnation and divinity of the Son of God, in contrast to the view of Unitarians such as Joseph Priestly and Theophilus Lindsey.

John Wesley's view of the atonement was that Christ: "was a Priest, who gave himself a sacrifice for sin, and still makes intercession for transgressors . . . that he is the Lord of all . . . but more peculiarly our Lord, who believe in him, both by conquest, purchase, and voluntary obligation."[13]

Although he associated with Arminian ideas, Wesley held a different view from them on the atonement. Their view was that Christ's death was a tribute to governmental justice, to show the seriousness of sin, and so to deter others from sin. For if Christ had indeed paid the penalty for the sin of all, then all would be forgiven. Christ's death shows us that forgiveness

---

10. Ibid., 1:291.
11. Wesley, *Standards*, 1:5, 6.
12. Rattenbury, *Hymns*, 191.
13. Jackson, ed., *Works*, 10:81.

is costly. Wesley had a more robust view. He taught that we suffer death because of our sin: "art thou ready to meet death and judgment?"[14] He preached that Christ is our only Savior: " . . . the Judge of all is also the Saviour of all . . . Hath he not bought you with his own blood, that ye might not perish, but have everlasting life? Oh make but proof of his mercy rather than his justice; of his love, rather than the thunder of his power!"[15]

Neither Whitefield nor Wesley taught that God as bound by an external law of justice. They recognized the personal nature of God's law, so that rebellion against the law is rebellion against God himself.

Wesley's view contrasts with that of William Law, whose ideas he had previously followed. For Law, "Christ's suffering on the cross is not regarded as a vicarious suffering for mankind. It was only a representational act in the name of mankind . . . Christ is a sacrifice to make the sacrifices of mankind acceptable to God."[16] For Wesley, Christ made "by that one oblation of himself, once offered, a full perfect, and sufficient sacrifice, oblation, and satisfaction for the sins of the whole world."[17]

While Wesley does acknowledge Christ's death as healing and victory, he applies these themes more naturally in the area of sanctification. And, more generally, whereas Whitefield applies the atonement to justification, Wesley applies it to sanctification. Maddox writes, "For Wesley, the value of justification was precisely its contribution to the higher goal of sanctification—our recovery of the Likeness of God."[18]

An increasing contrast between Wesley and the Calvinists on the atonement is that of the imputation of righteousness, as we will see. Wesley became nervous about using the expression, because he feared that if people thought they had Christ's righteousness, they would not bother pursing righteousness in their own lives. Wesley agreed that Christ's offering to the Father was that of his passive and active obedience: "for the sake of thy active and passive obedience, I am forgiven and accepted by God."[19] Yet he also made it clear that "Christ was a substitute only in suffering punishment, not in His fulfilling of the law."[20] He wanted to retain the express warnings in the New

---

14. Wesley, *Standards*, 21.
15. Ibid., 148.
16. Lindström, *Wesley*, 57.
17. Jackson, ed., *Works*, 10:277, a quotation from the Communion Service in the *Book of Common Prayer*.
18. Maddox, *Responsible Grace*, 172.
19. Wesley, *Standards*, 1:196.
20. Lindström, *Wesley*, 73.

Testament against laxness in Christian living, and his sermon on "The Great Assize" is an appropriate and powerful expression of this theme.[21]

Whitefield also preached Christ's passive and active obedience: "Here we see the meaning of the word righteousness. It implies the active, as the well as passive obedience of the Lord Jesus Christ. We generally, when talking of the merits of Christ, only mention the latter, viz.: his death; whereas the former, viz.: his life and active obedience, is equally necessary." [22]

Regeneration

Whitefield gained his first impression of the need of new birth or regeneration from Henry Scougal's *The Life of the God in the Soul of Man*, where he read that "true religion was union of the soul, with God, and Christ formed within us."[23] In 1737 he wrote that when he had preached, "The doctrine of the New Birth and Justification by Faith in Jesus Christ (though I was not so clear in it as afterwards) made its way like lightening into the hearer's consciences."[24] He soon printed his sermon, "On the Nature and Necessity of our Regeneration or New Birth in Christ Jesus," to spread his message more widely.[25] And he prayed for the people of Salisbury, "Raise up some true pastors amongst them, who may acquaint them with the nature and necessity of the new birth, and point them out to them the blessed Spirit, whereby they may have that repentance wrought in their heart, which the self-righteous Mr. Chubb falsely asserts may be wrought in them by a moral persuasion."[26]

Wesley similarly preached the need for new birth, for regeneration: "It is the great change which God works in the soul, when he brings it into life; when he raises it from the death of sin to the life of righteousness. It is the change wrought in the whole soul by the almighty Spirit of God . . . when the love of the world is changed into the love of God; pride into humility; passion into meekness; hatred, envy, malice, into a sincere, tender, disinterested love for all mankind . . . 'So is every one that is born of the Spirit.'"[27]

These were significant agreements between Whitefield and Wesley.

---

21. Wesley, *Standards*, 1:138–48.
22. Whitefield, *Sermons*, 3:4.
23. Whitefield, *Journals*, 47. See Scougal, *Works*, 3.
24. Ibid., 81.
25. Ibid., 86.
26. Ibid., 212.
27. Wesley, *Standards*, 1:451

Disagreements

Unfortunately, however, there were also disagreements, which not only damaged their ministries but also were personally painful. Charles Wesley had been a significant help to Whitefield at Oxford. Charles had befriended him, introduced him to his brother John—senior to them both—and brought him into the Holy Club. Whitefield was deeply indebted to them. Yet Whitefield had come to saving faith in Christ in 1735, before the two Wesleys in 1738. Whitefield had led the way in preaching outside church buildings, and introduced them to that ministry. And he had entrusted his ministry in England to Wesley when he went to in America in 1739. These were complicated relationships.

The Extent of the Atonement

Wesley and Whitefield disagreed on the extent of the atonement. At that time there were two Calvinist views on the extent of Christ's atonement. The stronger view was that Christ died only for the elect. This view was supported by the Westminster Confession, John Owen, and John Gill. Wesley critiqued Gill's hyper-Calvinism in his "Predestination Calmly Considered" of 1752.[28] The milder view was that Christ's atoning death was sufficient for all, but efficient only for the elect: that is, that Christ's death was sufficient for the sins of all humanity, but was only effective in the elect, who by God's free grace came to faith in Jesus Christ. John Newton and Charles Simeon took this milder view.[29]

Whitefield took the stronger view, yet was certainly not a hyper-Calvinist. He held to limited atonement: "But, blessed be God, our Lord knew for whom he died. There was an eternal compact between the Father and the Son. A certain number was given him, as the purchase and reward of his obedience and death. For these he prayed, John xvii, and not for the world. For these, and for these only, he is now interceding, and with their salvation he will be fully satisfied."[30]

---

28. Jackson, ed., *Works*, 10:204–58.

29. Newton: "That there is an election of grace, we are plainly taught; yet it is not said, that Jesus Christ came into the world to save 'the elect,' but that he came to save 'sinners' . . . And therefore the command to repent implies a warrant to believe in the name of Jesus, as taking away the sin of the world." Clifford, *Atonement*, 80, 81. Simeon: "To say that he died for the elect only, is neither scriptural nor true. He died for all: according as it is elsewhere said: 'we thus judge, that if one died for all, then were all dead: And that he died for all . . .'" Ibid., 81.

30. Whitefield, *Journals*, 587.

And he agreed that election and reprobation are consistent: "For, without doubt, the doctrine of election and reprobation must stand or fall together . . . I believe the doctrine of reprobation, in this view, that God intends to give saving grace, through Jesus Christ, only to a certain number, and that the rest of mankind, after the fall of Adam, being justly left of God to continue in sin, will at last suffer that eternal death, which is its proper wages."[31]

While for some this view of God's eternal covenant may have reduced their commitment to evangelism, Whitefield's theology was naturally expressed in evangelism: "Go home then, turn the words of this text into a prayer, and entreat the Lord to be your righteousness."[32]

To counter Whitefield's view, the Wesleys preached and sang universal atonement.[33]

> Help us Thy mercy to extol,
>
> Immense, unfathom'd, *unconfined*;
>
> To praise the Lamb who *died for all*,
>
> The general Saviour of mankind.
>
> Thy undistinguishing regard
>
> Was cast on Adam's fallen race;
>
> *For all* Thou hast in Christ prepared,
>
> Sufficient, sovereign, saving grace.[34]

However, they not only called on congregations to sing this positive message, but also called on them to sing anti-Calvinist words as well. Here is an example in which the congregation would attack Calvinism as asserting: "God could a helpless world create/ To thrust them into hell."[35]

---

31. Whitefield, *Journals*, 575, 74.

32. Whitefield, *Sermons*, 1:17.

33. By "universal atonement," Wesley meant that Christ died for all so that if all respond, then all will be saved. The expression is used with other meanings elsewhere.

34. Rattenbury, *Hymns*, 134. My italics.

35. As quoted in Kidd, *Whitefield*, 143.

Predestination

Predestination—the belief that that God has chosen those who will become believers, brings them to faith, and keeps them faithful to the end—was another related area of disagreement.[36] In 1739 John Wesley preached against Calvinism in his famous sermon on "Free Grace," and subsequently republished it with Charles Wesley's hymn "Universal Redemption" attached in 1740. By "free grace," Wesley means "the Grace or Love of God, whence cometh our Salvation, is free in all, and free for all."[37]

It is free in two ways: "First, it is free in all to whom it is given. It does not depend on any power or merit in Man; no, not in any degree, neither in whole, nor in part. It does not in any wise depend either on the good works or righteousness of the receiver; Not on anything he has done, or anything he is.[38]

He then asks the crucial question: "But is it free for all, as well as in all?" and describes the predestinarian view: "No: It is free only for those whom GOD hath ordained to Life; and they are but a little flock. The greater part of mankind GOD hath ordained to Death; and it is not free for them."[39] Wesley then argued that even those who focus on the election of grace still hold an implicit doctrine of reprobation: "By virtue of an eternal, unchangeable, irresistible decree of God, one part of mankind are infallibly saved, and the rest infallibly damn'd: It being impossible that any of the former should be damn'd, or that any of the latter should be saved."[40]

Wesley continued to explain the ramifications of holding such a doctrine: "But if this be so, then is all Preaching Vain . . . . It directly tends to destroy that holiness, which is the end [purpose] of all the ordinances of God . . . this doctrine tends to destroy the comfort of religion, the happiness of Christianity . . . this uncomfortable Doctrine directly tends to destroy our zeal for good works . . ."[41] Furthermore, predestination contradicts clear statements in the Bible. "For it is grounded on such an Interpretation of some Texts . . . as flatly contradict all the other texts, and indeed the whole scope and tenor of Scripture." [42]

---

36. See Best, *Charles Wesley*, 138–58.
37. Outler, ed., *Sermons*, 3:545.
38. Ibid., 3:545.
39. Ibid., 3:545.
40. Ibid., 3:547.
41. Ibid., 3:547–50.
42. Ibid., 3:552.

At the heart of the disagreements between Wesley and Whitefield lay the interpretation of Scripture, and the challenge of combining and cohering passages that emphasized divine freedom and sovereignty with those that emphasized human responsibility. Whitefield replied with an extensive critique of this sermon, published in February 1741.[43] He points out that preaching is the God-appointed means to bring people to salvation: "How is preaching needless to them that are elected; when the gospel is designated by God himself, to be the power of God unto their eternal salvation? And since we know not who are elect, and who reprobate, we are to preach promiscuously to all . . . "[44]

He denied that predestination precludes holiness. "A true lover of the Lord Jesus Christ would strive to be holy for the sake of being holy, and work for Christ out of love and gratitude, without any regard to the rewards of heaven, or fear of hell."[45]

Whitefield further contested the idea that predestination destroys the comforts of religion: "As for my own part, this doctrine is my daily support: I should utterly sink under a dread of my impending trials, was I not firmly persuaded that God has chosen me in Christ from before the foundation of the world, and that now being effectually called, he will suffer none to pluck me out of his almighty hand."[46]

He argued that God is just to judge all, and so is just to condemn some: "Surely Mr. Wesley will own God's justice, in imputing Adam's sin to his posterity; and also, that after Adam fell, and his posterity in him, God might justly have passed them *all* by, without sending his own Son to be a saviour for any one."[47]

Yet Whitefield misunderstood Wesley when he wrote, "You plainly make salvation depend not on God's free-grace, but on man's free will . . ."[48] Wesley's views were not Pelagian. It is a weakness in Whitefield that in his response to Wesley's "Free Grace" sermon, he does not deal with Bible passages that may be seen to oppose his view of limited atonement, such as 1 Timothy 1:15, John 1:29, 1 John 2:1–2, and 2 Corinthians 5:14. Nor does he mention Article Thirty-One, with its reference to Christ's death being "for the sins of the whole world, both original and actual." Nor does he reflect on the words of the Holy Communion service in the Book of Common Prayer,

---

43. Whitefield, *Journals*, 564–88.
44. Ibid., 575.
45. Ibid., 576.
46. Ibid., 578.
47. Ibid., 583.
48. Ibid., 587.

which refers to Christ's death as "a full perfect, and sufficient sacrifice, oblation, and satisfaction for the sins of the whole world." He does not deal with the evidence that contradicts his rejection of Wesley's views. He assumes the existence of the covenant between the Father and the Son, which defined who would be saved. As Wesley later asked, "I beseech you, where is this written? In what part of Scripture is this covenant to be found?"[49] This disagreement about predestination was linked to their disagreement about the extent of the atonement, as we have seen.

Prevenient Grace

A further area of great disagreement was prevenient grace. Prevenient grace is God's work within a believer that precedes regeneration, justification, faith, and conversion. Both Whitefield and Wesley asserted it, but with radically different meanings.

Whitefield held to the traditional Reformed view of prevenient grace. It was wholly God's initiative. Because humans were by nature sinful and depraved, it could not be God's response to anything we had done. Prevenient grace was God's free gift. It was free because it was not deserved, and free because it was God's free choice to give it. Prevenient grace meant that what God had done *for us* in Christ, he now did *within us* to apply Christ's atoning death to us. "Man is nothing: he hath a free will to go to hell, but none to heaven, till God worketh in him to will and to do after his good pleasure. It is God must prevent, God must accompany, God must follow by his grace, or Jesus Christ will bleed in vain."[50]

When Whitefield writes, "God must prevent," he means God must go before; God must initiate. "Prevent" here means "go before," hence the expression "prevenient grace." Prevenient grace is effective, as well as undeserved: "If you belong to Jesus Christ, he is speaking of you; for, says he, *I know my sheep*. I know them; what does that mean? Why, he knows their number; he knows their names, he knows every one for whom he died; and if there was to be one missing for whom Christ died, God the Father would send him down again from heaven to fetch him."[51]

Whereas for Whitefield prevenient grace was effective only in the elect, Wesley held a very different view. It was that God's prevenient grace was at work in every human being, and that it enabled people to respond to God's gospel invitation if they chose to do so. In fact, he believed that no one is

---

49. Jackson, ed., *Works*, 10:239.
50. Gillies, ed., *Works*, 1:90.
51. Whitefield, *Sermons*, 3:305.

absolutely and solely in the state of original sin and total depravity because God's prevenient grace is at work in all: "For allowing that all the souls of men are dead in sin by *nature*, this excuses none, seeing that there is no man that is in the state of mere nature; there is not man, unless he has quenched the Spirit, that is wholly void of the grace of God . . . But this is not natural; it is more properly termed "preventing grace." Every man has a greater or less measure of this, which waiteth not for the call of man."[52]

By "waiteth not," Wesley means that God's grace does not respond to or depend upon human initiative. He continues, "Therefore inasmuch as God works in you, you are now able to work out your own salvation. Since he worketh in you of his own good pleasure, without any merit of yours, both to will and to do, it is possible for you to fulfil all righteousness."[53] This then meant that every turning to God, every turning to Christ for salvation, depended firstly on God's prevenient grace and secondly on human response. God was at work in all: some responded to that internal work of God and were saved, and some did not respond, and were condemned. This view was not Pelagian or even semi-Pelagian, despite Calvinist accusations. It was not based on an optimistic, sin-free view of human nature; the power to cooperate with God's grace was not an inherent power but was itself a gift of that grace.

Wesley's doctrine of prevenient grace is simple, clear, and attractive. It protects God's love and emphasizes human responsibility. However, as he accused others of ignoring Scriptures in his sermon on "Free Grace," so his system can be accused of the same fault. He himself provided little exegetical support for his views.

Justification

What then about justification? It was an area of both agreement and disagreement. Whitefield preached the following on justification:

> Every man that is saved is justified three ways: *First, Meritoriously,* by the death of Jesus Christ: "it is the blood of Jesus Christ alone that cleanses us from all sin." *Secondly, Instrumentally,* by faith; faith is the means or instrument whereby the merits of Jesus Christ are applied to the sinner's heart. "Ye are all the children of God by faith in Christ Jesus." *Thirdly,* we are justified *Declaratively*: namely by good works: good works declare and prove to the world that our faith is a true saving faith.

52. Outler, ed., *Sermons*, 3:207.
53. Ibid., 3:207

"Was not Abraham justified by works?" And again, "Show me thy faith by thy works."[54]

Whitefield held that faith would produce good works in the elect, and that God had both imputed and imparted righteousness: "For the word *righteousness* in the text, not only implies Christ's personal righteousness imputed to us, but also holiness of heart wrought in us."[55] And Whitefield preached: "For, though faith alone justifies, yet, as the good old Puritans used to observe, that faith that is alone justifieth not."[56] Righteousness is imputed in justification, and imparted in sanctification.

Wesley preached along similar lines: "These things must necessarily go together in our justification: upon God's part, his great mercy and grace; upon Christ's part, the satisfaction of God's justice; and on our part, faith in the merits of Christ."[57] And again, "I cannot describe the nature of this faith better, than in the words of our own church. 'The only instrument of salvation, [whereof justification is one branch] is faith: that is, a sure trust and confidence that God both hath and will forgive our sins, that he has accepted us again into his favour, for the merits of Christ's death and passion . . . '"[58]

Both believed that justification was based on the atoning work of Christ. So Wesley wrote: "'Justification' . . . taken in the largest sense, implies a deliverance from guilt and punishment, by the atonement of Christ actually applied to the soul of the sinner now believing on him, and a deliverance from the power of sin through Christ 'formed in his heart.'"[59]

And again, ". . . God implants righteousness in every one to whom he has imputed it . . . They to whom the righteousness of Christ is imputed, are made righteous by the Spirit of Christ; are renewed in the image of God . . . "[60] In other words, both Wesley and Whitefield believe that those whom God justifies he also sanctifies.

Nonetheless, significant differences on justification arose between them. Whitefield believed that justification covered all the sins of the believer, before conversion, and also after conversion. "I fear, they understand justification in that low sense, in which I understood it in a few years ago, as implying no more than remission of sins: but it not only signifies remission

54. Whitefield, *Sermons*, 2:12.
55. Ibid., 3:13.
56. Ibid., 4:13.
57. Wesley, *Standards*, 1:194.
58. Ibid., 1:48.
59. Outler, ed., *Sermons*, 1:124
60. Ibid., 1:196.

of sins past, but also a federal right to all good things to come."[61] He preached righteousness as an everlasting righteousness: "Christ's righteousness was intended by the great God to extend to mankind even from eternity . . . because the benefit of it is to endure to everlasting life . . . "[62] Toplady quotes this saying: "The greater our satisfaction is, the more advanced we are in holiness, the more we shall feel our need of free justification."[63]

In contrast, Wesley taught that it was only pre-conversion sins that were covered by justification, so that the believer must approach God again for forgiveness of sins committed after conversion. And Wesley made it clear that although righteousness was imputed to believers, this will be of no value if they remain unrighteous: "O warn them that if they remain unrighteous, the righteousness of Christ will profit them nothing!"[64] Wesley later talked less of imputed righteousness and more of imparted righteousness, saying, "I am myself more sparing in the use of it [imputed righteousness] . . . because the Antinomians used it at this day to justify the grossest abominations."[65] For that reason too he later tended to refer to "imparted faith," rather than to "imparted righteousness," noting that the New Testament does not refer directly to "the imputing the righteousness of Christ."[66]

"Antinomianism," generally referring to those who opposed using the law of Moses as a directive for Christian behavior, could be held as a theological view by those of exemplary Christian behavior. But it could also be asserted as a justification for immorality: if I am justified, then I have a license to sin, without any consequences. This was Wesley's fear and accusation. He opposed Moravian antinomians as much as Calvinist antinomians. He called them "the most dangerous . . . of all the Antinomians now in England."[67]

Whitefield also opposed antinomians. They do not repent of their ongoing sins: "Some allow that there is mourning before, but no mourning after conversion; pray, who says so? None but an Antinomian, a rank Antinomian."[68] Rowland Hill, Calvinist and opponent of Arminianism, was also totally opposed to them. "The greatest curse that ever entered the

---

61. Whitefield, *Sermons*, 3:26.
62. Ibid., 2:34–36.
63. Toplady, *Works*, 598.
64. Outler, ed., *Sermons*, 1:462
65. Jackson, ed., *Works*, 10: 315.
66. Ibid., 10:314.
67. Ibid., 10:201.
68. Whitefield, *Sermons*, 1;100.

church of God is dirty Antinomianism."⁶⁹ So Wesley was not attacking straw men: but Whitefield and his fellow-Calvinists were as opposed to antinomian practice as Wesley was.

Wesley believed that those who were certain of their eternal justification would not strive for holiness. Whitefield believed that assurance of eternal justification stimulated the pursuit of holiness.

The Human Will . . . and God's Grace

At the heart of the dispute was a disagreement about the role and significance of the human will. Whitefield thought that the human will was so infected by sin that no one could turn to God or continue as a believer unless God made it happen. God calls us to faith and obedience, and makes and keeps us as believers. Wesley taught that while the human will was infected by sin, God's grace enables human response: "A measure of free will [is] supernaturally restored to every man."⁷⁰ So human free will was a necessary part of this response. For Wesley, human free will is fundamental. "Indeed, if man were not free, he would not be accountable, either for his thoughts, words or actions. If he were not free . . . he would be incapable either of virtue or vice, of being either morally good or bad."⁷¹

Wesley's view is grace-based, though some Calvinist critiques of Wesley do not recognize this. Wesley asks: "How is it more for the glory of God to save man irresistibly, than to save him as a free agent, by such grace as he may either concur with or resist?" ⁷² And he asserted, "Whatever grace we receive, it is a free gift from [Christ] . . . in consideration of the price he paid. We have this grace, not only from Christ, but in him."⁷³

Free will, or free grace, was at the center of the dispute. Free or sovereign grace was a key theme of Calvinists. God's grace was not deserved or earned by people, but a free gift of God, a free gift bestowed solely on God's initiative, and freely and thoroughly effective in providing salvation for us, and working that salvation in us. As Ian Maddock has shown, Wesley had taken over a Calvinist slogan, and used it against them: "Wesley's desire was to 'reclaim' the term 'free grace' from the Calvinists and reapply it on Arminian terms."⁷⁴

69. Shenton, *Hill*, 425.
70. Jackson, ed., *Works*, 10:229–30.
71. Ibid., 6:227.
72. Ibid., 10:231.
73. Ibid., 11:395.
74. Maddock, *Men of One Book*, 194.

What should we make of this disagreement? The word "grace" in the New Testament has two related but distinct meanings. In some contexts it means God's sovereign and decisive grace [monergism], and in some contexts it means God's enabling grace [synergism]. God's decisive grace is God's free grace, and God's effective grace. Here, faith is acceptance. In God's enabling grace, faith is empowered and cooperative commitment. However, Wesley's view is a subtle integration of both monergism and synergism, as Kenneth Collins has shown.[75] Here salvation is by grace alone, but the grace-enabled human response to God's work of grace within the believer is also recognized. A comprehensive doctrine of grace needs to include both the gratuitous, decisive free-gift of salvation, and also the enabling power of God's grace. It is significant that the monergistic New Testament references are to the gift of salvation,[76] and the synergistic references are to God's enabled ministry and endurance.[77] Of course, the order is significant: it is only those who have received the free gift of grace who will live the grace-enabled life and do the grace-enabled ministry.

To support his view, Wesley supported the Arminian reworking of the biblical doctrine of predestination. He famously explained Romans 8:29 by adding the words "as believers": "Who are predestinated? None but those whom God foreknew *as believers*."[78] A consequence of his view of free will was that even perfected believers, could lose their salvation. "But one who was sanctified by the blood of Christ may nevertheless go to hell."[79]

For Whitefield, Wesley's view tipped the balance too far away from God's freedom, and so too close to human effort. He warned of the danger of promoting human willpower. He preached, "If we deny election, we must, partly at least, glory in ourselves."[80] And again, "But as the Sovereign Lord of all, who is debtor to none, he has a right to do what he will with his own, and to dispense his favours to what objects he sees fit, merely at his pleasure."[81] He called on believers: "Build not on your own faithfulness, but on God's unchangeableness. Take heed of thinking you stand by the power of your own free will. The everlasting love of God the Father must be your only

---

75. Collins, *Theology of John Wesley*.
76. Rom 3:24; 5:2, 15–21; Gal 2:21; 5:4; Eph 1:6; 2:7–10; Tit 2:11–14; 3:7; 1 Pet 1:13.
77. Rom 12:3, 15:15, 16; Gal 2:9, 20, 21; 1 Cor 15:10; 2 Cor 12:7–10; Eph 4:7; 1 Pet 4:10; and the charismata of Romans 12 and 1 Corinthians 12.
78. Jackson, ed., *Works*, 6:229; my italics.
79. Ibid., 10:297.
80. Whitefield, *Sermons*, 3:19.
81. Whitefield, *Journals*, 585.

hope and consolation . . . "[82] Or again, "when you are justified before God, it is without any respect to your works, either past, present, or to come."[83] Whitefield accused Wesley, as we have seen, "You plainly make salvation depend not on God's *free-grace*, but on man's *free-will*."[84] Whitefield misunderstood the subtlety of Wesley's theology of grace.

We see Wesley's valuing of the human will in his description of sin as "a voluntary transgression of a known law." He wrote: "I believe there is not such perfection in this life as excludes these involuntary transgressions which I apprehend to the naturally consequent on the ignorance and mistakes inseparable from mortality . . . Such transgressions you may call sins, if you please: I do not . . . "[85] This modifies his claim to perfection, but the point here is that it is the exercise of free will which is important in sinning, as well as in faith and good works. We are, however, authentically and responsibly ourselves all the time, and not only when we are making conscious free choices.

The situation was further complicated by Wesley's ambivalence regarding the sinful state of those who had been perfected. Did the sinful nature remain, or had it been removed by God's grace?[86] And his use of the words "inherent righteousness" to signify "imparted righteousness" did little to reduce the possibility of confusion. We see this dependence on the human will in the Wesley Conference 1770 minutes:

> We have received it as a maxim that "a man is to do nothing in order to justification" [sic]. Nothing could be more false . . . Whoever repents should do "works meet for repentance." And if this is not to find favour, what does he do them for? . . . Is this not salvation by works? Not by the merit of works but by works as a condition . . . [87]

In his "Thoughts on Salvation by Faith" of 1779, Wesley goes further and writes:

> Those that hold, "Every one is absolutely predestined either to salvation or damnation," see no medium between salvation by words and salvation by absolute decree. It follows, that whosoever denies salvation by absolute decree, in so doing, (according

---

82. Whitefield, *Sermons*, 3:31.
83. Ibid., 4:113.
84. Whitefield, *Journals*, 587.
85. Jackson, ed., *Works*, 11:396.
86. McGonigle, *Sufficient Saving Grace*, 252.
87. Telford, *Wesley*, 286–87.

to their apprehension) asserts salvation by works. And herein I verily believe they are right. As averse I once was to the thought, upon further consideration, I allow there is, there can be, no medium. Either salvation is by absolute decree, or it is (in the scriptural sense) by works . . . You must either assert unconditional decrees, or (in a scriptural sense) salvation by works.[88]

Yet, as we have already seen, Whitefield also recognized the significance of good works in justification: "*Thirdly*, we are justified *Declaratively*: namely by good works: good works declare and prove to the world that our faith is a true saving faith. 'Was not Abraham justified by works?' And again, 'Show me thy faith by thy works.'"[89]

Parsing the relationship between the divine plan and human choice is of course notoriously difficult. As Whitefield tended to the view that God's plan is fulfilled against human choice, so Wesley tended to the view that God's plan is fulfilled when God's grace enables human choice. Both can be true. Fulfillment of God's plan and the exercise of human will are not mutually exclusive, even if their exact relationship is impossible to define.

Here is Whitefield's description of God's grace. "Salvation, everywhere through the whole Scripture, is said to be the free gift of God through Jesus Christ our Lord. Not only free, because God is a free sovereign agent, and therefore may with-hold it, on confer it on whom he pleaseth, but free, because there is nothing found in man, that can in any way induce God to be merciful to him."[90]

However the word "grace" is used with two meanings in the New Testament as we have seen, and Wesley's theology includes grace as free gift, and also grace as enabled response.

Reflections

How then can we characterize the theologies of Whitefield and Wesley? We could say that Whitefield's emphasis was on the sovereignty of God, and Wesley's on the love of God. Or that Whitefield focused on justification, and that Wesley focused on sanctification. This idea makes good sense when we note that Whitefield was an itinerant evangelist, while Wesley, though an able evangelist, also saw the need to promote the sanctification of the believers. And because he lived longer than Whitefield, he had much more scope to focus on this.

88. Jackson, ed., *Works*, 11:493, 94.
89. Whitefield, *Sermons*, 2:12.
90. Ibid., 1:175.

Whitefield is often described as a Calvinist and Wesley an Arminian. Both deserve a more subtle description. Whitefield was a Calvinist, and believed in sovereign grace, limited atonement, and predestination. However, he was also an activist evangelist, and the appeal for a decision often lasts for up to a third of the length of his sermons. Wesley was an Arminian, but held to a substitutionary view of the Christ's atonement, and to an entire dependence on God's grace.

Another way of thinking about the distinction between them is to ask the question, "What self-description is appropriate for a Christian believer?" We can characterize Whitefield's answer as, "a sinner saved by grace." We can characterize Wesley's answer as, "a saint saved by grace." Of course, both are true. And each answer may be a useful insight in different pastoral situations. The Calvinist emphasis on and acceptance of sinfulness and sinning could be imbalanced. Whitefield wanted to preserve God's sovereign grace and glory. Wesley wanted to urge sinners to pursue holiness. Both are legitimate aims. And God will finally achieve both!

What contributed to these disagreements between close friends and brothers in Christ? Misunderstanding, inconsistent theology, personal attack, and sin all appear to have played their part in these tensions. They tended to argue their case along the lines of theological and practical consistency, and fail to engage in careful exegesis of those passages in the Bible that appeared to contradict their views.

Confusion was caused by the difficulty in using biblical words for theological concepts. It is a constant problem in Christian theology. When using words to describe theological concepts we can either use non-biblical words, such as "Trinity," "Incarnation," "Person," "Substance," and "the Christian life," or we can use biblical words such as "faith," "justification," "sanctification," and "grace." The difficulty is that these words are used with a range of meaning in the Bible. "Grace" is used with two distinct meanings, as we have seen. The meanings of "faith" in the New Testament includes saving faith; a special gift of faith; enduring faith; the content of faith; and inactive faith.

"Justification" and "sanctification" are commonly used of the start and the continuation of Christian experience in theology, but have more particular meanings in different contexts in the New Testament. "Sanctification" in Hebrews, for example, includes what theology describes as "justification" and "sanctification." This causes endless confusion in theological communication, and in interpreting the New Testament, as it did in Whitefield and Wesley's thinking and communication. It also appears that the Wesleys and Whitefield did not always understand exactly what each other wrote. As Maddock observes, "Whitefield appears to have confused

Wesley's evangelical Arminian anthropology with semi-Pelagianism . . . conversely it appears that Wesley never truly understood Whitefield's brand of Calvinism."[91] Further, though Wesley claimed to have held the same views on perfection all through his ministry, in fact that was not the case. He did modify his views, and this increased confusion.

It must be admitted that not all of the debate was motivated by a zest for pure theology. There were personality disputes, there was a competition, especially for the patronage of the Countess of Huntingdon. There was resentment when people to whom Whitefield had ministered were then ministered to by Wesley and given a different message. There was resentment when some gospel workers were penalized or promoted for their views. There was envy and jealousy. In a word, there was sin.

And while they had much in common, there was still significant theological disagreement between them, even if they did not always diagnose it accurately. Their theological disagreements over predestination and perfection were significant, as were their disagreements about the extent of the atonement, and assurance of salvation. And these disagreements had pastoral consequences, and so shaped their ministries and messages. It is a feature of human life that we are most strongly aware of the disagreements we have with those with whom we agree on many points. Both Wesley and Whitefield felt this pain.

At times they preached and wrote against each other's views. While correcting error is a necessary part of Christian ministry, reaction against error alone is no way to find the truth. Those who react against others are in part defined by them. We must be defined by the Scriptures, not by our opponents. And while correcting error is a necessary element in Christian ministry, this task must not dominate our message. In the words of Henry Venn:

> It is a rule with me, to conclude any person who can be taken up with a desire to make men converts to any notion, not to Christ, or be zealous for any thing more than the life of faith and holiness from knowledge of Christ crucified, is a sounding empty professor, or, at best, in a very poor low state.[92]

We praise God for the lives and ministries of these men of God.

---

91. Maddock, *Men of One Book*, 192–93.
92. Venn, *Letters*, 263–64.

8

"Plain Truth for Plain People"

Wesley, Whitefield, and Homiletics

Martin Wellings

IN HIS MAGISTERIAL SURVEY of worship and theology in England from the Reformation to the late twentieth century, Horton Davies justifies devoting a chapter to the preaching techniques of John Wesley and George Whitefield on the grounds that "they transformed the function of the pulpit and also the religious life of England and North America."[1] In this assessment of their significance as preachers Davies echoed the plaudits of Thomas Haweis, who wrote a decade after Wesley's death: "Men more laborious . . . since the apostles' days will hardly be found . . . wherever they moved, they were as a flame of fire, and left a train of evangelical light behind them . . . thousands awaited and welcomed them, heard them with reverence, and received them as angels of God."[2]

Not all contemporaries were so positive: Wesley and Whitefield were caricatured by Hogarth, satirized by Samuel Foote, and described disdainfully by Horace Walpole.[3] But none could fail to be impressed by the sheer statistics of their endeavors. Over fifty years of itinerancy, Wesley traveled perhaps a quarter of a million miles, and preached 40,000 times, while Whitefield preached an estimated 18,000 sermons over thirty-five years, and addressed the largest crowds ever assembled in London and New England.[4]

---

1. Davies, *Worship and Theology*, 3:143.
2. Haweis, *An Impartial and Succinct History*, 3:235.
3. Davies, *Worship and Theology*, 3:176–79; Horace Walpole to George Montagu, 3 September 1748, in Lewis, *Horace Walpole's Correspondence*, 9:73–74; Walpole to John Chute, 10 October 1766, ibid., 35:119.
4. Downey, *Eighteenth Century Pulpit*, 156, 210. Slightly different figures may be

It is not surprising, therefore, that the preaching of both men has attracted hagiographers, in print and online, and that disentangling fact from myth is not a straightforward enterprise. Whitefield and Wesley, moreover, were themselves able advocates in their own cause, adept at using the press to tell their story through their letters, pamphlets and published journals. Furthermore, the trajectories of Wesleyan and Calvinistic Methodism, and of the Arminian and Reformed branches of the evangelical movement since the eighteenth century, have sometimes added a partisan flavor to the narrative of their work and the analysis of their impact, seen, for example, in the nuancing of Whitefield variously as passionate orator, theological novice, or theatrical egotist, or of Wesley as compelling evangelist, donnish expositor, or inanimate lecturer.[5]

These contrasting interpretations also serve as a reminder that placing Whitefield and Wesley together as progenitors of the evangelical revival should not occlude their differences in character, personality, and homiletic technique. Furthermore, a just recognition of their transformative and enduring impact on preaching in Great Britain and North America should not be allowed to divorce them from the wider setting in which they were shaped. The burgeoning discipline of sermon studies has underlined that the period between the Glorious Revolution and the death of Queen Victoria may be described as "a 'golden age' of sermon culture in Britain," and the same might be said of North America in the heyday of the New England pulpit.[6] Acknowledging the pervasiveness of preaching in this "sermonic society," and drawing on wider literary, cultural, and historical insights can add depth and breadth to the understanding of Wesley and Whitefield in their contexts, and in their preaching.

This essay will begin by looking at the sermon culture of the early eighteenth century, exploring the rhetorical, theological, and evangelical influences that formed, and then reformed, Wesley and Whitefield as preachers. After considering the sources for studying their homiletics, attention will then be given to their message, practice, performance, and influence.

Formation and Reformation: Whitefield, Wesley, and the Neoclassic Sermon

Thomas Jackson, the nineteenth-century editor of John Wesley's *Works*, appended to his biography of Charles Wesley and attributed to John and

found in Hughes, *Wesley and Whitefield*, 77, 80.

5. Hughes, *Wesley and Whitefield*, 139, 145–46.
6. Gibson, "The British Sermon 1689–1901," 5; Stout, *New England Soul*, 3–4.

Charles's father, Samuel, an anonymous pamphlet entitled *Advice to a Young Clergyman*, a letter addressed by an experienced incumbent to his new curate.[7] Jackson and Luke Tyerman were confident in the ascription of the pamphlet to Samuel Wesley.[8]

Even if their confidence was misplaced, the judgment of the anonymous author about the principal influences on late seventeenth- and early eighteenth-century English preaching has been endorsed by later scholars. Writing of the "glorious lights in the Church of God" in the reign of Charles II, the author affirmed, "In the first rank stood Bishop Wilkins, who may be almost said to have taught us first to preach; as his kinsman Archbishop Tillotson, to have brought the art of preaching near perfection."[9]

John Wilkins (1614–1672), first secretary of the Royal Society and Restoration Bishop of Chester, in successive editions of his *Ecclesiastes; or, a Discourse Concerning the Gift of Preaching as It Falls under the Rules of Art*, championed a plain style of pulpit oratory, in reaction against the elaborate "witty" style exemplified by Jacobean divines like Lancelot Andrewes and John Donne, as well as the scholastic and textual pedantry of the Puritans. Wilkins argued for clarity of language, simplicity of structure, and an avoidance of jargon and ostentatious learning: "The greatest learning is to be seen in the greatest plainnesse."[10]

This approach, buttressed by references to the classical rhetoric of Cicero and Quintilian, was echoed by the next generation of stylists, including Gilbert Burnet and Jonathan Swift, and it was powerfully demonstrated in the sermons of John Tillotson (1630–1694), Archbishop of Canterbury from 1691. Tillotson's influence as a model for homiletics was considerable during his lifetime, and endured long after his death, due to the growing appetite for published sermons: his widow sold the rights to print her husband's sermons for £2,500 in 1695; one hundred and sixty items were printed, some with print runs of over 2,000 copies; and his works were translated into Welsh and Irish.[11] Even preachers who disagreed with Tillotson's Latitudinarian theology emulated his homiletic method,[12] and where Tillotson led, other Anglican and dissenting preachers followed,

---

7. Jackson, ed., *Charles Wesley*, 2:499–534.

8. Tyerman, *Samuel Wesley*, 381–88.

9. *Advice to a Young Clergyman, in a Letter*, 45–46, in Jackson, ed., *Charles Wesley*, 2:521.

10. Wilkins, *Ecclesiastes, Or, a Discourse concerning the Gift of Preaching*, 128.

11. One of Whitefield's North American converts, a Savannah tradesman, owned seventeen volumes of Tillotson's *Sermons*: Whitefield, *Journals*, 404.

12. Gibson, "The British Sermon," 20 and Aston, "Rationalism, the Enlightenment, and Sermons," in Francis and Gibson, *Oxford Handbook of the British Sermon*, 391.

shaping a neo-classical approach that combined a plain style, a practical message and a natural mode of delivery.[13]

Samuel Wesley senior may not have written the anonymous *Advice to a Young Clergyman*, but he did compose a eulogy on the late Archbishop, describing him as "the standard... of English eloquence."[14] John Wesley was far less complimentary. He included some extracts from Tillotson's *Works* in his *Christian Library* (1749–1755), adding a typically caustic preface:

> I have the rather inserted the following Extracts for the sake of two sorts of people, —those who are unreasonably prejudiced for, and those who are unreasonably prejudiced against, this great man. By this small specimen it will abundantly appear, to all who will at length give themselves leave to judge impartially, that the Archbishop was as far from bring the worst, as from being the best, of the English writers.[15]

Whitefield was still more trenchant, notoriously condemning Tillotson's theology in vigorous terms: "[U]pon the maturest deliberation, *I* say again, what I have often said before, that Archbishop Tillotson *knew no more about true Christianity than Mahomet.*"[16]

Whitefield's strictures on Tillotson have been seen as an example of the brashness and arrogance of a young preacher achieving sudden celebrity. It is certainly true that Whitefield later expressed considerable regret at some of the apparently unguarded statements in his early letters and journals. It has also been suggested, however, that Whitefield deliberately used Tillotson as a foil for his own presentation of the gospel, creating a Latitudinarian straw man to stand against an evangelical message.[17] It has also been noted that both Whitefield and Wesley drew on significant elements of the neo-classical sermon style in their preaching, including plain vocabulary and a structure of text, argument, and application.[18] Wesley's reading in homiletics during his Oxford years included such examples of the plain style as Benjamin Calamy and William Tilly, as well as Tillotson himself. Wesley was also acquainted with, and sometimes critical of, the older homiletic schools represented by Thomas Playfere (1561?–1609) and

---

13. Lessenich, *Elements of Pulpit Oratory*, 234–35.

14. Tyerman, *Samuel Wesley*, 192.

15. "List of Works revised and abridged from Various Authors," in Jackson, ed., *Works*, 14:233.

16. George Whitefield, "To a Friend in London," 18 January 1740, in *Letters*, 505. Whitefield attributes the offending phrase to Wesley, speaking "in a private Society."

17. Lambert, "Whitefield and the Enlightenment," 70.

18. Edwards, *A History of Preaching*, 434.

Jeremy Taylor (1613–1667) for the "ornate" style, and Joseph Hall (1574–1656), Thomas Manton (1620–1677) and Samuel Annesley (1620?–1696), Wesley's maternal grandfather, for the Puritans.[19] Wesley's declaration in the preface to the first volume of his *Sermons on Several Occasions* (1746) that "I design plain truth for plain people" therefore aligned him with the eighteenth century's homiletic mainstream.[20]

Where Whitefield and Wesley parted company from Tillotson was in the evangelical experience and emphasis that governed the doctrine, purpose, and tone of their sermons. The Latitudinarian divines employed a plain style in the service of persuasive rhetoric, seeking to convince their hearers of the wisdom and benefits of moral behavior.[21] At least from the mid-1730s, Whitefield and Wesley sought in their preaching to bring people to an experience of the new birth through justification by faith, and to urge believers to grow in the life of holiness. It was the failure, as they saw it, of many clergy to preach the classic Reformation message of justification and sanctification, which led the revivalists to complain of sermons that were no more than "a little dead dry Morality"[22]; conversely, it was the revivalists' emphasis on conversion and reliance on experience which led their Anglican and Dissenting critics to scent enthusiasm and antinomianism, or, in the title of Hogarth's print of 1762, "credulity, superstition and fanaticism."

Text and Event: The Problem of Evidence

One of the difficulties inherent in studying Whitefield and Wesley as preachers is in teasing out the relationship between an oral sermon, a recollection of a sermon event, and a written or published text. Scholars have sometimes worked on the basis that Wesley and Whitefield's corpus of published sermons represents a good sample of the sermons they preached, more or less verbatim, and have then felt obliged to seek explanations for the lifelessness of the printed prose, for instance by suggesting that Whitefield's rich voice and dramatic delivery more than made up for the apparent deficiencies in his homiletic content.[23] It has also been observed that where publications were based on sermons as preached, contemporary accounts of the

19. Outler, ed., *Sermons*, 1:23–24.
20. Ibid., 1:104.
21. Lessenich, *Elements of Pulpit Oratory*, 110–13.
22. Whitefield, *Polite and Fashionable Diversions*, 8. Davies, *Worship and Theology*, 167–68, notes that Whitefield did not republish this provocative sermon.
23. Ibid., 150; Downey, *Eighteenth Century Pulpit*, 167.

preaching include illustrations, digressions, and topical references that do not appear in the printed texts.

More recent research, however, has shown that the relationships were far more complicated than has often been assumed. When Whitefield's preaching ministry began, he was a popular sensation, and there was considerable pressure to get sermons into print for a wider audience. Pirate versions appeared, and Whitefield had to act quickly to provide authorized texts, recognizing that these edited versions contained the "sum and substance" of his discourses, but were not "word for word" transcriptions.[24] Only a proportion of the sermons published in Whitefield's *Works* were checked and revised by the Grand Itinerant himself, and the vast majority of those date from the very beginning of his ministry: forty-six out of sixty-three were written before he was twenty-five years old.[25] Even then, however, it is possible to argue that Whitefield made sophisticated use of his printed sermons as published texts distinct from the oral event of his preaching. John Wesley, on the other hand, continued to write, revise, and publish sermons for most of his long life. Some of Wesley's printed sermons were published before they were preached, and were deliberately composed as teaching aids for the Methodist people, modeled on the Church of England's *Book of Homilies*. There were occasions when someone heard Wesley preach a sermon they had already read.[26] Printed texts, then, need to be handled with care, and not simply taken as transcripts of verbatim sermons.

Message and Method

Albert Outler has proposed for Wesley a key distinction between the purpose of an oral and a written sermon, suggesting that "the former is chiefly for *proclamation* and invitation; the latter is chiefly for *nurture* and reflection."[27] Wesley's own definition of "the best general method of preaching" in the *Large Minutes* was: "1. To invite. 2. To convince. 3. To offer Christ. 4. To build up: and to do this in some measure in every sermon."[28]

The emphasis, therefore, in oral preaching was to set out the basic Christian message, characterized by Horton Davies as "the three R's": ruin by the Fall, redemption through the cross of Christ, and regeneration by

---

24. Maddock, *Men of One Book*, 103–5.
25. Tyerman, *Whitefield*, 1:297.
26. "Notes on Wesley's Journal," 138.
27. Outler, ed., *Sermons*, 1:14; italics in original.
28. Rack, ed., *Methodist Societies*, 859.

the power of the Holy Spirit.[29] In the face of Enlightenment optimism about the human condition, Wesley held tenaciously to a traditional doctrine of the fall, and therefore maintained the inherent sinfulness of humankind. He affirmed that grace was at work in every person, creating the possibility of a response to the gospel, and was therefore confident in urging his hearers to appropriate the benefits of the atonement and to experience the new birth. For Wesley, the gift of regeneration was a stage on the way to the complete renewal of the individual in the image of God, a state he described variously as "entire sanctification" or "perfect love."[30] Wesley's message differed from Whitefield's partly in doctrine and partly in emphasis: Wesley's Arminian insistence on free grace "for all" was at odds with Whitefield's Calvinism, and Wesley's teaching on Christian perfection bewildered his Reformed colleagues; while the strongly ethical agenda of Wesley's *Sermons on Several Occasions*, addressing the lifestyle of the Methodist people, was not paralleled in Whitefield's published discourses. As a field preacher, Wesley sought to "offer Christ"; as the leader and guide of a network of religious societies, he was keen to inculcate holy living, and so he published sermons on such practical topics as the danger of riches, the education of children, charity, and dress, as well as an extended series of expositions on the Sermon on the Mount.

Whitefield shared Wesley's evangelical emphases, preaching on original sin, justification by faith, conversion, and the new birth. He insisted on the experience of inner renewal, echoing Wesley's affirmation that saving faith is "not barely a speculative, rational thing, a cold, lifeless assent, a train of ideas in the head; but also a disposition of the heart."[31] The distinction between formal religion and genuine Christianity recurred in Whitefield's preaching, as he urged his hearers to "close with Christ by a lively faith, so as to feel Christ in your hearts, so as to hear him speaking peace to your souls."[32] Whitefield's critics complained that he substituted emotion for rational persuasion, and that this made his preaching ultimately ineffective because he played on feelings, but failed to change minds. For Whitefield, however, the transformation of lives and minds came about through the regenerating work of the Holy Spirit, not through a process of calm reasoning, and this new birth was likely to be emotional and dramatic.

Eighteenth-century manuals of homiletics and rhetoric recognized the importance of unfolding an argument and building towards the application

---

29. Davies, *Worship and Theology*, 153.
30. See, for instance, the outlines of Wesley's theology in Wood, *Burning Heart*.
31. Outler, ed., *Sermons*, 1:120.
32. "The Method of Grace," in Whitefield, *Select Sermons*, 86.

at the end of the sermon. Wesley and Whitefield gave an evangelical inflection to this methodology, adopting some of the principles urged by contemporary homileticians but significantly modifying them in the process. Both aimed for clarity of structure, moving from a concise introduction of a text or theme through the argument to the application. Thus, for example, Whitefield's sermon "Christ the believer's wisdom, righteousness, sanctification and redemption" refers briefly to the biblical text (1 Corinthians 1:30), sets out the two principal divisions of the argument with sub-divisions, and then turns to urge the application.[33] Wesley, in his sermon on "Salvation by Faith," has three divisions and a very short application:[34] typically, Wesley's outline of a sermon includes the promise of "a few inferences" at the end. Where Wesley's sermons are reinforcing a doctrine, the application often simply concludes that the case is proved; where he is exploring Christian behavior, for instance in "On Obedience to Parents," the application is more specific and more detailed.[35]

It was in the substance and tone of the application, especially in their evangelistic preaching urging the new birth, that Wesley and Whitefield attracted particular criticism. Whitefield recorded in his *Journal* in January 1739 a controversy with "two clergymen of the Church of England" who were "strong opposers of the doctrine of the New Birth," and who, on hearing Whitefield's testimony of conversion, were inclined to "look upon me as a madman"[36]; Horace Walpole, listening to Wesley at Bath in 1766, complained that towards the end of the sermon he "exalted his voice and acted very vulgar enthusiasm."[37] Urging the new birth and the experience of conversion subverted the conventions of the early eighteenth-century *artes concionandi*.

One of Whitefield's particular gifts as a preacher was his ability to bring a Bible story to life through dramatic retelling. Very few of Wesley's sermons took this form,[38] but Whitefield preached and published sermons on Abraham and Isaac, Bartimaeus, the conversion of Saul, Zacchaeus, and other incidents in the Bible. His power to carry a congregation with him in exploring a narrative was the stuff of legend, with Lord Chesterfield apparently being sufficiently borne along by a story of a blind beggar draw-

33. Whitefield, *Select Sermons*, 96–115.
34. Outler, ed., *Sermons*, 1:118.
35. Ibid., 3:368–72.
36. Whitefield, *Journals*, 203.
37. Walpole to John Chute, 10 October 1766, in Lewis, *Horace Walpole's Correspondence*, 35:119.
38. One such, on "Dives and Lazarus," appeared in *Sermons on Several Occasions*: Outler, ed., *Sermons*, 4:4–18.

ing near to a precipice to leap to his feet at the denouement, crying "He's gone! He's gone!"[39] As a young man, Whitefield mocked the stories told in preaching by the Gloucester dissenter, Thomas Cole,[40] but his own sermons made sophisticated use of narrative, not just for illustration or even rhetorical effect, but to convey and embody converting power.[41]

Precept and Practice

Although Whitefield published a short discourse entitled "Directions: How to hear Sermons," explaining how people might hear sermons "with profit and advantage," he did not write explicitly on homiletics. Wesley, however, did address this subject, particularly in the published *Minutes* of the Methodist Conferences and in his abridgement of a seventeenth-century French treatise, *Directions concerning Pronunciation and Gesture* (1749). In turning attention to the advice and opinions expressed by Whitefield and Wesley on the art of preaching, and on the extent to which their practice corresponded with their precepts, it will be seen how far they adopted the guidance and priorities of contemporary stylists, and how far they challenged the norms of the eighteenth-century pulpit.

It was widely accepted in the early eighteenth century that preaching required thorough study and preparation.[42] A substantial part of John Wilkins's *Ecclesiastes*, for example, was devoted to a bibliography for preachers, while the author of the anonymous *Advice to a Young Clergyman* insisted on a thorough acquaintance with biblical languages and theologians from the Patristic era to the present day.[43]

In his more provocative moods, Whitefield was scornful of scholarship, declaring: "Our common learning, so much cried up, makes men only so many accomplished fools."[44] How far this was fideism, how far arrogance, and how far carefully-crafted polemic arguing for a "converted" ministry and against "formal" clergy is open to debate, but it is clear that Whitefield was nonetheless a conscientious student, and by 1750 he was expressing concern that some popular preachers would benefit from rest

---

39. Dallimore, *George Whitefield*. 2:388.

40. Ibid., 1:49.

41. See the analysis of Whitefield's sermon "Abraham offering up his son Isaac" in Emma Salgård Cunha, "Whitefield and Literary Affect," 200–206.

42. Lessenich, *Elements of Pulpit Oratory*, 151–54.

43. Anon., *Advice to a Young Clergyman*, 23–54.

44. Davies, *Worship and Theology*, 179.

and instruction, or else "for want of proper foundation [they] will run themselves out of breath."[45]

Wesley, while also emphasizing the primary need for spiritual qualifications for the clergy and warning the bibliophiles like Joseph Benson not to spend all their time with their books, also strongly advocated sound learning. In his *Address to the Clergy*, he wrote, "none can be a good Divine who is not a good textuary."[46] Methodist preachers were required to spend at least five hours a day reading, and Wesley described the opinion that a preacher need only read the Bible as "rank enthusiasm," adding in reply to one who objected, "'But I have *no taste* for reading.' Contract a taste for it by use, or return to your trade."[47] Here, too, Wesley practiced what he preached, reading widely and making a range of theological texts accessible to his people through the *Christian Library* and, later, the *Arminian Magazine*.

Learning once acquired was to be worn lightly, and not paraded in order to impress. Again, the neoclassic preachers inculcated clear thinking and plain language: Tillotson was reputed to have tested his sermons on an old servant, to ensure that he was avoiding jargon and obscurity.[48] Wesley followed suit,[49] and he urged the Methodist preachers to "choose the plainest texts you can," to "be sparing in allegorizing or spiritualizing," and to "take care of anything awkward or affected, either in your gesture, phrase, or pronunciation."[50] Wesley held up the First Letter of John as a model of clarity for young preachers, demonstrating "the strongest sense and the plainest language."[51] Contemporaries confirmed that Wesley's preaching style was "neat, simple, and perspicuous,"[52] and a lady who heard him preach in Lincoln in 1790 exclaimed in surprise: "Why, the poorest person in the chapel might have understood him!"[53]

Towards the end of his life, Wesley was reported to have overheard two women near Billingsgate market quarreling and "using language far more forceful than pious." When urged to beat a retreat, Wesley's response

---

45. Olson, "Whitefield's Conversion and Early Theological Formation," 30–45; Whitefield, *Journals*, 46–48; Elliott-Binns, *Early Evangelicals*, 371.
46. "Address to the Clergy," in Jackson, *Works*, 10:482, 486.
47. Rack, ed., *Methodist Societies*, 887–88.
48. Lessenich, *Elements of Pulpit Oratory*, 17.
49. Telford, ed., *Life of John Wesley*, 315–16.
50. Rack, ed., *Minutes of Conference*, 918.
51. 18 July 1765, in Ward and Heitzenrater, eds., *Journals and Diaries*, 22:13.
52. Whitehead, *Wesley*, 2:466.
53. "Anecdotes of the Wesleys," *Wesleyan Methodist Magazine*, 25.

to his companion was: "Stay, and learn how to preach."[54] Wesley's vigor in preaching might sometimes have struck critical contemporaries as enthusiastic, but nonetheless he advised his preachers: "Let your whole deportment before the congregation be serious, weighty, and solemn."[55] For Wesley, a plain style and an energetic and colloquial vocabulary must not slide into vulgarity. Whitefield, the raconteur and pulpit performer, who was much more adept with humor and repartee than Wesley, was more likely to cross this line, and this was picked up by the satirists, who mocked "the Rev. Dr. Squintum's Extemporary Sermons" and portrayed Whitefield admitting "I am a vulgar-mouth'd fellow."[56]

By the early eighteenth century it was expected that sermons would be written out in full. Some preachers read their manuscripts, which, when using duodecimo booklets, made the reading difficult for the preacher and very apparent to the congregation.[57] Others committed their sermons to memory; still others used notes or headings in the pulpit. Looking back from the late 1770s, Wesley recalled his first experience of involuntary extempore preaching at All Hallows', Lombard Street, in London, in 1735, standing in when the advertised preacher failed to appear: "This was the first time that, having no notes about me, I preached extempore." Wesley's Oxford diary, however, suggests that he had in fact begun preaching extempore at Oxford Castle in the previous November.[58] Whitefield had a similar experience of preaching without notes in Deptford in December 1737.[59] Thereafter both Whitefield and Wesley regularly spoke without notes, but this did not mean that they preached without preparation. One advantage of itinerancy was that they could prepare and practice material, and use it in different places. Benjamin Franklin claimed to be able to distinguish between Whitefield's newly-composed sermons and his well-rehearsed older ones, finding the latter "so improved by frequent repetition."[60] Horace Walpole, by contrast,

---

54. Tyerman, *Life and Times of the Rev. John Wesley*, 3:660.

55. Rack, ed., *Methodist Societies*, 918.

56. Davies, *Worship and Theology*, 180–82; see Haweis (*An Impartial and Succinct History*, 3:281) on humor that "pushed the ludicrous to the debasement of the dignity of the sacred ministry."

57. Chamberlain, "Parish preaching in the long eighteenth century," 48. Compare Hogarth's cartoon "The Sleeping Congregation."

58. Outler, ed., *Sermons*, 1:14; 28 January 1776, in Ward and Heitzenrater, eds., *Journals and Diaries*, 23:3.

59. Whitefield, *Journals*, 98.

60. Stout, *Divine Dramatist*, 104.

complained that Wesley's Bath sermon of 1766 was evidently too familiar, because it was delivered at speed and "like a lesson."[61]

Contemporary rhetoricians devoted much attention to the proper use of voice and gesture in public speaking. In both, extremes were to be avoided. Preachers should use sufficient variety of tone to counter Henry Fielding's acerbic definition of a sermon in his "Modern Glossary" (1752) as "a sleeping dose," without resorting to affectation or ecstasy.[62] Likewise, the preacher should be graceful and animated in gesture, but not histrionic.[63] Wesley's *Directions* echoed much of this advice, citing the example of Demosthenes practicing diction and gesture. As well as offering lots of specific guidance for developing the voice, overall Wesley emphasized "the natural key" and a varied, conversational tone.[64] Elsewhere, particularly in his correspondence, he consistently complained about preachers who forced their voices to an unnatural pitch or volume, describing and denouncing this as "screaming."[65] According to John Whitehead, Wesley's own voice was "not loud, but clear and manly."[66] With regard to gesture, Wesley commended the natural, advocated making eye-contact with the congregation, and deprecated thumping the pulpit: "Your hands are not to be in perpetual motion: This the ancients called the babbling of the hands."[67] Here again, Wesley seems to have united precept and practice: one observer of his preaching in Lincolnshire in July 1788 said that "but for the occasional lifting up of his right hand, he might have been termed a speaking statue."[68]

George Whitefield's practice was very different. The "Grand Itinerant" had exceptional gifts of voice and manner, and he used them to the full. As John Gillies, Whitefield's first biographer, recalled, "He had a strong and musical voice, and a wonderful command of it."[69] Whitefield was able to make himself heard in the open air by crowds numbering tens of thousands; his voice was not only clear and loud, but also rich and melodious, making him a spell-binding raconteur and a compelling orator. It was claimed that Whitefield could move a crowd to tears or laughter simply by vary-

61. Walpole to Chute, 10 October 1766, in Lewis, *Horace Walpole's Correspondence*, 35:119.

62. Jensen, *Covent-Garden Journal*, 153.

63. Lessenich, *Elements of Pulpit Oratory*, 128–49.

64. "Directions concerning Pronunciation and Gesture," in Jackson, *Works*, 13:518–27.

65. For example, Wesley to John King, 28 July 1775, in Telford, ed., *Letters*, 6:166–67.

66. Whitehead, *Life of Wesley*, 2:466.

67. Jackson, ed., *Works*, 13:527.

68. Kendall, "Mr. Wesley's Last Visit to Langham Row and Alford," 175.

69. Gillies, ed., *Memoirs*, 284.

ing his pronunciation of the word "Mesopotamia," and David Garrick was reported to have said enviously, "I would give a hundred guineas if I could only say 'O!' like Mr. Whitefield."[70] Whitefield could deploy passion and pathos, humor and invective, colorful anecdote and direct address. He was, moreover, a natural actor, and his innate dramatic instinct was honed by an early fascination with the stage. From the beginning of his preaching ministry, Whitefield's sermons were delivered with an intense physicality: a critical account of an early sermon on the new birth said that the preacher's animation was such that he seemed to be personally in labor.[71] The powerful combination of tone of voice, facial expression, and physical gestures may explain Whitefield's ability to communicate effectively with hearers who could not speak English, from monoglot Welsh communities to German immigrants in North America.[72]

Where Whitefield and Wesley departed from contemporary *artes concionandi* in both precept and practice was in their advocacy of itinerancy and field preaching. Eighteenth-century handbooks of homiletics assumed a settled pastorate, whether in the Church of England or in the dissenting denominations; Wesley and Whitefield were inveterate itinerants. Wesley saw this practice as not only necessary in order to reach people with the gospel, but also beneficial as a remedy against staleness and boredom, writing to Samuel Walker in 1756, "I know, were I myself to preach one whole year in one place, I should preach both myself and most of my congregation asleep."[73] Wesley's preachers, therefore, were kept on the move. As for field preaching, Wesley consistently defended the practice, reflecting in the *Large Minutes*, "Have we not used it too sparingly?" and replying: "It seems we have . . . Because we are particularly called, by going into the highways and hedges (which none else will) to compel them to come in."[74] Although he urged James Rea in 1766 to "Preach abroad in every place," Wesley remained a reluctant field preacher, admitting after thirty-three years, "To this day field-preaching is a cross to me. But I know my commission and see no other way of 'preaching the gospel to every creature.'"[75] Whitefield, too, acknowl-

70. Edwards, *History of Preaching*, 435.

71. Stout, *Divine Dramatist*, 40.

72. Beebe and Jones, "Whitefield and the 'Celtic' Revivals," 134; Stout, *Divine Dramatist*, 251.

73. Wesley to the Rev. Samuel Walker, 3 September 1756, in Campbell, *Letters*, 27:53. Walker had been ministering in Truro for ten years by the time Wesley advised him that a year's preaching in one place would create a somnolent congregation.

74. Rack, ed., *Methodist Societies*, 846.

75. Wesley to James Rea, 21 July 1766, in Telford, *Letters*, 5:23; 6 September 1772, in Ward and Heitzenrater, eds., *Journals and Diaries*, 22:348.

edged the gospel imperative, but also enjoyed the experience, and he planned his field preaching with care, creating a spectacle to maximize the impact of the event.[76] Wesley's approach was more low-key, paying attention to such pragmatic considerations as location and acoustics.[77]

Impact and Influence

Contemporary reactions to the preaching of Wesley and Whitefield varied considerably. There were the predictable critics: Horace Walpole, and other representatives of fashionable society, who rejected the evangelical message and accused its advocates of hypocrisy and cant;[78] the actors and playwrights who were incensed by Whitefield's attacks on their livelihood and responded in kind; and the clergy, Anglican and dissenting, who bridled at references to "mitred infidels" and "unconverted ministers,"[79] and who, at a deeper level, feared that the evangelicals were relying on rhetorical excitement and over-playing emotion and experience, rather than promoting solid, rational piety. Dr. Johnson spoke for the skeptics when he opined of Whitefield, "His popularity . . . is chiefly owing to the peculiarity of his manner. He would be followed by crowds were he to wear a night-cap in the pulpit, or were he to preach from a tree."[80]

Many disagreed with these strictures. Whitefield and Wesley were undoubtedly celebrities, and their fame, or notoriety, drew crowds, a point freely acknowledged by Wesley in his *Farther Appeal*, where he justified the novelty of field preaching by observing that it brought people "in droves" who would not go to hear the parish clergy.[81] In time, moreover, celebrity brought a measure of respectability, and their services were in demand for charity sermons from pulpits that had formerly been closed to them.[82] Beyond celebrity, many who were drawn by curiosity, or who came to scoff, discovered that the preacher's message "found" them. A "jocose and dissipated" youth who heard Wesley in Langham Row, Lincolnshire, in 1788,

76. Stout, *Divine Dramatist*, 79.
77. Heitzenrater, "John Wesley's Principles and Practice of Preaching," 16.
78. Walpole to George Montagu, 3 September 1748, in Lewis, *Horace Walpole's Correspondence*, 9:73; Walpole to Sir Horace Mann, 3 May 1749, ibid., 20:52, quoting Lady Townsend.
79. John Wesley to Charles Wesley, 19 August 1785, in Telford, *Letters*, 7:285. The phrase "heathenish priests and mitred infidels" was published by Charles Wesley in *An Elegy on the Death of Robert Jones, Esq.* in 1742; Whitefield, *Journals*, 470.
80. Boswell, *Life of Johnson*, 409.
81. Cragg, ed., *Appeals to Men of Reason and Religion*, 11:306–7.
82. Anonymous, *Pulpit Eloquence*, 53.

came "with an air of bravery: 'This fine Mr. Wesley! I shall hear him and I'll get converted.'" Apparently "the countenance of the preacher sufficed to put him into a more serious state of mind" and sixty years later the young man was still serving as a Primitive Methodist class leader.[83]

The testimony of those who adhered to the revival, while positive about the preachers overall, reflected differences of individual judgment and impact. John Hampson, a disgruntled ex-Wesleyan itinerant, found Wesley "often logical and convincing," but thought that he preached too often and told too many stories, while Whitefield was "more various" and "more popular."[84] Thomas Olivers heard Whitefield in Bristol, and was so moved that "I used to follow him as he walked the streets, and could scarce refrain from kissing the very prints of his feet."[85] George Story, on the other hand, visited the chapel in Tottenham Court Road and took notes of Whitefield's sermons, "but still nothing reached my case, nor had I any light into the state of my soul . . . nor could I discern any difference between Mr. *Whitfield's* preaching and seeing a good tragedy." After hearing some of Wesley's preachers, Story went to the 1762 Conference and found that Wesley's sermons were "in a peculiar manner calculated for establishing me in what I had lately experienced."[86] John Nelson, too, heard Whitefield at Moorfields, and "his preaching was pleasant to me . . . [B]ut I did not understand him." When Wesley came to preach, however, "I thought his whole discourse was aimed at me."[87]

Individual testimonies like these, with varying nuances and emphases, could be multiplied. Taken together, Whitefield and Wesley had an enduring influence on preaching in Britain and North America in at least three ways. First, they enforced and popularized an evangelical message, which became the common currency of much preaching for the rest of the eighteenth century and well into the nineteenth. When Adam Clarke, one of the most learned of Wesley's preachers, came to offer advice in *A Letter to a Methodist Preacher on his Entrance into the Work of the Ministry* (1800), he advised, "As to the matter of your preaching, I will only say: Preach Jesus: preach his atonement: preach his dying love: and through him proclaim a free, full, and present salvation."[88]

83. Kendall, "Mr. Wesley's Last Visit to Langham Row and Alford," 175.
84. Hampson, *John Wesley*, 3:172–73.
85. Olivers, "Account," 83, 85.
86. Wesley, "A Short Account of Mr. George Story," 70.
87. "The Journal of Mr. John Nelson," in Jackson, *Lives of Early Methodist Preachers*, 1, 13–14.
88. Clarke, *A Letter to a Methodist Preacher*, 19.

Secondly, they foregrounded an emphasis on evangelical experience, both on the part of the preacher and as the overriding objective of the sermon. Clarke began his *Letter* with a section "concerning the spirit in which you should do your work," underscoring "see that you retain a sense of God's mercy to your own soul," and insisting that "you preach, not merely to explain God's word, but to save souls: whenever you forget this, you go astray." Later he affirmed: "Carry your authority to declare the gospel of Christ not in your hand but in your heart."[89]

Thirdly, they exemplified the plain style, in terms of homiletic structure and vocabulary, and married this to a direct form of address to a congregation. However pure the literary composition and however lucid the style, visibly reading a manuscript was no longer acceptable. Effective preaching required a rapport with the congregation in a sermon-event open to improvisation and inspiration.

Conclusion

John Wesley and George Whitefield both brought to their preaching the shaping influences of the eighteenth-century pulpit, transfigured by the evangelical revival. Each sought to present "plain truth" to "plain people," proclaiming an evangelical message kindled and confirmed by personal experience. In many of their emphases, attitudes, and approaches, they were in full agreement.

But there were also differences. Some illustrated Phillips Brooks's famous definition of preaching as "truth mediated through personality," and contemporaries tried to capture the distinctions. For John Hampson, "Never was the contrast greater between public characters than between Mr. Wesley and Mr. Whitefield." In Hampson's judgment, Wesley was logical; Whitefield was sublime. Wesley was calm; Whitefield was passionate. "Mr. Wesley preached to the learned; Mr. Whitefield to the people."[90] Thomas Haweis, reflecting on two men who "both favoured me with their cordial regard," offered his own summary: Wesley, slightly built, "singularly neat and plain in his dress; . . . upright, graceful and remarkably active," with an understanding "naturally excellent and acute," was a scholar-preacher whose "mode of address . . . was chaste and solemn." Whitefield, growing stout with the years, blessed with "natural eloquence" and a "manner . . .

---

89. Ibid., 8, 9, 15.

90. Hampson, *John Wesley*, 3:172–73. This neat contrast is called into question by Wesley's commitment to preach to the poor, and Whitefield's entrée to Lady Huntingdon's drawing-room.

often highly graceful and oratorical" offered "coruscations of eloquence" which "left an impression on the mind never to be effaced."[91]

Besides the similarities of formation and the differences of character, there was also a difference of focus. Whitefield was almost exclusively an evangelist; Wesley developed a corpus of sermons that could guide the faith and life of the Methodist societies, and he sought to create a body of preachers who could continue to propagate the mission of Methodism beyond his own lifetime. This gave Wesley, his sermons, and his preachers a lasting institutional influence, which Whitefield neither sought nor possessed. Whitefield's reputation as a preacher, it may be suggested, lives on principally in his example and inspiration; Wesley's influence has survived in his movement and his teaching.

---

91. Haweis, *An Impartial and Succinct History*, 3:274, 278–89.

9

Freedom in the Atlantic World

John Wesley and George Whitefield on Slavery

GLEN O'BRIEN

THE PHILOSOPHER DAVID HUME in a footnote in his 1748 essay *Of National Characters* wrote about African slaves in ways that suggest the Enlightenment had made little inroads in checking the idea of the superiority of white people.

> I am apt to suspect the negroes and in general all other species of men (for there are four or five different kinds) to be naturally inferior to the whites . . . Not to mention our colonies, there are negro slaves dispersed all over Europe, of which none ever discovered any symptoms of ingenuity . . . In Jamaica indeed they talk of one negro as a man of parts and learning; but 'tis likely he is admired for very slender accomplishments like a parrot, who speaks a few words plainly.[1]

Such ideological dehumanization of Africans no doubt contributed to buttressing the slave trade, which lay at the heart of eighteenth-century

---

1 The research for this chapter was undertaken as part of a much larger research project and I am indebted to the following institutions and their staff for support received: Asbury Theological Seminary, Asbury University, Booth College, Catherine Booth College, The Center for Studies in the Wesleyan Tradition at Duke Divinity School, Manchester Wesley Research Centre, The John Rylands Library at the University of Manchester, Nazarene Theological College, Manchester, and The Oxford Centre for Methodism and Church History at Oxford Brookes University.

Garrett, "Hume's Revised Racism Revisited," 171–78. Note that throughout this chapter the apparently arbitrary use of capitalization often found in eighteenth-century sources, as well as archaic spelling, has in most instances been edited to conform to modern usage.

Britain's commercial prosperity and served as a major support to its Atlantic empire. Few voices had been raised against it before the 1780s. As late as the 1772 *Treatise upon the Trade from Great Britain to Africa*, the slave trade could be spoken of in glowing terms as "the foundation of [Britain's] commerce, the support of our colonies, the life of our navigation and the first cause of our national industry and riches."[2] Even the churches had their theological justifications for it, including the Rev. R. Harris's *Scriptural Researches on the Licitness of the Slave Trade, Shewing its Conformity with the Principles of Natural and Revealed Religion* (1788).[3] Though the slave trade created massive wealth for the aristocracy, it was also supported by ordinary people from the middle class and even lower working classes, ordinary "mom and pop investors" who might own only a single slave yet draw income from that investment.[4] Little wonder, then, that systematic campaigning against slavery, led largely by Quakers, did not get under way until the 1780s, with The Society for Effecting the Abolition of the Slave Trade not being set up until 1787.

Historians have traditionally seen the anti-slavery cause as strengthened by a moral argument that privileged humanitarianism and natural rights over the selfishness and greed of market forces. In 1944, Eric Williams in *Capitalism and Slavery* set out the more prosaic argument that once the sugar trade in the West Indies hit a downturn through inefficiency, slavery was set aside as no longer profitable.[5] More recent scholarship has tended to the opinion that Williams overstated his case and has once again returned to the religious and theological foundations of the anti-slavery movement.[6] Christopher Leslie Brown sees a new moral legitimacy given to the abolitionist cause as an expression of the need to recover national virtue in the wake of the loss of the American colonies.[7]

John Wesley and George Whitefield were each in their own way agents of empire, but there were stark differences in their views on the legitimacy of the slave trade that supported that empire.[8] When one compares Wesley

---

2. Prest, *Albion Ascendant*, 254.

3. Pinfold, *Slave Trade Debate*, 174–247.

4. *Britain's Forgotten Slave Owners: Episode 1*. See the University College London's *Legacies of British Slave-ownership* website for a database of the names of slave owners https://www.ucl.ac.uk/lbs/, accessed 7 December 2016.

5. Williams, *Capitalism and Slavery*, 178–96, where Williams argues that the role of humanitarianism in abolition has been "grossly exaggerated."

6. Pinfold, *Slave Trade Debate*, 10–12.

7. Brown, *Moral Capital*.

8. For Whitefield as one who "did not think much about empire" and yet "engaged in the culture of empire," and contributed to its expansion, see Pestana, "Whitefield and

and Whitefield on political liberty in the context of the American Revolution one finds that while both men shared similar political views, Whitefield was much more sympathetic to American grievances than Wesley, whose patience with the Americans ended once their rhetoric switched from "liberty" to "independence." Along with the architects of American Independence, Whitefield, "the forgotten founding father," failed to see the contradictions between the rhetoric of freedom and the continuance of slavery.[9]

Whitefield and Slavery in the Colony of Georgia

Whitefield's ownership and use of slaves was driven by the financial needs of the Bethesda Orphanage, described rather vividly by Boyd Schlenther as "an albatross-like incubus hanging on his person and ministry—a poorly considered project which thwarted much of his proclaimed prime purpose."[10] Wesley, on the other hand, whose *Thoughts on Slavery* (1774) was the first significant non-Quaker treatise on the topic, rejected any pecuniary considerations as a justification for slavery, seeing clearly the inconsistency of Americans crying for liberty while "ten thousand negroes in the American colonies" were enslaved and exploiting this logical lapse for his own rhetorical purposes in opposing it.[11]

Whitefield's approach to slaves was humane and compassionate early in his career, but he seemed unwilling to address the systemic evil of slavery though he argued for the humane and compassionate treatment of slaves. In his 1740 "Letter to the Inhabitants of Maryland, Virginia, North and South Carolina," Whitefield issued a plea for the "poor negroes" who were treated worse than dogs. "Whether it be lawful for Christians to buy slaves, and thereby encourage the nations from which they are brought, to be at perpetual war with each other, I shall not take it upon me to determine; but sure I

Empire," 82–97.

9. Stout, *Divine Dramatist*, 198–99.

10. Schlenther, "Whitefield's Personal Life and Character," 24. See also Choi, "Whitefield, Georgia, and the Quest for Bethesda College," 224–40.

11. Entry for 12 February 1772, Ward and Heitzenrater, eds., *Journal and Diaries*, 24:70; Wesley, "Thoughts upon Slavery (1774)," Jackson, ed., *Works*, 11:59–79. I have consulted the 1774 edition published in London by R. Hawes housed in the John Rylands Library at the University of Manchester. However in addition to the page numbers in that edition I have provided, for convenience, the page numbers in the more readily available "Jackson" edition of Wesley's *Works*. A volume on Wesley's *Social and Political Tracts* is in preparation as part of the new critical edition of the *Works* under the General Editorship of Randy Maddox. Until then most readers will need to rely on the older edition. For discussion of Wesley's sources see Baker, "The Origins, Character and Influence of John Wesley's *Thoughts upon Slavery*," 75–86.

am it is sinful; when bought, to use them as bad as, nay worse, than brutes."[12] He urged upon slave masters that they teach their slaves the Christian faith, for just as they were as much sinners as whites, so they were as much able to be saved. This letter was published by Benjamin Franklin and widely distributed in colonial newspapers. It appeared thirty-five years before Wesley's more famous *Thoughts upon Slavery* and represents an important early voice for the compassionate treatment of slaves.

In his published sermon *The Lord our Righteousness*, first preached in Boston in 1740, Whitefield concluded by addressing the slaves among his hearers.

> I must not forget the poor negroes: no, I must not. Jesus Christ has died for them, as well as for others. Nor do I mention you last, because I despise your souls, but because I would have what I shall say make the deeper impression upon your hearts. O that you would seek the Lord to be your righteousness! Who knows but he may be found of you? For in Jesus Christ there is neither male nor female, bond nor free; even you may be the children of God, if you believe in Jesus. Did you never read of the eunuch belonging to the queen Candace? A negro like yourselves. He believed. The Lord was his righteousness. He was baptized. Do you also believe, and you shall be saved.[13]

Arnold Dallimore, one of Whitefield's more hagiographical biographers, while conceding regretfully that Whitefield made no effort to abolish the system of slavery, provided an overwhelmingly positive description of his relationship with slaves.[14] In spite of his ownership of slaves, "the far greater weight of his influence was exerted for the welfare of the black man . . . declar[ing] to America the human dignity and spiritual worth of the negro."[15] He closes with the estimate of Charles Maxon, writing in 1920, that Whitefield was "the first great friend of the American negro."[16]

---

12. Whitefield, "A Letter to the Inhabitants of Maryland, Virginia, North and South Carolina," (23 Jan 1740) in Gillies, ed., *Works* 4:37 (39–41). See also Stout, *Divine Dramatist*, 100–101, 258, 272–73; Dallimore, *Whitefield*, 1:495–509.

13. Gillies, ed., *Works*, 5:234. This sermon was included among those published in *Select Sermons*, 116–38.

14. Dallimore, *George Whitefield*, 1:495–509. Dallimore draws a rather long bow, however, when he suggests that the invention of the "negro spiritual" may be traced to Whitefield's preaching, ibid., 1:508–9.

15. Dallimore, *George Whitefield*, 1:509.

16. Maxson, *Great Awakening*, 57, cited in Dallimore, *George Whitefield*, 1:509.

Boyd Stanley Schlenther provides a less sanguine evaluation, pointing out the role of the Bethesda orphanage in Whitefield's legitimation of slavery:

> Bethesda fatefully led to Whitefield's emerging the most energetic, and conspicuous, evangelical defender and practitioner of black slavery. From the time he first visited Georgia he opposed the Trustees' prohibition against slavery and proceeded to issue a veiled threat that if it were not legally permitted he would remove Bethesda to South Carolina. When in 1750 the Georgia Trustees finally allowed slavery, he produced a full-throated defence of the institution: 'As for the lawfulness of keeping slaves, I have no doubt', adding: 'Though liberty is a sweet thing to such as are born free, yet to those who never knew the sweets of it, slavery perhaps may not be so irksome'. He of course claimed that keeping blacks in slavery meant they could be exposed to the Christian gospel; however, Whitefield recorded in his manuscript journal that, while preaching, he vehemently told slaves that "their hearts were as black as their faces."[17]

In 1747 Josiah Smith wrote from Charleston, South Carolina that Whitefield's supporters had subscribed two hundred pounds sterling "to purchase and improve with Negroes a very good plantation."[18] Whitefield wrote to the trustees of the Orphan House on 6 December 1748 concerned about its precarious financial condition, "Had a negroe [sic] been allowed, I should now have had a sufficiency to support a great many orphans, without spending above half the sum which hath been laid out . . . Georgia never can or will be a flourishing province without negroes be allowed."[19]

Given this pecuniary motive, one wonders what Whitefield would have thought of his friend John Wesley's claim thirty years later that no slaver ever purchased a slave out of a motive of mercy, but only ever to make money.[20] The colony of Georgia was originally set up by James Oglethorpe on benevolent grounds so that slavery was disallowed in its original charter. Wesley was of the opinion that it was largely financial expedience that led to the eventual introduction of slavery.

17. Whitefield to the Georgia Trustees (6 December 1748), Whitefield to [Johann] B[oltzius] (22 March 1751), Gillies, ed., *Works*, 2:208–9, 404; George Whitefield manuscript journal, 1, 2 May 1748, in Whitefield, *Memoirs*, 165, 166, cited in Schlenther, "Whitefield's Personal Life and Character," 25.

18. Stout, *Divine Dramatist*, 198.

19. Whitefield, Letter DCCXIV "To the Honourable Trustees of Georgia," 6 December 1748, in Gillies, ed., *Works*, 2:208–9.

20. Jackson, ed., *Works*, 11:71–72.

> Mr. Oglethorpe you know went so far as to begin settling a colony without negroes, but at length the voice of those villains prevailed who sell their country and their God for gold, who laugh at human nature and compassion, and defy all religion, but that of getting money . . . But I fear [slavery] will not be stopped till all the kingdoms of the earth become the kingdoms of our God.[21]

John Wesley's *Thoughts upon Slavery* (1774)

John Wesley's *Thoughts upon Slavery* will be the focus of most of this chapter, not in order to privilege Wesley's views over Whitefield's, but simply because there is no comparable extended treatment in Whitefield's writings on the subject, which are more occasional in nature.

It is particularly significant that centers of Methodist activity were often also centers of the slave trade. Bristol was the headquarters of Methodist activity in the south west of the country and was also, after London and Liverpool, the largest slave market in the Atlantic trade in the 1770s.[22] This close proximity of Methodists to the slave trade raises the question of why John Wesley left it so late in his career to offer a formal treatise on the subject. It should be kept in mind that, though Wesley was strongly opposed to slavery from the time he first encountered it, he was primarily an evangelist and the founder of a religious movement. He was not a parliamentary evangelical like William Wilberforce with a dedicated focus on a particular social issue. His opposition to slavery was made in the midst of a busy itinerant ministry and the management of a diverse, and at times troublesome, community of Methodists.

Something of a polymath, Wesley had an opinion on almost every topic under the sun, and harnessed his voracious reading habit to produce an encyclopedic knowledge of an impressive array of subjects, including moral, historical, political, economic, scientific, and religious concerns. It is unsurprising that his opposition to slave trade would have to wait its turn. Coupled with this consideration is the fact already noted that organized opposition to slavery did not really get under way until the 1780s in any case. Writing to Granville Sharp in 1787, Wesley declared, "Ever since I heard of it first I felt a perfect detestation of the horrid Slave Trade."[23] I will attempt

---

21. Smith, *John Wesley and Slavery*, 53.

22. Morgan, *Bristol and the Atlantic Trade*, 145; Marquardt, "Social Ethics in the Methodist Tradition," 294. See also Marquardt, *John Wesley's Social Ethics*, 67–75.

23. Wesley to Granville Sharp, October 11, 1787, Telford, ed., *Letters*, 8:17.

to show here that Wesley's opposition to slavery did not undergo a change from passive acceptance to active opposition, but remained adamant from early in his career.

John and Charles Wesley had first met with the cruelty of slave-masters in South Carolina as Charles was returning to England in 1736.[24] Though it would be forty years before John would take up his pen for an extended opposition to the institution, there are several early references to his hatred of the institution. In 1755, while commenting on 1 Timothy 1:10 in his *Explanatory Notes upon the New Testament*, Wesley spoke of "Man-stealers" as "the worst of all thieves, in comparison of whom highwaymen and housebreakers are innocent! What then are most traders in negroes, procurers of servants for America . . ."[25]

While visiting South Carolina in April 1737, Wesley engaged in a long conversation with "Nanny," a West Indian slave, in the home of the Rev. Thompson. Though he spoke with her at length about her soul and assured her that heaven was a place where no one would ever beat her, he did not raise or mention in his journal entry the institution of slavery.[26] He did, however, recoil at the violence toward slaves that he encountered in Purrysburg, South Carolina at that time. 'O earth! How long wilt thou hide blood? . . . cover thy slain?'[27]

Once Wesley did take up his pen to address slavery in a more extended treatment he did so largely on humanitarian grounds, using what we would today call a natural law argument. *Thoughts upon Slavery* begins by drawing upon Anthony Benezet's *Some Historical Account of Guinea,* published in 1771, an early anti-slavery work that provides a historical over view of the institution of slavery from ancient times. This is probably the work to which Wesley refers in his journal entry for Wednesday 12 February 1772.[28]

> In returning [from Dorking], I read a . . . book, published by an honest Quaker, on that execrable sum of all villainies, commonly called the "slave trade." I read of nothing like it in the heathen world, whether ancient or modern. And it infinitely exceeds, in every instance of barbarity, whatever Christian slaves suffer in Mahometan countries.[29]

24. Ward and Heitzenrater, eds., *Journals and Diaries*, 18:181n74.

25. Wesley, *Explanatory Notes upon the New Testament*, 539.

26. Ward and Heitzenrater, eds., *Journals and Diaries*, 18:501–2.

27. Curnock, ed., *Journal*, 1:352–53.

28. Benezet's work was reprinted in 1968 as Benezet, *Some Historical Account of Guinea*. Wesley also drew on Hargraves's *Plea for Somerset the Negro*.

29. Ward and Heitzenrater, eds., *Journals and Diaries*, 22:307. Benezet was born

One of the frequently heard arguments in support of slavery was that the country from which slaves had been brought was so inhospitable that it had been a mercy to be delivered from it.[30] Wesley strongly rejected this as a falsehood and countered it with a description of the Guinea and Ivory Coasts as pleasant, rich, and fertile areas abundant in produce of all kinds. Though it may have been unhealthy to European visitors it was perfectly healthy to the native inhabitants.[31]

Wesley then turned to consider the kind of people who had been forced into slavery providing a very positive portrait of the "Jalof," "Fuli," and "Mandingo" peoples.[32] The Fulis were described as having a fair judicial system, and their rulers ruled with moderation. As strict "Mahometans" they drank no alcohol, and had a "good and quiet disposition," well taught in good deeds, and disapproving those who did evil. They did not procure more land than they could use and they cultivated the land with industry. If one of their number was enslaved by the Europeans the others banded together to redeem him. They looked after their aged and infirm and even helped the Mandingos during times of famine.[33] A similarly positive portrait of the Mandingos is given, and it is noted that they are devout Muslims with a "priest" [imam] in every village. Their worship is said to be modest, attentive, and reverent. All three nations practiced several trades including "smiths, saddlers, potters, and weavers."[34]

---

in France of Huguenot parents who fled to London. He became a Quaker at the age of fourteen, and in 1731 the family moved to America. He left business in 1742 to become a teacher in Philadelphia and first became concerned about slaves in 1750 after which he wrote a series of works on the subject that were influential on the anti-slavery work of Thomas Clarkson and influenced Wesley's involvement in the anti-slavery movement. These works are *A Short Account of that part of Africa inhabited by Negroes* (Philadelphia, 1762); *A Caution and Warning to Great Britain and her Colonies in a Short Representation of the Calamitous State of the Enslaved Negroes in the British Dominions* (Philadelphia, 1766); and *Some Historical Account of Guinea, its Produce and the General Disposition of its Inhabitants, with an Enquiry into the Rise and Progress of the Slave Trade, its Nature and Calamitous Effects* (Philadelphia, 1771). Ward and Heitzenrater maintain that it is this last which "is probably the one referred to" in Wesley's journal entry but without giving any evidence. Ward and Heitzenrater, eds., *Journals and Diaries* 22:307n40.

30. Jackson, ed., *Works*, 11:60.
31. Ibid., 11:60–61.
32. The reader should note that the names used for people groups in historical sources often differ from those in present use.
33. Ibid., 11:62.
34. Ibid.

Rousseau's view of the "noble savage" is discernible in Wesley's citation of Allanson's portrait of Africans, which Allanson had reported to the Royal Academy of Science in Paris from 1749 to 1753:

> Which way soever I turned my eyes, I beheld a perfect image of pure nature: An agreeable solitude, bounded on every side by a charming landscape; the rural situation of cottages, in the midst of trees; the ease and quietness of the Negroes, reclined under the shade of the spreading foliage, with the simplicity of their dress and manners: The whole revived in my mind the idea of our first parents, and I seemed to contemplate the world in its primitive state.[35]

Allanson even marveled at the Africans' knowledge of the heavenly bodies, reckoning them to be excellent astronomers, though in want of "proper instruments."[36] The inhabitants of the Gold and Slave Coasts, as well as of the kingdoms of Benin, Congo, and Angola, are all given a similarly positive description.[37] Far from being ignorant and cruel savages, for John Wesley, more "justice, mercy and truth" was to be found among these people than among Europeans.[38]

The discussion then turned to the manner in which slaves were procured and transported to America; the portrait Wesley provides is very confronting and disturbing in its cruelty. Many were procured by fraud, tricked into boarding vessels and then held there against their will. The Europeans persuaded the Africans to wage war with each other and then to sell their prisoners of war. Even small children had been kidnapped by blacks and sold to slavers. "That their own parents sell them is utterly false: Whites, not Blacks, are without natural affection."[39] Wesley provides evidence of these methods via extracts from a surgeon's journal in *Two Voyages to Guinea* (1724) and declares with delicious irony, "Thus the Christians preach the Gospel to the Heathens!"[40]

Wesley's description of the traps set for unsuspecting Africans is confirmed by the account given by Ancona Robin John in a letter to Charles Wesley in August 1774. He and his brothers had been members of a powerful slave-trading dynasty in "Old Calabar" (today's Nigeria). In the midst of

---

35. Ibid, 11:63.

36. Ibid.

37. Ibid., 11:63–65. That the people of Benin punish adulterers, both men and women, with death, is a sign for Wesley of their advanced morality (64).

38. Ibid., 11:64–65.

39. Ibid., 11:65–66.

40. Ibid., 11:66–67.

a dispute with a rival slaving clan, the brothers were betrayed into the hands of English slavers.

> My brother Ambo upon the first appearance of the fraud which was discovered by the Captain and mate coming in to the cabin with pistols which my brother saw and felt for the Capt. Stroke him on the head then my brother seized the Captain and men and threw them on the floor but behind him were those that were cutting him on the head and neck till he were spent and must all kill'd at which time he cried out O Capt. Bevans what fashion is this for white men to killed black men so he cried for mercy but obtained none but was thrown up to the hands of his enemies who cut off his head and on the side of the ship this being done they sunk the canoes and drowned more than we can tell.[41]

In becoming slaves, the Robin Johns experienced the horrors to which they had condemned so many others. But the experience also led them to conversion and they became devout Methodists. While enslaved in Virginia their owner suddenly died and Ancona took this as God's judgment upon his cruelties. An apparently sympathetic ship's captain offered to carry them to Bristol from where they could make their way home, only to clap them in irons and place them on another transport ship upon arrival. Eventually they were set free on a legal technicality after Ephraim Robin John corresponded with the Chief Justice, Lord Mansfield. Upon their release, they met Charles Wesley and at some point became devout Methodists.

> This account reminds us that slaves were not simply victims but people who drew on their own resources and will power to respond to the appalling experience that befell them. Not all of them had Ancona and Ephraim's opportunities and skills, but many acted in profoundly determined, resourceful and courageous ways to survive the experience of slavery.[42]

Wesley cited Anderson's *History of Trade and Commerce* for his estimate that 100,000 slaves were transported to America every year, of which number 30,000 died en route. Slaves were first examined by surgeons with men,

---

41. Ancona Robin John to Charles Wesley, 17 August 1774, cited in Cruickshank, "Charles Wesley," 8–16. This article examines letters to Charles Wesley from the converted African slaves, Ephraim Robin John and Ancona Robin John in 1774. These letters provide a first-hand description of the experience of conditions aboard a slave ship and a glimpse into the relationship between slaves and Methodists. See also Sparks, *Two Princes of Calabar*.

42. Cruickshank, "Charles Wesley," 16.

women, and children standing stark naked in full view of all. Those who were approved were separated out from the rest and branded with a hot iron, marked on the breast with a company logo. On board they were crowded, still naked, into tiny spaces where the heat, thirst, and stench were so bad it was little wonder so many perished on the journey.[43] The vessel upon which Ancona Robin John was transported provided a mere five square feet per slave and only 272 of the 336 captives survived.[44] One of the most powerful and widely-distributed images of anti-slavery propaganda was the depiction of the Liverpool vessel *Brookes*, published in 1789, which depicted rows and rows of slaves lying in the lower decks of the vessel, "dehumanised objects, passively submitting to their fate and being packed onto the ships like herrings in a barrel."[45]

When they arrived they were again paraded naked before the eyes of their purchasers before being separated and sent to various plantations, never to see each other again. "Here you may see Mothers hanging over their daughters, bedewing their naked breasts with tears, and daughters clinging to their parents, till the whipper soon obliges them to part. And what can be more wretched than the condition they then enter upon?"[46] They were separated forever from their family and country, and fed on only a few roots, yams, or potatoes. Clothed by inadequate rags that offered no real shelter from the cold or the heat, they were deprived of adequate sleep and worked continuously from dawn till dusk and beyond their strength so that their lives shortened well before their time. Watched over by overseers who whipped them until they were scarred from shoulders to waist, they were often not in their quarters until midnight due to extra duties. Going to bed hungry, they were required to return to their labors in the morning or else feel the lash. "Did the Creator intend," asked Wesley, "that the noblest Creatures in the visible world, should live such a life as this!"[47]

Sir Hans Sloan (1660–1753), physician and successor to Sir Isaac Newton as President of the Royal Society, from 1729–41, reported even worse punishments inflicted on slaves:

---

43. Jackson, ed., *Works*, 11:67. For a good discussion of the conditions on board slave ships, see Hochschild, *Bury the Chains*.

44. Cruickshank, "Charles Wesley," 11–12.

45. Pinfold, *Slave Trade Debate*, quotation 12, image 328–29, reproduced from *An Address to the Inhabitants of Glasgow, Paisley, and the Neighbourhood, concerning the African Slave Trade by a Society in Glasgow* (Glasgow, 1791), in Pinfold, 312–29.

46. Jackson, ed., *Works*, 11:67–68.

47. Ibid., 11:67.

> [T]hey frequently geld [castrate] them, or chop off half a foot: After they are whipped till they are raw all over, Some put pepper and salt upon them: some drop melted wax upon their skin: Others cut off their ears and constrain them to broil and eat them. For rebellion, (that is, asserting their native liberty, which they have as much right to as to the air they breathe) they fasten them down to the ground with crooked sticks on every limb, and then applying fire by degrees, to the feet and hands, they burn them gradually upward to the head.[48]

Given his public status as a scientist, the description Sloane gives of the treatment of slaves, for all of its graphic horror, is likely to have been reliable.[49]

Wesley next pointed out how the laws enacted in plantations were no safeguard against such cruelties. In Virginia, any slave freed by his master was required to be resold to another, and anyone was legally permitted to kill a slave in whatever way he saw fit. In Jamaica, a reward of fifty pounds was offered for anyone who killed or brought in a runaway slave. In Barbados, the killer of a slave need pay only a fifteen-pound penalty.[50] Wesley recalled, "One gentleman, when I was abroad, thought fit to roast his slave alive! But if the most natural act of 'running away' from intolerable tyranny, deserves such relentless severity, what punishment have these lawmakers to expect hereafter, on account of their own enormous offences?"[51]

---

48. Ibid., 11:68. Sloan was a trusted authority who had published widely in natural history and had been the attending physician of both Queen Anne and George II. A trustee of the Georgia colony he probably had had some contact with Wesley in this capacity. His natural history collection was sold to the nation and in 1753 an act was passed to receive it along with other collections as the foundation of the British Museum.

49. On 12 December 1759 Wesley spent part of the afternoon in the British Museum where he admired the collections of Sloane. "There is a large library, a great number of curious manuscripts, many uncommon monuments of antiquity, and the whole collection of shells, butterflies, beetles, grasshoppers, etc., which the indefatigable Sir Hans Sloane, with such vast expense and labour, procured in a life of four-score years!" Ward and Heitzenrater, eds., *Journals and Diaries*, 21:236, and see n95. Wesley displayed his more typical disdain of collecting for collecting's sake when he visited, on 22 October 1748, the Botanical Garden near Chelsea Embankment begun by Sloane and donated by him in 1721 to the Society of Apothecaries. "I spent an hour in observing the various works of God in the Physic Garden at Chelsea. It would be a noble improvement of the design if some able and industrious person were to make a full and accurate inquiry into the use and virtues of all these plants, without this, what end does the heaping them thus together answer but the gratifying an idle curiosity." Ward and Heitzenrater, eds., *Journals and Diaries*, 20:252.

50. Jackson, ed., *Works*, 11:69.

51. Ibid.

Wesley stated that he would develop his argument against slavery "setting the Bible out of the question," in other words, to use an argument from natural law, "on the principles of heathen honesty."[52] Aspects of his natural law argument had already appeared in the tract. For example, Wesley argued that human beings are "the noblest creatures in the visible world" and that, as such, they have as much right to natural liberty as to the air that they breathe. To seek to escape the tyranny of slavery is a "most natural act." In choosing to argue in this way, he may have had in mind that an appeal to the Bible would be futile since the biblical material was often used to defend the institution of slavery as divinely ordained. The discussion of "natural liberty" was an important part of public discourse in the eighteenth century, and its adoption here is likely to have extended Wesley's influence beyond those who subscribed to the normative authority of Scripture. The fact that slavery and the cruel practices associated with it were legal did not make them morally right. For Wesley, no law could make good evil or evil good, and slave holding could never be consistent with any degree of natural justice.

It is interesting to note in this connection that, in a letter to John Wesley in 1751, Whitefield drew upon scriptural "proofs" to defend the institution of slavery. (Unfortunately, Wesley's reply, if any, does not seem to have survived.) In this he was repeating arguments, and indeed partly copying verbatim, from his 1750 letter to the Georgia Trustees upon their finally allowing slavery in the colony.

> As for the lawfulness of keeping slaves, I have no doubt. Since I hear of some that were bought with Abraham's money and some that were born in his house. I also cannot help thinking that some of those servants mentioned by the apostles in their epistles were, or had been, slaves. It is plain that the Gibeonites were doomed to perpetual slavery . . . [53]

The great jurist William Blackstone (1723–1780) had argued that "the three origins of the Right of Slavery assigned by [the Emperor] Justinian, are all built upon false foundations." Wesley draws on this authority to reject these foundations. 1) Slavery is said to arise from captives taken in war. But we have no right to kill prisoners of war, only to restrain them until the war is over. 2) The idea that slavery may begin by one person selling himself to another fails the test of logic. A person may sell his labor but not his life. A sale is based on equivalence in value between what is bought and what is

---

52. Ibid., 11:70. For a discussion of *Thoughts upon Slavery* as a model of public theology, see Field, "John Wesley as a Public Theologian."

53. Brendlinger, "Wesley, Whitefield, a Philadelphia Quaker, and Slavery," 167.

paid, but there is no equivalent price for a person's life or liberty. 3) It is said that a person is a slave if born of slaves, but since this idea is built on the two former ideas so it must fall with them.[54]

Turning to a number of justifications for slavery, Wesley rejected each one in turn. Some, including the Liverpool salt merchant Henry Wilckens, writing in a slightly later period, would argue that slaves purchased as prisoners of war were spared death, as if it had been an act of mercy to enslave them. "The advantage which the Negroes, the objects of the slave trade, thus derive appear to me sufficient to justify the continuation of it; and ... the Europeans, by preserving the lives of the slaves, are very much entitled to their services."[55] Wesley forthrightly declared the falsity of such arguments and, as noted earlier, asserted that no slaver ever purchased a slave out of a motive of mercy but only ever to make money.[56] Others, including Whitefield, had argued that, while slavery may not be consistent with either mercy or justice, it was nonetheless necessary to purchase slaves to furnish plantations, which would be economically unviable without them. Such economic arguments formed the cornerstone of the anti-abolitionist position.[57] Wesley replied that while it may be necessary to that end, the end itself was not necessary. It would be better for land to remain uncultivated forever than that it should be worked by slaves. This was an approach that, twenty-four years earlier in 1750, Whitefield could not bring himself to take. "[I]t is plain to a demonstration that hot countries cannot be cultivated without Negroes. What a flourishing country might Georgia have been had the use of them been permitted years ago! How many white people have been destroyed for want of them, and how many thousands of pounds spent to no purpose at all!"[58]

Wesley took the view that European lives were no less expendable than African lives and that white people were just as well able to work the land as Africans. He offered as proof of this his and other's hard manual labor in Georgia. To the idea that slavery was necessary for the "trade, wealth, and glory" of the nation, Wesley responded that England would be better to have no wealth at all than to procure it through villainy, through the "tears, and sweat, and blood, of our fellow-creatures."[59]

---

54. Jackson, ed., *Works*, 11:70–71.

55. Wilckens, *Letters concerning the Slave Trade*, 4, cited in Pinfold, *Slave Trade Debate*, 20.

56. Jackson, ed., *Works*, 11:71–72.

57. Pinfold, *Slave Trade Debate*, 22.

58. Brendlinger, "Wesley, Whitefield, a Philadelphia Quaker, and Slavery," 167.

59. Jackson, ed., *Works*, 11:72–74.

Some had argued that it was necessary to treat slaves harshly to prevent them running away and because they would otherwise be idle due to their miserable "stupidity."[60] Wesley's use of the word "stupidity" here does not refer to intelligence but to a lack of verve, motivation, and energy brought on by their situation. Slaves had not been so sapped of energy or motivation for industry in their own countries but on the plantations they had not been given any opportunity for education or improvement.

> The inhabitants of Africa, where they have equal motives and equal means of improvement, are not inferior to the inhabitants of Europe: To some of them they are greatly superior ... Their stupidity, therefore, in our plantations is not natural; otherwise than it is the natural effect of their condition. Consequently, it is not their fault, but yours: you must answer for it, before God and man.[61]

As for the idea that cruel punishments were necessary because of the cunning, pilfering, and stubbornness of the slaves, again, these had been brought on by the conditions enforced by their owners. If "mildness and gentleness" were used there might be a different result, as is proven in the case of Hugh Bryan from "the borders of South Carolina," who treated his slaves with such kindness that they "loved and reverenced him as a Father, and cheerfully obeyed him out of love. Yea, they are more afraid of a frown from him, than of many blows from an overseer."[62]

The final section of *Thoughts upon Slavery* is given over to an application not made to the public at large, to the English nation in general, or to the Parliament, but a direct and pointed application aimed at those at the heart of the trade—"captains, merchants [and] planters."[63] Captains well knew the fine country the slaves had been removed from, the dignity and high moral quality of the Africans, and the cruel manner in which they had treated them when they shipped them to the plantations, and are reminded that there is a just God to whom an account must be given. Wesley asks the captains whether they had any heart, any compassion, or any sympathy at all for the Africans. There was still an opportunity for the captains to repent of their deeds and quit their horrible trade before the Day of Judgment

---

60. Ibid., 11:74.

61. Ibid.

62. Ibid., 11:75. Wesley had engaged in "necessary talk (religious)" with Bryan while in Georgia on 22 and 23 November 1736 and wrote to him from Oxford on 28 April 1738 after his return to England. Ward and Heitzenrater, eds., *Journals and Diaries*, 18:449, 577 (diary entries).

63. Jackson, ed., *Works*, 11:75–76.

came upon them.[64] Merchants were in the same situation. If they had any compassion at all, they should follow the example of the Liverpool slaver who, when asked by one of his slaves how he would feel if his own wife and child were taken away by Africans, immediately left the slave business. "Be you a man! Not a wolf, a devourer of the human species!"[65]

In 1750 Whitefield had written to Wesley, laying out the argument that one may as well make a positive, practical use of the system of slavery, and that the guilt lay at the door of the procurer and the seller rather than the buyer of slaves.

> Though it is true that they are brought in a wrong way from their own country, and it is a trade not to be approved of, yet, as it will be carried on whether we will or not, I should think myself highly favoured if I could purchase a good number of them in order to make their lives comfortable, and lay a foundation for breeding up their posterity in the nurture and admonition of the Lord. I had no hand in bringing them into Georgia, though my judgment was for it, and I strongly importuned thereto; yet I would not have a Negro upon my plantation till the use of them was publicly allowed by the colony. Now this is done, let us diligently improve the present opportunity for their instruction.[66]

Wesley took a very different position in *Thoughts upon Slavery*. As for plantation owners, buyers of slaves were equally as guilty as their sellers. It was not enough for purchasers to say that they had bought their goods honestly and were not concerned about how they were procured. Since the purchasers' money keeps the slavers in their trade they must share in the guilt of the crimes committed.[67]

As he moved to the end of his treatise, once again Wesley returned to the concept of freedom as a natural right, this time with added scriptural allusions.

> Liberty is the right of every human creature, as soon as he breathes the vital air. And no human law can deprive him of that right, which he derives from the law of nature . . . Away with all whips, all chains, all compulsion! Be gentle toward all men; and see that you invariably do unto ever one, as you would he should do unto you.[68]

64. Ibid., 11:76–77.
65. Ibid., 11:77–78.
66. Brendlinger, "Wesley, Whitefield, a Philadelphia Quaker, and Slavery," 167.
67. Jackson, ed., *Works*, 11:78–79.
68. Ibid., 11:79.

The treatise closes with a prayer to the God of love, that God would have compassion on the slaves who are the work of God's own hands and for whom Christ shed his blood. For all of their differences on the institution of slavery Whitefield and Wesley at least shared this compassionate motive in common. He asks that God would stir their hearts to cry for their deliverance and also turn the hearts of the slavers to have compassion upon their charges.

> The servile progeny of Ham
>
> Seize as the purchase of thy blood!
>
> Let all the Heathens know thy name:
>
> From idols to the living God
>
> The dark American convert,
>
> And shine in every pagan heart![69]

Late Career Views of Whitefield and Wesley

Arnold Dallimore believed that Whitefield's approval of slavery was a "grievous" fault that lasted until his death in 1770.[70] Five years after Whitefield's death, the Quaker abolitionist Anthony Benezet, who had known Whitefield well and had visited him at Bethesda, expressed the view to Selina, Countess of Huntingdon, that Whitefield remained obstinate in his support of slavery through a process of attenuation.[71] It is possible, of course, that Whitefield may have changed his views on slavery if he had lived beyond 1770 when the period of anti-slavery agitation began to gather steam.

It is in my view unlikely, however, given Whitefield's broad attitude of support for the emerging American cry for independence. On his seventh and final voyage to America in 1769, Whitefield, motivated by a growing sensitivity to the tension between Britain and her American colonies, turned to a study of constitutional histories of England and the theme of liberty. In the wake of the Stamp Act and with British troops en route to Boston, Whitefield headed in a decidedly Whiggish direction, with the colonial patriot cause ever closer to his heart. It is difficult to imagine him adopting an anti-slavery platform during a time when the institution formed part of the economic backbone of the emerging new republic.

---

69. Ibid.
70. Dallimore, *George Whitefield*, 2:520–21.
71. Brendlinger, "Wesley, Whitefield, a Philadelphia Quaker, and Slavery," 168–70.

The British slave trade was naturally disrupted after the American War of Independence broke out. Wesley preached at Liverpool on 14 March 1777 and noted the impact of the war on the trade.

> I preached about noon at Warrington, and in the evening at Liverpool, where many large ships are now laid up in the docks which had been employed for many years in buying, or stealing, poor Africans and selling them in America for slaves. The men-butchers now have nothing to do at this laudable occupation. Since the American war broke out there is no demand for human cattle. So the men of Africa, as well as Europe, may enjoy their native liberty.[72]

In his *Serious Address to the People of England* (1788) Wesley took note of those who complained that Britain had "lost our Negro trade." As far as Wesley was concerned, good riddance to it: "Never was anything such a reproach to England since it was a nation, as the having any hand in this execrable traffic."[73] In a Postscript at the end of the *Serious Address*, Wesley noted the decrease in trade in the West Indies and saw this loss as something to be celebrated. The final destruction of slavery there would be cause for rejoicing, "tho' all our Sugar-Islands (so [long as] the inhabitants escaped) were swallowed up in the depths of the sea." England may well prosper without such an evil trade. "Certain it is, that England may not only subsist, but abundantly prosper without [the West Indies]: may increase in population, agriculture, manufactures, and all other articles above-mentioned, though we no more suck the blood and devour the flesh of the less barbarous Africans."[74]

On Thursday 6 March 1788, Wesley preached against slavery at Bristol, from Genesis 9:27, a text often used to legitimize slavery as divinely instituted with its prophecy that God would "enlarge Japheth, and he shall dwell in the tents of Shem; and Canaan shall be his servant."[75] The account in his journal shows that for Wesley, the controversy over slavery went beyond earthly courts, economies and politics, but was a war being waged among the principalities and powers in spiritual places. The room was packed when, in the middle of the sermon, a sudden and inexplicable noise like thunder was heard, shooting through the crowd like lightning and sending

---

72. Ward and Heitzenrater, eds., *Journals and Diaries*, 23:46.

73. Jackson, ed., *Works*, 11:144–45.

74. Wesley, *Serious Address*, 28. The postscript from which the quotation is drawn appears in the 1778 edition but does not appear in the Jackson edition. *A Serious Address to the People of England* appears in Jackson, ed., *Works*, 11:140–49.

75. Gen 9:27 (Authorized Version).

the people into a general panic. The crowd climbed over the top of each other violently and the benches were broken in the melee. After about six minutes the noise ceased and Wesley calmly continued. He considered this strange phenomenon to be a sign that the powers of evil were resisting the effort to end the slave trade.

> It was the strangest incident of the kind I ever remember and believe none can account for it without supposing some preternatural influence. Satan fought lest his kingdom should be delivered up. We set Friday apart as a day of fasting and prayer that God would remember these poor outcasts of men and (what seems impossible with men, considering the wealth and power of their oppressors) make a way for them to escape and break their chains in sunder.[76]

Only a month before this, in February 1778, the parliamentary reformer William Wilberforce (1759–1833) had given notice of a motion to introduce an abolition bill. Before he could introduce the bill, however, he experienced a breakdown and an attack of colitis. He urged his friend William Pitt to take up the cause and, on May 9, Pitt moved that the House of Commons investigate the slave trade.[77] Wilberforce called upon Wesley on Tuesday 24 February 1789 and the latter described their "agreeable and useful conversation" and considered it a "blessing for Mr. P[itt] to have such a friend as this."[78] Wilberforce himself noted, "I called on John Wesley, a fine old fellow."[79] One of the last letters Wesley wrote (24 February 1791) was to encourage Wilberforce, in his fight to end the slave trade.

> Unless the divine power has raised you up to be as *Athanasius contra mundum* [Athanasius against the world] I see not how you can go through your glorious enterprise in opposing that execrable villainy, which is the scandal of religion, of England, and of human nature. Unless God has raised you up for this very thing, you will be worn out by the opposition of men and devils. But if God be for you, who can be against you? Are all of them together stronger than God? O be not weary of well doing. Go on, in the name of God and in the power of His might, till even

---

76. Ward and Heitzenrater, eds., *Journals and Diaries*, 24:70.

77. Pollock, *Wilberforce*, 77–83.

78. Ward and Heitzenrater, eds., *Journals and Diaries*, 24:121, 273 (diary). Wesley was a strong and uncritical supporter of William Pitt. See Telford, ed., *Letters*, 8:113.

79. Curnock, ed., *Journals*, 7:471n, cited in Ward and Heitzenrater, eds., *Journals and Diaries*, 24:121n60.

> American slavery (the vilest that ever saw the sun) shall vanish away before it.
>
> Reading this morning a tract wrote by a poor African, I was particularly struck by that circumstance, that a man who has a black skin, being wronged or outraged by a white man, can have no redress; it being a law in all our Colonies that the oath of a black against a white goes for nothing. What villainy is this!
>
> That He who has guided you from youth up may continue to strengthen you in this and all things is the prayer of, dear sir,
>
> Your affectionate servant[80]

A great deal more has been made of this letter than is perhaps justified. Though Wesley's opposition to the institution of slavery was unflagging, he was too busy with his evangelistic work to be a full time activist like Wilberforce. At the same time his preaching may well have contributed to a change in the tide of public opinion against slavery. In 1792, 519 petitions to end slavery were presented to the Parliament with 400,000 signatures (13 percent of the adult male population) representing every English county.[81] In spite of this popular wave of support, the interposition of the war with France worked against the anti-slavery cause, as mass petitioning and popular movements were seen as harbingers of revolution. Conservative politicians supported slavery, fearing a loss of West Indian possessions to the French or the Americans. Eventually, 1805 saw the abolition of slavery in new British possessions but it would not be until 1807, sixteen years after Wesley's death, that the slave trade was finally declared illegal in Britain. Anti-slavery naval patrols were needed to check the illegal trade for a further sixty years.

Conclusions

Across the long careers of John Wesley and George Whitefield there appeared to be no discernible shift in their attitude toward slavery.

Wesley's earliest statements on the subject were damning and this continued throughout his career, though he only took it upon himself to write an extended treatment of the subject in 1774. Rather than seeing *Thoughts*

---

80. Wesley to William Wilberforce, 24 February 1791, http://wesley.nnu.edu/john-wesley/the-letters-of-john-wesley/wesleys-letters-1791/#Eighteen, accessed 12 December 2016. The "tract by a poor African" to which Wesley refers was that of the African slave Gustavus Vassa, which had been read to Wesley on the morning of 22 February 1791. Born in 1745, he was kidnapped and sold into slavery in Barbados. He traveled to England in 1757 and was baptized in St. Margaret's, Westminster, in 1759.

81 The figures are from Pinfold, *Slave Trade Debate*, 8.

upon Slavery as a response to organized resistance to the slave trade, it should be seen as an early contribution to the debate and one that, though by no means an altogether original piece of work, significantly contributed to the later reform movement.

In 1740, Whitefield was not prepared to say unequivocally that the slave trade was a moral evil, and he urged the compassionate treatment of slaves. By 1750 he was congratulating the colonial governors for having introduced slavery to Georgia, and wrote to them and to John Wesley, defending the institution on economic and scriptural grounds. When he died in 1770, he was an active participant in the political culture that birthed a new nation in which neither political nor natural liberty was to be extended to slaves.

Both these founding Methodists gloried in the strength of Britain's Protestant maritime empire, sharing in the "cult of commerce" that marked this period of British expansion.[82] Though they were themselves frugal, almost monkish men in their own patterns of self-denial, and often spoke against the evils of greed and luxury, they exhibited no in-principal opposition to economic prosperity as such. The health of British trade meant greater security for its Atlantic Protestant empire and served as a bulwark against foreign incursion and the loss of Protestant liberties.[83] Whitefield in particular benefitted from riding the waves of this Atlantic world (both figuratively and literally) becoming the most prominent transatlantic religious personality of the age. Wesley, however, was willing to see Britain's financial prosperity collapse rather than support a lucrative slave trade that kept human beings in lifelong servitude.

Both these Methodist leaders, close personal friends in spite of their sometimes-strained relationship over theological differences, spoke eloquently against the ill treatment of slaves. Whitefield issued one of the earliest protests against the cruelty of slave masters, and saw the African as the object of God's redeeming love. Yet slavery was for Whitefield a more personally confronting issue, as he could see no other way for his beloved Bethesda orphanage and proposed college to succeed. The colony of Georgia was established on a principle of social benevolence and slavery was initially outlawed there so that Whitefield's petitioning of the colonial government to allow slavery was ultimately self-serving.

The conclusion seems inescapable that Whitefield's rationale for keeping slaves was primarily economic and that, notwithstanding his plea for

---

82. Colley, *Britons*, 55–100.

83. For the manner in which independent traders challenged the Charter granted to the Royal Africa Company in order to obtain their share in the prosperity made available through the slave trade see Pettigrew, *Freedom's Debt*.

mercy toward slaves, Whitefield shared in a racist culture that exploited the labor of a people considered to be inferior for its own commercial benefit. What for John Wesley was an "execrable villainy" that could not be countenanced under any circumstances for George Whitefield was a necessary economic arrangement and a means to an end that needed only to be protected against brutality. Both men shared a passionate conviction about the spiritual freedom provided in the new birth; they differed, however, on the extent to which freedom should be considered a basic human right. Where freedom was a non-negotiable natural right in Wesley's Atlantic world, for Whitefield freedom was a matter contingent upon the circumstances of birth, race, and economic expediency.

10

Cultivating True Religion

The Nature and Dynamics of the Means of Grace

Tom Schwanda

Spirituality was foundational to the life and ministry of John Wesley and George Whitefield.[1] One indicator of this was their early participation in the "Holy Club," more accurately known as Oxford Methodism.[2] First Wesley and later Whitefield were leaders of this highly disciplined group that gathered for the cultivation of Christian fellowship through study and meditation, discussion of devotional classics, prayer, fasting and self-examination, visiting prisoners and providing for the poor.[3]

To guide our awareness of how Wesley and Whitefield understood spirituality this chapter will first examine the nature of true religion. This leads to an exploration of holiness as the goal of the spiritual life. The largest section of this chapter focuses on the means of grace, or spiritual disciplines, which guide believers in the sanctification process. The chapter concludes with an assessment of how Wesley and Whitefield emphasized specific means of grace. Wesley placed greater emphasis upon the Lord's Supper and fasting, while Whitefield stressed the value of meditation and observing God's providence. Despite these differences, both men sought to encourage believers to mature in Christ.

---

1. On Wesley, see Mursell, *English Spirituality*, 86–103; Whaling, *John and Charles Wesley*; and Watson, "Methodist Spirituality," 217–53, 263–70. On Whitefield, see Haykin, *Revived Puritan*; Gordon, "Jonathan Edwards and George Whitefield," 53–66; and Jones, "George Whitefield and Heart Religion."

2. Heitzenrater, *Mirror and Memory*, 81.

3. Ibid., 81–105.

Language of Spirituality[4]

Religion was the typical word used by Wesley, Whitefield, and other eighteenth-century evangelicals to express what we call spirituality today. In a 1734 letter to Richard Morgan Sr., the father of one of the Oxford Methodists, Wesley addressed the nature and dynamics of religion. He confessed that he had "providentially cast his eyes upon" the letter that Richard sent his father.[5] Wesley sought to correct the inaccuracies of young Richard with his clarification: "I take religion to be, not the bare saying over so many prayers morning and evening, in public or in private; not anything superadded now and then to careless or worldly life; but a constant ruling habit of soul; a renewal of our minds in the image of God; a recovery of the divine likeness; a still-increasing conformity of heart and life to the pattern of our most holy Redeemer."[6]

This reveals three significant principles for Wesley.[7] First, religion is not something added to one's life or external practices devoid of sincere conviction. Wesley frequently warned against the hypocrisy of the Pharisees who displayed this behavior. Second, there is a continuous interior pursuit that seeks to renew one's mind after the image of God. Third, the goal of this ever-expanding maturity is the imitation of Christ.[8] Throughout this description one recognizes the frequent biblical references that undergirded Wesley's thinking. The centrality of this is reinforced by his 1756 correspondence in which he declared, "I have one point in view--to promote, so far as I am able, vital, practical religion; and by the grace of God to beget, preserve, and increase the life of God in the souls of men."[9] Wesley's adjectives clarify the nature of a true religion in contrast with the moralistic and anemic religion that was common in his time.

Likewise, when Whitefield was nineteen he recorded his conversion using similar language. Charles Wesley's gift of Henry Scougal's *The Life of God in the Soul of Man* (1677) provided the impetus. Whitefield confessed "At my first reading it, I wondered what the author meant by saying, 'That some falsely placed religion in going to church, doing hurt to no one,

---

4. While there are various means to study a person's spirituality, this chapter focuses on the spiritual teachings of Wesley and Whitefield. Scholars caution that there are few reliable sources to understand their personal spirituality. See Rack, *Reasonable Enthusiast*, 544–50; and Jones, "So Much Idolized by Some, and Railed at by Others," 8.

5. Baker, ed., *Letters*, 25:367.

6. Ibid., 25:369.

7. For a variation on this, see Mursell, *English Spirituality*, 91–93.

8. Hammond, "John Wesley and 'Imitating' Christ."

9. Telford, ed., *Letters*, 3:192, cf. 194.

being constant in the duties of the closet, and now and then reaching out their hands to give alms to their poor neighbours." Confused, Whitefield wrote, "if this be not true religion, what is?" Finally, he confessed his liberating discovery: "true religion was union of the soul with God, and Christ formed within us."[10]

While briefer than Wesley's description, Whitefield also realized the necessity of Christ being formed within the believer (Gal 4:19). In his sermon "The Benefits of an Early Piety" Whitefield offered an expanded understanding of religion as "a thorough, real, inward change of nature, wrought in us by the powerful operation of the Holy Ghost, conveyed to and nourished in our hearts, by a constant use of all the means of grace, evidenced by a good life, and bringing forth the fruits of the spirit."[11] Whitefield stressed the dynamic interaction of agency between the Holy Spirit's operation and the person's use of the means of grace. It mirrors Jesus' teaching that you will know a person by the behavior of his or her life, which originates from a "real, inward change of nature" (Luke 11:39–40).

While religion was the dominant term, the language of spirituality was not absent. Wesley used spirituality to compare the righteousness of a Christian with a Scribe or Pharisee. He concluded, "Above all, let thy righteousness exceed theirs in the purity and spirituality of it."[12] Similarly, Whitefield employed spirituality to speak of the interiority of life. In one sermon, he stressed the essential occupation of the believer was the care of their soul. He insisted "Happy are they, who in the crowd of business do not lose something of the spirituality of their minds, and of the composure and sweetness of their tempers."[13]

Wesley and Whitefield both affirmed that holiness or sanctification was the goal of spirituality.[14] Maddock cautions that identical language of Wesley and Whitefield can communicate very different theology.[15] This is particularly evident regarding the pursuit of holiness. In a 1734 letter

---

10. Whitefield, *Journals*, 46–47. Whitefield sent Scougal's book to a friend to clarify the nature of true religion. Gillies, ed., *Works*, 1:6. On Scougal, see Olson, "Whitefield's Conversion and Early Theological Formation," 30–33 and McVickers, "Study of the Contemplative Life of George Whitefield." 171–72, 176–204.

11. Gillies, ed., *Works*, 5:161.

12. Outler, ed., *Sermons*, 1:570, cf. 552. Whitefield also used spirituality in discussing the Scribes and Pharisees. Whitefield, "Self-Inquiry Concerning the Work of God," 708.

13. Gillies, ed., *Works*, 5:456.

14. Wesley's concept of sanctification is complex. For helpful overviews see Collins, *Theology of John Wesley*, esp. 6–16, 288–303; and Tyson, *Way of the Wesleys*, 41–54.

15. Maddock, *Men of One Book*, 176, 179.

to his father, Wesley defined holiness as "not fasting, or bodily austerity, or any other external means of improvement, but that inward temper to which all these are subservient, a renewal of the soul in the image of God. I mean a complex habit of lowliness, meekness, purity, faith, hope, and love of God and man."[16] Wesley consistently reiterated that "Scriptural holiness is the image of God; the mind which was in Christ; the love of God and man."[17] Consistent with his definition of religion is the centrality of recovery of the image of God.

Part of the challenge of grasping Wesley is that he freely used holiness, sanctification, entire sanctification, and Christian perfection interchangeably.[18] In his sermon "On Perfection" Wesley taught that "perfection is another name for universal holiness—inward and outward righteousness—holiness of life arising from holiness of heart."[19] Wesley described the radical transformation that occurred at the new birth; when a person was changed from "inward sinfulness to inward holiness." Inward holiness was understood as a complete renovation of the person's soul. The selfish love and desires of a person were stopped mid-stream and redirected to God. Indeed, "the earthly, sensual, devilish mind gives place to 'the mind that was in Christ Jesus.'"[20] Outward righteousness was another name for social holiness. More specifically, Wesley wrote that "the essential part of Christian holiness is giving the heart wholly to God," yet he is realistic to remind his correspondent that life "will still be encompassed with numberless infirmities; for you live in an house of clay."[21]

Wesley's missionary journey to Georgia was motivated, in part, to cultivate an increasing "degrees of holiness."[22] He later revised this and maintained that there were no degrees of inner holiness but only outward holiness.[23] Despite these claims Wesley warned in 1786 the danger of friendship with the world. That person "can hardly avoid decreasing in holiness" and will ultimately "lose one degree of inward or outward holiness."[24] Shortly before his death, Wesley bemoaned that many still did not understand the nature of holiness. He articulated, "Many take holiness and harmlessness

---

16. Baker, ed., *Letters*, 25:399.
17. Jackson, ed., *Works*, 10:203.
18. See also McEwan's discussion of Christian perfection in chap. 6.
19. Outler, ed., *Sermons*, 3:75. See also ibid., 2:104.
20. Ibid., 3:174.
21. Telford, ed., *Letters*, 5:56.
22. Baker, ed., *Letters*, 25:441.
23. Telford, ed., *Letters*, 6:189.
24. Outler, ed., *Sermons*, 3:137, 179.

to mean one and the same thing." He insisted that "holiness . . . is the true wedding garment," and, "In a word, holiness is having 'the mind that was in Christ', and the 'walking as Christ walked.'"[25] Taken together, Wesley claimed that holiness consisted of "the love of God and our neighbour; the image of God stamped on the heart; the life of God in the soul of man; the mind that was in Christ, enabling us to walk as Christ walked."[26]

Initially Whitefield shared Wesley's language of degrees of holiness. He counseled others to "aspire after the utmost degrees of inward purity and holiness."[27] Speaking autobiographically, he attested that "I am athirst for holiness myself."[28] In sharp contrast to Wesley, this language disappeared after 1741, and Timothy Smith correctly observes, "Whitefield had backed away somewhat from the emphasis . . . on a holy life."[29] No doubt this was a result of his growing conviction of Calvinism and reticence to embrace Wesley's insistence on Christian perfection and measuring the stages of holiness.[30]

Unlike Wesley, Whitefield did not use the terms outward or social holiness. However, Whitefield did not ignore social needs or minimize the necessity of holiness and affirmed its consistency with his Calvinism.[31] In 1746 Whitefield wrote to Herbert Jenkins who was experiencing difficult "sifting times." Amid this confusion Whitefield counseled him, "But Jesus knows what is best for us. He shortens or lengthens out our trials as He sees will best promote inward sanctification of the heart."[32] Whitefield revealed his continued interest in holiness in a 1755 letter to Lady Huntingdon: "O for growth in grace! O for the total destruction of self and selfishness! Alas, what inward purgations and martyrdoms must be undergone! LORD JESUS, we are the clay, and thou art the potter; stamp thine image in what way thou pleasest!"[33] While this reference lacks the

---

25. Ibid., 4:146, 147. Wesley believed some people misunderstood holiness as merely avoidance of unhealthy behavior. Jackson, ed., *Works*, 7:456.

26. Jackson, ed., *Works*, 3:341.

27. Gillies, ed., *Works*, 1:339, 345–46, 350, 356.

28. Ibid., 1:345; see also 237, 356.

29. Smith, *Whitefield & Wesley on the New Birth*, 122.

30. Jones, "George Whitefield and Heart Religion," 99. Jonathan Edwards within his Calvinist context continued to stress thirsting after holiness. Edwards, *Religious Affections*, 382; see also 104.

31. Whitefield, *Journals*, 576–77. See also Jones, "George Whitefield and Heart Religion," 93, 109, 110, 111.

32. Christie, "Newly Discovered Letters," 162, 163.

33. Gillies, ed., *Works*, 3:148, 153.

specific words of holiness and sanctification, it captures the biblical principle of dying to self and mortification.

The following correspondence from 1763 attests to Whitefield's persistent commitment to holiness. He encouraged a friend in intentional love and service to God, saying, "Who knows but our latter end may yet increase? If not in public usefulness, LORD JESUS, let it be in inward heart–holiness, that we may daily ripen for the full enjoyment of thyself in heaven!"[34] In reality, Whitefield would affirm the pursuit of holiness prepares one for heaven.

The Nature of the Means of Grace

Wesley and Whitefield agreed that the means of grace were essential for growing in holiness.[35] Wesley's "The Means of Grace" sermon was motivated by the "stillness controversy" of the Moravians, who maintained a person should not engage in spiritual disciplines until they had reached a place of settled faith.[36] This marginalization of spiritual practices prompted Wesley to defend their importance. He defined the means of grace as "outward signs, words, or actions ordained by God, and appointed for this end--to be the *ordinary* channels whereby he might convey to men preventing, justifying, or sanctifying grace."[37] He understood the possible abuses and danger of confusing the means with the ends and insisted that apart from the Spirit of God there was no profit in the means of grace; nor could anyone be saved except by the blood of Jesus.[38]

Wesley lived over thirty years longer than Whitefield and produced more extensive sources than his younger counterpart. In particular, he created an elaborate understanding of three different forms of grace. He differentiated between the "general" means of grace (obedience, obeying the commandments, self-denial and taking up one's cross daily, noticing God's presence), "instituted" means of grace (what is revealed in Scripture and expected of every believer to practice), and the "prudential" means (that which

---

34. Ibid., 3:293.

35. Literature on Wesley's teaching on the means of grace is abundant. Helpful sources include: Knight, *Presence of God in the Christian Life*; Campbell, "Means of Grace and Forms of Piety"; Tyson, *Way of the Wesleys*, 129–43; and Chilcote, *John and Charles Wesley*, 182–207.

36. Outler, ed., *Sermons*, 1:376.

37. Ibid., 1:381.

38. Ibid., 1:382.

is implicit from Scripture and prudent for wise people to practice).[39] Wesley also distinguished between works of piety and works of mercy.[40]

Whitefield used this language more sparingly and did not provide a succinct definition of the means of grace as Wesley did. He did, however, speak of "the instituted means of grace, as prayer, fasting, hearing and reading the word of GOD, receiving the blessed sacrament, and such-like."[41] Whitefield also referenced the nature of the prudential means.[42] While his language was limited on the instituted and prudential means, he addressed the importance of a proper theological foundation more fully. Early during their time at Oxford, both men struggled to grasp the nature and proper balance between justification and sanctification. Wesley confessed, "I was utterly ignorant of the nature and condition of justification. Sometimes I confounded it with sanctification."[43] This confusion remained until 1738.[44] Wesleyan scholar John R. Tyson observes that the means of grace also corrected Wesley's distorted theology of works righteousness.[45]

The effects of this confusion were even greater for Whitefield. As a member of the Oxford Methodists, he engaged in such strenuous asceticism to win God's favor that it almost literally killed him. During Lent in 1735 he lost any sense of healthy balance and suffered an illness for seven weeks. Whitefield eventually left the university to recuperate at home.[46] Through his lengthy spiritual ordeal, Whitefield experienced his conversion three years before Wesley.

Not surprisingly, this discovery of the proper ordering of justification and sanctification inspired both men. Whitefield quickly reminded his listeners that spiritual practices did not automatically produce an experience with God. Just because a person employed the "outward means of grace" did not mean they possessed "a saving experimental knowledge of JESUS CHRIST."[47] Elsewhere, Whitefield argued that spiritual disciplines "are means; but then they are only means; they are part, but not the whole of religion." He stressed that if the means were automatic then the Pharisees

---

39. Knight, *Presence of God in the Christian Life*, 5. Space prevents treatment of the prudential means of grace but included attending class meetings and prayer meetings, visiting the sick, doing good deeds, etc.

40. Outler, ed., *Sermons*, 2:166.

41. Gillies, ed., *Works*, 6:266.

42. Ibid., 2:363.

43. Jackson, ed., *Works*, 8:111. See also Tyson, *Way of the Wesleys*, 41, 44.

44. Collins, *Theology of John Wesley*, 169.

45. Tyson, *Way of the Wesleys*, 130.

46. Whitefield, *Journals*, 53, 57, 59.

47. Gillies, ed., *Works*, 5:138. See also ibid., 6:269.

would have been the most religious of all people.[48] Nevertheless, when the "powerful operations of the Holy Spirit" enlivened the means of grace, the result was the "fruits of the spirit."[49]

Similarly, Wesley warned of the danger of confusing the means with the ends. He asserted that spiritual practices guarantee nothing: "*before* you use any means let it be deeply impressed on your soul: There is no *power* in this." Additionally, the means of grace does not create any merit since that is solely in Jesus Christ.[50] Like Whitefield, Wesley also affirmed the essential role of the Holy Spirit, for there is no profit in engaging the means without depending upon the Holy Spirit.[51]

The Means of Grace to Cultivate True Religion

First in order of publication, and most significant for Whitefield, was his "Walking with God" sermon.[52] He acknowledged the devastating effects of sin and how it creates an "averseness to prayer and holy duties." He also provided hope, asserting that once a person was reconciled to God the means of grace could guide a person in walking with God more intimately.[53] Whitefield examined seven practices to encourage this spiritual progress: reading Scripture, prayer including ejaculatory prayers, frequent meditation, observing God's providential dealings, watching the motions of the Holy Spirit, making full use of God's ordinances, and keeping company with other Christians who are walking with God.

In comparison, Wesley's "Means of Grace" sermon enumerates three practices: prayer, Scripture (including hearing, reading and meditating on it) and the Lord's Supper (including self-examination).[54] However, in the Annual Conference Minutes known as the "Large Minutes" of 1791, Wesley delineated five spiritual disciplines that were to be used within the bands, classes and societies.[55] They are framed as questions and illustrate Wesley's perennial concern for accountability. This was a critical distinc-

48. Ibid., 6:266.
49. Ibid., 5:161.
50. Ibid., 1:396.
51. Ibid., 1:382.
52. Ibid., 5:21–37.
53. Ibid., 5:24, 26.
54. Outler, ed., *Sermons*, 1:381, 384–90.
55. Jackson, ed., *Works*, 8:322–33. The 1765 version is slightly expanded, but since the 1791 edition was edited before Wesley's death it is used here and throughout this chapter. Compare with Rack, ed., *Methodist Societies*, 10:855–57.

tion between our two evangelical preachers, since self-examination was less significant in Whitefield. In addition to the three practices from his "Means of Grace" sermon, Wesley added fasting and Christian conference to these instituted means of grace.[56]

Scripture is Whitefield's first practice and he included a lengthy list of biblical passages that stress the necessity and benefit of regular interaction with the Bible. If a person neglects Scripture and allows anything else to take its place as the supreme guide in life, they are deluded and in danger of making a "shipwreck of [their] faith." Using Luke 10:39, he instructed, "We must make his testimonies our counsellors, and daily, with *Mary*, sit at JESUS feet, by faith hearing his word." This regular pattern prepares a person to daily grow in awareness until they met Jesus face-to-face.[57]

In his sermon "The Great Duty of Family-Religion," Whitefield stressed the critical importance of reading Scripture as the first responsibility of the father or what he calls the "governor" of the house. He understood without the words of Scripture deeply planted within a person's heart they were ill equipped to speak to their children or others in life.[58] Whitefield's most detailed treatment on reading the Bible is his sermon "The Duty of Searching Scripture."[59] Among other things, he stressed the necessity of approaching the Bible with a "humble child-like disposition,"[60] making personal application of the reading to your own life and continually searching the treasures of Scripture daily. Two of his principles relate to the partnership between the reader and the Holy Spirit. Since the Holy Spirit is the author of the Bible, one must "labor to attain that Spirit" to properly comprehend and guide one into all truth. One should also ask Jesus to send the Spirit to guide a person that the words that have been read "may be inwardly engrafted in your hearts, and bring forth in you the fruits of a good life." Additionally, Whitefield counseled his listeners to "pray over every word and verse."[61]

Unlike Whitefield, whose published sermons mostly came early in his career, Wesley often addressed themes throughout his long and productive life. This creates a greater abundance of material in comparing and contrasting their instruction on the means of grace. Reading Scripture was Wesley's second practice. Both men stressed Jesus' command in John 5:29 to search

---

56. Rack, ed., *The Minutes of the Conference*, 10:855.
57. Gillies, ed., *Works*, 5:27, 28.
58. Ibid., 5:56.
59. Ibid., 6:79–88.
60. Ibid., 6:83.
61. Ibid., 6:85, 86.

the Scriptures.[62] Wesley's questions from the "Large Minutes" contained these prompts for

> searching the Scriptures by, (i.) Reading: Constantly, some part of every day; regularly, all the Bible in order; carefully, with the Notes; seriously, with prayer before and after; fruitfully, immediately practicing what you learn there? (ii.) Meditating: At set times? By any rule? (iii.) Hearing: Every morning? Carefully; with prayer before, at, after; immediately putting in practice? Have you a New Testament always about you?[63]

Reading and meditating suggest a personal use, while hearing signified a public engagement with Scripture. Campbell observes that Wesley's directions would be called "devotional biblical study" today.[64] Therefore, it is not surprising that Wesley's deep desire was for Christ's words to "take up its stated residence" and dwell within the believer.[65] Wesley also counseled readers to compare parallels passages of Scripture, meditate upon the word, and if any confusion existed to consult with others, which were his own personal practices.[66]

Wesley and Whitefield shared an appreciation for Matthew Henry's commentary of the Bible. Whitefield confessed his method of sermon preparation consisted of praying on his knees with Scripture and Henry.[67] Similarly, Wesley extoled the value of Henry's commentary but felt its large size and cost prevented many average people from affording it, so he sought to make it "*plainer* as well as shorter."[68]

This reveals another significant distinction between our two revivalists. Wesley had a proclivity to borrow and adapt any writings he found helpful from others.[69] Wesley concluded his preface with six practical suggestions for reading the Bible: (1) to set apart a time in the morning and evening; (2) to read a chapter of the Old and New Testaments, or if that was not possible to read a shorter portion; (3) to read the Bible with a "single eye" to "know the whole will of God"; (4) to read with the "anal-

---

62. The best overviews of Wesley's teaching on searching the Scripture are Knight, *Presence of God in the Christian Life*, 148–59; and Maddox, "Rule of Christian Faith, Practice, and Hope," 1–35.

63. Jackson, ed., *Works*, 8:323.

64. Campbell, "Means of Grace and Forms of Piety," 284.

65. Knight, *Presence of God in the Christian Life*, 149.

66. Outler, ed., *Sermons*, 1:106.

67. Whitefield, *Journals*, 60, 62.

68. Jackson, ed., *Works*, 14:248.

69. Outler, ed., *Sermons*, 1:55; and Mursell, *English Spirituality*, 90.

ogy of faith,"[70] which was essentially a christological exegesis to recognize the harmony of the entire sweep of Scripture; (5) to always approach Scripture with "earnest prayer" and seek the guidance of the Holy Spirit who authored these inspired words;[71] and, (6) to periodically pause and examine themselves so the word could be applied to their hearts.[72] Wesley had inserted "Advice on Spiritual Reading" to his abridgement of Thomas á Kempis's *Imitation of Christ*.[73] This reflected a meditative way of reading that likely shaped his own practice.

Even more succinctly, Wesley summarized his basic guidance for reading Scripture in a 1772 correspondence: "Read a little, pray and meditate much."[74] Similarly, Whitefield offered an example of his contemplative experience when he spoke of his "sweet communion" that had "carried [him] out beyond myself when sweetly meditating in the fields!"[75]

Whitefield's second means was secret prayer. This was reminiscent of the three-fold structure of Puritan spiritual practices: secret prayer was the individual alone with God, private prayer described a small gathering such as a family, and public spoke of the larger church gathering in worship.[76] Personal prayer was instrumental in cultivating intimacy with God because it was the "fan of the divine life, whereby the spark of holy fire kindled in the soul by God, is not only kept in, but raised into flame."[77] This served as a protection against temptation, and the person who neglected it was more likely to experience spiritual diseases.

Whitefield summarized this practice, challenging his listeners to develop both a habitual practice of "set prayer" and to "be much in ejaculatory prayer" as they went about their daily activities.[78] Whitefield appreciated both the formal structure of the Book of Common Prayer and the extempore prayer from the heart as any need presented itself. Whitefield counseled a man about the benefits of this practice, "if you could be brought once to love secret prayer, and to converse feelingly with GOD in his word, your heaven will begin on earth; you will enjoy more pleasure than in all manner

70. See Maddox, "Rule of Christian Faith, Practice, and Hope," 21–24; and Knight, *Presence of God in the Christian Life*, 154–57, 231.

71. Maddox, "Rule of Christian Faith, Practice, and Hope," 13–15, 33.

72. Jackson, ed., *Works*, 14:253.

73. Whaling, *John and Charles Wesley*, 88–89.

74. Telford, ed., *Letters*, 6:7.

75. Whitefield, *Journals*, 61. This was not an isolated experience for Whitefield. I am planning to explore his understanding of sweet communion in a future article.

76. Schwanda, *Soul Recreation*, 82, 29.

77. Gillies, ed., *Works*, 5:28.

78. Ibid., 5:28–29.

of riches."[79] This demonstrates both the benefit of prayer in increasing one's intimacy with God and also the overflow of disciplines, how one practice was often connected with another—in this case prayer and reading Scripture, but elsewhere it took many other forms.

Whitefield described how secret prayer worked together with "*self-examination, and receiving the blessed sacrament*."[80] In his "Temptation of Christ" sermon, he quoted Luther's dictum that "prayer and meditation, reading and temptation, make a minister."[81] He also championed the importance of family prayer.[82] While Whitefield typically preached extemporaneously and often stressed the same in prayer he was enough of an Anglican clergyman to appreciate set forms of prayers. In fact, he taught, "christianity does not require us to cast off all outward forms; we may use forms, and yet not be formal: for instance, it is possible to worship GOD in a set form of prayer, and yet worship him in spirit and truth."[83]

Prayer was Wesley's first means of grace.[84] From the "Large Minutes" he challenged Wesleyans: "Prayer; private, family, public; consisting of deprecation [i.e., confession], petition, intercession, and thanksgiving. Do you use each of these? Do you use private prayer every morning and evening? If you can, at five in the evening; and the hour before or after morning preaching? Do you forecast [i.e., predict or estimate] daily, wherever you are, how to secure these hours? Do you avow it everywhere? Do you ask everywhere, 'Have you family prayer?' Do you retire at five o'clock?"[85]

Wesley grasped the centrality of prayer not only as a "the grand means of drawing near to God" but also as it enabled other spiritual activities.[86] His first publication, *A Collection of Forms of Prayer for Every Day in the Week* (1733),[87] was a distillation of his own personal prayer manual that included morning and evening prayers for each day of the week. Each prayer focused on different themes—love of God and neighbor, humility, thankfulness,

---

79. Gillies, ed., *Works*, 1:335.
80. Whitefield, *Letters*, 490.
81. Gillies, ed., *Works*, 5:271.
82. Ibid., 5:57–58.
83. Ibid., 5:376.
84. Borgen, *John Wesley on the Sacraments*, esp. 106–11; and Knight, *Presence of God in the Christian Life*, esp. 116–20, 160–64.
85. Jackson, ed., *Works*, 8:322–23.
86. Telford, ed., *Letters*, 4:90.
87. Jackson, ed., *Works*, 11:203–37.

mortification—and, characteristic of Wesley, began with a series of questions to prepare the person. Wesley even included prayers for the dead.[88]

Like Whitefield, Wesley's appreciation for written prayers did not prevent him from also using extemporaneous prayers.[89] Unlike Whitefield, who rarely mentioned the Lord's Prayer, Wesley devoted a full sermon to it. There he defined prayer as "the lifting up of the heart to God: all words of prayer without this are mere hypocrisy. Whenever therefore thou attemptest to pray, see that it be thy one design to commune with God, to lift up thy heart to him, to pour out thy soul before him."[90] Wesley continually warned against the hypocrisy of the Pharisees and heathen, who felt that God measured prayers by their length.[91] He also observed the difference between the two versions of the Lord's Prayer and instructed that Matthew 6:9 provided a model for what to pray while Luke 11:2 was an exact form to follow.[92] Additionally, Wesley counseled that one should avoid vain repetitions since prayers are not to inform God of what God already knows but rather to lodge the requests more deeply within the heart to cultivate a "continual dependence" on God, who is the only person who can satisfy our requests.[93] Wesley employed Luke 18:1–5 and the necessity of asking "in faith, nothing wavering, nothing *doubting*" to teach that prayers must be persistent.[94]

Unlike Wesley, Whitefield separated frequent meditation from reading Scripture as his third means of grace. Perhaps this suggests a more critical appreciation of meditation for Whitefield? Whitefield reordered Luther's famous dictum, but this time concluded with meditation to reinforce that practice.[95] He repeated the same in a letter written in 1749: "prayer, temptation, and meditation, says *Luther* are necessary ingredients for a minister."[96] In his treatment of extemporaneous preaching, Whitefield referred to Luther's dictum again and confessed that while he had no written notes for his preaching that should not mean he did not prepare. In fact, he declared, "I love to study, and delight to meditate."[97]

---

88. Ibid., 11:223, 232, cf. 9:55 and 10:9–10 for Wesley's justification of praying for the dead.

89. Ibid., 8:321, cf. 7:30 and Telford, ed., *Letters*, 2:77, 241; 3:146.

90. Outler, ed., *Sermons*, 1:575.

91. Ibid., 1:575–76.

92. Ibid., 1:577.

93. Ibid., 1:576, 577.

94. Ibid., 1:385, 386.

95. Gillies, ed., *Works*, 5:29.

96. Ibid., 2:245.

97. Ibid., 4:216.

Whitefield also compared meditation to the digestion of food for the body. It gathers the spiritual nutrients from Scripture, encounters with God, and interactions with others to internalize and nourish the soul. He used the biblical examples of David and Isaac (Gen 24:63).[98] Whitefield does not detail the subject of meditation, but it would be based on Scripture. More eloquently, he contended that meditation "is a kind of silent prayer, whereby the soul is frequently, as it were, carried out of itself to GOD, and in a degree made like unto those blessed spirits, who by a kind of immediate intuition always behold the face of our heavenly Father."[99] His description is reminiscent of the earlier Puritans, who frequently spoke of the soul being ravished by God, and reflects the contemplative–mystical piety of the Puritans.[100] Due to these benefits, Whitefield urged his listeners to frequently engage in meditation since it could both kindle "the fire of divine love" and "maintain a close and uniform walk with the most-high GOD."[101] He also taught that this must be practiced daily to discover "the words of eternal life" that leads one to know God's "heavenly treasure."[102]

Whitefield's sixth discipline, making full use of the ordinances, could include various spiritual practices but typically referred to baptism and the Lord's Supper. Whitefield asserted that God's ordinances for believers were "conduit-pipes, whereby the infinitely condescending *Jehovah* conveys his grace to their souls."[103] This expresses Whitefield's high view of the Lord's Supper, that it communicated grace to the participant. He urged a correspondent to consistently make use of God's ordinances for "by-and-by the loving Savior may pass by and visit your soul."[104] The ordinances are an expression of God's tokens of love sent through his Holy Spirit.[105] In the summer of 1742 Whitefield preached at Cambuslang, Scotland. This long weekend gathering, known as sacramental occasions, culminated in the celebration of the Lord's Supper. Whitefield employed the bridal imagery of Isaiah 54:4 to woo individuals to receive Jesus as their husband.[106] Of the seven practices to cultivate walking with God, this was Whitefield's shortest and least developed.

98. Ibid., 5:29.
99. Ibid., 5:29.
100. Schwanda, *Soul Recreation*, esp. 163–96.
101. Gillies, ed., *Works*, 5:29.
102. Ibid., 6:87.
103. Ibid., 5:31.
104. Ibid., 1:251.
105. Ibid., 5:74.
106. Kidd, *George Whitefield*, 163–66.

Whitefield's stark treatment of communion is dwarfed even more when placed alongside Wesley's third category of the Lord's Supper.[107] In keeping with the means of grace, Wesley instructed his listeners that "all who desire an increase of the grace of God are to wait for it in partaking of the Lord's Supper." Like Whitefield, Wesley maintained that God conveys "spiritual grace" to those who participate in the Lord's Table. Following 1 Corinthians 11:23–26, Wesley declared the necessity of first examining for one's self whether one "understand[s] the nature and design of this holy institution."[108] He was deeply influenced by Daniel Brevint, a seventeenth-century Anglican sacramental writer, and abridged his treatise on the sacraments as a preface to the Wesley's *Hymns on the Lord's Supper* (1745).[109] Wesley declared there were three dimensions to the Lord's Supper: to represent the sufferings of Christ as a memorial; to convey the first fruit of these graces as the means; and to assure a person of God's glory for the future as a pledge.[110] This nicely reflects the past, present, and future nature of the Lord's Supper. The Holy Spirit was instrumental not only as an agent in the Supper but also received by those who partook of it.[111]

Due to the importance of the Lord's Supper, Wesley devoted an entire sermon to the "Duty of Constant Communion." While he asserted its originality, it was heavily dependent upon Robert Nelson, another Anglican liturgical author.[112] Wesley urged his listeners to receive the Lord's Supper as frequently as possible, since it was a command of Christ.[113] While the expectation of the Church of England was to commune three times a year, Wesley personally received the Lord's Supper more frequently than once a week.[114] He summarized its nature as a "continual remembrance of the death of Christ."[115] Since his concern was to correct the distorted understanding of those who neglected frequent celebration due to their unworthiness, he devoted three fourths of this message to refuting a wide range of objections

---

107. Borgen, *John Wesley and the Sacraments*, esp. 183–217. See also Knight, *Presence of God in the Christian Life*, 130–48.

108. Outler, ed., *Sermons*, 1:389.

109. Space does not permit an examination of the importance of hymns in Wesley's understanding of the Lord's Supper. See Tyson, *Way of the Wesleys*, 148–57.

110. Borgen, *John Wesley on the Sacraments*, 86; and Borgen, "John Wesley: Sacramental Theology No Ends without the Means," 70–72, 78–81.

111. Borgen, *John Wesley on the Sacraments*, esp. 208, also 183, 184, 195–97, 201 and Knight, *Presence of God in the Christian Life*, 131, 132, 139.

112. Outler, ed., *Sermons*, 3:427.

113. Ibid., 3:428–29

114. Rack, *Reasonable Enthusiast*, 418.

115. Outler, ed., *Sermons*, 3:430.

to this. His most creative resolution was that failure of constant communion was the equivalent of renouncing your baptism, where you had promised to obey all of God's commands.[116] He concluded that unworthiness was never a legitimate excuse because everyone is unworthy.[117] Clearly one essential reason for emphasizing the necessity of frequent participation at the Lord's Table is that "This is the food of our souls: this gives strength to perform our duty, and leads us on to perfection."[118]

In typical Wesley fashion and totally unlike Whitefield, Wesley provided a series of questions for self-examination in preparation for communion. "Do you use this [i.e., the Lord's Supper] At every opportunity? With due preparation? i.e., with solemn prayer? with careful self-examination? With deep repentance suited thereto? With earnest and deliberate self-devotion? Do you in communicating discern the Lord's Body? Do you afterward retire, not formally, but in earnest?"[119] Yet another contrast between the two early Methodists is Wesley's strong assertion that the Lord's Supper was a converting ordinance.[120]

The seventh means of grace for Whitefield was keeping company with other Christians. Whitefield knew his church history and realized, like Wesley, the instructive value of primitive Christianity. He also recognized how "christian societies, and fellowship meetings" guided believers over the centuries in walking with God.[121] His first sermon preached was "The Necessity and Benefits of Religious Societies." Whitefield also addressed some letters specifically to the religious societies to motivate and guide them in their maturity in Christ. However, over time Whitefield radically reduced his interest in the creation and supervision of these societies. This is a very complex issue that requires more detailed analysis.[122] Arnold Dallimore was one of the first to conjecture that Whitefield marginalized his leadership of these groups for many reasons, including his constant transatlantic journeys that prevented

---

116. Ibid., 3:435.

117. Ibid., 3:439.

118. Ibid., 3:429.

119. Rack, ed., *Methodist Societies*, 10:856; see also Outler, ed., *Sermons*, 3:430, on the importance of preparation.

120. Borgen, *John Wesley on the Sacraments*, 197–98; Tyson, *Way of the Wesleys*, 146–48; and Maddox, *Responsible Grace*, 219–21.

121. Gillies, ed., *Works*, 5:31.

122. See my forthcoming article "Origin, Growth and Divergent Perspectives within the Religious Societies of John Wesley and George Whitefield," which will examine this topic more fully.

regular contact with the societies and the bitter competition and tensions that produced deep pain in his relationship with Wesley.[123]

If religious societies decreased in importance for Whitefield then they significantly increased in value for Wesley, who placed Christian conference as his fifth and final means of grace.[124] Next to the questions posed on prayer, this was the second longest section of examination. Wesley asked: "Are you convinced how important and how difficult it is to 'order your conversation right?' Is it 'Always in grace? seasoned with salt? meet to minister grace to hearers?' Do not you converse too long at a time? Is not an hour commonly enough? Would it not be well always to have a determinate end in view; and to pray before and after it?"[125]

While Wesley named conferences as an instituted means, his all-important system of class and band meetings was included under the prudential means of grace. When Wesley wrote the history of early Methodism, he framed the three early periods of development around the religious societies.[126] The most prominent document was "The Nature, Design, and General Rules, of the United Societies" (1743). There he clearly articulated the purpose of the society as "a company of men 'having the form, and seeking the power of godliness,' united in order to pray together, to receive the word of exhortation, and to watch over one another in love, that they may help each other to work out their salvation."[127]

Wesley's high valuation of conferences and societies revealed the ongoing intensity of conflict between the two evangelicals. In 1778, almost a decade following Whitefield's death, Wesley still criticized his late friend: "But those who were more or less affected by Mr. Whitefield's preaching had no discipline at all. They had no shadow of discipline; nothing of the kind. They were formed into no societies: They had no Christian connection with each other, nor were ever taught to watch over each other's souls. So that if any fell into lukewarmness, or even into sin, he had none to lift him up: He might fall lower and lower, yea, into hell, if he would, for who regarded it?"[128]

Whitefield's fourth discipline was paying attention to providential dealings. Earlier Whitefield instructed his auditors to search the Scriptures for God's guidance to notice how God directs and provides for humanity

---

123. Dallimore, *George Whitefield*, 2:249.

124. The literature on this topic is extensive. See, for example, Knight, *Presence of God in the Christian Life*, 95–116.

125. Jackson, ed., *Works*, 8:323.

126. Heitzenrater, *Wesley and the People Called Methodists*, 33–95.

127. Davies, ed., *Methodist Societies*, 9:69.

128. Outler, ed., *Sermons*, 3:598.

through providence. The significance of this doctrine was reinforced in that Whitefield named his South Carolina plantation "Providence."[129] Providence teaches that God is ever present and upholds and governs all of creation; nothing is by chance because of God's daily awareness and involvement. In a letter written from Dublin in 1751, Whitefield offered a succinct definition, asserting: "I find that providence has wonderfully prepared my way, and over-ruled every thing for my greater acceptance."[130]

While it is one thing to receive the benefits of God, it is another thing to accept that "every cross has a call in it, and every particular dispensation of divine providence, has some particular end to answer in those to whom it is sent."[131] In 1736, Whitefield reminded his correspondent that all of the "dispensations of providence" are an expression of God's love and that afflictions are "not so much to punish, as to purify your soul."[132] Therefore, Whitefield taught his listeners to carefully observe the movements of providence in order to walk more closely with God. From his collection of prayers, he demonstrated the necessity for sailors to be attentive and responsive to God's providential care. He wrote: "Grant me a lively persuasion, that thy providence ruleth all things; that thou intendest every thing for my good, and enable me therefore patiently to tarry thy leisure, and to give thee thanks for all things that befall me, since it is thy will in CHRIST JESUS concerning me."[133]

Whereas observing the movements of God's providence was an external operation, Whitefield's fifth practice stressed the importance of recognizing the Spirit's guidance within a person's heart. This had been foundational to him from the beginning of his ministry. Kidd correctly observes that this "emphasis on the Holy Spirit would be a consistent theme in Whitefield's career, although he would in time back away from claims for his immediate guidance."[134] On one occasion, he reported that he had "expounded to a large roomful of people, and with such power and demonstration of the Spirit as I never saw before."[135] Elsewhere he confessed in correspondence (1741) that it was a "glorious privilege to be led by the spirit of GOD."[136]

---

129. Gillies, ed., *Works*, 2:119. See also Kidd, *George Whitefield*, 199.
130. Gillies, ed., *Works*, 2:409, 273.
131. Ibid., 5:29.
132. Ibid., 1:21.
133. Ibid., 4:484.
134. Kidd, *George Whitefield*, 36.
135. Whitefield, *Journals*, 259.
136. Gillies, ed., *Works*, 1:254.

Critics seized upon Whitefield's dependency upon the Spirit as another reason to criticize him and other early Methodists. Whitefield defended himself when he clarified "the *sensible* operations of the Holy Ghost" referred to the "operations of the Spirit of God."[137] To walk with God required a believer to become like a child and develop the humble posture that is receptive to guidance, much like a "little child gives its hand to be led by a nurse or parent."[138] Conscious of his critics, Whitefield instructed "though it is the quintessence of enthusiasm, to pretend to be guided by the Spirit without the written word; yet it is every christian's bounden duty to be guided by the Spirit in conjunction with the written word of GOD." Recognizing the potential for abuse, he wisely instructed that every motion or impression of the Spirit must be tested against the "unerring rule of GOD's most holy word" to guide one from erring either on the side of enthusiasm or deism.[139] This essential balance between Word and Spirit was common already in the early Protestant Reformation.

Though Whitefield did mention fasting in relation to the means of grace, he did not include it in his "Walking with God" sermon. It is likely Whitefield's extreme asceticism nearly killed him during his Oxford days moderated his emphasis upon fasting. In contrast, this was Wesley's fourth practice. The fasting question from the "Large Minutes" is the shortest in Wesley's five means of grace: "Fasting: How do you fast every Friday?"[140] He devoted a full sermon to this and, among other things, acknowledged that fasting, more than any other means of grace, was prone to extremes.[141] Indeed, some perceived that Wesley and the early Oxford Methodists encouraged "fanatical practices of fasting."[142] Initially he fasted on Wednesdays and Fridays, but eventually designated Fridays, which was the Anglican norm. Wesley's intense asceticism included vegetarianism and apostolic poverty as well.[143]

Over time, Wesley developed greater pastoral sensitivity and recognized that there must be degrees of fasting that could include abstinence

---

137. Whitefield, *Journals*, 301.

138. Gillies, ed., *Works*, 5:30; also 1:446.

139. Ibid., 5:30. Whitefield was often accused of enthusiasm. Ibid., 4:203; 5:381. See also Kidd, *George Whitefield*, 101–2, 172–73, 181–82. The same charges were leveled against Wesley, Mursell, *English Spirituality*, 87.

140. Jackson, ed., *Works*, 8:323.

141. Outler, ed., *Sermons*, 1:593.

142. Heitzenrater, *Wesley and the People Called Methodists*, 47. See also Heitzenrater, *Diary of an Oxford Methodist*, 22–23.

143. Hammond, *John Wesley in America*, 48–49. See also Telford, ed., *Letters*, 2:285 and 7:151.

when people were limited due to "sickness or weakness." The lowest form of fasting was "abstaining from pleasant food."[144] He taught there were five reasons for fasting: avoidance of food, sorrow for sin, reduction of lust and sensuality, punishment for misusing God's gifts, and as an aid to prayer.[145] Ultimately the "Christian [should] fast from sin, and not food." The primary purpose for fasting was to recognize one's total dependence upon God for all of life's provisions and thereby grow in greater humility.

Wesley acknowledged that fasting had both a physical and spiritual component and maintained that fasting should afflict one's body and also "be a season of devout mourning, of godly sorrow for sin."[146] Wesley also warned his followers to consider their motivation and practice fasting for the glory of God rather than the praise of others.[147] Once again, this reflects Wesley's perennial desire to avoid the hypocrisy of the Pharisees. Reflective of earlier Puritans, Wesley connected alms with fasting.[148] In 1790, shortly before he died, Wesley lamented the "almost universally neglected" practice of fasting among the Methodists.[149]

This chapter has examined the means of grace specifically identified by Wesley and Whitefield. Neither list should be seen as exhaustive.[150] Whitefield would likely include the importance of listening to sermons, illustrated by his "Directions How to Hear Sermons."[151] And Wesley would certainly add the centrality of hymns as a means of grace.[152] Limitations of space permit only a brief comment on the works of mercy that could result from these works of piety. Wesley continued to demonstrate acts of social compassion to the poor, treatment of the sick, visiting prisoners, and the establishment of schools. Whitefield also revealed a deep concern for the education of children, his orphanage in Georgia, visitation of the sick and prison ministry. Sadly, he did not share Wesley's strong stance against slavery.[153]

---

144. Outler, ed., *Sermons*, 1:595.

145. Ibid., 1:597–601. Wesley stressed the combination of prayer and fasting frequently. See Telford, ed., *Letters*, 7:301, 352; and Borgen, *John Wesley on the Sacraments*, 111–12, 118–19.

146. Outler, ed., *Sermons*, 1:604, 609.

147. Ibid., 1:608.

148. Ibid., 1:610. On the Puritan practice, see Webster, *Godly Clergy*, 61.

149. Telford, ed., *Letters*, 8:243. Wesley expressed similar frustration in 1785. Ibid., 7:256, 259.

150. For a broader treatment of early evangelical spiritual disciplines, see Schwanda, *Emergence of Evangelical Spirituality*, 153–95.

151. Gillies, ed., *Works*, 5:418–27.

152. See Knight, *Presence of God in the Christian Life*, esp. 163–67.

153. For Wesley, see Yrigoyen, *John Wesley*, 57–73. For Whitefield, see Kidd, *George Whitefield*, 235, 238–41, 243–44.

Assessment and Conclusion

A number of themes emerge from this summary of Wesley and Whitefield's approach to the means of grace.

Similarities can be seen between the two. Both men were deeply passionate about their relationship with God. For Wesley, that translated personally into a "neurotic 'grid' system" in which he sought to continually measure his devotional zeal.[154] Similarly, Whitefield was relentlessly "taking his spiritual temperature," gauging his love for Christ by his persistent activism.[155] Both shared a common understanding of true religion and the nature and dynamics of the means of grace. They also agreed that the goal of holiness was growing in the image of God.

However, here the contrasts begin to emerge. Sanctification developed differently for them due to their conflicting views on the nature of sin. This produced a sharp distinction when Whitefield's early theology of holiness radically shifted after 1741 and he became more convinced of his Calvinism. As previously stressed, this did not diminish the importance of sanctification in his view but created a more Calvinistic version of it.

A number of other contrasts become visible as we read these men side-by-side. Wesley emphasized fasting and the Lord's Supper to a greater degree, both personally and corporately. Whitefield had a deeper appreciation for noticing the movement of God's providence and meditation, at least in relation to the means of grace. While both men were deeply formed by their early reading of the Puritans, Whitefield continued his appreciation later in life, which perhaps encouraged greater emphasis upon meditation.

However, the deepest fissure relates to their structures for sanctification. Wesley rebuked Whitefield more for his neglect of ignoring religious societies than he did for his teaching on predestination.[156] Likely, Wesley's strong-armed authoritarianism and reticence to share power with others contributed to this. [157] This intersected with Whitefield's greater flexibility and tendency towards compromise to preserve peace. Positively, this created the beneficial accountability for Wesley through his religious societies and multitude of self-examination questions. But one wonders how much Whitefield's waning emphasis on the societies was affected by his desire to seek peace with his old friend John Wesley.

---

154. Rack, *Reasonable Enthusiast*, 95.
155. Gordon, "Jonathan Edwards and George Whitefield," 58.
156. Jackson, ed., *Works*, 7:411.
157. Rack, *Reasonable Enthusiast*, 246–48.

11

"Companions in the Way"

Mentoring in the Ministry of Wesley and Whitefield

Rhys S. Bezzant

It has often been the case in times of rapid social change, and in moments of the church's history when the institution has been maligned or impotent, that the significance of one-on-one personal work has increased. In the medieval era, the growth of auricular confession demonstrates this observation. In the sixteenth century, Luther's theological breakthrough came at least partly as a result of the mentoring he received in his Augustinian order in Erfurt by Johannes Staupitz. In the Puritan tradition, which had been marginalized in the university of Cambridge or Oxford, home seminaries were cultivated; these trained clergy outside of the normal means of leadership development, and this often in the context of small groups of relational intensity. Richard Greenham in Dry Dayton is an example of such alternative models of training.

The eighteenth century was another turning point for the ministry of mentoring. The word "mentor" was used in modern literature for the first time in François Fénelon's novel *Les aventures de Télémaque*, written in 1699. In this story of a young man's travels in the ancient world, the hero Telemachus was groomed for leadership of his inherited kingdom through experiences that were discussed and interpreted by his educational companion, Mentor. As a private arrangement, the practice of mentoring is often difficult to document, but the word's first English usage in 1750 in the writing of Lord Chesterfield is a clear indication of an ancient practice being reinvented in the modern world.

The eighteenth century was, after all, a period in which the social and intellectual implications of the Enlightenment began to take root in ministry expectations and structures. This was the age in which individual autonomy was validated through prioritizing human rationality, encapsulated in Descartes's slogan, *cogito ergo sum*: I think, therefore I am. In some quarters, the Enlightenment shaped Christians when they preached literary essays rather than exhortatory sermons, but in other circles it was the doctrine of regeneration and the power of a felt experience of conversion that promoted Enlightenment sentiment. The category of personal agency took on new dimensions, as individuals made more economic decisions in a world of growing capitalist opportunity, and as increased wealth enabled travel and mobility within regions and internationally as well. This was, in turn, supported by the movement from the countryside to the towns in old and new England, where traditional patterns of relationships were being replaced by relationships of elective affinity. A new kind of literature was invented, called the novel, built around fictional letters that were assembled to create a storyline and as a by-product a new kind of personal sensibility and communication, as long as you had the time and money to sit down and read something longer than a poem. All these features of life in the eighteenth century created the preconditions for a new understanding of personhood, and thereby a new approach to personal work.

These cultural developments form the essential backdrop to the ministries of John Wesley and George Whitefield, who in turn promoted the conditions required to crystalize a new appreciation of mentoring during the revivals of the eighteenth century. While itinerants like Whitefield and Wesley engaged in extensive field preaching and long-distance travel, some type of regular personal work or opportunity for intentional interaction with individuals was still possible.

Mentoring had been part of their experience from the earliest days. When Whitefield arrived to study in Oxford at Pembroke College in 1732, he was taken under wing by Charles Wesley and began to attend the Holy Club.[1] Whitefield in turn invested spiritually in James Habersham, who accompanied him later to Georgia.[2] John Wesley had been mentored by William Law, who was described as "a kind of oracle" to him, though latterly they had fallen out over the place of philosophy in theological reflection.[3] Charles Delamotte was a "son in the Gospel" to John Wesley and traveled with him to America, where he "did much good, and endured great hardships for the sake of Jesus Christ."[4] The convenient thing about relation-

---

1. Kidd, *George Whitefield*, 27–28, 252.
2. Ibid., 50.
3. Campbell, ed., *Letters*, 27:207; Henderson, *Model for Making Disciples*, 22, 121.
4. Whitefield, *Journals*, 291.

ships of these kinds is that they can be undertaken simultaneously with other activities, even on the road.

However, personal work like mentoring did undergo change as a result of the revivals, and Wesley and Whitefield may not have been the most outstanding practitioners of the art. Reinventing an ancient tradition and encouraging a modern form of individuation,[5] leaders of the revivals reinterpreted the interplay between authority and agency in pastoral ministry, and charged their followers to pursue an agenda for growth in the human soul that would have distinctive eighteenth century features. The breath of revivalistic preaching would fan into flame the embers of nominal faith, and the appointed means of grace were supplemented with personal accountability to promote an individual's growth and leadership capacity, drawing together biblical priorities with ministry opportunities and cultural conditions.

The Methodist movement in the British Empire of the eighteenth century provides a rich vein in which to mine the possibilities of one-on-one work in the modern world. While the precise dynamics of a personal mentoring relationship may be hard to track at a distance of several hundred years, the following features of Methodism certainly aided the personal work of Wesley and Whitefield, and are worthy of highlighting to draw attention to an often overlooked spiritual practice.

Methodist Origins: Encouragement and Accountability

In origin, the Methodists were Anglicans who worked to establish a small group program in parallel to the more regular means of grace—such as services, sermon, and sacraments—that defined and shaped the Church of England, for example. As clergy, Wesley and Whitefield encouraged members of their society to keep attending Sunday services in their local parish church, and as leaders they resisted planning other events at the time of the parish Lord's Supper. Wesley had inherited from his father "an interest in the role of religious societies in the spiritual and moral renewal of English church and society,"[6] and later recounted the genesis of the Holy Club, where "Methodist" undergraduates met for mutual edification:

> In the year 1725, a young student at Oxford was much affected by reading Kempis's "Christian Pattern," and Bishop Taylor's "Rules

---

5. Hindmarsh, "Reshaping Individualism," 73, 79.
6. Vickers, *Wesley: A Guide for the Perplexed*, 11.

of Holy Living and Dying." He found an earnest desire to live according to those rules, and to flee from the wrath to come. He sought for some that would be his companions in the way, but could find none; so that, for several years, he was constrained to travel alone, having no man either to guide or to help him. But in the year 1729, he found one who had the same desire. They then endeavoured to help each other; and, in the close of the year, were joined by two more. They soon agreed to spend two or three hours together every Sunday evening. Afterwards they sat two evenings together, and, in a while, six evenings, in the week; spending that time in reading the Scriptures, and provoking one another to love and to good works.[7]

Ministry in small-group settings had been a staple of Pietists in Germany from their earliest days, following the directions of Jakob Spener to form *collegia pietatis*, or "colleges of piety," where church members might cultivate spiritual practices to raise their spiritual temperature.[8] Though John Wesley was later to fall out with the Moravians over their spiritual passivity,[9] their example of heart religion hot-housed in small groups became for him an abiding commitment. His intentional structure for small groups, comprising classes for catechesis, societies for accountability, and bands for warm affective faith, was one where intimate relationships might grow.[10]

Behind the later organization of small groups, of varying composition and aim, lay the desire to provide pastoral care for vast numbers of outliers, who might not otherwise have benefited from the more traditional means of care available in the parish church.[11] This was an age in which the Church of England was falling behind in its outreach to the newly minted working class, and was terrified of enthusiasm (the denial of means), which had become synonymous with the upheavals and fissiparousness of the Puritan interregnum of the seventeenth century. Religion of the heart was associated with religious dissent, not Anglican conformity. With the emergence of outdoor preaching as a means of conversion, small groups were a reflex reaction to accommodate the growth.[12] The agenda for pastoral care in small groups reflected a new kind of personal agency, in which lay members of groups took up responsibility for others, exercising a ministry of care,

---

7. Outler, ed., *Sermons*, 3:580–81.
8. See Kohl, "Spener's Pia Desideria," 61–78.
9. Kidd, *George Whitefield*, 139.
10. Henderson, *Model for Making Disciples*, 83–126.
11. See Schmidt, "Pattern of Revival," 84.
12. Vickers, *Wesley: A Guide for the Perplexed*, 18.

teaching, hospitality, and accountability otherwise not offered. Expression of the affections in the small group format furthered just such activity:

> Methodists stressed the free agency of each individual, and his or her ability to enter Christ's kingdom as a citizen of heaven on equal footing with others. Methodist success in emphasizing individual agency, and in using emotion to create a sense of that agency, put pressure on other churches . . . [13]

Empowerment of the laity was a deliberate Methodist ecclesiological strategy. This period saw the churches increasingly impacted by the absolutist claims of the state, so the slogan (much used by the revivalists) "the power of godliness" represented an aspiration for more satisfying personal experiences, and for the capacity to make a contribution to the life of the church, which rank and file members of Methodist societies craved.

The culture of Methodist societies was massively influenced by women, who constituted a majority of those signed up. Though men dominated the leadership of the movement and women were not frequent preachers or exhorters in public settings, the empowering that women received through their membership provided further environmental stimuli to cultivate pastoral care in general, and mentoring in particular. Noll explains how the revivals enhanced the pastoral ministry of both men and women:

> Where conversion liberated women from the entanglements of oppressive relationships and bestowed personal agency, for men it provided a countervailing liberation from the excesses of agency and opened the possibilities of relational being.[14]

While the activation of the laity was rooted in the reform agenda of the sixteenth century, its eighteenth century expression was nonetheless a significant breakthrough, for it was now able to project its existential and religious concerns onto political and economic screens.[15] As Mark Noll states, "Evangelicals also successfully adapted themselves to major transformations in secular society that further promoted the activity of the laity."[16]

In this world of increasing individual autonomy, generated by political, economic, and religious pressures, one of the most significant outcomes was the development of the principle of voluntary association. Indeed, this turned out to be not just a matter of small group membership, but more

---

13. Porterfield, *Conceived in Doubt*, 134.

14. Noll, "National Churches, Gathered Churches," 148.

15. Trueman, "Reformers, Puritans and Evangelicals," 33. See also Vickers, *Wesley: A Guide for the Perplexed*, 51.

16. Noll, "National Churches, Gathered Churches," 139.

and more defined the experience of denominationalism, especially in the New World. At heart, the voluntary principle marginalized the authority of an institution and tradition, and supported the agency of an individual to choose which kind of faith expression best suited circumstances and preferences.[17] This was an age of elective affinities, which subverted the imprimatur of the church hierarchy, and promoted the value of local structures of accountability, for example friendships, which were private, intense, and voluntary. As Nehamas writes:

> In early modern Britain, friendship was inseparable from favoritism, patronage, and clientage . . . At the very end of the sixteenth century, however, friendship began to be transformed from a public into a private good . . . The place of friendship in the private realm was cemented gradually, in large part through the broad economic, political, and philosophical developments of the eighteenth century.[18]

Not surprisingly, theological reflection on the ministry of the Holy Spirit in conversion "seemed irresistibly to trivialize the importance of institutions once widely held to mediate regeneration." What is more, "to exalt the converted person's use of the Bible as the most important religious authority was implicitly to devalue the elaborate edifices protecting scriptural interpretation that prevailed in all the historic European churches."[19] With the possibility of subjectivizing hermeneutics, Pelikan has named this development the "affectional transposition of doctrine."[20] It is not just that the emergence of small groups for maturity added an extra movement to the symphony. The whole symphony was now being played in a new key.

But the conductor still maintained control. Wesley was thoroughly committed to communitarian disciplines, but his more authoritarian tendencies in terms of church order had to be accommodated within the disruptive power of personal assurance and decentralized accountability. A tension emerged (which was never fully resolved) between individualistic expressions of the faith, which the revivals had encouraged, and Wesley's own particular psychology and gifts as centralizing founder of the movement. His "strong democratic impulse" was not easily squared with the way he "ran the Methodist societies in an overtly hierarchical fashion."[21] Methodist ecclesiology encouraged intense yet accountable experiences alongside the

---

17. Trueman, "Reformers, Puritans and Evangelicals," 19.
18. Nehamas, *On Friendship*, 40, 42, 48.
19. Noll, "National Churches, Gathered Churches," 145–46.
20. Pelikan, *Christian Doctrine and Modern Culture*, 119.
21. Vickers, *Wesley: A Guide for the Perplexed*, 3.

provision of regular means of grace. It may have been occasionally unstable, but this kind of ecclesiology did give permission for new patterns of growth and expectations of personal piety, while designed to inhibit antinomian tendencies. The genius of Methodism, its combination of communal with personal disciplines,[22] was well suited to the spirit of the age, and the practice of personal work benefitted from the collaboration.

Methodist Spirituality: Integrative Aspirations

One of the great features of Methodist spirituality was its integrative character, which sought to draw together a variety of strands of Christian piety such as Moravian, Catholic, Anglican, or Puritan. Under the theme of Christian perfection, growth in holiness was resourced through manifold means, for example, through reading spiritual classics. These books might have been written before the Reformation, like Thomas à Kempis's *Imitation of Christ* (1418–1427), or after the Reformation, like Puritan spiritual manuals such as Henry Scougal's *The Life of God in the Soul of Man* (1677). Some were written within the lifetime of the revivals, for example William Law's *A Serious Call to a Devout and Holy Life* (1729), which emphasized spiritual disciplines rather than the nature of conversion or experiences of grace.[23] The earnest pursuit of heart religion, in the context of an academic institution, with the accountability of friends and commitment to serve the needy, demonstrate a rich, multi-layered spiritual experience. In the following extract, we note Wesley's summary of the variegated achievements of the Holy Club:

> But if these things are so, may we not well say, "What hath God wrought!" For such a work, if we consider the *extensiveness* of it, the *swiftness* with which it has spread, the *depth* of the religion so swiftly diffused, and its *purity* from all corrupt mixtures, we must acknowledge cannot easily be paralleled, in all these concurrent circumstances, by anything that is found in the English annals, since Christianity was first planted in this island.[24]

When unified in the "primitive . . . religion of love" and seeking "to flee from the wrath to come," the movement was bound together effectively.[25] Wesley aimed to avoid the extreme dangers of antinomianism and en-

---

22. Hempton, *Methodism*, 31.
23. Kidd, *George Whitefield*, 24–27.
24. Outler, ed., *Sermons*, 3:588.
25. Ibid., 3:592, 581.

thusiasm, and to create a centrist synthesis, in which the physical and the spiritual, the intellectual and the practical, and freedom with discipline were smelted into one. His brand of Christian perfection may have been innovative and frequently misunderstood by Whitefield, but it did in the end serve as a useful spiritual glue to manage disparate pressures and priorities in the Christian life.

Whitefield's appeal to an integrative spirituality is witnessed when he vilifies the type of insipid religion that never reaches the heart. In early ministry in the American colonies, he rebuked putatively unconverted leaders at Harvard, who displayed only a cerebral and not heart faith, demonstrating a form of godliness but denying its power.[26] Further, he adopted a homiletic strategy that was not rationalistic but profoundly affective, appealing to the will and the emotions, not just the mind.[27] Not only was this achieved through his fine oratory, but the "performative" dimensions to his preaching, in which he literally put his body on the line with boisterous gestures, reunited physically what rationalist religion had pulled apart conceptually, that is, the mind from the body. Surrender involved all of a person's life, and was therefore profoundly integrative, as Reklis summarizes:

> Surrender to God's sovereignty was to understand oneself as consummated in the divine unity of all things, and therefore beautified by participation in God's relational being, over and against the increasingly fragmented and self-interested community that was being created in the confluence of early Enlightenment philosophy and early global capitalism . . . [28]

The bands themselves were an organizational strategy to sustain moral accountability, doctrinal unanimity, and affectional warmth. Without them, isolation would threaten the movement by providing no checks and balances to maintain its integrative character. When powerful conversion experiences were accompanied by bodily expressions of release, instruments of order proved their worth: "The particular interest of the eighteenth-century writings on conversion experiences arises from the fact that such experiences were regarded as important opportunities for soul care . . . it was thought that a danger to be avoided at all costs was isolation, with its temptation to self-diagnosis."[29] Companionship, on the other hand, involved the interaction of bodies, minds, and hearts, with face-to-face responsibilities and reality checks, encouraging the possibility of deep mutuality.

26. Stout, *Divine Dramatist*, 120–21.
27. Stout, *New England Soul*, 189–95.
28. Reklis, *Theology and the Kinesthetic Imagination*, 3.
29. Clebsch and Jaekle, *Pastoral Care in Historical Perspective*, 283, 284.

Wesley could highlight the importance of such relationships in writing to his niece on 31 March 1781: "But you must needs have some companions in the way; for how can one be warm alone? I wish you to be acquainted with Miss Johnson, who lodges in Oxford Street at No. 368 . . ."[30] More programmatically, the whole aim of his Methodist Societies was for the sake of creating a "company of people associating together to help each other to work out their own salvation."[31] Mentoring was one such practice to achieve this end.

Commitment to integrative spirituality is also to be seen in the power of hymnody, which consists in its capacity to join heads and hearts, individuals and a community, liturgy with a measure of vocal spontaneity, time, and eternity, all in one. John Wesley chose to translate a hymn by Johann Scheffler (1624–1677), with an integrative theme as its climax: "Give to my eyes refreshing tears | Give to my heart chaste, hallow'd fires | Give to my soul, with filial fears | The love that all heaven's host inspires | That all my powers, with all their might | In thy sole glory may unite."[32] Whitefield was also a compiler of hymns, though his *Collection* of 1753 is not very well known today. It consisted of composers from a great range of denominational traditions, including Roman Catholics, and allowed for a mixture of metrical expression. The spirituality it engendered was significant:

> In its metres, the hymnbook did not sever connections with traditional forms, but it also blended those forms with a wide variety of new expressions. In the same way, the spirituality that Whitefield represented grew out of strong Protestant traditions, but then—in form as well as substance—expanded, altered riffed, remixed, enlivened, and (above all) personalized those traditions.[33]

Further, Whitefield combined correspondence with choruses, as it were, in a couple of letters penned during the peak season of the revivals. In 1741, on December 24, in Abergavenny, he wrote to the Right Honourable the Lord L— and to the Right Honourable Lady Mary H—, to encourage their faith commitments. It appears that His Lordship, the Earl of Leven and Melville, was near to becoming a Christian, and so Whitefield offered to him some verses that he might sing as a sign of his conversion. First of all: "Men call'd me Christian, and my heart | On that delusion fondly staid | Moral my hope, my Saviour self | Till mighty grace the cheat display'd." Then conclusively: "Glad, I

---

30. Telford, ed., *Letters*, 7:54.
31. Outler, ed., *Sermons*, 3:584.
32. Wesley, "Translations of Some German Hymns," 97.
33. Noll, "Whitefield, Hymnody, and Evangelical Spirituality," 248.

forsook my righteous pride | My moral, tarnish'd, sinful dress | Exchang'd my loss away for Christ | And found the robe of righteousness."[34]

In his letter to Lady Mary Hamilton, he again quotes hymns, but this time he explains that these are spiritual overflows from his own heart, and apologizes that he has interrupted the flow of the letter to sing: "But whither am I going? Your Ladyship will excuse me; whilst I am writing, the fire kindles: Thro' all eternity to God | A grateful song I'll raise | But O eternity's to [sic] short | To utter all his praise."[35] Such interruptions are a sign of the informal style of letter writing, invented in the eighteenth century, which was commonly used by the revivalists to stress their relational proximity and commitment to a cause common to both writer and reader.[36] These two letters otherwise deal with travel arrangements, spiritual growth, and assurance of prayers. Their mixture of genres and themes bespeaks an integrative agenda, though their expression is somewhat formulaic.

It should be noted as well that, though Wesley and Whitefield do not agree on all points of doctrine, most notably the doctrines of grace, they are still able to apply the adjective "Methodist" to their labors. There may be theological differences, but there are methodological convergences in their common approach to a spirituality that is integrative, built on discipline and anthropological convictions. In 1756, Whitefield can wish, for example, that future leaders in his movement might be able to

> direct a careless unthinking world into a *holy Method* of dying unto themselves, and living unto God! This is the only Methodism I desire to know. And that this may meet with an universal flow amongst Ministers and people of all denominations I am sure thou wilt join us in praying . . .[37]

John Wesley could summarize their movement in terms appealing to external practices:

> The regularity of their behavior gave occasion to a young gentleman of the college to say, "I think we have got a new set of *Methodists*,"—alluding to a set of Physicians, who began to flourish at Rome about the time of Nero, and continued for several ages.[38]

The deep shape and the visible behaviors both relate to practical Christian living, and bind their increasingly disparate theological agendas in one

---

34. Whitefield, *Letters*, 348.
35. Ibid., 352.
36. See Anderson and Ehrenpreis, "The Familiar Letter"; and Dierks, *In My Power*.
37. Whitefield, *Journals*, 32.
38. Outler, ed., *Sermons*, 3:581.

evidently integrative spirituality. Though Wesley was to use the phrase later, it was Whitefield who first owned the phrase "the world is my parish," extending the reach of the work of God beyond the boundaries of a local church and enabling a vision that was cosmic and coherent.

One final example of their integrative aspirations should be noted. For both Wesley and Whitefield, Oxford men, the value they placed on education was significant. The transformative role of education in Whitefield's personal experience, and the value of education in the stabilization of the Wesleys' Methodist ministry, contributed significantly to the character of the movement as a whole.[39] Further, Whitefield spent all his days raising money for his beloved orphanage, Bethesda, in Georgia. In all his itinerations he never failed to call on others to give generously to this ministry to the poor. At one level, he was imitating the Apostle Paul and his own collection for the saints in Jerusalem, but at another he was expressing his hope that a community, in which children would be taught and catechized, and would labor and pray, would be a community of healthy spirituality and Christian virtue, raising up leaders for the American church. Wesley, though not engaged in raising money for an orphanage, raised money for the poor, and educated Methodist leaders by publishing Christian classics. The circulation of the minutes of his conferences was also a form of schooling for lay leadership. Recognizing pedagogical priorities, these leading revivalists of the eighteenth century were not obscurantists. They instead prized observation, interpretation, and exhortation, and their integrative worldview was nurtured by this academic agenda.

Methodist Communication: Exhortative Practices

As much as Wesley or Whitefield might have aspired to integrative spirituality, one of the most significant impediments to their mentoring was that they were both itinerants, spending large spans of time on the road, and not seeing possible mentees with any degree of regularity. They naturally worked with individuals along the way, answering questions and stimulating new visions for sanctified living, but to meet with an individual occasionally is not the same as mentoring an individual intentionally. Furthermore, itinerancy was itself in the eighteenth century a transgressive practice, undermining traditional authority and the relationship between the parson and his people, so any mentoring that may have been undertaken would not have assumed either stable notions of social propriety, or communication built on

---

39. See Vickers, *Wesley: A Guide for the Perplexed*, who underscores Wesley's significance in the stabilization of the confessional state in eighteenth-century England.

an ordered world guaranteed by ecclesiastical office.[40] Wesley or Whitefield would appeal instead to charismatic authority, validated not through logic or divine design but through the spiritual effectiveness of their warnings and admonitions. There was some sense of hierarchy among Methodists, but the movement's attractiveness was located in its provision of a new sense of agency rather than an old sense of deference to social superiors.

As itinerating evangelists, Wesley and Whitefield concentrated on a ministry of exhortation rather than a ministry of nurture. It is interesting to note in some letters of pastoral counsel, for example, how quickly Wesley focused on a particular issue, reducing the presenting pastoral conundrum to a clear exhortation or parcel of advice. In a letter to Mrs. Bennis on 25 July, 1767, he recognized that she might yet be "encompassed with numberless infirmities," but the way forward was: "Believe, and feel him near."[41] On 5 January 1772, to Philothea Briggs, who was apparently overwhelmed by circumstances, Wesley first explains reductionistically that "you have all things in one, the whole of religion contracted to a point . . . 'walk in love,'" then exhorts her to "be filled with the faith that worketh by love."[42] In another, to Ann Loxdale on 12 April 1782, Wesley acknowledged that the Christian life is an arduous pilgrimage, but nevertheless provided a simple quotidian exhortation: "the essence of religion . . . is no other than humble, gentle, patient love . . . I do not know whether all these are not included in that one word resignation. For the highest lesson our Lord (as man) learned on earth was to say, *Not as I will, but as You will.*"[43] Humility in our circumstances is of course thoroughly Christian, but resignation may not be the last word a pastor should offer to someone struggling with the nature of Christian holiness. In these letters, Wesley does not reveal anything of his own heart as a man, and the language of "we" is conspicuously absent.

An exhortative default can also be witnessed in the ministry of Whitefield. He built his own identity around significant characters from the biblical narrative, upon whom salvation history hinges, and thereby saw himself and others playing a role in the grand plan to promote the advance of salvation history. He made a parallel between his life and Jonah, Abraham, Paul, and of course Christ himself,[44] and in so doing sets himself within a "kind of spiritual and moral space," in which his pastoral identity was to some

40. See for example Hall, *Contested Boundaries*.
41. Telford, ed., *Letters*, 5:56.
42. Ibid., 5:299.
43. Ibid., 7:120.
44. See Whitefield, *Journals*, 506, 515, 530, 37. See also Bezzant, "Whitefield's Voice."

degree *bestowed*, obviating the need to negotiate contextually determined relationships or pastoral needs.[45] The voice he heard the morning after his ordination, calling on him to "Speak out, Paul," authorized him to build his identity on scriptural characters and to limit his identity to that of preacher.[46] In a letter, to J. W., presumably to John Wesley, written on 25 August 1740, he confirmed that "my business seems to be chiefly in planting."[47] Such focus is seen in his *Journal* on Saturday 15 November 1740. He recounts the week past, in which many were converted after earlier conviction, though he lamented how he can not do the follow up he would like, and trusts in the Lord to raise up workers to do that instead of him. He wrote:

> My chief business was now to build up and to exhort them to continue in the grace of God. Notwithstanding, many were convicted, almost every day, and came to me under the greatest distress and anguish of soul . . . Being so engaged, I could not visit them as I would, but I hope the Lord will raise me up some fellow-labourers, and that elders will be ordained in every place . . .[48]

In fact, Whitefield did not draw attention to any human intermediaries when he was trained for service: "Thus did God, by a variety of unforeseen acts of providence and grace, train me up for, and at length introduce me into, the service of His church."[49] His Pauline primitivism encourages him to give priority not to pastoral demands but evangelistic outcomes. Miniatory and hortatory appeals call listeners to make a decision and join his story. Wesley and Whitefield did not aspire to a full gamut of pastoral giftings, but concentrated on just a few.

The eighteenth century was the great age of friendship and the personal dimension of ministry was highly prized in the revivals, given their appeal to charismatic rather than institutional validation, yet for both of these men friendship did not come easily. For example, their own marriages were neglected due to their extensive travel. One particularly horrendous occasion in Whitefield's marriage came when he traveled first from America to Barbados, then back to Britain, leaving his wife Elizabeth James in Georgia, though later she followed him by herself.[50] Whitefield's public persona, cultivated through his experience on the stage and in the pulpit, may have created a barrier to the enjoyment of closeness. It was not so much that he

45. Hindmarsh, "Reshaping Individualism," 81.
46. Mahaffey, *Preaching Politics*, 33.
47. Whitefield, *Letters*, 205.
48. Whitefield, *Journals*, 493.
49. Ibid., 70.
50. Schlenther, "Whitefield's Personal Life and Character," 18.

confected an external identity that was divorced from his heart, but his public role was a powerfully formative device to reinforce personal weaknesses. Henry Rack reviews Wesley's life and makes these concluding observations on his capacity for intimate relationships:

> It is hard to escape the impression that Wesley behaved most graciously to those who were either submissive to his guidance or were in various ways naturally inferior to him . . . He continued to like the old tutorial relationship, suitably adapted and seen essentially as a relationship between superiors and inferiors . . . But Hampson is perhaps on stronger ground when he says that Wesley "had no attachments, so far as we have been able to discover, that partook of the genius of friendship" . . . Wesley was in a solitary position, forbidding to intimacy . . . an essentially lonely man, despite his vast range of human contacts.[51]

As for Whitefield, we discover frequent recognition of friends in his *Journals* and letters, such as: "I find we must be tried by friends, as well as by foes"; "the blessed Jesus hath been the author of our friendship, and therefore it will be blessed"; " . . . in order to express how sincerely I value your friendship"; "true friendship needs no apology"; "the good Lord sanctify my friendship to you, and grant we may go hand in hand to heaven"; "openness is the best preservative of spiritual friendship."[52] Despite these claims, we have to recognize the possibility that linguistic usage didn't necessarily mean psychological attachment. Even the little correspondence we have between him and his wife, presumably his closest friend, is perfunctory.[53]

It can be admitted, however, that letters function as a kind of epistolary "presence." In the eighteenth century, personal hand-writing represented a person's agency, the cost of paying the postman when a letter arrived served to valorize a relationship, and content highlighting the power of godliness reminded family and friends that, though apart physically, spiritual (if not emotional) unity might still be enjoyed. And such is the case in letters by Wesley and Whitefield, though little that is truly personal and a lot that is transactional are featured. The exhortative wins.

Further, of the four classic functions of pastoral care, namely healing, sustaining, guiding, and reconciling,[54] the pastoral ministry of Wesley and Whitefield certainly focused most on the nature of decision-making and therefore the value of advice-giving, falling under the canopy of guiding.

---

51. Rack, *Reasonable Enthusiast*, 542.
52. Whitefield, *Letters*, 450, 33, 140, 160, 181.
53. Ibid., 405.
54. Clebsch and Jaekle, *Pastoral Care in Historical Perspective*, 32.

While there may have been a *therapeutic* edge to the physical manifestations of the Spirit's filling, and Wesley did carry with him a medical bag of herbal *remedies*, these would not be sufficient to describe their pastoral ministry as centered on healing. Perhaps more appropriate is the term *maieutic*, serving like spiritual midwives by bringing new life to birth when they preached a sermon or wrote a letter. With the world as their parish, and therefore a sense of self that was expansively spatial, the notion that they were midwives fits well, for any new birth represents new occupation of space in the world. Offering help for acute crises, not chronic conditions, suggests a limited scope for pastoral engagement. If the hierarchical world that was being superseded thought in terms of *up and down*, the world that was being born imagined life in terms of *in and out*. Someone was needed at the bedside to exhort those in labor to keep pushing.

It is evident, then, that the revivals of the eighteenth century provided fertile soil for ministries of mentoring to take root. With intensity in personal relationships, the expectation of dynamic growth in the Spirit's power, a culture that increasingly prized friendships, and assumptions about the possibilities of impression and example, these were days when a new form of case-by-case instruction could emerge.[55] It is certainly true that Wesley and Whitefield received this kind of ministry, and they encouraged it in others too. However, their own modeling of mentoring was less potent. For their advocacy of integrative and exhortative ministries, we can be thankful, even if by personality and circumstances their own contribution was not fully orbed. When it comes to Methodist mentoring, Wesley and Whitefield were, in terms of their practice, kindred spirits and "companions in the way," even if on matters doctrinal their paths may have diverged.

---

55. Schwanda, *Emergence of Evangelical Spirituality*, 153.

12

The Hymnody of John Wesley and George Whitefield

Robert S. Smith

Neither John Wesley nor George Whitefield are typically remembered as hymn writers. Both, however, were passionate singers, promoters, collectors, compilers, editors, publishers, and (in Wesley's case) translators of hymns, with a shared concern that Christian people "be inspired and warmed with a like divine Fire whilst singing below, and be translated after Death to join with them in singing the Song of Moses and the Lamb above."[1]

In comparing Wesley and Whitefield's approaches to hymnody, then, their common concerns and convictions warrant both acknowledgement and exploration. At the same time, several key differences need to be identified and discussed. These include differences in style and theology, the pedagogical breadth of their respective hymnals, differences regarding the inviolability of the intellectual property of other hymn writers, and a major disparity in their output of publications.

However, before looking further into the hymnody of either man, and in order to set their respective contributions in context, it is necessary to outline the basic features of congregational singing in English churches at the beginning of the eighteenth century. This will sharpen our appreciation of Wesley and Whitefield's influences and antecedents, and also the significance and extent of their achievements.

---

1. Whitefield, *A Collection of Hymns for Social Worship*, Preface.

The Development of Evangelical Hymnody

Congregational Singing in Eighteenth-Century England

At the time of John Wesley's first encounter with the Moravians, the Church of England remained committed to the Calvinistic practice of singing only metrical versions of the psalms in the common tongue. Indeed, "the public singing of texts not directly from the Bible was still regarded by many as an 'error of popery.'"[2] Furthermore, in numerous country parishes, where many were illiterate, the psalms were sung by "lining out."[3] This involved a clerk reading each line aloud, so that the congregants could commit it to memory, before they all sang it together. Like Isaac Watts before him, Wesley abhorred this tedious practice, describing it as "disgusting tuneless repetition."[4] He was equally scathing of the quality of verse contained in Sternhold and Hopkins's 1562 metrical paraphrase of the Psalms (often referred to as the "Old Version"); lambasting it as "miserable, scandalous doggerel."[5]

In the last decade of the seventeenth century, a number of significant attempts to improve psalmody and introduce hymnody took place in nonconformist circles—especially among the Particular Baptists. The most notable innovator, and the man who is to be credited as the first to introduce regular hymn singing into the life of an English congregation, was Benjamin Keach (1640–1704); minister at Horselydown, Southwark. His views, however, were not shared by all of his contemporaries. A sharp debate thus ensued, with some claiming that set hymns were as bad, if not worse, than set prayers. Such attacks moved Keach to write a thorough defense of hymn singing with the instructive title: *The Breach Repaired in God's Worship: or, Singing of Psalms, Hymns and Spiritual Songs, proved to be an Holy Ordinance of Jesus Christ. With an Answer to all Objections* (1691).

Keach was not only a prolific author (publishing some 43 works), but also a prolific hymn-writer. His two major compilations were *Spiritual Melody* (1691) and *Spiritual Songs* (1696) which, between then, contained a total of 400 hymns, all Keach's own compositions. While few, if any, of these hymns are sung today, his emphasis on the joy of hymn singing and his desire to move the affections show him to be a precursor of the evangelical revival.[6]

---

2. Wilson-Dickson, *Story of Christian Music*, 110.
3. Gillman, *Evolution of the English Hymn*, 198.
4. Nuelson, *John Wesley and the German Hymn*, 21.
5. Telford, ed., *Letters*, 3:227.
6. Vaughn, "Public Worship and Practical Theology," 352.

Isaac Watts: The "Liberator" of the English Hymn

Notwithstanding the importance of Keach's patient pioneering, at the turn of the eighteenth century it was Isaac Watts who stood against the deplorable state of church music like no other before him. Although not the "father" of English hymnody (as he is often called), he was certainly "the liberator" of the English hymn.[7] As Louis Benson memorably put it: "He does not stand alone, but his personality commands the situation, his mind plans the remedy purely from personal resources, and his strong will overcomes the force of tradition, of conviction, of sacred associations, of habit, of prejudice, and, not least, of indifference."[8]

Watts's most significant publication was his *Hymns and Spiritual Songs* (1707), a collection of 210 original compositions. The opening sentence of his "Preface" reveals the purpose of the volume and the problem is sought to solve: "While we sing the Praises of our God in his Church, we are employ'd in that part of Worship which of all others is the nearest a-kin to Heaven; and 'tis pity that this of all others should be perform'd the worst upon Earth."[9]

The other piece in Watts's "single System of Praise"[10] was his *The Psalms of David Imitated in the Language of the New Testament*" (1719). The brilliance of this work lay in the way "Watts took the Hebrew and recast it, as if the psalmist were writing in the Christian era."[11] His aim, as he explained in the "Preface," was to give "an evangelic turn to the Hebrew sense" and in so doing "to accommodate the book of Psalms to Christian worship."[12]

As an Independent, Watts's most immediate influence was upon Nonconformists. Nevertheless, his concerns were shared and his hymns cherished by many in the Church of England—not least a young John Wesley and an even younger George Whitefield. Of particular appeal was Watts's ability to write both for "the common man" and "those of more refined taste," and his "free use of the first person singular as the predominant voice of the verse texts." These characteristics gave his hymns "a sense of immediacy and familiarity not characteristic of the older psalmody."[13]

---

7. Routley, *Hymns and Human Life*, 64.
8. Benson, *English Hymn*, 217.
9. Watts, *Hymns and Spiritual Songs*, iii.
10. Benson, *English Hymn*, 209.
11. Watson, *English Hymn*, 153.
12. Watts, *Psalms of David Imitated*, iv, xvi.
13. McNearney, "Ah, Lovely Appearance of Death," 63.

The hymnody of John Wesley

Life in the Epworth rectory

The impact of Isaac Watts upon the young Wesley brothers was clearly significant, but it was far from the only contributor to their love of hymnody. The Wesleys were, in fact, a family of poets. Samuel, the father, published several volumes of poems and also "showed himself as by no means an incapable hymn writer."[14]

The Wesley family also engaged in the social singing of the psalms. This was somewhat unusual, even for a rectory household, for many had been put off the practice by the "sorry Sternhold Psalms" (as Samuel called them) and the vileness of their tunes.[15] Nevertheless, as he wrote to Samuel junior, Samuel senior regarded church music as "a great help to our devotion, as it notably raises our affections towards heaven."[16] He thus strongly advocated psalm singing, both in public and in private, especially the newer strains of Tate and Brady's Psalter ("the New Version").

Although it is unclear just how much John, as a child, understood or shared his father's convictions, it is not difficult to determine the origin of many of his later views, particularly regarding the use and abuse of psalmody, the value of hymnody and the need for church music reform. Nor is it surprising that the singing of psalms and hymns became a feature of meetings of the Holy Club from its earliest days in 1729.

The Influence of the Moravians

Among the passengers who accompanied John and Charles Wesley on their voyage to Georgia in 1735 were a group of twenty-six Moravian colonists. As John records in his *Journal*, he "began to learn German in order to converse with the Germans, six-and-twenty of whom we had on board."[17] An additional motivation was to join them in their daily worship and, in particular, to sing from their new hymnbook, published by Nicholas Ludwig von Zinzendorf, *Das Gesang-Buch der Gemeine in Herrnhut* (*The Songbook of the Congregation in Herrnhut*).

---

14. Benson, *English Hymn*, 221.
15. Ibid, 221–22.
16. Letter to Samuel Wesley (Jr.), "Epworth, August 15, 1706," cited in Torpy, *Prevenient Piety of Samuel Wesley, Sr.*, 89.
17. Ward and Heitzenrater, eds., *Journals and Diaries*, 18:137.

Throughout the voyage, both Wesleys were deeply affected by the singing of the Moravians, who not only sang passionately but in harmony. The effect of this exposure "was to make an indelible impression of the spiritual possibilities of the Hymn and of a fervid type of hymn singing far removed from the dull parochial Psalmody or congregational praise of Nonconformist chapels. The fervor and spontaneity of this Moravian song was ultimately to be reproduced in the hymn singing of Methodist meetings."[18] The worship practices of the Moravians also persuaded John of the importance of incorporating hymns of "human composure" into Sunday church services.

A Translator of Continental Hymns

While John's interest in hymn singing clearly predated his voyage to Georgia, "the Moravian Singstunde (singing meeting) awakened in Wesley a love for hymns that was never quenched."[19] He was so struck by the content of *Gesang-Buch* that by 27 October 1735, less than a week after having set sail from Gravesend, he had already began translating several of its hymns. Two years later, when he produced his "Charlestown hymnbook,"[20] five of his translations were included.

John's 1738 visit to the Moravian headquarters in Herrnhut, Germany, only deepened his appreciation of continental hymns. Consequently, five more of his translations appeared in *Collection of Psalms and Hymns* (1738), an additional twelve in *Hymns and Sacred Poems* (1739), and a further six in the 1740 edition of the same title. At this point, however, things changed rather dramatically. This can be seen in the third edition of *Hymns and Sacred Poems* (1742), which contained only one new German translation and none of the previous twenty-eight! The obvious explanation for this absence was the split between the Moravian and Methodist societies in 1740.

When later editions of the Wesleys' hymnbooks are counted, most Wesley scholars are agreed that John published a total of thirty-three of his translations of German hymns.[21] It is unknown how many were never published. John also tried his hand at translating a small number of French and Spanish hymns. However, it was the German hymns that captured his attention, at least until 1740. The significance of this early fascination is well summarized by James Watson:

18. Benson, *English Hymn*, 224.
19. Hammond, "John Wesley's Relations with the Lutheran Pietist Clergy in Georgia," 142.
20. Wesley, *A Collection of Psalms and Hymns* (1737).
21. Nuelsen, *John Wesley and the German Hymn*, 27.

Wesley's choice of these writers, and his affinity with them, suggests that he was in pursuit of a religious pattern of behaviour more in keeping with seventeenth-century mysticism and Puritanism than with the Latitudinarian theology of his own day.[22]

A Publisher of Hymnals

As important as his translations were, it is his work as a compiler, editor, and publisher of hymnals that is, arguably, Wesley's greatest contribution to the development of the English hymn. By the end of his life in 1791, John (often in conjunction with Charles) had published some sixty separate hymnals, thirty-six of which contained his and Charles's hymns alone.

A cursory glance at these publications reveals two things. First, the Wesleys understood the importance and power of hymn singing to inform and transform both seeker and saved. This understanding guided them in their inclusion decisions, and also in their own hymn composition. As Benson remarks: "The composition of the hymns was thus closely related to the progress of the Revival which they in turn did much to foster; and the long series of books and tracts in which they appeared are an essential part of the Revival records."[23]

Second, whilst the thematic range of each publication varied—some narrower (like *Hymns on the Trinity*, 1767) and others wider (like *Hymns and Spiritual Songs Intended for the Use of Real Christians of All Denominations*, 1753)—the theological and liturgical breadth of the entire corpus is staggering. Soteriological themes dominate (especially the work of Christ and the doctrines of grace—albeit with an Arminian edge), but few, if any, major doctrinal heads are left unexplored. Furthermore, the pastoral and ecclesial concerns addressed by various hymns and, in some instances, whole publications (for example, *Hymns on the Expected Invasion*, 1759),[24] indicate a deep desire for theology to be applied personally and practically.

Indeed, John's claim in the "Preface" of *A Collection of Hymns for the Use of the People Called Methodists* (1780)—that "The hymns are not carelessly jumbled together, but carefully ranged under proper heads, according to the experience of real Christians. So that this book is, in effect, a little body of experimental and practical divinity"[25]—is not only true of that pub-

22. Watson, *English Hymn*, 205.
23. Benson, *English Hymn*, 230.
24. Prompted by the growing threat of a French invasion of England.
25. Wesley, *A Collection of Hymns for the Use of the People Called Methodists*, Preface, paragraph 4.

lication, but of his entire corpus. Thus, the "Wesleyan hymnals are among the most important of the publications from the movement, and while a few of the hymnals are monumental classics, we should not forget that smaller hymn collections came out at a rate of more than one per year."[26]

A Writer of Hymns

What made these frequent publications possible was the fact that Charles Wesley was "an unstoppable fountain of song,"[27] penning somewhere "between six thousand and nine thousand hymns and sacred poems (depending upon what one is willing to call a hymn or poem)."[28]

But what of John? How many hymns came from his pen? Like other hymnals of the time, the authorship details of individual hymns were not included in the Wesleyan publications. It is thus notoriously difficult to determine exactly how many should be attributed to him. Because of this, many Wesley scholars adopt the "traditional practice" of ascribing everything to Charles.[29] Other sources, however, confidently list John as the sole author of the following:[30]

1. Author of Life Divine (1746)
2. How Happy Is the Pilgrim's Lot (1747)
3. We Lift Our Hearts to Thee (1741)
4. Servant of God, Well Done! (1770)[31]
5. Unclean of Life and Heart Unclean (no date)

Furthermore, there are several good reasons to think that John authored more than these five hymns. For instance, "a number of the early hymnbooks of the brothers were described on the title pages as 'by John and Charles Wesley.'"[32] Added to that, there is "some evidence that the brothers

---

26. Sanders, *Wesley on the Christian Life*, 91.
27. Ibid., 91.
28. Tyson, *Assist Me to Proclaim*, vii–viii.
29. For example, Herbert, *John Wesley as Editor and Author*, 61.
30. For example, the "Hymntime" website: http://www.hymntime.com/tch/bio/w/e/s/wesley_j.htm.
31. This hymn is of particular interest for this essay, as it was written in response to Whitefield's death (September 1770) and appeared at the end of the published version of Wesley's funeral sermon, preached (at Whitefield's request) on Sunday, 18 November 1770.
32. Watson, *English Hymn*, 214.

agreed not to distinguish their several contributions of the hymns published jointly."[33] To complicate matters further, not only did John often edit and revise Charles's hymns, but both are known to have contributed stanzas to the same hymns and, according to their associate, Samuel Bradburn, made a compact not to reveal their respective verses.[34] So the "source critical" puzzle is virtually impossible to solve.

Or is it? In his detailed study of *The Hymns of Methodism in their Literary Relations*, Henry Bett suggests a number of "marked peculiarities" that, in his view, indicate that a hymn has come from John's pen. For example: (1) "A strong preference for the simpler measures, particularly four-line or six-line stanzas of eight-syllabled lines"; (2) "A considerable use of lines rhymed consecutively"; (3) "A tendency to divide the octosyllabic line into equal clauses of four syllables, with a pause between"; (4) "the tendency to elaborate and repeat a thought"; (5) "the tendency to begin a succession of lines with a series of parallel expressions"; and (6) "A habit of carrying over a sentence from one line to another, ending, or pausing heavily, at the *second* syllable of the second line." [35]

These and other consideration enable Bett to attribute a further nine hymns to John.[36] However, not all Wesley scholars share Bett's confidence,[37] and Bett himself concedes that, in the end, his case can't be proved. Nor does he wish to throw doubt on the correctness of the general impression that "most of the hymns are unquestionably the work of Charles Wesley."[38] This is confirmed by none other than John, who, in regard to the 1780 *Collection*, was adamant that "but a small part of these hymns is of my own composing."[39] Exactly how small that "small part" is remains a mystery.[40]

---

33. Benson, *English Hymn*, 220.

34. Bett, *Hymns of Methodism in their Literary Relations*, 129.

35. Ibid, 130–33.

36. Ibid, 134.

37. See, for example, Rattenbury, *Evangelical Doctrines of Charles Wesley's Hymns*, 23, 337; Baker, *Charles Wesley's Verse: An Introduction*, 97; Beckerlegge and Hildebrandt, eds., *A Collection Hymns*, 7:38.

38. Bett, *Hymns of Methodism*, 135.

39. Wesley, *A Collection of Hymns for the Use of the People Called Methodists*, Preface, paragraph 4.

40. What can be said, according to Benson, is that "Charles Wesley's hymns owe much to the strong hand of his brother, not only for the winnowing they so much needed, but for the verbal revision to which he subjected them insistently, before their first appearing and after it." *English Hymn*, 247.

A Teacher of Theology through Hymnody

Capitalizing on his brothers' remarkable poetic gifts, John made it his business to get his (and others') hymns into the hands and mouths and hearts of "a people called Methodists" and anyone else he could reach. For "[h]ymns, more than any other source except the Bible, were the means by which the ordinary Methodist could obtain a knowledge of what Wesley thought Methodism taught."[41]

What, then, did Methodism teach? One way of answering this question is by examining the contents of the 1780 *Collection*, for the book's very structure, according to Henry Rack, "takes the user through the Methodist plan of salvation."[42] Clearly a detailed analysis of the volume is not possible in this essay, but David Hempton's summary successfully captures the main themes:

> Part one was an exhortation to return to God by describing the pleasantness of religion, the goodness of God, death, judgement, heaven and hell . . . Part two of the *Collection* describes the difference between formal and informal religion; part three contains prayers for repentance and recovery from backsliding; part four envisages the believer rejoicing, fighting, praying, watching, working, suffering, groaning for full redemption, and interceding for the world; part five includes hymns of corporate life, celebrations of Methodist community.[43]

Throughout, the person and work of a fully-divine-fully-human-Christ is ever-present. Moreover, it is the atoning death of Christ—"the blood" in Charles's language—that is of central importance. In this sense, Wesley was a poet-preacher of Christ alone, as he was also of faith alone. This latter point explains his frequent stress on salvation as *conditional*—that is, the benefits of Christ's death are received only by those who believe. Further, the Wesleys regarded saving faith as living and active; that is, a faith that patiently pursues a path of sanctification. Robert Cushman, thus, sums up the soteriological "system" of the Wesleyan hymns as follows:

> On the one hand, there was justification or forgiveness of sins by grace through faith received; on the other hand, the "new birth" carried with it a life vocation, namely Christian perfection, inward and outward holiness as an inescapable obligation. Together, these constitute "the ordinary condition of final

---

41. Rack, *Reasonable Enthusiast*, 414.
42. Ibid.
43. Hempton, *Methodism: Empire of the Spirit*, 69–70.

salvation." Yet always Wesley teaches that this is God's doing by his preventing and saving grace.[44]

The importance of the hymns for the theology of the Methodist movement and for the theological formation of Methodist believers cannot for overstated; "for, unlike John's reasoned writings, they were read and sung by all Methodist people and so penetrated their hearts, illumined their minds and expressed in striking and memorable phrase the saving truths which were believed and preached."[45]

Furthermore, it was not only Methodists who made use of the Wesleys' hymns. As Mark Noll has observed, the early evangelical hymns in particular "possessed an almost magical power to smooth over the often sharp theological differences that emerged within the movement."[46] Key to this broad ecumenical appeal was the fact that Charles's hymns are so steeped in Scripture that, "A skillful man, if the Bible were lost, might extract much of it from Wesley's Hymns."[47] Evidence of this is found in the latest critical edition of *A Collection of Hymns for the Use of the People Called Methodists* (1780), where the "Index of Scriptural Allusions" contains some 2,500 entries drawn from every biblical book with the exceptions of Nahum and Philemon.[48]

Not all of the Wesleys' hymns, however, were of an ecumenical spirit. Some were deliberately provocative and combative. This is not really surprising, for neither their opposition to Calvinism nor their views on sanctification were secret. Indeed, Charles (like John) regarded "Universal Redemption and Christian Perfection as the two great truths of the everlasting Gospel."[49] Thus, at various points, "polemical poetry" of a more "vituperative tone" can be found in the Wesleyan corpus.[50] The hymn, "Universal Redemption," which accompanied the published version of John's 1739 sermon, "Free Grace," is a case in point.[51] In it the Wesleys turn their guns on the doctrine of predestination, directly challenging George Whitefield's affirmation of limited atonement and unconditional election.

---

44. Cushman, *John Wesley's Experimental Divinity*, 48.
45. Rattenbury, *Evangelical Doctrines of Charles Wesley's Hymns*, 63.
46. Noll, "The Defining Role of Hymns in Early Evangelicalism," 13.
47. Rattenbury, *Evangelical Doctrines of Charles Wesley's Hymns*, 48.
48. Dudley-Smith, "Why Wesley Still Dominates Our Hymnbook," 31.
49. Charles Wesley, *Journal of the Rev. Charles Wesley, M.A.*, 1:286.
50. Dean, *A Heart Strangely Warmed*, 125.
51. The authorship of "Universal Redemption" is, once again, a matter of some dispute. Some of its thirty-three verses may well have been written by John. Most scholars, however, favor attributing it to Charles.

An Instructor in Hymn Singing

As we have seen, it is impossible to explore John's approach to hymnody apart from Charles's prodigious output. If Charles, however, was the principal composer of the movement's songs, John was very much the chief choirmaster—instructing his congregations not only *what* to sing but *how* to sing. As Davies avers: "The great editor of the Methodist collection of hymns was as deeply concerned with the method of singing as with the content."[52]

How, then, did this work out in practice? Detailed instructions were often enunciated by the Wesleyan leadership at various Methodist Conferences. "In 1746, it suggested the following to its preachers. 1) To be careful to choose hymns proper to the congregation. 2) To choose hymns of praise or prayer. 3) To beware of singing too much—though many Wesleyan hymn texts were very long, no more than 5–6 verses were to be sung at a time. 4) To regularly stop the singing and ask the people if they knew the meaning of what they had just sung. This was one of John Wesley's favorite techniques."[53]

The best-known list of John's directions, however, is found on the last page of *Select Hymns with Tunes Annext*: (1761).[54] The purpose of the "Directions" is provided in an opening statement: "*That this part of Divine Worship may be the more acceptable to God, as well as the more profitable to yourself and others, be careful to observe the following directions.*" The substance of the "Directions," may be summarized and explained as follows: (1) Learn these tunes first; (2) Sing them exactly as they are printed; (3) "Sing *All*"—that is, everyone sing and sing frequently; (4) "Sing *lustily* [i.e., confidently and enthusiastically] and with good courage"; (5) "Sing modestly"—that is, blend in with the rest of the congregation; (6) "Sing in *Time*," neither running ahead nor falling behind the lead voices; and (7) "Above all sing *spiritually*"—that is, aim to please God more than others by attending to the words you're singing and by continually offering your heart to him.

A number of interrelated concerns are reflected in these instructions. The first is the importance of the fit between words and music. As Steven Kimbrough Jr. notes: "the Wesleys had come to understand the power of the wedding of text and tune as the most vital way of celebrating and remembering faith, Scripture, theology, and the task of social service."[55] To

---

52. Davies, *Worship and Theology in England*, 203.

53. Shaw, "Music of the Early Methodist Church," 3.

54. Throughout their lifetimes, the Wesleys published a total of four different hymn books with tunes: (1) *A Collection of Tunes set to Music, as they are commonly Sung at the Foundery* (1742); (2) *Hymns on the Great Festivals and other occasions* (1746); (3) *Select Hymns with Tunes Annext* (1761); (4) *Sacred Harmony* (1781).

55. Cited in Young, *Music of the Heart*, 73.

this end, John was disparaging of complexity, counterpoint, or harmony, regarding these as enemies of naturalness and music's true power.[56]

The second concern is for what Davies calls "a more democratic type of worship."[57] That is, Wesley desired the whole congregation to sing, not just a trained choir. This was one of the reasons he despised anthems, as these gave a small group a monopoly on the praise.[58] All must be engaged and give themselves to praise with sustained energy. To this end, he advised: "Let not a slight degree of weakness or weariness hinder you. If it is a cross to you, take it up, and you will find it a blessing" (Direction III). Furthermore, "Beware of singing as if you were half dead, or half asleep" (Direction IV). And yet, if *all* are going to sing well *together*, it is important that the members "Do not bawl, so as to be heard above or distinct from the rest of the congregation, that [they] may not destroy the harmony; but strive to unite [their] voices together, so as to make one clear melodious sound" (Direction V).

The third concern is to avoid formality in order to promote spirituality. This was another reason Wesley despised anthems, particularly those that pandered to (what he regarded as) "the shocking custom of modern music," where "different persons sung different words at one and the same moment."[59] Behind this criticism lay a concern that people's hearts be "not carried away with the sound, but offered to God continually" (Direction VII). This reveals that Wesley's "primary concern was for the spiritual well-being and development of the emerging Methodist societies."[60] It also reveals that music, for Wesley, was ultimately a means to an end: whole-hearted worship of God through clear-minded singing of his word. To this end it is vital "to attend strictly to the sense of what you sing" (Direction VII).

Concluding Thoughts on Wesley

The Wesleyan hymns that came to be such a key feature of Methodist worship fulfilled at least four distinct functions.[61] First, they gave free expres-

---

56. See, in particular, points 11 and 12 of Wesley's, "The Power of Music," 768–69.

57. Davies, *Worship and Theology in England*, 201.

58. In a letter "To A Friend. On Public Worship" on 20 September 1757, he is scathing of "the screaming of boys, who bawl out what they neither feel nor understand, or the unseasonable and unmeaning impertinence of a voluntary on the organ." Cited in Brewer, *Pleasures of the Imagination*, 555–56.

59. Ward and Heitzenrater, eds., *Journals and Diaries*, 22:152.

60. Clarke, *John Wesley and Methodist Music in the Eighteenth Century*, 145.

61. This list is adapted from Davies, *Worship and Theology in England*, 201.

sion to the warmth and reality of gospel-generated emotions. Second, they served a pedagogical function, effectively teaching evangelical doctrine and functioning as "sung creeds." Third, they were aesthetically and poetically superior to the sad doggerel characteristic of Sternhold and Hopkins's metrical Psalter. Fourth, they were truly democratic, allowing the whole congregation to contribute to the common worship of God.

But they did more than this. "No one can turn from the earlier hymns to the Wesleyan without being conscious of a change of atmosphere, a heightening of emotion, a novelty of theme, a new manner of expression."[62] The net result, therefore, was not merely an enrichment of the stores of English hymns, nor simply a modification of the ideal English hymn, but a range of new types of hymns: hymns that sounded a new evangelical and experiential note, that set a new liturgical and literary standard.[63] In sum, "Wesley's lifelong efforts to standardize the rhetoric and music of congregational song—the unity of emotion and the cognate, the head and the heart—became a distinctive mark of the eighteenth century Methodist revival in Britain."[64]

The Hymnody of George Whitefield

Due to the sheer volume of the Wesley brothers' output, there might seem to be comparatively little to be said about the hymnody of George Whitefield. But this is not so. While it is true that Whitefield "had nothing of Wesley's impulse and ability to organize his followers, and indeed no ambition beyond that of preaching the gospel far and wide,"[65] he clearly saw the advance of evangelical hymnody as a key part of the gospel enterprise. This explains "the importance of hymns in George Whitefield's rhetoric, the centrality of their christological focus, and their ubiquity throughout his public life."[66] It also explains his desire to publish his own *A Collection of Hymns for Social Worship* in 1753.

---

62. Benson, *English Hymn*, 247.
63. Ibid, 244–55.
64. Young, *Music of the Heart*, 74.
65. Benson, *English Hymn*, 315.
66. Noll, "Whitefield, Hymnody and Evangelical Spirituality," 260.

A Promoter of Hymn Singing

At John Wesley's urging, Whitefield made his first visit to the North American colonies in February 1738. As we have seen, this year marked a major turning point for the new hymns being produced in England with the publication of the Wesley brothers' *A Collection of Psalms and Hymns*. Unbeknown to Whitefield, John had returned to England the day before he set sail.[67] Whitefield, nonetheless, continued his journey and, once in Georgia, picked up where Wesley had left off.

Like Wesley, Whitefield made good use of the hymns of Isaac Watts in his ministry, encouraging their singing both as an act of private devotion and as a form of public witness-bearing.[68] He was also keen to promote the use of evangelical hymns throughout the colonies. Consequently, during a visit to Northampton, in 1741, he gave Jonathan Edwards a copy of Watts's *Hymns and Spiritual Songs* and *Psalms of David Imitated*. Within a year, Edwards reported that his congregation "sang nothing else, and neglected the Psalms wholly."[69]

In addition to this, as the awakening gained traction throughout the region, personal and congregational use of Watts's hymns was increasingly supplemented by their use in public evangelistic events. This practice, plus Whitefield's personal connections in both England and New England, enabled him to create "an intercolonial evangelical network during the revival through which he transmitted Watt's psalms and hymns as well as his own influential collection of English Evangelical hymns."[70]

Furthermore, greatly helped by the sonority, timbre, and penetration of his voice, Whitefield frequently took it upon himself to lead the singing at the outdoor revival meetings. For this he was often abused, assaulted, and sometimes arrested.[71] Nevertheless, the "effect achieved in these highly theatrical, emotionally charged spaces was remarkable, galvanizing supporters and opponents alike."[72] This only aided the spread and popularity of the revival hymns—so much so that after Whitefield had preached to immense crowds in Philadelphia in 1739, Benjamin Franklin remarked how

---

67. Burnett, *In the Shadow of Aldersgate*, 28
68. Tyerman, *Life of George Whitefield*, 1:241.
69. Cited in Marini, *Sacred Song in America*, 78.
70. Marini, *Sacred Song in America*, 316.
71. Ibid.
72. Phillips, "Cotton Mather Brings Isaac Watts's Hymns to America," 220.

"one could not walk through Philadelphia in the evening without hearing psalms sung in different families of the street."[73]

As the revival continued to spread through Whitefield's ministry, so Watts's "System of Praise" spread through New England, creating a phenomenon of congregational worship on a scale hitherto unknown.[74] By 1770, thanks to the efforts of William Billings, a new American synthesis of sacred song was beginning to emerge. *The New-England Psalm-Singer* contained one hundred and twenty-six tunes, all Billings's own compositions. The metrical texts, however, were almost entirely those of Watts. Billings was clearly greatly indebted to Whitefield (who died in the same week that Billings wrote his Preface) and expressed his gratitude by publishing what he thought was one of Whitefield's own hymns: "Ah! Lovely Appearance of Death."[75]

A Writer of Hymns?

But was Whitefield in fact that author of "Ah! Lovely Appearance of Death"? Immediately following his death in Newburyport in 1770, numerous pamphlets appeared not only containing the words of the hymn but claiming Whitefield as their author.[76] Some further claimed that it was "designed to have been sung over his corpse, by the orphans belonging to his tabernacle in London, had this great, pious, and learned man died there."[77] The hymn was, in fact, composed by Charles Wesley in 1746, and appeared in the first edition of the Wesleys' *Funeral Hymns*, published that same year. So Whitefield was most certainly not its author.

But that does not mean that Whitefield wrote nothing. In 1755, he published *A Communion Morning's Companion. By George Whitefield, A.B., late of Pembroke College, Oxford, and Chaplain to. the Right Honourable the Countess of Huntingdon. London, 1755.* Among other liturgical elements, the book contains fifty-nine Sacramental Hymns, and seventeen Doxologies. Except for a few which were written by the Wesleys, most of the hymns,

---

73. Reported in Tyreman, *Life of the Rev. George Whitefield*, 1:338.

74. Phillips, "Cotton Mather Brings Isaac Watts's Hymns to America," 207. In fact, Whitefield's promotion of Watts's hymns resulted in at least six American reprints of his works within five years.

75. Marini, *Sacred Song in America*, 78.

76. McNearney, "Ah, Lovely Appearance of Death," 57.

77. Ibid., 57.

according to Luke Tyerman, are "pious doggerel." Nevertheless, the book was extremely popular and passed through several editions.[78]

What is of particular interest, for our purposes, is the following remark found in Whitefield's Preface:

> There is but little in this "Communion Morning's Companion" of my own; and, as it is intended purely for the assistance of the professed members of the Church of England, I thought it most advisable to extract the meditations and practical remarks on the public form of administration from our own bishops.[79]

The statement "but little . . . of my own" suggests there is some of Whitefield own work in the publication. However, once the Wesley hymns are excluded, it is impossible to determine how many of the hymns that remain may have come from Whitefield's pen.

A similar problem pertains to his 1753 publication, *A Collection of Hymns for Social Worship*. Of the *Collection*'s one hundred and eighty-one hymns, the authors of only one hundred and forty-nine are able to be identified.[80] This leaves the authorship of thirty-two hymns unconfirmed. Could Whitefield have written some of these? The revelation provided in the "Preface" to his *Communion Morning's Companion* might suggest an affirmative answer.

At first glance, further support appears to be found in Whitefield's publication of a companion volume to *Hymns for Social Worship*; a book of texts and tunes titled: *The Divine Musical Miscellany, being a Collection of Psalm and Hymn Tunes: great part of which were never before in print* (1754). Of the 67 hymns contained in the volume, Whitefield's initials appear at the bottom of nineteen! The problem, however, is that "eleven of them are known to be the work of others, and none of the remaining eight can be positively attributed to Whitefield."[81]

This leads Ronald Byrnside to pose the following questions: "Was he being deliberately deceitful? Was this some sort of perverse ego trip? Did he feel that hymns bearing his name would help promote the book?"[82] Such questions, however, are needlessly dramatic. What is far more likely is that the anonymous editor of the volume was indicating the source from which the nineteen hymns were taken—that is, Whitefield's *Hymns for Social Wor-*

---

78. Tyerman, *Life of the Rev. George Whitefield*, 2:344.
79. Cited in ibid., 2:344.
80. Noll, "Whitefield, Hymnody, and Evangelical Spirituality," 249.
81. Byrnside, *Music in Eighteenth-Century Georgia*, 91.
82. Ibid., 92.

ship. In other words, the presence of Whitefield initials at the end of these hymns ought not to be confused with a claim to authorship.[83]

That Whitefield dabbled in hymn writing is likely. Indeed, Clayton McNearny believes we have "dozens of examples of his own doggerel verse to be found scattered throughout his letters and journals."[84] If this is so, what can be said is that, while Whitefield could preach like no other, when it came to verse making he was no Charles Wesley.

A "Mender" of Hymns

By contrast with his reputation as a hymn writer, Whitefield's reputation as hymn alterer or "mender" is well-deserved. He was, of course, far from alone in engaging in such a practice. For hymns, in the eighteenth century, were virtually regarded as public property. All who published collections took certain liberties with the texts of the hymns they included.[85] Indeed, Isaac Watts encouraged such changes, writing in the "Preface" to the second edition of *Hymns and Spiritual Songs*, "where any unpleasing word is found, he that leads the worship may substitute a better; for (Blessed be God) we are not confined to the words of any Man in our public solemnities."[86]

The Wesleys, however, clearly believed their hymns were beyond either poetic or doctrinal improvement. Hence in the "Preface" of *A Collection of Hymns for the Use of the People called Methodists* (1780), John pleads with those who would publish the Wesleys' hymns to "print them just as they are" and "not attempt . . . to mend either the sense or the verse."[87] Doubtless, these remarks were elicited by numerous instances of unwelcome editorial alterations, most of which are unknown.

One that is known, however, concerns Whitefield's changes to the hymn we now know as "Hark the Herald Angels Sing." Written by Charles Wesley in 1739, its opening lines originally read: "Hark how all the Welkin rings / Glory to the King of Kings."[88] Whitefield evidently thought that several alterations were in order and so reworked the opening two lines into

---

83. That this is almost certainly the correct explanation has been confirmed to me in a private email from Professor Stephen Marini, dated 25 April, 2017.

84. McNearney, "Ah, Lovely Appearance of Death," 65.

85. Görlach, *Text Types and the History of English*, 169.

86. Cited in ibid., 169.

87. Wesley, *A Collection of Hymns for the Use of the People called Methodists*, Preface, paragraph 7.

88. Both the word "welkin" (an old English term for "sky" or "heavens") and the opening line, seems to have been adapted from a poem about fox hunting called "The Chase," written in 1735 by William Somerville. See Watson, "Welkins," 80.

their now familiar form. He also changed "Universal Nature say / 'CHRIST the LORD is born to Day!'" to "Nature rise and worship him, / Who is born at Bethlehem."[89] Finally, in keeping with his claim to be "no great Friend to long Sermons, long Prayers, or long Hymns,"[90] he dropped out the last half of verses four and five, creating a new composite verse four.

Charles, reportedly, "refused to sing Whitfield's [sic] reworking of his words, furious that he had presumed to alter them to suit his own ends."[91] But the making of such alterations, as we've noted, was a common and accepted practice of the time, as was the listing of an "alterer" as co-author. Interestingly, it is Whitefield's version that John Wesley included in the "Supplement" section *of A Collection of Hymns for the Use of the People called Methodists* (1780).[92]

A Publisher of Hymn Texts

In 1739, soon after returning from his first visit to Georgia, Whitefield made his initial sortie into the realm of hymn publishing. In so doing, he was, evidently, inspired by the release of the Wesley brothers' third compilation, *Hymns and Sacred Poems* (also 1739), if not by a desire to publish a theologically superior volume.

Whitefield's publication carried the lengthy title: *Divine Melody: or, A Help to Devotion. Being, A Choice Collection of Hymns, Psalms, and Spiritual Songs for the Use of the Pious and Sincere Christian. Selected, Approved and Recommended by the Rev. Mr. George Whitefield*. Like the Wesleys' volume, it was built around a selection of devotional poems by George Herbert (1593–1633). However, whereas the Wesleys' was filled out by various continental poems, metrical psalms by Samuel Snr. and hymns by Charles, Whitefield's was laden with the more overtly Calvinist hymns and psalm imitations by Isaac Watts. According to Stephen Marini: "This doctrinal differential in their early devotional poetry collections prefigured the Calvinist-Arminian break between Whitefield and the Wesleys that would shortly ensue."[93]

Whitefield's next publication was *A confession of faith, sung by all the brethren and sisters at the general love-feast, November 4th, 1744. in the Tabernacle, London*. This was a single hymn, published in pamphlet form,

---

89. In 1760, Martin Madan further altered these lines to "With angelic hosts proclaim / Christ is born in Bethlehem."
90. Whitefield, *Hymns for Social Worship*, Preface.
91. Giles, *O Come Emmanuel*, 100.
92. Listed as "Hymn 602: The Incarnation of Christ," on page 555.
93. Marini, "Whitefield's Music," 111.

consisting of nine verses in 8.8.8.8.8.8 meter. It is generally assumed to have been penned by Charles Wesley,[94] and was composed for a gathering of Wesleyans, Moravians, and Calvinistic Methodists who met for a "general love feast" on the date nominated in the title.[95] The title also reveals that "men and women met and sang together in the service."[96]

It wasn't until 1753, however, when the new Tabernacle was opened, that Whitefield produced his next major hymnal: *Hymns for social worship, collected from various authors, and more particularly design'd for the use of the Tabernacle Congregation in London. By Georg Whitefield, A.B., late of Pembroke College, Oxford, and Chaplain to the Rt. Hon. The Countess of Huntingdon, London: printed by William Strahan, and to be sold at the Tabernacle, near Moorfields. M DCC LIII.* Although clearly designed for the Tabernacle congregation, it had a broader reach, running to "at least 15 editions during Whitefield's lifetime, including a Philadelphia reprinting in 1768, to 32 printings by 1788, and remained in print into the nineteenth century."[97]

Such popularity is not surprising, as it was one of the first compilations to include the hymns of both Isaac Watts (eighty-four) and Charles Wesley (twenty-five)—despite being over a decade since Whitefield's split with the brothers. Other contributors included Whitefield's former associates, now turned Moravians, John Cennick (fourteen) and William Hammond (five).[98] In addition to this, the collection displayed a remarkable degree of (what Noll calls) "denominational promiscuity" in its range of authors.[99] Such ecclesiastical breadth was partly a reflection of Whitefield's natural ability to get on well with all kinds of people,[100] but mostly of his desire that the anthology maintain "a broadly orthodox concentration on the fact and implications of Christ's redeeming sacrifice."[101]

The contents thus "focused, refocused, and focused again on two main subjects: the character and work of Christ the redeemer, and the believer's

---

94. Interestingly, Kimbrough Jr. and Beckerlegge list it under "Hymns and Poems of Doubtful Authorship." See *Unpublished Poetry of Charles Wesley*, 3:455.

95. Jackson, *Centenary of Wesleyan Methodism*, 187.

96. Marini, "Whitefield's Music," 107. It probably also performed an ongoing role in the Moorfields congregation, not only accompanying their love feasts but functioning as a kind of statement of faith for the Tabernacle society.

97. Ibid., 111. In fact, according to Tyerman, the English hymnologist and bookseller, Daniel Sedgwick (1814–1879), counted a total of thirty-six editions between 1753 and 1796. *Life of George Whitefield*, 2:294.

98. Noll, "Whitefield, Hymnody and Evangelical Spirituality," 249.

99. Ibid.

100. Davies, *Worship and Theology in England*, 145.

101. Noll, "Whitefield, Hymnody and Evangelical Spirituality," 256.

response to the redeeming transaction between a loving Trinity and sinful humanity."[102] This is not to say that other themes were entirely absent. Indeed, either as a "peace offering or peace challenge," Whitefield chose to include Charles Wesley's 144-line poem on Christian unity, "The Communion of Saints."[103] Several other hymns also explored the intimate nature of the fellowship of the redeemed. But the genius of the volume was that it simultaneously captured what most evangelicals believed while steering away from issues over which they disagreed.

Such "evangelical ecumenicity" was entirely consistent with Whitefield's gospel-centered Calvinism, for although ready and able to publicly defend Calvinistic doctrine, Whitefield clearly saw such debates as intramural, not fellowship-fracturing, discussions. To this end, the hymns in his collection were "so altered in some Particulars" that "all may safely concur in using them"[104]—a remark that refers both to his attempts to remove all controversial theological or sectarian references and to his insertion of first-person-plural pronouns to include all members of his denominationally diverse connection.[105]

In terms of Whitefield's intention for his hymnbook, Benson's summary is apt: "Whitefield aimed at a standard of Praise combining the doctrine and dignity of Watts with the evangelical fervor of Charles Wesley and his own colleagues."[106] While he did not attempt the same degree of pedagogical breadth as did Wesley in his 1780 *Collection*, the popularity and influence of *Hymns for Social Worship* would suggest that the anthology was every bit as useful to the evangelical world of his day.[107]

A Publisher of Hymn Tunes

We come, finally, to consider the importance of Whitefield's 1754 publication: *The Divine Musical Miscellany, being a Collection of Psalm and Hymn Tunes: great part of which were never before in print*. This was "a substantial anonymous tune book featuring a thorough introduction to musical theory and performance, as well as 68 psalm and hymn tunes arranged in two parts for melody and bass with first-stanza text underlay and thorough-bass

---

102. Ibid., 252.
103. Ibid., 256.
104. Whitefield, *Hymns for Social Worship*, Preface.
105. Marini, "Whitefield's Music," 111–12.
106. Benson, *English Hymn*, 319.
107. Indeed, Benson writes, "Its greatest permanent importance lay in its influence with the early Evangelical clergy of the Church of England." Ibid., 319.

notation for keyboard accompaniment."[108] Given Whitefield's interest in music theory, "it is possible that he wrote the eleven pages in question."[109] If so, it is less likely that Whitefield was responsible for any of the tunes, although "the composers of most of them remain unknown."[110]

In publishing such a volume, Whitefield was by no means a pioneer. The Wesleys had produced their first tune book some twelve years earlier: *A Collection of Tunes set to Music, as they are commonly Sung at the Foundery* (1742). However, "most Evangelicals, especially in London, had not encountered a collection of tunes that reflected more recent musical developments at both Moorfields and the Foundery. *The Divine Musical Miscellany* was thus the first printed tune book to provide that new repertory."[111] Consequently, fifty-seven of the sixty-eight tunes were either new variants or totally new compositions.[112] It is also noteworthy that at the end of *The Divine Musical Miscellany* music for four "dialogue hymns," designed to be sung in gendered antiphonal or responsorial style, is found.[113]

One of the chief things *The Divine Musical Miscellany* reveals is that, like the Wesleys, Whitefield was aware of the importance not just of hymn texts but of hymn tunes, and, most of all, of getting the pairing right. And many agreed he had got it right. For example, a number of London's dissenters "began to embrace the Whitefieldian collection's original text and tune pairings."[114]

Concluding Thoughts on Whitefield

It is well recognized that Whitefield lacked the organizational genius of Wesley and had limited interest in creating a sectarian movement among the evangelical Calvinists. And yet, he evidently had a clear ecumenical vision for evangelicalism which extended into the realm of hymnody and which had a major impact on the ecclesiastical landscape of his day. So much so that, at the time of his death in 1770, *Hymns for Social Worship* had never ceased to be in print, his music was being sung across the evangelical world, and a dozen of the new and variant tunes from *The*

---

108. Marini, "Whitefield's Music," 112.
109. Byrnside, *Music in Eighteenth-Century Georgia*, 91.
110. Marini, "Whitefield's Music," 112.
111. Ibid., 113.
112. Ibid., 115.
113. Byrnside, *Music in Eighteenth-Century Georgia*, 92.
114. Marini, "Whitefield's Music," 128.

Divine Musical Miscellany "had become standards among Wesleyan and Evangelical Calvinists alike."[115]

Furthermore, as well as pioneering the practice of singing at public outreach events, Whitefield's creation of an intercolonial evangelical network not only enabled the effective transmission Watts's work, but "provided the post-revolutionary constituencies for the singing school, whose early tune books represented the most intense outburst of Evangelical music publication until Sankey's gospel hymns."[116] Moreover, the impact of the tunes from *The Divine Musical Miscellany* is seen in that almost a quarter of them were reprinted more than a hundred times in the fifty years after Whitefield's death, albeit attached to different texts. This, as Marini suggests, is "entirely in keeping with Whitefield's legacy as the most protean and least institutionalized force in the formation of Anglo-American Evangelicalism and its sacred song."[117]

Final Reflections

While temperamentally very different, when it came to hymnody, Wesley and Whitefield were men of "like passions." Therefore, Benson's claim that there was "no one on the Evangelical side who shared to the full John Wesley's deep sense of the importance of the Hymn, his delight in hymn singing, or his skill in administering it as a Christian ordinance,"[118] is an uncharacteristic overstatement. Although he published considerably less than Wesley, Whitefield was every bit as much a lover, singer, and promoter of hymns, and equally convinced that "we never resemble the Blessed Worshippers above more than when we are joining together in public Devotions, and with Hearts and Lips unfeigned, singing Praises to him who sitteth upon the Throne for ever."[119]

Moreover, although Wesley and Whitefield differed on several important theological questions (for example, predestination, the imputation of Christ's righteousness, and the scope of forgiveness), they were agreed that the core of the gospel consisted of three non-negotiable doctrines: original sin, justification by faith, and spiritual regeneration.[120] Consequently, it was these doctrines, and the proper response to them, that lay at the

---

115. Marini, "Whitefield's Music," 133.
116. Marini, *Sacred Song in America*, 316.
117. Marini, "Whitefield's Music," 134.
118. Benson, *English Hymn*, 315–16.
119. Whitefield, *Hymns for Social Worship*, Preface.
120. Maddock, *Men of One Book*, 237–38.

heart of their hymnals. While significant divisions eventually developed between the Wesleyans and Whitefieldians, this common body of gospel-centered-hymnody helped to breed "an unusually broad, unexpectedly gracious, ecumenicity"[121] among the burgeoning evangelical movement of the eighteenth century.

In America, similarly, the net effect of Wesley and Whitefield's various compendiums was a remarkable "hymnological accumulation of Calvinist and Arminian divinity" that, in time, produced "a group of consensus hymns that circulated in virtually all evangelical denominations and articulated a common ground of belief and practice for early American popular religion."[122] Cruciocentrism was the chief hallmark. As Noll puts it: "a Christ-centered picture of redemption is the scarlet thread running through these hymns."[123] Wesley and Whitefield can jointly take credit for this focus on singing "our great redeemer's praise."

In regard to the output of publications, however, Whitefield was no match for the Wesley brothers. He did, of course, have the likes of John Cennick and William Hammond in his corner, but as long as John had the ever-prolific Charles in his, Whitefield could not hope to compete. Nor did he really try.

There was also a major disparity between the thematic breadth of the Wesleyan and Whitefieldian hymnals. As the title of his 1753 *Collection* reveals, Whitefield only included songs suitable for "Social Worship." For him, this meant that they "ought to abound much in Thanksgiving, and to be of such a Nature, that all who attend may join in them without being obliged to sing Lies, or not sing at all."[124] He consequently steered away from more subjective hymns, or pluralized the pronouns, and maintained a focus on God and the gospel.

John Wesley, as we've seen, was no less concerned for "common praise," but in his major hymnals (at least) sought to do more than Whitefield. As he wrote in the "Preface" to *A Collection of Hymns for the Use of the People called Methodists* (1780), his intention was to provide a "distinct and full" account of scriptural Christianity." This, of course, would not have been possible without Charles. For "there is no principal element of Christianity, no main article of belief, as professed by Protestant Churches . . . no moral or ethical sentiment, peculiarly characteristic of the Gospel . . . that does not

---

121. Noll, "We Are What We Sing," 39.
122. Marini, "Hymnody as History," 285–86.
123. Noll, "We Are What We Sing," 39.
124. Whitefield, *Hymns for Social Worship*, Preface.

find itself emphatically, and pointedly, and clearly conveyed in some stanza of Charles Wesley's hymns."[125]

Nevertheless, between them, with others to assist them, and standing on the shoulders of those who went before them, John Wesley and George Whitefield helped to establish the day of the evangelical English hymn. The evidence of this was everywhere to be seen or, more to the point, heard. For

> Whether the early revivals in Northampton, Massachusetts, the Wesleys' ministry in Georgia, the white-hot meetings of Pentecostal intensity in London during 1738 and 1739, the itinerant preaching of Whitefield, Wesley and so many others, the society meetings in all forms of Methodism, the gatherings of redeemed ex-slaves in South Carolina or Nova Scotia or Sierra Leone, the Sunday schools from the 1770s, the social gatherings at Clapham, the ships that carried evangelical missionaries overseas—all were marked by the robust singing of mostly new evangelical hymns.[126]

---

125. Taylor, *Wesley and Methodism*, 91.
126. Noll, *Rise of Evangelicalism*, 274.

Bibliography

Adamthwaite, Murray R. *Through the Christian Year with Charles Wesley: 101 Psalms and Hymns*. Eugene, OR: Wipf and Stock, 2016.
Anderson, Howard, and Irvin Ehrenpreis. "The Familiar Letter in the Eighteenth Century: Some Generalizations." In *The Familiar Letter in the Eighteenth Century*, edited by Howard Anderson et al., 269–82 Lawrence: University of Kansas Press, 1966.
"Anecdote of Mr Wesley." *Wesleyan Methodist Magazine* 48 (1825) 25.
Anonymous. *A Brief and Impartial Account of the Character and Doctrines of Mr. Whitefield and Mr. Wesley: In a Letter from London, September 1743*. Edinburgh: n.p., 1743.
———. *Pulpit Eloquence: Or, Characters and Principles of the Most Popular Preachers, of Each Denomination, in the Metropolis and Its Environs*. London: Loade, 1782.
Anstey, Roger. *The Atlantic Slave Trade and British Abolition, 1760–1820*. London: Macmillan, 1975.
Arminius, Jacobus. *Works of James Arminius*. 3 vols. Grand Rapids: CCEL, n.d.
Armistead, M. Kathryn, et al., eds. *Wesleyan Theology and Social Science: The Dance of Practical Divinity and Discovery*. Newcastle upon Tyne: Cambridge Scholars, 2010.
Atherstone, Andrew. "Commemorating Whitefield in the Nineteenth and Twentieth Centuries." In *George Whitefield: Life, Context, and Legacy*, edited by Geordan Hammond and David Ceri Jones, 278–99. Oxford: Oxford University Press, 2016.
Ayling, Stanley. *John Wesley*. New York: Collins, 1979.
Baker, Frank. *Charles Wesley's Verse: An Introduction*. London: Epworth, 1964.
———. *John Wesley and the Church of England*. 2nd ed. London: Epworth, 2000.
———. "The Origins, Character and Influence of John Wesley's *Thoughts upon Slavery*." *Methodist History* 22 (1984) 75–86.
———. "Whitefield's Break with the Wesleys." *Church Quarterly* 3 (1970) 103–13.
Baker, Frank, ed. *Letters I–II*. Works of John Wesley: Bicentennial Edition 25–26. Nashville: Abingdon, 1980–1982.
Balleine, George R. *A History of the Evangelical Party in the Church of England*. London: Longmans, 1911.
Bebbington, David W. *Evangelicalism in Modern Britain: A History from the 1730s to the 1980s*. London: Routledge, 2004.

Beckerlegge, Oliver A., and Franz Hildebrandt, eds. *A Collection of Hymns for the Use of the People Called Methodists*. Works of John Wesley: Bicentennial Edition 7. Nashville: Abingdon, 1983.

Belden, Albert D. "George Whitefield: His Influence on His Time." *Evangelical Christian* (1961) 2–4, 19–20.

Benezet, Anthony. *Some Historical Account of Guinea: A New Impression of the Edition of 1788*. London: Cass, 1968.

Benson, Louis F. *The English Hymn: Its Development and Use*. London: Hodder & Stoughton, 1915.

Best, Gary. *Charles Wesley: A Biography*. Peterborough: Epworth, 2006.

Bett, Henry. *Hymns of Methodism in their Literary Relations*. London: Epworth, 1913.

Bezzant, Rhys S. "Whitefield's Voice: Heroic, Apostolic, Prophetic." In *Paul as Pastor*, edited by Brian S. Rosner and Andrew S. Malone. London: T. & T. Clark, 2016.

Bishop of London's Pastoral Letter against LukeWarmness and Enthusiasm. London, 1739.

Book of Common Prayer, 1662 Edition. Cambridge: Cambridge University Press, 2005.

Borgen, Ole E. *John Wesley on the Sacraments: A Theological Study*. Zurich: United Methodist Church, 1972.

———. "John Wesley: Sacramental Theology No Ends without the Means." In *John Wesley: Contemporary Perspectives*, edited by John Stacey, 67–88. London: Epworth, 1988.

Boswell, James. *The Life of Samuel Johnson*. Oxford: Oxford University Press, 1980.

Brendlinger, Irv. "Wesley, Whitefield, a Philadelphia Quaker, and Slavery." *Wesleyan Theological Journal* 36, no. 2 (2001) 164–73.

Brewer, John. *The Pleasures of the Imagination: English Culture in the Eighteenth Century*. Abingdon, UK: Routledge, 2013.

Britain's Forgotten Slave Owners: Episode 1 Profit and Loss, written and presented by David Olusoga, first shown on BBC television 15 July 2015.

Brown, Christopher Leslie. *Moral Capital: Foundations of British Abolitionism*. Chapel Hill: University of North Carolina Press, 2006.

Brown-Lawson, Albert. *John Wesley and the Anglican Evangelicals of the Eighteenth Century*. Edinburgh: Pentland, 1994.

Bryant, Barry E. "Original Sin." In *The Oxford Handbook of Methodist Studies*, edited by William J. Abraham and James E. Kirby, 522–39. New York: Oxford University Press, 2009.

Burnett, Daniel L. *In the Shadow of Aldersgate: An Introduction to the Heritage and Faith of the Wesleyan Tradition*. Eugene, OR: Wipf and Stock, 2006.

Byrnside, Ronald L. *Music in Eighteenth Century Georgia*. Athens: University of Georgia Press, 1997.

Campbell, Ted A, ed. *Letters III, 1756–1765*. The Works of John Wesley: Bicentennial Edition 27. Nashville: Abingdon, 2015.

———. "Means of Grace and Forms of Piety." In *Oxford Handbook Methodist Studies*, edited by William J. Abraham and James E. Kirby, 280–91. Oxford: Oxford University Press, 2009.

———. *Wesleyan Beliefs: Formal and Popular Expressions of the Core Beliefs of Wesleyan Communities*. Nashville: Kingswood, 2010.

Chadwick, Owen. *The Victorian Church*. Vol. 1. 3rd ed. London: A. & C. Black, 1971.

Chilcote, Paul Wesley. "Charles Wesley and the Language of Faith." In *Charles Wesley: Life, Literature and Legacy*, edited by Kenneth G. C. Newport and Ted A. Campbell, 299–319. Petersborough: Epworth, 2007.

———. *John and Charles Wesley: Selections from Their Writings and Hymns—Annotated and Explained*. Woodstock, VT: SkyLight Paths, 2011.

Chilcote, Paul Wesley, and Kenneth J. Collins, eds. *Doctrinal and Controversial Treatises II*. The Works of John Wesley: Bicentennial Edition 13. Nashville: Abingdon, 2013.

Choi, Peter. "Whitefield, Georgia, and the Quest for Bethesda College." In *George Whitefield: Life, Context, and Legacy*, edited by Geordan Hammond and David Ceri Jones, 224–40. Oxford: Oxford University Press, 2016.

Christie, John W. "Newly Discovered Letters of George Whitefield" *Journal of the Presbyterian Historical Society* 32, no. 3 (1954) 159–86.

Church, Leslie F. *Knight of the Burning Heart: The Story of John Wesley*. London: Epworth, 1938.

Claghorn, George S., ed. *Letters and Personal Writings*. Works of Jonathan Edwards 16. New Haven: Yale University Press, 1998.

Clark, Stuart Henry. *George Whitefield: Wayfaring Witness*. Nashville: Abingdon, 1957.

Clarke, Adam. *A Letter to a Methodist Preacher on his Entrance into the Work of the Ministry*. London: Butterworth and Baynes, 1800.

Clarke, Adam, ed. *Memoirs of the Wesley Family: Collected Principally from Original Documents*. New York: Bangs and Mason, 1824.

Clarke, Martin V. *John Wesley and Methodist Music in the Eighteenth Century: Principles and Practice*. PhD diss., Durham University, 2008.

Clarkson, George E. *George Whitefield and Welsh Calvinistic Methodism*. Lewiston, NY: Mellen, 1996.

Clebsch, William A., and Charles R. Jaekle. *Pastoral Care in Historical Perspective*. Lanham, MD: Rowman & Littlefield, 1994.

Clifford, Alan C. *Atonement and Justification: English Evangelical Theology 1640–1790: An Evaluation*. Oxford: Clarendon, 1990.

Colley, Linda. *Britons: Forging the Nation, 1707–1837*. New Haven, CT: Yale University Press, 2009.

Collins, Kenneth J. "Other Thoughts on Aldersgate: Has the Conversionist Paradigm Collapsed?" *Methodist History* 30, no. 1 (1991) 10–25.

———. *The Scripture Way of Salvation: The Heart of John Wesley's Theology*. Nashville: Abingdon, 1997.

———. *The Theology of John Wesley: Holy Love and the Shape of Grace*. Nashville: Abingdon, 2007.

Collins, Kenneth J., and John H. Tyson. *Conversion in the Wesleyan Tradition*. Nashville: Abingdon, 2001.

Como, David. "Predestination and Political Conflict in Laud's London." *Historical Journal* 46, no. 2 (2003) 263–94.

Coppedge, Allan. *John Wesley in Theological Debate*. Wilmore, KY: Wesley Heritage, 1987.

Cragg, Gerald R., ed. *The Appeals to Men of Reason and Religion and Certain Related Open Letters*. Works of John Wesley: Bicentennial Edition 11. Nashville: Abingdon, 1989.

———. *The Church and the Age of Reason*. Baltimore: Penguin, 1966.

Crofford, J. Gregory. *Streams of Mercy: Prevenient Grace in the Theology of John and Charles Wesley.* Lexington, KY: Emeth, 2010.

Cruickshank, Joanna, "Charles Wesley, The Men of Old Calabar, and the Abolition of Slavery." *Aldersgate Papers* 7 (2009) 8–16.

Curnock, Nehemiah, ed. *The Journal of the Rev. John Wesley, A.M.* 8 vols. 1905–1916. Repr., London: Epworth, 1938.

Cushman, Robert E. *John Wesley's Experimental Divinity: Studies in Methodist Doctrinal Standards.* Nashville: Kingswood, 1989.

Dallimore, Arnold. *George Whitefield: The Life and Times of the Great Evangelist of the 18th Century Revival.* Vols. 1 and 2. Edinburgh: Banner of Truth, 1970, 1980.

Danker, Ryan. *Wesley and the Anglicans: Political Division in Early Evangelicalism.* Downers Grove, IL: IVP Academic, 2016.

Darsey, Steven. "John Wesley and Hymn and Tune Editor: The Evidence of Charles Wesley's 'Jesus Lover of My Soul' and Martin Madan's Hotham." *Hymn* 47, no. 1 (1996) 17–24.

Davie, Martin, et al., eds. *New Dictionary of Theology: Historical and Systematic.* 2nd edition. Downers Grove, IL: InterVarsity, 2016.

Davies, Horton. *Worship and Theology in England.* Vol. 3, *From Watts and Wesley to Maurice.* Princeton: Princeton University Press, 1961.

Davies, Rupert E., ed. *The Methodist Societies: History, Nature, and Design.* Works of John Wesley: Bicentennial Edition 9. Nashville: Abingdon, 1989.

De Blasio, Marlon. "Conversion, Justification, and the Experience of Grace in the Post-Aldersgate Wesley: Towards an Understanding of Who Is 'a Child of God.'" *Asbury Journal* 66, no. 2 (2011) 18–34.

Dean, Jonathan. *A Heart Strangely Warmed: John and Charles Wesley and their Writings.* London: Canterbury, 2014.

Dickson, David. "The Sum of Saving Knowledge." In *The Confession of Faith, the Larger and Shorter Catechism, with the Scripture Proofs at Large, Together with the Sum of Saving Knowledge,* 321–44. Ross-shire: Free Presbyterian Church of Scotland, 1976.

Dierks, Konstantin. *In My Power: Letter Writing and Communications in Early America.* Early American Studies. Philadelphia: University of Pennsylvania Press, 2009.

Dixon, Leif. *Practical Predestinarians in England, c. 1590–1640.* Burlington, VT: Ashgate, 2014.

Dowley, Tim. *Christian Music: A Global History.* Oxford: Lion, 2011.

Downey, James. *The Eighteenth Century Pulpit.* Oxford: Clarendon, 1969.

Dudley-Smith, Timothy. "Why Wesley Still Dominates Our Hymnbook." *Christian History* 31 (1991) 11.

Dutton, Anne, "A Discourse upon Walking with God." In *Selected Spiritual Writings of Anne Dutton: Discourses, Poetry, Hymns, Memoir,* edited by Joann Ford Watson, 1–74. Macon, GA: Mercer University Press, 2004.

Edwards, Jonathan. *The Religious Affections.* Edited by John E. Smith. New Haven: Yale University Press, 1959.

Edwards, O. C., Jr. *A History of Preaching.* Nashville: Abingdon, 2004.

Field, David. "John Wesley as Public Theologian: The Case of *Thoughts upon Slavery.*" *Scriptura* 114 (2015) 1–13.

Finley, C. Stephen. *Nature's Covenant: Figures of Landscape in Ruskin.* University Park: Pennsylvania State University Press, 1993.

BIBLIOGRAPHY

Francis, Keith A., and William Gibson, eds. *The Oxford Handbook of the British Sermon, 1689-1901*. Oxford: Oxford University Press, 2012.

Fox, Adam, *English Hymns and Hymn Writers*. London: Collins, 1947.

Garrett, Aaron. "Hume's Revised Racism Revisited." *Hume Studies* 26, no. 1 (2000) 171–78.

Gatiss, Lee. "The Anglican Evangelist: George Whitefield." In *Positively Anglican: Building on the Foundations and Transforming the Church*, edited by Lee Gatiss, 27–41. London: Church Society, 2016.

Gatiss, Lee, ed. *The Sermons of George Whitefield*. 2 vols. Wheaton, IL: Crossway, 2012.

Gibson, William. "Whitefield and the Church of England." In *George Whitefield: Life, Context, and Legacy*, edited by Geordan Hammond and David Ceri Jones, 46–63. Oxford: Oxford University Press, 2016.

Giles, Gordon. *O Come Emmanuel: A Musical Tour of Daily Readings for Advent and Christmas*. Brewster, MA: Paraclete, 2006.

Gillies, John. *Memoirs of the Life of the Reverend George Whitefield, M.A.* London: E. & C. Dilly, 1772.

Gillies, John, ed. *The Works of the Reverend George Whitefield, M.A.* 7 vols. London: E. & C. Dilly, 1772.

Gillman, Frederick John. *The Evolution of the English Hymn*. London: Allen, 1927.

Gledstone, James. *George Whitefield, M.A.: Field Preacher*. London: Hodder & Stoughton, 1901.

Goodwin, Charles H. "Setting Perfection Too High: John Wesley's Changing Attitudes toward the 'London Blessing.'" *Methodist History* 36, no. 2 (1998) 86–96.

Gordon, James M. "Jonathan Edwards and George Whitefield." In *Evangelical Spirituality: From the Wesleys to John Stott*, edited by James M. Gordon, 53–66. London: SPCK, 1991.

Görlach, Manfred. *Text Types and the History of English*. Berlin: de Gruyter, 2004.

Graham, Thomas C. G., ed. "George Whitefield and Friends: The Correspondence of Some Early Methodists." *National Library of Wales Journal* 27, no. 2 (1991) 175–203.

Green, Richard, ed. *The Works of John and Charles Wesley: A Bibliography*. London: Kelly, 1896.

Grotius, Hugo. *The Truth of the Christian Religion in Six Books*. Translated by John Clark. Edited by Jean Le Clerc. London: Baynes, 1829.

Gunter, W. Stephen. "John Wesley, a Faithful Representative of Jacobus Arminius." *Wesleyan Theological Journal* 42, no. 2 (2007) 65–82.

———. *The Limits of "Love Divine."* Nashville: Kingswood, 1989.

Hall, Timothy D. *Contested Boundaries: Itinerancy and the Reshaping of the Colonial American Religious World*. Durham: Duke University Press, 1994.

Hammond, Geordan. "John Wesley and 'Imitating' Christ." *Wesleyan Theological Journal* 45, no. 1 (2010) 197–212.

———. *John Wesley in America: Restoring Primitive Christianity*. Oxford: Oxford University Press, 2014.

———. "John Wesley's Relations with the Lutheran Pietist Clergy in Georgia." In *The Pietist Impulse in Christianity*, edited by Christian T. Collins Winn et al., 135–45. Cambridge: Clarke, 2012.

Hammond, Geordan, and David Ceri Jones, eds. *George Whitefield: Life, Context, and Legacy*. Oxford: Oxford University Press, 2016.

Hampson, John. *Memoirs of the late Rev. John Wesley, A.M.* Sunderland, UK: Graham, 1791.

Harding, Alan. *The Countess of Huntingdon's Connexion.* Oxford: Oxford University Press, 2003.

Harrington, Susan. "Friendship Under Fire: George Whitefield and John Wesley, 1739-1741." *Andover Newton Quarterly* 15, no. 2 (1974) 167-81.

Hatfield, James T. "John Wesley's Translations of German Hymns." *Proceedings of the Modern Language Association* 11, no. 2 (1896) 171-99.

Haweis, Thomas. *An Impartial and Succinct History of the Rise, Declension, and Revival of the Church of Christ.* London: Mawman, 1800.

Haykin, Michael A. G. *The Revived Puritan: The Spirituality of George Whitefield.* Dundas, OT: Joshua, 2000.

Heitzenrater, Richard P., ed. *Diary of an Oxford Methodist Benjamin Ingham, 1733-1734.* Durham, NC: Duke University Press, 1985.

———. "John Wesley's Principles and Practice of Preaching." In *Beyond the Boundaries. Preaching in the Wesleyan Tradition*, edited by Richard Sykes, 12-40. Oxford: Applied Theology, 1998.

———. *Mirror and Memory: Reflections on Early Methodism.* Nashville: Kingswood Books, 1989.

———. *Wesley and the People Called Methodists.* 2nd edition. Nashville: Abingdon, 2013.

Hempton, David. *Methodism: Empire of the Spirit.* New Haven: Yale University Press, 2005.

Henderson, D. Michael. *A Model for Making Disciples: John Wesley's Class Meeting.* Nappanee, IN: Asbury, 1997.

Henry, Stuart C. *George Whitefield: Wayfaring Witness.* New York: Abingdon, 1957.

Herbert, Thomas W. *John Wesley as Editor and Author.* Eugene, OR: Wipf and Stock, 2008.

Higgins, Nicholas. "Achieving Human Perfection: Benjamin Franklin contra George Whitefield." *Journal of American Studies* 50 (2016) 61-80.

Hindmarsh, D. Bruce. *The Evangelical Conversion Narrative: Spiritual Autobiography in Early Modern England.* Oxford; New York: Oxford University Press, 2005.

———. "Reshaping Individualism: The Private Christian, Eighteenth-Century Religion and the Enlightenment." In *The Rise of the Laity in Evangelical Protestantism*, edited by Deryck W. Lovegrove, 67-84. London: Routledge, 2002.

Hochschild, Adam. *Bury the Chains: Prophets and Rebels in the Fight to Free an Empire's Slaves.* Boston: Houghton Mifflin, 2005.

Hood, Jared C. "'I Never Read Calvin': George Whitefield, a Calvinist Untimely Born." *Churchman* 125, no. 1 (2011) 7-20.

———. "The Methodical George Whitefield: A 'Most Excellent Systematic Divine'?" *Churchman* 126, no. 4 (2012) 311-22.

———. "Whitefield: The Heart of an Evangelist." *Reformed Theological Review* 69, no. 3 (2010) 164-79.

Hynson, Leon O. "George Whitefield and Wesleyan Perfectionism: A Response." *Wesleyan Theological Journal* 19, no. 1 (1984) 86-90.

Jackson, Marion A. "An Analysis of the Source of John Wesley's 'Directions for Renewing Our Covenant with God.'" *Methodist History* 30, no. 3 (1992) 176-84.

Jackson, Thomas. *Centenary of Wesleyan Methodism: A Brief Sketch of the Rise, Progress, and Present State of the Wesleyan Methodist Societies throughout the World*. New York: T. Mason & G. Lane, 1839.

———. *The Life of the Rev. Charles Wesley, M.A.* 2 vols. London: Mason, 1841.

Jackson, Thomas, ed. *The Journal of the Rev. Charles Wesley, M.A.* 2 Vols. London: Wesleyan-Methodist Book room, 1849.

———. *The Works of John Wesley*. 14 vols., 3rd ed. 1872. Reprint, Kansas City: Beacon Hill, 1979.

James, William. *The Varieties of Religious Experience: A Study in Human Nature*. New York: Penguin, 1982.

Jensen, Gerard E., ed. *The Covent-Garden Journal*. New Haven: Yale University Press, 1915.

Jones, David Ceri. "George Whitefield and Heart Religion." In *Heart Religion: Evangelical Piety in England and Ireland, 1690–1850*, dited by John Coffey, 93–112. Oxford: Oxford University Press, 2016.

———. "'So Much Idolized by Some, and Railed at by Others': Towards Understanding George Whitefield." *Wesley and Methodist Studies* 5 (2013) 3–29.

Karlberg, Mark W. *Covenant Theology in the Reformed Perspective: Collected Essays and Book Reviews in Historical, Biblical, and Systematic Theology*. Eugene, OR: Wipf and Stock, 2000.

Kendall, Henry. "Mr. Wesley's Last Visit to Langham Row and Alford." *Primitive Methodist Magazine* 31 (1850) 173–75.

Kidd, Thomas S. "America's Spiritual Founding Father: Whitefield's Life and Legacy." *Credo Magazine* 4, no. 3 (2014) 20–27.

———. *George Whitefield: America's Spiritual Founding Father*. New Haven: Yale University Press, 2014.

Kimbrough, S. T., Jr., and Oliver A. Beckerlegge. *The Unpublished Poetry of Charles Wesley*. Vol. 3. Nashville: Kingswood, 1992.

Knight, Henry H., III. *The Presence of God in the Christian Life: John Wesley and the Means of Grace*. Metuchen, NJ: Scarecrow, 1992.

———. "The Transformation of the Human Heart: The Place of Conversion in Wesley's Theology." In *Conversion in the Wesleyan Tradition*, edited by Kenneth J. Collins and John H. Tyson, 43–55. Nashville: Abingdon, 2001.

Kohl, Manfred Waldemar. "Spener's Pia Desideria: The Programschrift of Pietism." *Covenant Quarterly* 34, no. 4 (1976) 61–78.

Lambert, Frank. "The Great Awakening as Artifact: George Whitefield and the Construction of Intercolonial Revival, 1739–1745." *Church History* 60, no. 2 (1991) 223–46.

———. *"Pedlar in Divinity": George Whitefield and the Transatlantic Revivals, 1737–1770*. Princeton, NJ: Princeton University Press, 1994.

Larsen, Timothy. "Defining and Locating Evangelicalism." In *The Cambridge Companion to Evangelical Theology*, edited by Daniel J Treier and Timothy Larsen, 1–14. Cambridge: Cambridge University Press, 2007.

Lee, Harper. *To Kill a Mockingbird*. New York: Harper & Row, 1961.

Lessenich, Rolf P. *Elements of Pulpit Oratory in Eighteenth Century England (1660–1800)*. Cologne: Böhlau, 1972.

Lewis, W. S., et al., eds. *The Yale Edition of Horace Walpole's Correspondence*. London: Oxford University Press, 1937–83.

Lightwood, James T. *Methodist Music of the Eighteenth Century*. London: Epworth, 1927.

Lindbeck, George A. *The Nature of Doctrine*. Philadelphia: Westminster, 1984.

Lindström, Harald, *Wesley and Sanctification: A Study in the Doctrine of Salvation*. London: Epworth, 1950.

Lloyd, Gareth. *Charles Wesley and the Struggle for Methodist Identity*. Oxford: Oxford University Press, 2007.

Mack, Phyllis. *Heart Religion in the British Enlightenment: Gender and Emotion in Early Methodism*. Cambridge: Cambridge University Press, 2008.

Maddock, Ian. "George Whitefield: Christian Perfectionist?" *Reformed Theological Review*, 74, no. 3 (2015) 147–61.

———. *Men of One Book: A Comparison of Two Methodist Preachers, John Wesley and George Whitefield*. Eugene, OR: Pickwick, 2011.

———. "Solving A Transatlantic Puzzle? John Wesley, George Whitefield and 'Free Grace' Indeed!" *Wesley and Methodist Studies* 8, no. 1 (2016) 1–15.

Maddox, Randy L. *Aldersgate Reconsidered*. Nashville: Kingswood, 1990.

———. *Responsible Grace: John Wesley's Practical Theology*. Nashville: Kingswood, 1994.

———. "The Rule of Christian Faith, Practice, and Hope: John Wesley on the Bible." *Methodist Review* 3 (2011) 1–35.

Maddox, Randy L., ed. *Doctrinal and Controversial Treatises I*. Works of John Wesley: Bicentennial Edition 12. Nashville: Abingdon, 2012.

Mahaffey, Jerome Dean. *Preaching Politics: The Religious Rhetoric of George Whitefield and the Founding of a New Nation*. Studies in Rhetoric and Religion 3. Waco, TX: Baylor University Press, 2007.

Marini, Stephen A. "Hymnody as History: Early Evangelical Hymns and the Recovery of American Popular Religion." *Church History* 71, no. 2 (2002) 273–306.

———. *Sacred Song in America: Religion, Music, and Public Culture*. Urbana: University of Illinois Press, 2003.

———. "Whitefield's Music: Moorfields Tabernacle, The Divine Musical Miscellany (1754), and the Fashioning of Early Evangelical Sacred Song." *Yale Journal of Music and Religion* 2, no. 1 (2016) 101–34.

Marquardt, Manfred. "Christian Conversion: Connecting Our Lives with God." In *Rethinking Wesley's Theology for Contemporary Methodism*, edited by Randy L. Maddox and Theodore Runyon, 99–111. Nashville: Kingswood, 1998.

———. *John Wesley's Social Ethics: Praxis and Principles*. Nashville: Abingdon, 1991.

———. "Social Ethics in the Methodist Tradition." In *T. & T. Clark Companion to Methodism*, edited by Charles Yrigoyen Jr., 292–308. London: T. & T. Clark, 2010.

Martin, Hugh. "The Baptist Contribution to Early English Hymnody." *Baptist Quarterly* 19 (1962) 195–208.

Maxson, Charles Hartshorne. *The Great Awakening in the Middle Colonies*. Chicago: University of Chicago Press, 1920.

McCall, Thomas H. "'But a Heathen Still': The Doctrine of Original Sin in Wesleyan Theology." In *Adam, the Fall, and Original Sin: Theological, Biblical, and Scientific Perspectives*, edited by Hans Madueme and Michael Reeves, 147–66. Grand Rapids: Baker, 2014.

McConnell, F. J. *Evangelicals, Revolutionists and Idealists: Six English Contributors to American Thought and Action*. Port Washington, NY: Kennikat, 1942.

Bibliography

McCoy, Charles S., and J. Wayne Baker. *Fountainhead of Federalism: Heinrich Bullinger and the Covenantal Tradition*. Louisville: Westminster John Knox, 1991.

McEwan, David B. *The Life of God in the Soul: The Integration of Love, Holiness and Happiness in the Thought of John Wesley*. Milton Keynes: Paternoster, 2015.

———. *Wesley as a Pastoral Theologian: Theological Methodology in John Wesley's Doctrine of Christian Perfection*. Milton Keynes: Paternoster, 2011.

McGonigle, Herbert. "John Wesley—Exemplar of the Catholic Spirit." In *Ecumenism and History: Studies in Honour of John H. Y. Briggs*, edited by A.R. Cross, 50–68. Bletchley: Paternoster, 2002.

———. *Sufficient Saving Grace: John Wesley's Evangelical Arminianism*. Carlisle: Paternoster, 2001.

McGrath, Alister E. *A Scientific Theology*. Vol. 3, *Theory*. London: Continuum International, 2006.

McKnight, Scot, and Hauna Ondrey. *Finding Faith, Losing Faith: Stories of Conversion and Apostasy*. Waco, TX: Baylor University Press, 2008.

McNearney, Clayton L. "Ah, Lovely Appearance of Death." *Soundings: An Interdisciplinary Journal* 65, no. 1 (1982) 57–77.

Meredith, William Henry. *The Real John Wesley*. Cincinnati: Jennings and Py, 1903.

A Methodist Preacher. *John Wesley, the Methodist: A Plain Account of His Life and Work*. New York: Methodist Book Concern, 1903.

Miller, Josiah. *Singers and Songs of the Church: Being Biographical Sketches of the Hymn-Writers in all their Principal Collections*. London: Longmans, Green, 1869.

Milton, John. *Complete Poems and Major Prose*. Edited by Merritt Y. Hughes. Indianapolis: Hackett, 2003.

Monk, Robert C. *John Wesley: His Puritan Heritage*. London: Epworth, 1966.

Morgan, Kenneth. *Bristol and the Atlantic Trade in the Eighteenth Century*. Cambridge: Cambridge University Press, 1994.

Murray, Iain. *Wesley and the Men Who Followed*. Edinburgh: Banner of Truth, 2003.

Murray, John. *The Life of Rev. John Murray*. 4th ed. Boston: Marsh, Capen and Lyon, 1832.

Mursell, Gordon. *English Spirituality: From 1700 to the Present Day*. Louisville: Westminster John Knox, 2001.

Nehamas, Alexander. *On Friendship*. New York: Basic, 2016.

Noble, Thomas A. *Holy Trinity: Holy People: The Historic Doctrine of Christian Perfecting*. Eugene, OR: Cascade, 2013.

Nock, Arthur Darby. *Conversion: The Old and the New in Religion from Alexander the Great to Augustine of Hippo*. Baltimore: Johns Hopkins University Press, 1933.

Noll, Mark A. "The Defining Role of Hymns in Early Evangelicalism." In *Wonderful Words of Life: Hymns in American Protestant History & Theology*, edited by Richard J. Mouw and Mark A. Noll, 3–16. Grand Rapids: Eerdmans, 2004.

———. "National Churches, Gathered Churches, and Varieties of Lay Evangelicalism, 1735–1859." In *The Rise of the Laity in Evangelical Protestantism*, edited by Deryck W. Lovegrove, 134–52. London: Routledge, 2002.

———. *The Rise of Evangelicalism: The Age of Edwards, Whitefield and the Wesleys*. Downers Grove, IL: InterVarsity, 2003.

———. "We Are What We Sing: Our Classic Hymns Reveal Evangelicalism at its Best." *Christianity Today* (July 12, 1999) 37–41.

———. "Whitefield, Hymnody, and Evangelical Spirituality." In *George Whitefield: Life, Context, and Legacy*, edited by Geordan Hammond and David Ceri Jones, 241–60. Oxford: Oxford University Press, 2016.

Nuelsen, John L. *John Wesley and the German Hymn*. Translated by Theo Parry, Sydney H. Moore and Arthur Holbrook. Calverley, UK: Holbrook, 1972.

O'Brien, Glen, "George Whitefield, John Wesley, and the Rhetoric of Liberty." *Religion in the Age of Enlightenment* 6 (2016) 76–100.

Oden, Thomas C. *Christ and Salvation: John Wesley's Teachings*. Grand Rapids: Zondervan, 2011.

———. *John Wesley's Scriptural Christianity: A Plain Exposition of His Teaching on Christian Doctrine*. Grand Rapids: Zondervan, 1994.

Oden, Thomas C. *John Wesley's Teachings*. Vol. 2, *Christ and Salvation*. Grand Rapids: Zondervan, 2012.

———. *John Wesley's Teachings*. Vol. 3, *Pastoral Theology*. Grand Rapids: Zondervan, 2012.

Olson, Mark K. "Exegeting Aldersgate: John Wesley's Interpretation of 24 May 1738." PhD diss., University of Manchester, 2016.

———. "Whitefield's Conversion and Early Theological Formation." In *George Whitefield: Life, Context, and Legacy*, edited by Geordan Hammond and David Ceri Jones, 29–45. Oxford: Oxford University Press, 2016

Olson, Roger E. *Arminian Theology: Myths and Realities*. Downers Grove, IL: InterVarsity, 2006.

Outler, John, ed. *John Wesley*. New York: Oxford University Press, 1980.

———. *Sermons*. Works of John Wesley: Bicentennial Edition 1–4. Nashville: Abingdon, 1984–1987.

Packer, J. I. *Honouring the People of God: The Collected Shorter Writings of J. I. Packer*. Carlisle: Paternoster, 1999.

Parr, Jessica. *Inventing George Whitefield: Race, Revivalism, and the Making of a Religious Icon*. Jackson: University Press of Mississippi, 2015.

Peckham, Colin N. *John Wesley's Understanding of Human Infirmities*. Ilkeston, UK: Wesley Fellowship, 1997.

Pelikan, Jaroslav. *Christian Doctrine and Modern Culture (since 1700)*. Vol. 5 of *The Christian Tradition: A History of the Development of Doctrine*. Chicago: University of Chicago Press, 1989.

Pestana, Carla Gardina. "Whitefield and Empire." In *George Whitefield: Life, Context, and Legacy*, edited by Geordan Hammond and David Ceri Jones, 82–97. Oxford: Oxford University Press, 2016.

Peterson, Robert A., and Michael D. Williams. *Why I Am Not an Arminian*. Downers Grove, IL: InterVarsity, 2004.

Pettigrew, William A. *Freedom's Debt: the Royal African Company and the Politics of the Atlantic Slave Trade, 1672–1752*. Chapel Hill: University of North Carolina Press, 2013.

Philip, Robert. *The Life and Times of the Reverend George Whitefield, M.A.* New York: Appleton, 1838.

Phillips, Christopher N. "Cotton Mather Brings Isaac Watts's Hymns to America; or, How to Perform a Hymn without Singing It." *New England Quarterly* 85, no. 2 (2012) 203–21.

Piette, Maximin. *John Wesley in the Evolution of Protestantism*, translated by Joseph Bernard Howard. New York: Sheed & Ward, 1937.

Pinfold, John, ed. *The Slave Trade Debate: Contemporary Writings for and against.* Oxford: Bodleian Library, 2007.

Pollock, John. *Wesley the Preacher*. Eastbourne: Kingsway, 1988.

———. *Whitefield the Evangelist*. Eastbourne: Hodder and Stoughton, 1972.

———. *Wilberforce*. London: Constable, 1977.

Poole-Connor, E. J. *Evangelicalism in England*. 2nd edition. Worthing: Walter, 1966.

Porterfield, Amanda. *Conceived in Doubt: Religion and Politics in the New American Nation*. American Beginnings, 1500–1900. Chicago: University of Chicago Press, 2012.

Prest, Wilfred. *Albion Ascendant: English History 1660–1815*. Oxford: Oxford University Press, 1998.

Rack, Henry D., ed. *The Methodist Societies: The Minutes of the Conference*. Works of John Wesley: Bicentennial Edition 10. Nashville: Abingdon, 2011.

———. *Reasonable Enthusiast: John Wesley and the Rise of Methodism*. 3rd ed. Peterborough, UK: Epworth, 2014.

Rambo, Lewis R. "Conversion Studies, Pastoral Counseling, and Cultural Studies: Engaging and Embracing a New Paradigm." *Ex Auditu* 25 (2009) 1–16.

———. *Understanding Religious Conversion*. New Haven, CT: Yale University, 1993.

Rattenbury, J. Earnest. *The Evangelical Doctrines of Charles Wesley's Hymns*. London: Epworth, 1941.

Reist, Irwin W. "John Wesley and George Whitefield: A Study in the Integrity of Two Theologies of Grace." *Evangelical Quarterly* 47 (1975) 26–40.

Reklis, Kathryn. *Theology and the Kinesthetic Imagination: Jonathan Edwards and the Making of Modernity*. New York: Oxford University Press, 2014.

Rivers, Isabel. "Whitefield's Reception in England, 1770–1839." In *George Whitefiled: Life, Context, and Legacy*, edited by Geordan Hammond and David Ceri Jones, 261–77. Oxford: Oxford University Press, 2016.

Rodes, Stanley J. *From Faith to Faith: John Wesley's Covenant Theology and the Way of Salvation, Distinguished Dissertations in Christian Theology*. Eugene, OR: Pickwick, 2013.

Routley, Erik. *Hymns and Human Life*. London: Murray, 1952.

Runyon, Theodore. *The New Creation: John Wesley's Theology Today*. Nashville: Abingdon, 1998.

Rupwate, Daniel. "The Covenant Theology of John Wesley." *Canadian Methodist Historical Society Papers* 9 (1991) 79–90.

Sanders, Fred. *Wesley on the Christian Life: The Heart Renewed in Love*. Wheaton, IL: Crossway, 2013.

Schlenther, Boyd Stanley. "Whitefield's Personal Life and Character." In *George Whitefield: Life, Context, and Legacy*, edited by Geordan Hammond and David Ceri Jones, 12–28. Oxford: Oxford University Press, 2016.

Schmidt, Darren. "The Pattern of Revival: John Wesley's Vision of 'Iniquity' and 'Godliness' in Church History." In *Revival and Resurgence in Christian History: Papers Read at the 2006 Summer Meeting and the 2007 Winter Meeting of the Ecclesiastical History Society*, edited by Kate Cooper and Jeremy Gregory, 142–53. Studies in Church History 44. Woodbridge: Boydell, 2008.

Schwanda, Tom, ed. *The Emergence of Evangelical Spirituality: The Age of Edwards, Newton, and Whitefield.* The Classics of Western Spirituality. Mahwah, NJ: Paulist, 2016.

———. *Soul Recreation: The Contemplative-Mystical Piety of Puritanism.* Eugene, OR: Pickwick, 2012.

Schwenk, James L. *Catholic Spirit: Wesley, Whitefield, and the Quest for Evangelical Unity in Eighteenth Century British Methodism.* Lanham, MD: Scarecrow, 2008.

———. *George Whitefield: A Guided Tour of His Life and Thought.* P & R, 2015.

———. "'And the Holy Catholic Church': A Paradigm for Evangelical Catholicity." *Evangelical Journal* 18, no. 2 (2000) 74–89.

Scougal, Henry. *The Works of Henry Scougal, 1650–1678.* Morgan, PA: Soli Deo Gloria, 2002.

Seymour, Aaron. *The Life and Times of Selina Countess of Huntingdon.* 2 vols. London: Painter, 1839.

Shaw, Scott. "Music of the Early Methodist Church." *Reihai to Ongaku* Autumn (2004) 1–9.

Shenton, Tim. *The Life of Rowland Hill: "The second Whitefield."* Darlington, UK: Evangelical, 2008.

Smith, Timothy L. "George Whitefield and Wesleyan Perfectionism." *Wesleyan Theological Journal* 19, no. 1 (1984) 63–85.

———. *Whitefield and Wesley on the New Birth.* Grand Rapids: Asbury, 1986.

Smith, Warren Thomas. *John Wesley and Slavery.* Nashville: Abingdon, 1986.

Snyder, Howard. *The Redical Wesley and Patterns for Church Renewal.* Downers Grove, IL: InterVarsity, 1980.

Sparks, Randy. *Two Princes of Calabar: An Eighteenth-Century Odyssey.* Cambridge: Harvard University Press, 2004.

Spurgeon, Charles H. *C. H. Spurgeon's Autobiography.* Vol. 1. London: Passmore & Alabaster, 1899.

———. "John Wesley." *Banner of Truth* 70 (1969) 54–58.

———. *The Metropolitan Tabernacle: Its History and Work.* London: Passmore & Alabaster, 1876.

Stanglin, Keith D., and Thomas H. McCall. *Jacob Arminius: Theologian of Grace.* Oxford: Oxford University Press, 2012.

Steed, Robert. *An Epistle concerning Church Singing*, 1691

Stout, Harry S. *The Divine Dramatist: George Whitefield and the Rise of Modern Evangelicalism.* Library of Religious Biography. Grand Rapids: Eerdmans, 1991.

———. *The New England Soul: Preaching and Religious Culture in Colonial New England.* New York: Oxford University Press, 1986.

Taylor, Isaac. *Wesley and Methodism.* London: Longman, Brown, Green, and Longmans, 1851.

Telford, John, ed. *The Letters of the Rev. John Wesley.* 8 vols. London: Epworth, 1931.

———. *The Life of John Wesley.* London: Epworth, 1924.

Thomas, Graham C. G., ed. "George Whitefield and Friends: The Correspondence of Some Early Methodists." *National Library of Wales Journal* 27, no. 2 (1991) 175–203.

Toon, Peter. *The Emergence of Hyper-Calvinism in English Nonconformity, 1689–1765.* Eugene, OR: Wipf & Stock, 2011.

Toplady, Augustus. *The Works of Augustus Toplady.* London: Chidley, 1837.

Bibliography

Torpy, Arthur Alan. *The Prevenient Piety of Samuel Wesley, Sr.* Lanham, MD: Scarecrow, 2009.
Tracy, Joseph. *The Great Awakening: A History of the Great Awakening in the time of Edwards and Whitefield.* Edinburgh: Banner of Truth Trust, 1842.
Tripp, David H. *The Renewal of the Covenant in the Methodist Tradition.* London: Epworth, 1969.
Trueman, Carl R. "Reformers, Puritans and Evangelicals: The Lay Connection." In *The Rise of the Laity in Evangelical Protestantism,* edited by Deryck W. Lovegrove, 17–35. London: Routledge, 2002.
Tyacke, Nicholas. "Puritanism, Arminianism and Counter-Revolution." In *The Origins of the English Civil War,* edited by Conrad Russell, 119–43. London: Macmillan, 1973.
Tyerman, Luke. *The Life and Times of the Rev. John Wesley.* London: Hodder & Stoughton, 1870.
———. *The Life of the Rev. George Whitefield.* 2 vols. London: Hodder & Stoughton, 1876.
Tyson, John H. "John Wesley's Conversion at Aldersgate." In *Conversion in the Wesleyan Tradition,* edited by Kenneth J. Collins and John H. Tyson, 27–42. Nashville: Abingdon, 2001.
Tyson, John R. *Assist Me to Proclaim: The Life and Hymns of Charles Wesley.* Grand Rapids: Eerdmans, 2007.
———. *The Way of the Wesleys: A Short Introduction.* Grand Rapids: Eerdmans, 2014.
Tyson, John R., ed. *Charles Wesley: A Reader.* Oxford: Oxford University Press, 1989.
Van Til, Cornelius. "Covenant Theology." In *New 20th Century Encyclopedia of Religious Knowledge,* edited by J. D. Douglas, 240–41. Grand Rapids: Baker, 1991.
Vaughn, James Barry. "Public Worship and Practical Theology in the Work of Benjamin Keach (1640–1704)." PhD diss., University of St. Andrews, 1989.
Venn, John. *The Life and Selection from the Letters of the late Rev Henry Venn.* London: Hatchard, 1837.
Vickers, Jason E. *Wesley: A Guide for the Perplexed.* Continuum Guides for the Perplexed. London: T. & T. Clark, 2009.
———. "Wesley's Theological Emphases." In *The Cambridge Companion to John Wesley,* edited by Randy L. Maddox and Jason E. Vickers, 190–206. Cambridge: Cambridge University Press, 2010.
Vincent, William. *Considerations on Parochial Music.* London: Cadell, 1790.
Wallace, Charles Jr., ed. *Susanna Wesley: The Complete Writings.* Oxford: Oxford University Press, 1997.
Walls, Jerry L. "John Wesley on Predestination and Election." In *The Oxford Handbook of Methodist Studies,* edited by William J. Abraham and James E. Kirby, 619–32. New York: Oxford University Press, 2009.
Walls, Jerry L., and Joseph R. Dongell. *Why I Am Not a Calvinist.* Downers Grove, IL: InterVarsity, 2004.
Ward, W. Reginald. *Early Evangelicalism: A Global Intellectual History, 1670–1789.* Cambridge: Cambridge University Press, 2006.
Ward, W. Reginald, and Heitzenrater, Richard P., eds. *Journal and Diaries I–VII.* Works of John Wesley: Bicentennial Edition 19–24. Nashville: Abingdon, 1988–1997.
Watson, David Lowes. "Methodist Spirituality." In *Protestant Spiritual Traditions,* edited by Frank C. Senn, 217–70. Mahwah, NJ: Paulist, 1986.

Watson, John R. *The English Hymn: A Critical and Historical Study*. Oxford: Clarendon, 1999.

———. "The Welkins." *Hymn Society of Great Britain and Ireland, Bulletin*, July 2000, 80.

Watts, Isaac. *Hymns and Spiritual Songs*. London: J. Humphreys, for John Lawrence, 1707.

———. *The Psalms of David Imitated in the Language of the New Testament and Applied to the Christian State and Worship*. London: Clark, 1719.

Webster, Tom. *Godly Clergy in Early Stuart England: The Caroline Puritan Movement c. 1620–1643*. Cambridge: Cambridge University Press, 1997.

Wesley, Charles. *The Journal of Charles Wesley*. 2 vols. London: Mason, 1849.

Wesley, John, ed. "An Account of the Life of Mr. Thomas Olivers, written by Himself." *Arminian Magazine* 2 (1779) 77–85.

Wesley, John. *A Collection of Hymns, for the Use of the People Called Methodists*. London: Mason, 1780.

———. *A Collection of Psalms and Hymns*. Charlestown, UK: Printed by Timothy Lewis, 1737.

———. *The Complete English Dictionary Explaining Most of Those Hard Words, Which Are Found in the Best English Writers*. London: Strahan, 1753.

———. *Explanatory Notes upon the New Testament*. New York: Soule and Mason, 1818.

———. *Explanatory Notes upon the Old Testament*. Salem, OH: Schmul, 1975.

———. "John Wesley's Translations of Some German Hymns." In *John and Charles Wesley: Selected Prayers, Hymns, Journal Notes, Sermons, Letters and Treatises*, edited by Frank Whaling, 90–98. London: SPCK, 1981.

———. *Serious Address to the People of England*. London, 1778.

———. *Wesley's Doctrinal Standards. Part 1: The Sermons*. Salem, OH: Schmul, 1967.

Wesley, John. "A Short Account of Mr. George Story." *Arminian Magazine* 5 (1782) 14–20, 70–78, 122–25.

Whaling, Frank. *John and Charles Wesley: Selected Writings and Hymns*. Ramsey, NJ: Paulist, 1981.

Whitefield, George. *Additional Sermons, The Works of George Whitefield*. Shropshire: Quinta, 2000

———. *A Collection of Hymns for Social Worship: More Particularly Design'd for the Use of the Tabernacle Congregation, in London*. London: Strahan, 1753.

———. *A Communion Morning's Companion*. London: Strahan, 1755.

———. *Divine Melody: Or, a Help to Devotion. Being, a Choice Collection of Hymns, Psalms, and Spiritual Songs for the Use of the Pious and Sincere Christian. Selected, Approved and Recommended by the Rev. Mr.. George Whitefield*. London: Rayner, 1739.

———. *The Divine Musical Miscellany, Being a Collection of Psalm and Hymn Tunes: Great Part of Which Were Never Before in Print*. London: Smith, 1754.

———. *Eighteen Sermons Preached by the Late Rev. George Whitefield*. Edited by Joseph Gurney. London: Gurney, 1771.

———. *George Whitefield's Journals*. Edinburgh: Banner of Truth, 1960.

———. *George Whitefield: Sermons*. Vols. 1–4. New Ipswich, NH: Pietan, 1991–2008.

———. *The Polite and Fashionable Diversions of the Age Destructive to Soul and Body. A Sermon Preached at Blackheath*. London: Whitefield, 1740.

———. *Select Sermons of George Whitefield*. Edinburgh: Banner of Truth, 1958.

———. "Self-Inquiry Concerning the Work of God." In *Sermons on Important Subjects*. London: Tegg, 1841.

———. *The Works of the Reverend George Whitefield, M.A., Late Chaplain of Pembroke-College, Oxford, and Chaplain to the Rt. Hon. The Countess of Huntingdon*. London: Printed for E. and C. Dilly, 1771.

Whitehead, John. *The Life of the Rev. John Wesley, M.A*. London: Couchman, 1796.

Wilckens, Henry. *Letters concerning the Slave Trade and with Respect to Its Intended Abolition*. Liverpool, 1793.

Williams, A. H. "The Leaders of English and Welsh Methodism, 1738–91, Pt. II." *Bathafarn: The Journal of the Historical Society of the Methodist Church in Wales* 17 (1962) 5–26.

Wilson-Dickson, Andrew. *The Story of Christian Music: From Gregorian Chant to Black Gospel, An Authoritative Illustrated Guide to All the Major Traditions of Music for Worship*. Oxford: Lion, 1992.

Witherington, Ben, III. "New Creation or New Birth? Conversion in the Johannine and Pauline Literature." In *Conversion in the Wesleyan Tradition*, edited by Kenneth J. Collins and John H. Tyson, 103–18. Nashville: Abingdon, 2001.

Wood, A. Skevington. *The Inextinguishable Blaze: Spiritual Renewal and Advance in the Eighteenth Century*. Grand Rapids: Eerdmans, 1960.

Young, Carlton R. *Music of the Heart: John and Charles Wesley on Music and Musicians*. Carol Stream, IL: Hope, 1995.

Yrigoyen, Charles, Jr. *John Wesley: Holiness of Heart and Life*. Nashville: Abingdon, 1996.

www.ingramcontent.com/pod-product-compliance
Lightning Source LLC
Chambersburg PA
CBHW051517230426
43668CB00012B/1648